Praise for *Philosophy: An Innovative Introduction*

"This is an exciting book that promises to invigorate courses in philosophy, ethics, and the humanities. . . . The authors offer a robust conception of 'fictive narrative philosophy'— one that treats seriously the power of fiction in philosophical discourse. The authors' innovative approach pairs the philosophies of major figures with short stories that engage those figures in thought-provoking ways. The result is that the philosophical tradition is brought to life for students as abstract ideas become vivid and compelling."

—Linda Furgerson Selzer, Penn State University

"Boylan and Johnson return philosophy to its original home—the story. By blending narrative with other philosophical discourses, they create an approach that engages ambiguity in order to attain wisdom."

—Marc Conner, Washington and Lee University

"In the acknowledgements Charles Johnson quotes Camus, 'If you want to be a philosopher, write novels.' While an extravagant claim, Boylan and Johnson have conceived and brought to life an 'innovative' new introductory philosophy text that richly demonstrates what Camus calls for. . . . The text offers numerous helpful aids for the classroom, but most importantly it uniquely blends traditional philosophical argumentation with provocative fictive narratives (stories) that promise to engage students more fully, thus bringing philosophy alive in ways more traditional texts can only approximate."

—Richard E. Hart, Bloomfield College

"This unusual introduction to philosophy has broad appeal without sacrificing intellectual rigor."

—Felicia Nimue Ackerman, Brown University

"This book is a *tour de force*. . . . Designed not only to inform but also to stimulate our feelings and imagination, the creative imagery of the fictional stories accompanying the philosophical texts succeed in instantly transporting us to the everyday lives of these famous philosophers. We walk with Socrates as he struts around the Agora of Athens animated in the midday sun talking about justice. We wait in Kant's living room as he changes his tie before answering the door to welcome guests to yet another of his Friday dinner soirées. Like Platonic dialogues, this wonderful and timely book works not only with words but with powerful, visceral imagery."

—Edward Spence, Centre for Applied Philosophy and
Public Ethics, Charles Sturt University

D0162104

PHILOSOPHY

An Innovative Introduction

PHILOSOPHY

Fictive Narrative, Primary Texts, and Responsive Writing

MICHAEL BOYLAN

Marymount University

CHARLES JOHNSON

University of Washington

WESTVIEW
PRESS
A Member of the Perseus Books Group

Published by Westview Press,
A Member of the Perseus Books Group

Find us on the World Wide Web at www.westviewpress.com.

Every effort has been made to secure required permissions to use all images, maps, and other art included in this volume. Credits appear on pages 327–329, which constitutes a continuation of the copyright page.

Westview Press books are available at special discounts for bulk purchases in the United States by corporations, institutions, and other organizations. For more information, please contact the Special Markets Department at the Perseus Books Group, 2300 Chestnut Street, Suite 200, Philadelphia, PA 19103, or call (800) 810-4145, ext. 5000, or e-mail special.markets@ perseusbooks.com.

Designed by Trish Wilkinson
Set in 10.5 point Adobe Garamond

Library of Congress Cataloging-in-Publication Data

Boylan, Michael, 1952–
    Philosophy : an innovative introduction : fictive narrative, primary texts, and responsive writing / Michael Boylan, Charles Johnson.
        p.   cm.
    Includes bibliographical references and index.
    ISBN-13: 978-0-8133-4448-5 (alk. paper)
    ISBN-10: 0-8133-4448-4 (alk. paper)
    1. Philosophy—Textbooks. I. Johnson, Charles Richard, 1948–
II. Title.
B74.B69 2010
100—dc22   2009040401

10 9 8 7 6 5 4 3 2 1

CONTENTS

PREFACE

This is a new and unconventional introduction to philosophy. Like traditional, conventional texts, this book is linked by common themes and a historical presentation. Students learn to reconstruct direct-deductive arguments and then evaluate them. The texts represent some of the major figures in the canon, along with some new faces—Buddha, Hannah Arendt, Iris Murdoch, and Martin Luther King Jr.—who contribute to a more multicultural and inclusive presentation of the field of philosophy.

In addition to the conventional deductive array, this text uniquely presents a narrative component. From Chapters 1 to 3 in Part 1 (on writing direct- and indirect-discourse responses to philosophical arguments), to the short stories that lead off the readings in each of Chapters 4 to 13, to the creative writing exercises that follow each of the readings—narrative is brought forward in a manner that engages students in a compelling fashion. This second mode of presentation—reading and writing fictive narrative—connects to students in ways that complement the direct-discourse model. It has been our experience that the mixture of narrative with direct-discourse presentation touches the right- and left-brain perspectives of students in a powerful way, unmatched by any other textbook with which we are familiar.

In particular the unique features of this book are these:

- Three introductory chapters on the time-honored and essential role of narrative fiction in philosophy (Chapter 1), constructing direct logical responses to claims (Chapter 2), and constructing indirect fictive-narrative responses to claims (Chapter 3).
- Ten chronologically arranged chapters pertaining to key figures in ancient and medieval philosophy (Plato, Aristotle, Buddha, Aquinas) and modern and contemporary philosophy (Descartes, Kant, Marx, Heidegger and Arendt, Murdoch, King).
- A short story in Chapters 4 to 13 that focuses on a key insight into that chapter's featured philosopher.
- Short, primary, direct-discourse texts in Chapters 4 to 13 that connect to the subject of the story. In addition to readings from the featured philosopher in each of these chapters, primary texts are also included from Gottfried Leibniz, Christian Wolff, David Hume, and G. W. F. Hegel.

- Double chapters (Chapters 9 and 10), dealing with Kant and Marx that also include primary texts by other philosophers, providing a historical and intellectual context for the featured philosopher. (Double chapters also have double class assignments.)
- Probing reading and discussion questions that help students identify and focus on essential arguments in both the short stories and the primary texts.
- Class exercises: writing assignments in both the direct and narrative formats.
- Suggested midterm and final assignments in both the direct and narrative formats.
- Games (exercises) in philosophy (in the appendix) that are broadly representative of the discipline.
- A glossary of key philosophical terms, placed in the front matter, where it is easily found and consulted by students.

Furthermore, the reading selections—both the short stories and the primary texts—have been chosen for their cogency in developing certain themes as well as for their accessibility to the introductory student. The themes developed in the readings cover all four of the traditional branches of philosophy: ethics, epistemology, metaphysics, and logic:

- *From ethics and social and political philosophy,* the readings consider the duty to obey or disobey unjust laws. Among the primary direct-discourse texts, for example, Plato's "Crito" exhorts us to obey even unjust laws, whereas Aquinas (in his "Natural Law") calls upon us to obey the natural law over unjust human laws. Two readings by Marx ("Alienated Labor" and "Private Property and Labor") urge us to change unjust social structures, but Eichmann (in Arendt's "An Expert on the Jewish Question") advocates following orders in one's sovereign state. Likewise, in a more contemporary vein, Murdoch ("Ludwig's Conundrum") sympathetically repeats the "Crito" argument, while King's "Letter from a Birmingham Jail" sympathetically repeats Aquinas's argument.
- *From epistemology,* the readings present contending perspectives on the role of a priori and a posteriori input in forming judgments in one's mind about the world. This tension between perspectives is represented among the primary texts of this book by Aristotle's functional account of mind that is materially oriented, by Descartes's rationally leaning account, by Leibniz's and Wolff's mixed accounts leaning toward rationality, by Hume's empiricism based on mitigated skepticism, and by Kant's critical empiricism.
- *From metaphysics,* the readings ponder the role and nature of Being, as described, for example, in Plato's Charioteer myth in the context of a theory of Forms. Likewise, Buddha situates Being in the context of not being; Aquinas

assumes transcendent Being in his presentation; Hegel describes a mode of being in *Geist* ("spirit"); Marx attacks Hegel; Heidegger modifies Hegel through his analysis of Being through a questioning process on the Being of a being; and King (like Aquinas) assumes transcendent Being.

- *From logic*, the student is required in each chapter to outline deductive arguments presented in both the primary readings and the short stories. This recurring task requires developing skill in informal logic, guidelines for which are provided in Chapter 2.

This book, then, introduces narrative not only in order to present in a vivid format various keen philosophical moments in the lives of the writers featured but also as a response mode to both direct and indirect discourse. It is the experience of the authors (based on their combined sixty plus years of teaching) that using narrative feedback, along with conventional direct discourse, engages students more fully in their inquiry into philosophical issues and evaluating claims. It also makes them participants in the exploration of esthetics (another recognized area of philosophy).

We hope that this dual-presentation mode will usher in more usages of narrative in philosophy classes in its traditional place alongside direct logical discourse presentations and truly make philosophy *live* for a wider audience!

Michael Boylan
Charles Johnson

ACKNOWLEDGMENTS

From Michael:

I want to thank Charles Johnson for sending me some of these stories as they were being written. They inspired the basic idea of this book. I have enjoyed working with Dr. Johnson. I also want to thank my audience at the Association for Professional and Practical Ethics for their input at a talk I gave there in 2008. Further, I'd like to thank Mount St. Mary's College in Los Angeles for inviting me to give their Larkin Lecture (2008), in which I explored fictive-narrative philosophy.

From Charles:

I cannot thank Michael Boylan enough for the tremendous labor he has invested in this book. From its conception through all its changes, he has done the heavy lifting and infused the text with his exuberant, expansive spirit. My contribution is minimal compared to his. He understands so well what Albert Camus wrote in his *Notebooks* (1935–1942): "Feelings and images multiply a philosophy by ten." And, "People can think only in images. If you want to be a philosopher, write novels." Dr. Boylan is exactly the kind of philosopher/storyteller Camus had in mind, as well as an outstanding educator, so it has been the greatest of pleasures and a true privilege for me to work with him on this innovative, imaginative project.

From both authors:

We would like to thank Karl Yambert and the entire production team at Westview for putting forth a fine effort in order to turn out the best possible book.

GLOSSARY

Philosophy is such a diverse field that no practitioner or school defines all terms in precisely the same way. The following represents a set of definitions that are meant to be in keeping with general readings for an introductory audience.

a posteriori—This term from epistemology covers that sort of knowledge obtained from empirical experience. For example, the conclusions of modern science obtained via the experimental method would be a posteriori. See also *a priori*.

a priori—This term from epistemology covers that sort of knowledge obtained from a source other than from our empirical experience (technically, logically prior to experience). For example, in plane geometry the concepts of point, line, and plane are posited and used in constructions. However, because they are not three-dimensional objects and because such objects cannot be sensed, they are posited from a source other than our experience in the world—for example, by some power of reason and the imagination. See also *a posteriori*.

alienation (Marx)—Alienation according to Marx is a state in which a worker finds him- or herself as isolated and set apart from the person he or she wants to or naturally should be. The worker is diminished and his or her life becomes miserable. Alienation comes about through the operation of industrial capitalism as it grinds down the working class. Marx posits four levels of alienation.

analytic proposition (Kant)—An analytic proposition is one in which the predicate term does not expand our knowledge of the subject term. For example, in the proposition "All bachelors are unmarried males," the predicate term (unmarried males) gives us no new information about the subject term. If we understand the subject term (bachelors), then we already know that they are unmarried males. See also *synthetic proposition*.

antithesis (Plato, Kant, Hegel, Marx)—This term has slightly different meanings according to the philosopher using it. For Plato, antithesis is the generating proposition for a reductio ad absurdum argument. The antithesis for Plato is generally an opponent to Socrates. Following from this antithesis leads to an absurdity; therefore, the antithesis is rejected in favor of its opposite (the thesis). In Kant, the thesis-antithesis combination is most famously used in the *Critique of Pure Reason* during the section on the antinomies of pure reason (part of the "Transcendental

Dialectic"). Kant puts forth arguments for a thesis and an antithesis (side by side) to show that certain problems that reason entertains show only that reason is bounded and cannot address with certainty all possible problems. For Hegel (and, by extension, Marx), the antithesis is the negation of the abstract description that begins the first dialectical moment. Through a back-and-forth between increasingly concrete opposites (antithesis and thesis), a middle position (the synthesis) that is both concrete and universal is arrived at.

assertion—An assertion is a justification of a premise in a direct-deductive logical argument that refers merely to the say-so of the speaker who is making a claim.

Association, Law of (Hume)—Hume argues that the rationalist philosophers' (Descartes, Leibniz, Wolf, and others) account of cause is unfounded. A more reasonable account of causation is the more modest claim of there merely being a constant conjunction of two events under a law of association instead of assuming a mechanical necessity between cause and effect. In everyday language, one can still say "x caused y," but this locution merely means constant conjunction.

Being (Heidegger)—Being is the ontological ground of some x's (a being's) existence. It depicts the general phenomenon of a living entity's existence that is only revealed via an examination of a particular kind of being's activity, *Dasein* (the being that we humans, ourselves, are). See also *being* (Heidegger), *Dasein* (Heidegger).

being (Heidegger)—A being is a particular living entity that exists in the world. To understand its meaning requires a process of examination. The phenomenological revelation of that being is in terms of its ontological ground, Being. This occurs via the examination of a particular kind of being, *Dasein* (the being that we humans, ourselves, are). See also *Being* (Heidegger), *Dasein* (Heidegger).

claim—A claim is a proposition set out by a speaker to his or her audience. For philosophers, claims must be supported by either a direct-discourse logical argument or an indirect-discourse argument. The terms *point of contention* and *conclusion* are closely aligned to the notion of a claim.

conclusion—The conclusion is the point of contention within the structure of an argument that expresses the claim. In deductive arguments, acceptance of the conclusion follows from the truth of the premises (also called soundness) and the strength of the justificatory inferences (also called validity). When an argument is sound and valid, then the conclusion must necessarily be accepted.

Contradiction, Law of (Kant)—see *Noncontradiction, Principle of* (Leibniz)

cosmology—This is a subcategory of metaphysics that discusses how the various modes of being relate to one another.

critical philosophy (Kant)—Critical philosophy (as opposed to dogmatic philosophy) operates from a standpoint that begins with experience (a posteriori propositions) and then examines the possibility of experience within the framework of logically necessary boundary conditions. Dogmatic philosophy, on the other hand, begins with a priori propositions and uses these to describe our experience of the world.

Within this context the philosophers Leibniz and Wolff are dogmatic philosophers while Kant and Hume are critical philosophers.

Dasein (Heidegger)—*Dasein* is the being that we humans, ourselves, are. *Dasein* finds itself already existing in an environment that is rich in a cultural/spiritual/valued context. *Dasein* exists within a temporal context that goes beyond mere time as measured by a clock. *Dasein*'s being refers to the existential reality of its moment of "thrownness" in the world in which the subject "temporalizes" himself by returning to what has been (as it orients itself for the future).

deductive logic—This is a method of presenting a claim (or point of contention or conclusion) that follows necessarily from the acceptance of the premises.

dialectic—The term *dialectic* has at least two clear historical meanings. The first comes from Plato. In this sense dialectic means opposite positions that come into conflict. Most of the Socratic dialogues are of this design. Socrates confronts his antagonist. The process works out such that Socrates (with one exception) wins the argument, but the final outcome may be a positive statement of Socrates's position (however modified), or it may be merely the defeat of the opponent's position. Here the meaning of dialectic comes from *dia-logos*, meaning going through the words or logical account in verbal exchange. The second key historical meaning comes from Hegel. In Hegel the dialectic operates through a series of "moments." The beginning of the dialectic is a statement of some abstract notion (thesis) that is then negated to an opposite—and slightly more concrete—counterstatement (antithesis) that conceptually frames the first. The moments progress until a stopping point is reached at the concrete universal (the synthesis).

direct logical discourse—This is the presentation of claims through deductive logic such that the conclusion follows necessarily from the acceptance of the premises.

empiricism—A term from epistemology, empiricism can refer broadly to theories of knowledge that have as their primary (or sole) source the subject's sensory experience in the world. Some thinkers in this category only allow unaided sensory experience (naive empiricists), while most others allow instruments that enhance sensory exploration—ranging from microscopes to polymerase chain reaction machines used in DNA sequencing. Many empiricists also employ a priori concepts related to the association of ideas to evaluate sensory experience critically. What is important is that it all begins with sensation, and in cases of dispute, it is there we must return. See also *rationalism*.

enthymeme—An enthymeme is an added premise that must be provided in order to make an inference tight and acceptable (meaning that it follows logically). Enthymemes are typically put in square brackets to indicate that they are not explicit in the original text but are only implicit (suppressed).

Epicurean(ism)—This is the philosophical position attributed to the Greek philosopher Epicurus (341–270 BCE) and his followers (such as Lucretius). The position most cited by later philosophers is the position of ethical hedonism. Under this doctrine it is asserted that what makes one ultimately happy in life is the simple moral life. But because "happiness" or "pleasure" is taken as the standard, many misread the position as advocating unrestrained hedonism (going after as much wanton pleasure as possible).

epistemology—This is one of the four traditional branches of philosophy that concerns what we can properly know and believe.

ethics—This is one of the four traditional branches of philosophy that concerns the study of what is considered to be right and wrong in human action.

existential—This refers to insights into the human condition that begin with one's existence in the world. All subsequent conclusions must follow from the foundational beginning of our being mortal creatures with various natural and artificial constraints upon us.

fact—A fact is an agreement (whether actual or assumed) between the speaker and the audience in the presentation of a direct or indirect argument. Generally, facts refer to empirically based propositions that have been inductively generated from real-world experience.

fictive-narrative discourse—This is storytelling. When the story makes clearly recognizable claims, then the discourse becomes philosophy (hence the label "fictive-narrative philosophy").

fictive-narrative philosophy—This is fictive-narrative discourse in which the story itself makes claims (also known as themes).

Form (Plato)—A Form is a principle in metaphysics primarily and epistemology secondarily. Plato believed that one way we understand some particular thing in front of us is to subsume the object into various logical types of things. These types are the Ideas, or Forms. In a number of passages, Plato indicates that these forms have a sort of independent existence apart from the particular thing at hand. For example, I see a chair in front of me that comes from another country and is designed unlike the chairs in my country. However, the "chairness" of this object is ascertained by shape and function: what do you do with this thing in front of me? You sit on it to rest your knees and back in order to engage in a variable series of tasks. For Plato, Forms are always described in very general terms as "types of things." The Form that connects all other Forms is called the Form of the Good.

indirect discourse—This is an argument form in which the conclusion (the claim or point of contention) seems to be the most reasonable assessment from the data given. It creates a belief on the part of the reader but not knowledge (since the acceptance of this claim is not necessary).

inductive logic—This is an indirect argument form that creates probable (rather than necessary) conclusions based on empirical data.

inference—This is a justification of a premise in a direct-deductive logical argument. One or more prior premises cause the audience to agree to the premise in question on the basis of their prior acceptance of the earlier premise(s).

intersubjective—This is the widespread acceptance of various truisms within a shared community worldview.

logic—This is one of the four traditional branches of philosophy that concerns the rules of validity and soundness in deductive logic, whose conclusions are necessary, and how one can form a posteriori empirically based conclusions that are probable in inductive logic.

mechanics (of inference)—This is the process of deriving a conclusion or subconclusion that follows logically and necessarily from the acceptance of prior premises.

metaphysics—This is one of the four traditional branches of philosophy that concerns the nature of being (ontology) and how the various modes of being relate to one another (cosmology).

modality of necessity (Leibniz)—The modality of necessity for Leibniz refers to the strength of a propositional claim and a description of the realm of its application. In the first instance, one considers whether the claim can be otherwise. If it can, then that tells against its strength. If the claim cannot be otherwise (such as, given the laws of plane Euclidean geometry, a triangle is only ever a closed plane figure wherein the sum of the interior angles equals 180°), then the propositional claim has achieved one important level of necessity. The second level of necessity concerns whether one might imagine any other possible universe in which the claim might be false. In the case of the triangle, one can imagine a non-Euclidean space in which a plane might have positive or negative curvature. In this case the triangle's interior angles might be greater or less than 180°. Thus, on this second level, the proposition is not necessary because it could be the case that in another possible universe, the conclusion might be otherwise. The strongest sort of proposition is one that is necessary in all possible universes.

Noncontradiction, Principle of (Leibniz)—The Law of Noncontradiction states that it is impossible to conjoin a proposition and its logical complement, or opposite. In common language, you cannot conjoin "Joan is pregnant" and "Joan is not pregnant" at the same time and place. Either Joan is or is not pregnant but not both.

objectification (Marx)—This is the process whereby a person externalizes him- or herself in the world. This can be positive in the instance of meaningful work, friendships, and supportive social relations. Objectification can become alienation when the objectified individual confronts an alien oppressive power that sets a person apart from what he or she wants to be or naturally is. See also *alienation*.

ontology—This is one of the subcategories of metaphysics that concerns the nature of being (what it is and its modality of existence).

phenomenology—This is a movement in philosophy in the twentieth century characterized by the central figures Edmund Husserl, Martin Heidegger, Emmanuel Levinas, Maurice Merleau-Ponty, and Jacques Derrida. Each of these practitioners and their followers define the phenomenological method slightly differently, but in general it refers to the quality of mental states. This quality or property is phenomenologically meaningful if and only if the mental property corresponds to a concrete state that one lives in. For example, emotions have a phenomenology because we can be "angry," "in love," or "envious," and so on. Belief statements (such as "Washington, D.C., is the capital of the United States") do not have a phenomenology because there is no concrete state that allows us to be Washington, D.C., the capital, or the United States. Proponents of this approach emphasize this sort of examination of lived experience as the starting point of philosophy.

philosophy—This is the study of first principles in order to gain conceptual clarity in order to understand the structure of any area of human understanding. Traditionally, the field comprises ethics, logic, metaphysics, and epistemology. Today, there is also a list of subareas of human understanding that are more proximately examined—such as art (philosophy of art, or aesthetics), science (philosophy of science), economics (philosophy of economics), and so on.

point of contention—This is the claim that the speaker wishes to prove to his or her audience via a direct-discourse logical argument or an indirect-discourse argument. Once the claim or point of contention takes on its formal guise in a deductive logical argument, inductive logical argument, or reductio ad absurdum argument, it is called the conclusion of the argument. In narrative philosophy, the point of contention is often called the theme.

predicate-in-subject theory (Leibniz)—Leibniz's predicate-in-subject posit is important to his construction of monad theory (his comprehensive metaphysical system). This is how it works: truth is said to be a proposition in which the predicate is contained within the subject. Kant called such propositions "analytic." An example would be "All bachelors are unmarried males." If one knows either the subject or the predicate, then one has the other half as well. In this case, Leibniz is inclined to begin with the predicate, such as "unmarried males." Thus, if one understands the predicate, then he already has the subject, "bachelors," as well.

premise—This is a proposition set in a deductive or inductive argument that causes one to accept the conclusion. In the case of deductive argument, the premises must be true. In the case of inductive arguments, the premises must be likely and operate according to laws of probability and currently accepted scientific method.

proposition—This is a declarative sentence with truth-value. Each proposition in an argument must be justified as either an assertion (the say-so of the speaker), fact (the agreement between speaker and audience), or inference (the logical connection between premises that in deductive arguments necessarily compels the audience to accept the consequent subconclusion). In inductive arguments, the connection between premises in an inference is probable but not necessary.

rationalism—This is a term in epistemology. Rationalists believe that our sensory experience of the world should be seen through preexistent rational categories that can call into question the veracity of various sensory reports. What we know best are a priori guidelines for experience that shape how we understand and classify our sensory representation of the world. Important is that in cases of controversy, it is to a priori categories that we must turn for our answers. See also *empiricism*.

reconstruction—This refers to reconstruction of a claim or argument that, in direct logical discourse, begins with the point of contention and then works backwards to set out a deductive argument with premises that are justified as fact, assertion, or inference. In fictive-narrative philosophy, however, reconstruction of a claim operates rather more like induction, as it gathers the particular facts presented to it in such a way that the claim emerges from the process of careful attention to details in the context of the reader's personal worldview.

reductio ad absurdum—This is a demonstration that a given proposition would, if followed to its logical conclusion, result in an absurdity.

skeptical philosophy (Hume)—Hume parsed skepticism into two general categories: radical skepticism and mitigated skepticism. In the former category, he puts thinkers like Descartes, who attempt to doubt everything (or so Hume claims). This is problematic because if we doubt everything, it is difficult to know how we can move forward. The more plausible approach, Hume argues, is mitigated skepticism, which accepts the givens of matters of fact and matters concerning relations of ideas. If these are accepted as starting points, then further inferences from these should be doubted unless conclusively proven.

soundness—This is a property of a logical deductive argument in which the premises are all true. See also *validity* and *conclusion*.

subconclusion—This is a premise that follows mechanically (logically and necessarily) from one or more preceding premises in the argument and will also, itself, be a part of the conclusion's inference.

Sufficient Reason, Principle (or Law) of (Leibniz)—Leibniz believes that for every predicate that is true of a subject there must be some other predicate or proposition that constitutes a sufficient reason for its being true. Nothing happens without a reason. Unless this principle were true, then there would be no sense to anything.

syllogism—This is a special form of the deductive logical argument that contains two premises and a conclusion (arranged according to special rules that dictate valid and invalid forms).

synthesis—see *antithesis*

synthetic proposition (Kant)—Synthetic propositions for Kant are those propositions in which the predicate term of the proposition enlarges one's understanding of the subject term. For example, one might take the proposition "The boiling point of water is 100°C at sea level." One's understanding of the subject term, "water," would merely constitute understanding the chemical definition of water, H_2O, and the appropriate chemical bonding. When one adds that it boils at 100°C, then one is providing new information, which expands one's understanding of the subject term and makes the proposition more applicable to the real world in which we live.

theme—This is the claim or point of contention within the context of fictive-narrative philosophy.

thesis—see *antithesis*

validity—This is a property of a logical deductive argument in which the inference justifying the conclusion cannot be rationally doubted.

PART I

DIRECT AND INDIRECT DISCOURSE IN PHILOSOPHY

CHAPTER ONE

Direct and Indirect Discourse in Philosophy

Consider the following facts and conclusion:

Fact 1: Two planes have just crashed into the Twin Towers of the World Trade Center in New York City, killing many hundreds of civilians in the towers and on the planes.

Fact 2: The passenger manifests and bodies from the wreckage show that known members of terrorist organizations were on board the planes.

Fact 3: A radical extremist, Osama bin Laden, leader of a terrorist group named al-Qaeda, has claimed responsibility for the attack on the World Trade Center.

Fact 4: Under international law, the killing of civilians (noncombatants) is wrong in situations of war and non-war alike; it is murder.

Conclusion 1: Osama bin Laden and all who helped him are murderers and should receive the strictest sentence under the law (life in prison under international law).

But consider also how the situation might change with the addition of another fact:

Fact 5: Some of the terrorists (perhaps including even the leader) have motivations—personal stories—for their acts that might mitigate our judgment of them.

Conclusion 2: Using judicial discretion that takes into account the context of the crime and other mitigating factors, we might decide the punishment of at least some of the terrorists should amount to something less than life in prison.

Conclusions 1 and 2 differ significantly. Why is this? The first case focuses upon the *empirical* facts of the crime at hand. The reasoning is cut-and-dried, leading directly from agreed-on facts to a (seemingly) necessary conclusion: civilians were killed, terrorists killed them, it was al-Qaeda terrorists in particular who killed the civilians, and the killing of civilians is murder; therefore, the responsible members of al-Qaeda are murderers and should be punished severely as such. In situations in which the facts are widely agreed upon or might at least be tested and proven, a particular conclusion is commonly best presented by marshalling the facts that lead compellingly to that conclusion.

The straightforward method of presentation—choosing and arranging the facts that lead to a given conclusion—is *direct logical discourse*. It is *discourse* because it is communication of thoughts. It is *logical* because it arrays facts and assertions (that are structured as simple declarative sentences with truth-value, that is, propositions) in such a way that the collection of these propositions according to certain rules will yield conclusions that cannot be doubted: philosophers say that such conclusions are "necessarily accepted." *Facts* are justifications of propositions that indicate that the speaker and her audience are in accord about states of affairs. *Assertions* are justifications of propositions that indicate that the force for accepting the proposition is merely the say-so of the speaker. In direct discourse, propositions (in the context of an argument, they are called *premises*) are set together to compel a conclusion that follows reasonably from the premises. And it is *direct* because a given proposition builds on the previous facts, and the chain of facts leads straight to the conclusion. The force of the presentation is *necessary* because it cannot be logically doubted.

In the case of Conclusion 2, however, the facts are less agreed upon; they are certainly less testable. They carry a stronger tinge of uncertainty. Once the terrorists' individual motivations became known to us, we might (or might not) admit that those particular motivations mitigated our view of their actions, and we might (or might not) conclude that the appropriate punishment for the terrorists (if they were caught) should be less severe than life in prison, at least for certain of the individuals, if not in all of them. In such an instance, our understanding of the facts (and the conclusions that we base upon those facts) depends less on a simple chain of direct logical reasoning and more on a multifaceted sense of nuanced and possibly complicated factors. In turn, our appreciation of those factors and contingencies depends not just on a series of logically connected statements but on the life experiences and the personal values with which we respond to the situation at hand.

In practical terms, such nuance—such weighing of complicating and mitigating factors—is often difficult or impossible to distill into direct discourse. It is at that point that *indirect discourse* can step in. Indirect discourse is a way of making claims that are persuasive but not necessary. They amount to the "best account available." As such they can generate belief but not knowledge (where knowledge is the necessary acceptance of a claim). There can be several subcategories of indirect discourse: from variants of the deductive argument such as *reductio ad absurdum* to the *argument from remainders*. Other subcategories include *inductive argument* (which creates probable or cogent conclusions based on empirical data that are interpreted according to the rules of scientific inquiry) and *fictive-narrative philosophy*. The following list helps us quickly put this classification scheme into context.

The Contrast Between Direct and Indirect Discourse in Philosophy

Direct-Discourse Philosophy

- In deductive logical argument, the speaker proves his claim to his audience by mustering simple declarative sentences with truth-value (propositions) that are individually justified as fact, assertion, or inference (these act like subconclusions). The conclusion is derived by inference from the premises and is necessarily true if the mechanics of the argument are handled correctly and the premises are all true.

Indirect-Discourse Philosophy

- Reductio ad absurdum is a variant of direct logical argument and refers to taking the proposition of the objector (antithesis) as a starting point for examination and then showing that the antithesis leads to an absurdity (this is how Socrates argued in the early Platonic dialogues).
- Argument from remainders is a hybrid of direct logical argument and inductive logical argument and begins by asserting that the number of outcomes is finite—say A, B, and C. When A and B are eliminated, then C is said to be the result.
- Inductive logical argument is a category unto itself. It refers to arguments that are generally based on empirical (sense-derived) data that are systematized via the scientific method to generalizations or specific conclusions that are highly probable but not necessary.
- Fictive-narrative philosophy makes claims differently. Rather than relying on a narrow series of propositions and facts to make a point or establish a claim, as direct logical discourse and the other forms of indirect discourse do, indirect discourse ideally makes vibrant, "ah-ha" connections to the reader or audience's wider experiences and values (also know as the worldview of the audience).

Storytelling, or *fictive-narrative discourse*, is one form of indirect discourse. In this sense, the indirect discourse is a *narrative* because it is a story, and it is *fictive* because the story is made up for the occasion, rather than purporting to relate something that actually happened. This sort of discourse becomes *philosophy* when it also makes a *claim*. Think, for example, of Aesop's fable of the hare and the tortoise, in which the slow but persistent tortoise finishes the race ahead of the fleet, but inconsistently attentive, hare. The conclusion to the fable is spelled out in the moral, to the effect that "slow and steady wins the race," but that conclusion is not derived from a set of tightly linked, mutually supportive facts and propositions, as a direct-discourse conclusion would be. Rather, it is implicit in the actions and results of the story. Readers can accept the conclusion to the degree that they can identify with the events and characters of the story. Readers might, for example, recall situations in their own lives in which they were more tortoiselike or more harelike and remember how they came out ahead or behind in certain instances. They might extrapolate "slow and steady" to situations beyond mere physical exertion, such as running in a race, to other kinds of effort and achievement, such as solving a difficult problem at work. According to their own experiences, then, they might accept the moral to a greater or lesser degree. (For example, one might take to heart the validity of the fable's moral in general, while also maintaining that "fast and steady"—combining the best traits of both the hare and the tortoise—would be an even better formula for winning a race.)

Or consider another story, Jesus's parable of the Good Samaritan (in Luke 10:25–37):

And, behold, a certain lawyer stood up and asked Jesus, "Master, what shall I do to inherit eternal life?"

Jesus said unto him, "What is written in the law? How readest thou?"

And the lawyer, answering, said, "Thou shalt love the Lord thy God with all thy heart, and with all thy soul, and with all thy strength, and with all thy mind; and love thy neighbor as thyself."

And Jesus said unto him, "Thou hast answered right. This do, and thou shalt live."

But the lawyer, willing to justify himself, said unto Jesus, "And who is my neighbor?"

And Jesus, answering, said, "A certain man went down from Jerusalem to Jericho, and fell among thieves, which stripped him of his garments, and wounded him, and departed, leaving him half dead. And by chance there came down a certain priest that way, and when he saw the man, he passed by on the other side of the road. And likewise a Levite, when he was at the place, came and looked on him, and passed by on the other side. But a certain Samaritan, as he journeyed, came where the man was, and when he saw him, he had compassion on him, and went to him, and bound up his wounds, pouring in oil and wine, and set him on his own donkey, and brought him to an inn, and took care of him. And on the morrow when he departed, he took out two pence and gave them to the host, and said unto him, 'Take care of him, and whatsoever thou spendest more when I come again, I will repay thee.' Which now of these three, thinkest thou, was neighbor unto him that fell among the thieves?"

And the lawyer said, "He that showed mercy on him."

Then said Jesus unto him, "Go, and do thou likewise."

Notice how this is a double narrative, a story within a story. The first is a framing story, written down by Saint Luke, in which Jesus induces a questioning lawyer to recite a version of the Golden Rule ("love thy neighbor as thyself," or "do unto others as you would have them do unto you") as an answer to the lawyer's own question about how to achieve eternal life. The lawyer's statement, which he has memorized from older scriptures ("the law"), is a true one, according to Jesus. But simply having accurately memorized a religious truth does not satisfy the lawyer's need to internalize—to truly understand—the key to salvation. So the lawyer presses Jesus for further elaboration. In response, Jesus does not recite additional religious precepts. Instead, he tells the lawyer a parable (the story within Luke's story) about a traveler beaten by thieves, then rescued by a passing Samaritan.

From his own experiences of life in ancient Judaea, the lawyer would be keenly aware of the parable's nuances. He would understand immediately the considerable risk of assault and robbery that anyone of the time took when traveling alone. He would sense instinctively the helplessness of stricken travelers in an age before 911 calls, highway patrols, and ambulances. And he would be struck by the fact that it is the distressed man's ostensibly religious fellow Jews (the priest and the Levite) who ignore him, but it is a Samaritan (a traditional enemy of the Jews) who goes out of his way to come to the beaten man's aid.

Note, then, that Jesus himself does not directly express the lesson to be drawn from the parable. Rather, the situations and characters in the story resonate with the lawyer in such a way that he can then, on his own, extract from the story the essential point that the person who shows mercy and compassion for others, regardless of their condition or social status, is one who loves his neighbors as himself—and is therefore eligible for eternal life. Jesus's story brings to life for the lawyer the holy, but otherwise sterile, admonition to "love thy neighbor as thyself." That is the purpose of fictive narratives in philosophy: to make connections with readers through their life experiences and their deeply held values and to lead them to draw conclusions from the story accordingly.

This introduction to philosophy will concentrate on the dualism in types of presentation between direct logical discourse (on the one hand) and narrative-based philosophy (on the other hand). Direct logical philosophy operates mechanically via premises that bind us to a conclusion (see Chapter 2 for more details). Narrative philosophy uses stories that make claims and persuade us through indirect discourse (see Chapter 3 for more details). Thus, narrative-based philosophy operates differently from direct-discourse philosophy.

What Is Direct-Discourse Philosophy?

In direct-discourse philosophy, one attempts to look at facts in the world and their impact on other events *intersubjectively*, that is, in a manner widely agreed upon by, or comprehensible to, many people. In this way, direct discourse is a very public medium. It depends on there being public facts and events about which most people might reasonably agree. In the Western tradition, the philosopher Aristotle stands as the formal originator of direct discourse in this sense through his *The Prior Analytics*. In this groundbreaking book, Aristotle invents a system of direct-discourse logic that stood relatively unchanged for 2,300 years—quite an achievement. How would you like to be able to put on your resume that you invented logic?

In *deductive logic* we create a series of declarative sentences that have truth-value (propositions). When the speaker presents these propositions, they become *facts* when the audience agrees without significant controversy that they are true. When controversy arises, the proposition is not tagged as fact but rather as an *assertion* (the bald say-so of the speaker to his audience).

Premises are linked together to support a conclusion (also known as the claim or point of contention). The proper linking of premises that follow various rules of deduction is called an *inference*. All conclusions are propositions that are justified by an inference. The propositions and their conclusion together constitute a *logical argument*. A very simple logical argument that has two premises and a conclusion with a special set of rules is called a *syllogism*. A sample might be diagrammed in the following form:

1. All artifacts that depict the reality of the human condition are masterpieces—Fact
2. All plays of Shakespeare depict the reality of the human condition—Assertion

   _____

3. All plays of Shakespeare are masterpieces—(Inference from premises 1 and 2)

In this example, the conclusion (listed under the line as statement 3) is a necessary inference based solely and directly on the information given in propositions 1 and 2 together: if all artifacts that depict the reality of the human condition are masterpieces, and if all the plays of Shakespeare depict the reality of the human condition, then no reasonable person can disagree with the conclusion that all the plays of Shakespeare are masterpieces.

This relationship between propositions and conclusions is characterized by tight logical connections. It is very mechanical and is subject to intersubjective scrutiny. That is, reasonable people can read and agree with the propositions and agree that the conclusion follows necessarily from the propositions. Whenever it is possible to do so in establishing a philosophical contention, one should employ direct discourse because of its compelling logical arguments and intersubjective validity.

But sometimes, despite its logical power, direct discourse is not the best way to persuade people. Situations that are complex and that involve degrees of nuance, ambiguity, contradiction, or interpretation often lend themselves instead to fictive narrative.

What Is Fictive-Narrative Philosophy?

A narrative is a story. When the story is structured toward a logically sequential conclusion (such as Conclusion 1 in the World Trade Center example at the opening of the chapter), then direct discourse is the option of choice. However, when the nuances of the story become too complicated or lie beyond intersubjective verification, then fictive-narrative philosophy might be called for. Fictive-narrative philosophy can make *claims* that are too complicated or unverifiable ever to be suitable for direct logical discourse. Thus, the *sort of question that is being addressed* can be one reason for choosing fictive narrative as a means to make a philosophical point.

A fictive narrative can argue for a conclusion but does so through a narrative that is rich in detail about the characters who act within the story. That detail is important. It makes a strong connection to the lived experience of the reader. As we have seen in the example of the Good Samaritan, many of the great religious texts of the world have made use of narratives in the form of parables and very short stories to deliver a conclusion that is more spontaneously accessible to people than a precise but narrow direct-discourse syllogism would be. Thus, a second reason for selecting a fictive narrative to deliver a philosophical argument lies in the *way fictive narrative communicates.*

Why Narrative-Based Philosophy?

The following elements appear in the communications flow of both direct and indirect discourse:

The Communication Flow of Direct and Indirect Philosophical Discourse

- Speaker (author)
- Audience (those listening to or interacting with the speaker)
- Point of contention/claim/conclusion (aka the theme in storytelling)
- Direct or indirect argument (including philosophical narrative)
- Common body of knowledge (the given facts and values within a society)

In direct discourse, we first confront the point of contention (conclusion/claim), and then the other elements follow suit. Indeed, as you read the primary texts in this volume, you should start with the conclusion and then work backward to the supporting premises.

However, in fictive narrative, as a form of indirect discourse, the order is reversed—rather perversely. Not only is the point of contention hidden, but it is the mission of the enterprise to engage (conscript) readers in discovering it. Thus, the reader who confronts fictive-narrative philosophy must acknowledge all the elements in the communications flow in order to ferret out a conclusion.

Though philosophy today is largely about direct-deductive discourse, this has not always been the case. The most famous practitioner of narrative as a vehicle for philosophical discourse is Plato. In his early dialogues, Plato often employs engrossing fictive action to draw his audience into a dramatic scene in which they engage his argument. An example of this comes from Book One of *The Republic*.

> "Very good, Cephalus," I said. "But what is the definition of Justice? Is it to tell the truth and to pay your debts? No more? And is this definition even correct? Suppose a friend deposits his weapons with me. When he did this he was perfectly in control. Later, when he is mad he asks for them back. Should I give them to him? Nobody would sanction this or call such an action right anymore than they would require me to always speak the truth to my mad friend."
>
> "This is true," he said.
>
> "But then we were not right to say that Justice is telling the truth and repaying that which had been previously given."[1]

In this example of fictive narrative, Plato takes the claim of his foe (called the *antithesis*) and shows that absurdity follows from this. By the reductio ad absurdum strategy of indirect discourse (given in a fictive context), the conclusion is rejected.

Fictive narrative is employed by the early Platonic dialogues to present issues in ethics, epistemology, and metaphysics, and those dialogues are often used nowadays as readings in introductory college courses. One reason for this is that students are more likely to get the point of Plato's presentation than they would of (say) presentations by Aristotle or Kant (who do not employ fictive narrative). Why is this?

One's reactions to the dialogues are fashioned within the context of one's personal worldview—a worldview that combines one's scientific understanding of the world with one's values about beauty, ethics, and truth (often understood through religion). When we are confronted with claims that aspire to be about our experience in the world, we try to fashion our understanding of each claim and our responses to it from our personal worldview.

Fictive narratives stimulate various aspects of our consciousness in a synergistic manner. Lots of material is left out of a fictive narrative precisely because this is the presentation mode of indirect discourse. It is up to readers to fill in the gaps, thus requiring them to participate actively in interpreting the narrative—which takes the form of a dialogue between the text and readers' personal worldview. That is, narrative-based claims require readers not only to reconstruct the claims within the narrative context of the presentation but also within their own real-life experience. In the context of philosophical narrative, *to reconstruct* means that one takes on the elements of the story as given and then engages in a creative process of reassembling those elements to make sense of them all. Where a direct-deductive logical presentation consciously limits itself to

---

1 Plato, *Republic* I, 331c[1]–d, translated by Michael Boylan.

straightforward propositions and inferences that can be verified through empirical examination, narrative-based philosophy creates the possibility of a more open-ended exploration of a problem from a particular point of view.

One distinctive characteristic of fictive narrative is that the presentation evokes various sensory possibilities. In traditional fiction these sensory possibilities lie on the page. In film and theater, they are presented in various forms that are more stimulating to the audience's perception. To the degree that they are effective, such presentations are closer to our lived experience. We can describe this confrontation with the particularity of the characters and their situations, along with the sensory-rich backdrop, as being "empirically suggestive."

We are all, by nature, drawn to such presentations in a most compelling way. Thus, the empirically suggestive narrative-based-philosophy presentation is more gripping than is the more simple architecture of direct-deductive philosophy because it connects to the personal worldview in more ways than does a simple, abstract, rational presentation. The more contacts or touch points the presentation establishes with readers' personal worldview, the more real the presentation seems to them. The *real* in this context is that which is easier to project into one's personal worldview and thus to imagine in all of its potential significance. The act of worldview projection allows the reader to imagine more completely the claims presented in a narrative.

Think for yourself. If you read about the genocide in Rwanda, and if you saw the movie *Hotel Rwanda*, how did each affect you? On the one hand, the factual newspaper accounts depict horrific events, but on the other, the movie confronts you with actors who are able to stimulate your imagination so that you can take in more particularistic detail: you see a character in front of you *now*, and your reactions to the characters and unfolding events of a particular time and place are visually reinforced. The story in the movie has an impact that the facts in a newspaper account, appalling though they are, might not convey as vividly. The same may be said about newspaper accounts of the war in Iraq against movie depictions of the same, and so forth.

In the case of Platonic dialogues, Plato employs the character of his former teacher, Socrates, to enter into dramatic conversations (the so-called dialogues) with real people who lived in that period. Like the movie example, the particularity of the presentation gives it a popular connection to its readers. But what exactly happens when Plato presents one of his dialogues? Some would say that, in Plato, it is the straightforward direct-deductive argument or the indirect reductio ad absurdum argument (that goes on between Socrates and the person he is talking to in any given dialogue) that is most important. This argument is *all* the philosophy that is taking place (some would say). Everything else is merely noise or pretty trappings, but it is not philosophy. Those who hold such views about deductive-based philosophy make their case based on the fact that direct logical philosophy is grounded in hard-nosed empirical truth. Such proponents of direct discourse might characterize narrative-based presentations as mere entertainment.

However, it might well be that on some of the central issues of philosophy, there are voids in what we can argue effectively through deductive-based philosophy. That is, for some topics, some of the geography of truth may be hidden from direct physical inspection, and there is a consequent necessity for a mode of expression that is suggestive of that hidden territory. Narrative-based philosophy is the best candidate to put these sorts of these conjectures forward.

Presenting Narrative-Based Philosophy

Plato often has rather complex messages. He wants readers to accept major worldview alterations. This is a tough task. Whereas straightforward deductive presentations are persuasive for minor alterations of worldview architecture, they are not very good for major changes. Instead, we need a more holistically engaging form of presentation: fictive narrative. Only with an empirically suggestive presentation can philosophers really change readers in a fundamental way.

One can classify fictive narrative in philosophy on a continuum. *Level one* operates as Plato does, with a very didactic presentation set in a fictive venue. The story is subservient to the message delivered. Other examples of level one are the parables of Jesus and Buddha and the fables of Aesop. In this volume, the primary texts for Plato meet this standard, as do the selections from the *Dhammapada*.

At *level two*, there is a balance between the story and the philosophical message. Many people think that C. S. Lewis's *Chronicles of Narnia* are at this level. A few of the short stories in this volume are also at this level (such as "Aristotle the Outsider").

Finally, *level three* consists of stories that stand on their own *as stories*. Their "meaning" and philosophical message are hidden under the doctrine of "show, don't tell." The reader must do the work in discovering and reconstructing the message presented. The primary text on Iris Murdoch and many of the short stories in this volume operate in this way (such as "The Queen and the Philosopher"). At level three, it takes some careful reconstruction on the part of the reader to discover the clues laid down by the author that all point to the intended philosophical claim. Readers know they are on the right track in reconstruction when the various sources for clues—story, character, description, motifs, and so on—all point in a common direction toward a theme that makes a declaration about some aspect of the good, the true, or the beautiful.

Any author who wants to create major worldview change on the part of his audience will be more effective when employing some form of narrative at one of the three levels because of the suggestive empirical content that the fictive presentation brings forward. Suggestive empirical content helps most people understand a claim to such an extent that they can project it into their personal worldview. Because of its greater number of contact points, empirically suggestive, narrative-based philosophy is able to engage the personal worldview of most readers more strongly than direct, deductive-based presentations (which offer fewer worldview contact points). It also sits as an invitation for personal reconstruction in ways not entirely controlled by the author.

Not all works of fiction are examples of narrative-based philosophy. For example, works that merely intend to imitate nature without taking a clear position are not narrative-based philosophy. Nor are books or movies that seek merely to stimulate, describe, or entertain. Most genre fiction and genre movies fall into this category (romance, romantic comedy, situation comedy, murder mystery, spy movies, and so forth).

Narrative-based philosophy creates a stronger partnership between author and reader. The structure of fictive claims can be discovered within the text through the examination of various narrative devices—such as carefully crafted plot situations or dialogue between characters that present truth claims. The boundaries of these claims will be less precise than in deductive presentations, but they are many times more engaging to readers. The greater the suggestiveness of the narrative, the greater the audience engagement and cooperative ownership are likely to be. This cooperative engagement is useful when the author seeks to explore issues that are obscure and inconclusive to direct logical discourse.

Conclusion

Narrative-based philosophy works on the principle of empirically suggestive indirect discourse. It makes claims that amount to explanations that are "likely stories." This is because it highlights ranges of truth that are not amenable to direct, deductively based discourse. When choosing narrative-based philosophy (in contrast to direct-deductive discourse), however, one loses the exact precision of argumentative support that leads to a necessary conclusion. At the same time, one gains (in contrast to direct-deductive discourse) an ability to engage the personal worldview of the audience uniquely. This gain derives from the empirical suggestiveness of narrative. It transports us to another way of thinking about things more effectively than any other vehicle.

■ READING AND DISCUSSION QUESTIONS

1. What separates direct logical philosophy from fictive-narrative philosophy?
2. What is fictive-narrative philosophy?
3. Why would one employ fictive-narrative philosophy rather than direct logical philosophy?
4. What are the three levels of fictive-narrative philosophy?
5. Do all fictive narratives make philosophical claims? Why or why not?

CHAPTER TWO

How Can I Respond to Claims Using Direct Logical Discourse?

In this book argument is presented in one of two ways: through deductive logical argument (direct discourse) and through fictive-narrative philosophy (indirect discourse). This chapter will address three questions concerning direct-discourse response:

1. How does direct logical discourse work?
2. When is direct logical discourse appropriate?
3. How do I go about preparing a response using direct logical discourse?

The answers to these three questions about direct-discourse responses will structure this chapter. (Chapter 3 deals with indirect-discourse responses.)

How Does Direct Logical Discourse Work?

Direct logical discourse works mechanically. What makes it mechanical are the clear rules of logic that specify how the collection of several sentences (which we will call *premises*) necessarily cause us to accept another sentence (called the *conclusion* or *point of contention*). The process that allows this to happen is a justification called an *inference*. Inference lies at the heart of direct logical discourse. It is the strongest form of justification that one can give for accepting a premise. When applied to the argument as a whole, logical inference can generate a valid argument mechanically, in much the same way that answers are derived in mathematics: for example, 7 + 5 = 12. That is, "12" is said to follow mechanically from one's understanding of "7," "5," "+," and "=." See, for example, the following example of logical inference:

1. All humans are mortal—Fact
2. Socrates is a human—Fact

_____

3. Socrates is mortal—1, 2 Inference

Premises 1 and 2 are justified by *fact* (here taken to mean the agreement between speaker and audience). The other standard sort of justification, called an *assertion*, is the mere say-so of the speaker of the argument. In Figure 2.1 the conclusion (proposition 3) is justified by one's acceptance of premises 1 and 2 (which are facts). When one accepts premises 1 and 2, then one must accept proposition 3. The justification of the conclusion is one's previous acceptance of premises 1 and 2. One's assent to each causes one to accept proposition 3. Such intrapremise dynamics are called an *inference*. An inference can occur as a justification of a *premise* (often called a *subconclusion*), and it is always the justification of a *conclusion* (or else we would not have logical arguments). The intrapremise dynamics can be diagrammed as in Figure 2.1.

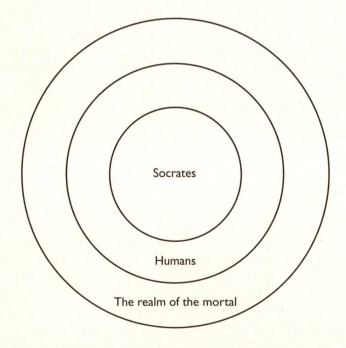

Socrates

Humans

The realm of the mortal

Figure 2.1 The mechanics of inference.

We can see from Figure 2.1 that within the realm of the mortal (meaning capable of death), humans are a subset. (There are other possible subsets of things that die, such as flowers, insects, snakes, and so on.) Looking at the middle circle, Socrates is one human, but there are certainly others—such as Lucy, Jemal, Petra, or any other person you can think of—who also belong in that circle. In mapping the first premise in this chart and then the second, you will find that you have already shown the conclusion—that is, Socrates is subsumed within the set of "humans" as well as within the set of things contained in "the realm of the mortal." Mechanically, it is impossible to disbelieve the conclusion (that Socrates is mortal) if you have already accepted the two premises (that humans are mortal and that Socrates is human).

At heart, this is what direct discourse is all about: creating a formal or informal reconstruction of an argument according to rules of inference that create deductively necessary conclusions. A reconstruction of an argument via the direct mode is transference of one's reading of a direct or indirect text in the form of a deductive argument containing numbered premises and a numbered conclusion. Each premise must have a justification (fact, assertion, or inference, indicated by listing previous numbered premises that logically compel the reader to accept this premise as true). When a premise (not the conclusion) is justified by an inference, it is called a *subconclusion*. Every conclusion must be justified by an inference.

The process of reconstruction begins with the conclusion (point of contention or claim). Each time you read a passage, write down what you think its point is. This will be the conclusion. Then go back and try to determine just what supported that conclusion: what evidence is there for the claim? Try to assemble the evidence in the form of numbered premises (each with a justification—fact, assertion, or inference).

When Is Direct Discourse Appropriate?

Direct discourse works best in situations in which the premises can be verified by empirical reports. This makes fact- and assertion-based premises alike amenable to examination and agreement by reasonable people according to their own observations of the world. In this way the truth of the premises is intersubjectively justified: reasonable people can all see and measure them and come to common conclusions about their truth or falsity. When there are minor gaps in the argument or it is necessary to accept other underlying worldview positions, then these missing or suppressed premises, called *enthymemes*, are indicated by putting the premise into brackets ([ ]). Consider the following argument about the best baseball team in history:

1. The best baseball team in history is the one that has won the most World Series titles—Assertion

---

2. The New York Yankees are the best baseball team in history—1 (Inference)

Here, the conclusion does not follow from premise 1. Something is missing between the premise and the conclusion. Can you figure out what it is?

"The New York Yankees have won the most World Series titles in history." The speaker left this second premise out, but it is necessary to make the inference to reach the conclusion. We should not be too hard on the speaker. It is very common to leave out a premise that seems obvious. But in direct-deductive argument reconstruction, each premise must be represented so that we can properly evaluate the argument. So, let us rewrite the argument with the missing premise (the enthymeme) in brackets.

1. The best baseball team in history is the one that has won the most World Series titles—Assertion
2. [The New York Yankees have won the most World Series titles in history]—Fact

---

3. The New York Yankees are the best baseball team in history—1, 2

The use of brackets shows that certain additional material is necessary to create the mechanical inference. The reader's responsibility is to provide such enthymemes in an effort to create a valid argument (meaning that the truth of the conclusion follows necessarily from inferences that come from the preceding premises).

In this introduction to philosophy, almost all of the primary-text readings are direct logical discourses fully amenable to this sort of reconstruction. Fictive-narrative philosophy is also amenable to this sort of response. Thus, when presented with either direct-deductive logical argument or fictive-narrative philosophy, one avenue of reconstruction and response is direct logical argument.

How Do I Go About Preparing a Response Using Direct Discourse?

In responding to direct discourse, a reader must first find the claim being made in the selection. The claim (also known as the point of contention or the conclusion) requires some support to be accepted. For the purposes of this exercise, we will focus on deductive logical support. Once you have determined what the passage is about (the point of contention or conclusion), then write it out in the form of a proposition. Propositions are short declarative sentences with truth-value.

The next step is to set down propositions that tend to support the conclusion. These propositions, called premises, will be sequentially numbered and must possess a justification at the end—either as an assertion, a fact, or an inference (as indicated in a list of the numbers of the previous premises that directly support a particular premise at hand). Sometimes propositions are about empirically verifiable statements or agreed-on values in the world. We will agree to call these premise justifications facts. Thus, for our purposes the term *fact* will be used to identify the justification of a proposition whenever (1) there is agreement between the speaker (the one making the claim) and the audience (the one listening to the claim), and (2) there is a real or theoretical possibility of intersubjective verification of the proposition. For example, if the speaker were to say that the boiling point of water at sea level is 100°C, we would call this a fact. Skeptics could (if they were so inclined) test the proposition by using a measuring device (that we all agreed was accurate) to check the temperature of boiling water.

An example of an agreed-on value might be that it is wrong to commit murder. However, there is no similar empirical test for values like there is for boiling water, apart, say, from an opinion survey.

At other times, the support is merely the say-so of the speaker. In this case there may be doubt in the minds of the audience. We will agree to call such justifications *assertions*. An example might concern who is best suited for some particular public office. Mr. A might declare that Jamal is the best, while Ms. B might support Sarah. There is no real test that would cause A or B to change his or her mind. We are left with the mere declared beliefs of the speakers.

For our purposes, we will rely upon the native rationality of each reader to determine whether a proper inference has been made or not. We will substitute formal rules for informal sensibility concerning the *tightness* or *looseness* of a proposed inference. The example above of enthymemes shows how sometimes we must supplement the presented argument from the text with bracketed statements so that each step of the deductive presentation holds. As per our example of the New York Yankees, you should put these additions into brackets so that your readers know that you are adding something that fits the spirit of the original text but is not explicitly present in it.

To summarize briefly:

1. Arguments can be found wherever there are claims (be it via direct or via indirect discourse).
2. Arguments are understood by forming the claim into a proposition that will be called the point of contention or conclusion.
3. Conclusions need to be supported by other propositions, called premises (each of which requires its own justification as fact, assertion, or inference—indicated by citing premise numbers).
4. A conclusion must always be justified by an inference.
5. Inferences are very special and must be tight in order for the argument to be logically correct (valid).
6. Sometimes one must add a premise or two in order to transform a weak inference into a tight one. These additions, called enthymemes (missing or suppressed premises), are put into brackets.

Examples of Response Using Direct Logical Discourse

Now let us try a couple of examples. The passages in this book are short by design in order to support a reading approach that requires multiple rereads. On the first reading you should go through the text completely without stopping. On the second reading you should try to find the principal claim the text is making. On the third reading you should try to locate the supporting evidence for the claim. Then, on the fourth and all subsequent readings you should try to set the argument into clear logical order.

A Direct Logical Response to a Direct Logical Passage

Consider this (simplified) claim about friendship (originally by Aristotle):

> There are several sorts of friendships that can be made in life. Each form of friendship owes its existence to a particular category. The categories are: utility, pleasure, and goodness. Thus, one sort of friend is someone you interact with because each of you gives the other a tangible, material benefit. This relationship will end as soon as the tangible, material benefit ends. The second form is similar to the first. The benefit, however, is immaterial: pleasure. Because of its immaterial nature, some interaction between the essential worldviews of the participants occurs. However, like utility, when the pleasure ends, so does the relationship. The final form is goodness. In this sort of friendship, it is the ability of each reciprocally to improve the moral excellence of the other that occasions the relationship. When you are with such a friend, then you know that you are better: becoming all that you can be. Each individual is permanently affected for the better. Thus, the friendship based upon goodness is the best sort of friendship.

Okay. Let us go through the routine.

1. Read the passage for overall meaning.
2. Find the principal claim: "The best sort of friendship is one based upon goodness."
3. What is the evidence for the claim?
4. Put the evidence into logical form using the methodology advocated above.

Start with writing down the conclusion. Then find subconclusions that may support it:

Conclusion: "The best sort of friendship is one based upon goodness"—conclusion (principal claim).

Consider these key points:

- There are three sorts of friendship: utility, pleasure, and goodness.
- Utility-based friendship fails when the utility ends.
- Pleasure-based friendship fails when the pleasure ends.
- In pleasure-based friendships, the worldviews of the participants interact.

- Interactive goodness makes each party more excellent.
- Each individual is permanently affected for the better.

Provide enthymemes necessary for the inferences:

- Long-term relationships are better than short-term ones.
- Interactive touching of a worldview is a worthwhile and positive event.
- All of us, by nature, desire most of all to be more excellent.
- Goodness and its expression are long term.

From these observations we are prepared to outline the argument according to the following form:

1. There are three sorts of friendships based (respectively) upon utility, pleasure, and goodness—A(ssertion)
2. Utility friendships fail when the benefit that is the basis of the friendship ends—F(act)
3. [Long-term relationships are better than short-term ones]—A
4. [Changes in utility are frequent and characteristic of a short-term relationship]—A
5. Utility friendships are not the best—1–4 (Inference)
6. Pleasure relationships fail when the pleasure ends—F
7. Pleasure relationships interactively touch the worldviews of the participants—A
8. [Interactive touching of a worldview is a worthwhile and positive event]—A
9. Pleasure relationships are not the best, but they are better than utility friendships—3, 6, 7, 8
10. Goodness relationships are characterized by interactive goodness—A
11. Interactive goodness makes all parties permanently more excellent—A
12. [All of us, by nature, desire most of all to be more excellent]—F
13. [Goodness and its expression are long term]—A
14. Goodness relationships are better than those based on pleasure—9–13

_____

15. The best sort of friendship is one based on goodness—5, 9, 14

This is an example of a logical outline according to the rules set forth. Please note that there is more than one "acceptable" direct reconstruction of a logical argument. This is because of ambiguity in language and the personal worldview of the reader (audience).

After you have reconstructed an argument in direct-deductive logical form, you are now in a position to create an *evaluation* of an argument. It is often the case that students want to jump to evaluation right after reading a text. This is a mistake because this sort of haphazard approach leads to an unbalanced evaluation and often encourages prejudicial focus on points perhaps not central to the argument. Thus, it is important first to find out in exact detail what the author is saying and why before one ventures to evaluate the claim.

To create a short, direct evaluation of an argument, find one or two premises that you think are controversial and then either take a "pro" or a "con" standpoint. For either, set out your understanding of the controversial premise(s), keeping in mind what others who disagree with you might say. Develop your essay in an interactive fashion. This means that if you are pro, you might anticipate the arguments that detractors of the pivotal premises might make and then develop premises that counter those objections. Conversely, if you are con, you should consider various replies that a supporter might make and then develop premises to meet and defeat those objections. End your essay with some discussion of the significance of this problem both in its original context and for today.

A Direct Logical Response to an Indirect Fictive Narrative

Consider this fable, retold from Aesop:

> The North Wind and the Sun had an argument about which was more powerful. They squabbled with no positive outcome. Then they saw a man who happened to be walking down the road. The man was wearing a light coat.
>
> The North Wind said, "Well, here's a perfect test for our argument. I'll wager that I can force that man to take off his coat more quickly than you can."
>
> "You're on," said the Sun. "You go first."
>
> The North Wind blew a frigid blast at the man so that he pulled his coat even tighter to his body. Then the North Wind blew harder and harder so that ice showers fell upon the unfortunate man. His hands began to shake with the cold and his teeth rattled, but the poor fellow hugged his light coat even tighter. The man was not going to take off his coat.
>
> "Now it's my turn," said the Sun.
>
> The Sun came out from behind the cloud and shined his heat with a radiant glow.
>
> At first the man stopped where he was. He looked up and smiled. Gradually his shivers and chattering teeth gave way to a more relaxed posture. Soon he decided to rest under the shade of a tree and he took off his coat.
>
> Thus, it was that the Sun won the bet.

The first step in reconstructing the fable's argument is to determine what claim it makes. There are several possible versions of a conclusion—such as it is easier to persuade with kindness than with bullying. For our purposes let us assume the following conclusion: "It is easier to get one's way with 'soft power' (gentle persuasion) than with 'hard power' (sheer force)."

Step two, then, would be to create a logical outline according to the rules set out here.

1. The North Wind represents "hard power" and the Sun represents "soft power"—A
2. The empirical test of disrobing a random person of his coat is taken as a conclusive test of the veracity of the general principle expressed in premise 1—F
3. The North Wind fails to disrobe the person while the Sun is successful—F

---

4. Soft power is more effective than hard power—1–3

Step three would be to examine the premise—premise 2—that might provoke the most disagreement. It is very possible that the test proposed in premise 2 does not really prove anything. Objectors might cite (or at least imagine) various other empirical tests that could render the inference in the conclusion invalid. On the other hand, supporters of premise 2 might counterclaim that the most enduring instances of political change have been as the result of the exercise of soft power over hard power, such as (for example) through the use of nonviolent civil disobedience by leaders such as Mohandas Gandhi and Martin Luther King Jr.

The use of direct discourse as a way to analyze fictive-narrative philosophy will look something like this. Because this mode strips away much of the fundamental character of a fictive narrative, some might object that this method of exposing the key arguments of a narrative is too artificial. Even with the addition of bracketed enthymemes, these objectors might insist that something is missing. But this is not a problem in this context. The direct logical reconstruction approach never pretends to comprehend everything presented in the text. In the direct logical discourse mode, the imperative is to *prove the claim using the rules of logical deduction*. Anything that does not move toward this goal is superfluous. The approach is ruthlessly efficient.

Thus, supporters will respond that what is on the table is the essential, stripped-bare claim and its direct-deductive explanation.

Conclusion

This is a very compact overview, but it should aid you in your quest to outline logical arguments (from whatever source, be it direct-deductive discourse or fictive-narrative philosophy) and begin a direct-deductive response of your own. To be perfectly clear, one may make a direct logically deductive response both to the primary texts in this book (largely delivered in this mode) and to the indirect fictive philosophical discourses in the book (including all the short stories and even several of the primary-text readings, such as Plato's "The Myth of the Charioteer," the *Dhammapada*, or Iris Murdoch's "Ludwig's Conundrum," which are in the form of indirect discourse). The response mode of direct discourse can be used to reconstruct and respond to every sort of discourse (written or visual). This book suggests that it is valuable to learn various response skills. For a quick primer on indirect-discourse response skills, turn to Chapter 3.

Suggested Rubric for Evaluating Direct-Discourse Philosophy

- Have you found the point of contention or claim in either the direct-discourse selection or the fictive-narrative philosophy selection?
- Does your essay highlight the point of contention in the context of controversial premises?
- Do you take a clear pro or con attitude toward the conclusion via the examination of the controversial premises in your evaluation?
- How well does your defense (pro essay) or refutation (con essay) of the author hang together? Does your essay move from surface problems to more fundamental philosophical principles?

■ READING AND DISCUSSION QUESTIONS

1. When is direct logical discourse the most effective way to respond to a philosophical claim?
2. Describe the process of creating a pro or a con argument. Use a step-by-step presentation.
3. How can one use a logical outline to help structure either a pro or a con argument?
4. How is the process of direct logical discourse as a response mode different when one is evaluating another work of direct logical discourse as opposed to fictive-narrative philosophy?

CHAPTER THREE

How Can I Respond to Claims Using Indirect Fictive-Narrative Discourse?

The second way that argument is presented is via fictive-narrative philosophy (a form of indirect discourse). This chapter addresses ways to respond to texts (of both direct and indirect discourse) using the approach of fictive-narrative philosophy. To this end the chapter addresses three questions:

1. How does indirect-narrative discourse work?
2. When is indirect-narrative discourse appropriate?
3. How do I go about preparing a response using indirect-narrative discourse?

How Does Indirect Discourse Work?

Fictive-narrative philosophy tells a story that makes a *claim* (that is, a *conclusion* or *point of contention* generally called a *theme* in fiction) that is expressed on one of three levels:

1. Level one, in which the claim dominates the story.
2. Level two, in which the claim and the story operate on a par.
3. Level three, in which the claim lies hidden within the dominant story.

The tale itself comprises various elements. When the claim presented is philosophical in nature (dealing with the good, the true, or the beautiful), then the indirect narrative is perforce philosophical. Chapter 1 suggested that plot, character, and narrative detail are means by which fictive-narrative philosophy works. Charles Johnson puts this list more systematically as

> (1) a story with logically plotted sequences; (2) three-dimensional characters—that is, real people with real problems; (3) sensuous description, or a complete world to which readers can imaginatively respond; (4) dialogue with the authenticity of real speech; (5) a strong narrative voice; (6) rhythm, musicality, and control of the cadences in their fiction; and finally, (7) originality in theme and execution.[1]

These categories would describe a well-wrought fictive narrative. It is perhaps fanciful to expect that you must master them all immediately. Nonetheless, you (and, indeed, all writers of fiction) would do well to consult Johnson's list and strive continually to make some progress in as many areas as possible.

When Is Indirect Discourse Appropriate?

Chapter 1 argued that when a claim is amenable to full intersubjective, empirical scrutiny, you are well advised to choose direct logical argument (guidelines for which were given in Chapter 2). Most of the primary-text readings in this volume are themselves direct logical arguments and, as such, lend themselves well to direct logical responses.

However, there are other situations in which part of the terrain upon the geography of truth is obscured. These are principles that cannot be decided by common agreement or scientific verification. For example, say one wished to create an argument around the claim that humans are basically bad. Because so much empirical evidence for this claim can be interpreted in contradictory ways—that is, as either supporting or denying the claim—no generally agreed-on logical conclusion can be drawn. Thus, the claim is a good candidate for fictive narrative. In fact, there have been many stories, novels, plays, and movies on this very topic—or on topics closely aligned to it, like "man's inhumanity to man."

Or take another case akin to the last example. "Which is the best way to motivate someone—through the use of kindness (carrots) or through the use of force (sticks)?" If one could answer this question in a logically necessary fashion, then think how much easier foreign policy might be. We'd know whether the use of belligerence and war (sticks) was superior in all cases to foreign aid and development (carrots). But because direct-deductive logical argument cannot answer this claim with certainty, another mode of making claims is necessary: fictive-narrative philosophy.

---

1. These seven categories come from Charles Johnson's essay "A Boot Camp for Creative Writing (Uncut)," *Writers Digest* (January 30, 2009), online reprint of "Boot Camp for Creative Writing," *Chronicle for Higher Education* 50, no. 10 (October 31, 2003): B7–B10.

How Do I Go About Preparing a Response Using Indirect Discourse?

So, now you have decided to create a response or to form an original claim via fictive-narrative philosophy. Each of the subsequent chapters of this book challenges you to do just that. You may be required to respond to two sorts of texts using this method:

1. A direct logical discourse text (including most of the primary texts in this volume).
2. A selection of fictive-narrative philosophy (including a few of the primary texts in this volume and all of the short stories).

Let us revisit the examples of each from Chapter 2 and see how responses using indirect discourse might work.

Fictive-Narrative Responses to Direct Logical Discourse

Consider the following discourse on friendship, based on an original argument by Aristotle:

> There are several sorts of friendships that can be made in life. Each form of friendship owes its existence to a particular category. The categories are: utility, pleasure, and goodness. Thus, one sort of friend is someone you interact with because each of you gives the other a tangible, material benefit. This relationship will end as soon as the tangible, material benefit ends. The second form is similar to the first. The benefit, however, is immaterial: pleasure. Because of its immaterial nature, some interaction between the essential worldviews of the participants occurs. However, like utility, when the pleasure ends, so does the relationship. The final form is goodness. In this sort of friendship, it is the ability of each reciprocally to improve the moral excellence of the other that occasions the relationship. When you are with such a friend, then you know that you are better: becoming all that you can be. Each individual is permanently affected for the better. Thus, the friendship based upon goodness is the best sort of friendship.

Chapter 2 sketched this argument via the response mode of deductive logical outline (direct discourse). Now let us take the very same direct logical text and try another response mode: indirect fictive-narrative philosophy.

Establish a Claim
The first step in creating an indirect narrative response to a direct logical presentation is to set out the claim. In this case the claim is that the best form of friendship is based on a mutual interaction toward the ethical betterment of each—that is, on "goodness." Create a statement of a claim in your own words (that is consistent with the text) and that you can understand through your own life experience. Sometimes this latter requirement can be difficult if the claim includes issues that you have never lived through. In those cases try to connect with analogous experiences—even if the connection is rather remote. For example, if

you were trying to understand what a general might be thinking in a claim involving war (and you have never been in the army or experienced military combat), you might imagine your experiences on the football team or some other arduous physical community project.

Find Something Missing in the Direct Presentation

The second step in creating an indirect narrative response to a direct logical presentation is to think carefully about the argument and ferret out what you believe is missing. Base your reaction on your own experience in life. Do you think that Aristotle's direct presentation is in any way lacking? Do his logical arguments miss something vital about how friendships work in the real world? This is important. *Remember, the point of fictive-narrative philosophy is to provide something that the direct logical approach leaves out.* Read your direct-discourse response to the Aristotle passage (or whatever other direct-discourse passage you are responding to) and then ask yourself, What would real people say in such a situation? or How would accepting Aristotle's recommendations really affect their lives? These are the sorts of questions that indirect discourse demands.

Imagine a Scene with Characters

Once you have a handle on what you think is missing in direct discourse, the third step is to think about the specific question at hand. In most cases this is a partially constructed scene about real people in the world. Your task is to create a fictive narrative. This means that you need to decide whose story it is and create whatever characters you need to make the scene come alive. This requires some work. Most professionals at fiction go through considerable background thinking on each character so that the character will appear real to the reader (see Johnson's list above). In the situation of a classroom assignment you will not be able to be quite as comprehensive, but you need to *know* your principal characters. Then create an action sequence that will make a claim (as per the methodology cited in Chapter 1).

Choose a Narrative Level

The fourth step is to decide at what level of fictive-narrative philosophy you wish to write: level one (principally didactic), level two (claim and story share the stage), or level three (the story takes the lead and the claims are very indirectly presented via Johnson's seven points). For most undergraduate students, the best level to attempt initially is usually level one, because it requires fewer fictive skills and is structurally simpler to construct. Those intrepid few who want to go further might start at level one and then venture to levels two and three according to their success at lower levels.

In the above example on friendship, you may want to tell the story of three friendships: John and Michelle, Felicia and Kenshana, and Marielle and Jemal (for example). The first friendship might be an instance of the utility friendship. It might be efficient to highlight this relationship just as it is starting or breaking up (in order to show what creates it or what destroys it). Second, there is the pleasure relationship. You might choose to look at this relationship in the middle of its course, before it ends, but then contrast it to the last kind of friendship, based on goodness—also in the middle of its course. Write down ideas about how you think you can mix all three stories into one single narrative. Will it be three sets of coworkers on the job or three sets of students in an introduction to philosophy class? Or might it involve some other situation? Setting out the characters and their initial situation is the first step. Then you have to structure a story using all three relationships and their various rationales and outcomes. The creation of a story often involves setting the scene with characters and then introducing a problem. The problem generates the action to follow. As you structure your problem and basic action, you cannot forget the claims you wish to represent. How will you present the claims? The easiest method is probably through the dialogue of the characters, as in Plato's dialogues. But you might also consider using a third-person narrator who comments on the text (like Jane Austen or Charles Dickens). The choice is yours.

Evaluate Your Story

Once you have constructed your story (the fifth and final step), then you need to have means to evaluate it. The means for evaluating your story are these:

1. Does your narrative make a claim? How well do you do present it via clarity and nuance? *Clarity* means that the reader can readily understand the claim from reading the story. *Nuance* is the indirect artfulness of such a presentation (the difference between step one and step two and again between step two and step three).
2. Are there any shortcomings in the narrative presentation (obvious contradictions, underdeveloped characters or actions, and so on)?
3. How well have you met the expectations set out in Johnson's list of seven points? (The more complete and fully executed, the better.)

When you give a fictive-narrative response to a direct philosophical presentation, it is important to be able to show something without necessarily expressing it explicitly in your story. The "unsaid" is that which is depicted indirectly. After all, one typically chooses the fictive-narrative response precisely in order to present aspects of a philosophical problem that do not lend themselves well to being completely spelled out in direct discourse. Thus, it is important to make sure that your creative presentation leaves room for your readers to reach certain conclusions for themselves.

Fictive-Narrative Response to Fictive-Narrative Philosophy

Consider (again) the following fable, retold from Aesop:

> The North Wind and the Sun had an argument about which was more powerful. They squabbled with no positive outcome. Then they saw a man who happened to be walking down the road. The man was wearing a light coat.

The North Wind said, "Well, here's a perfect test for our argument. I'll wager that I can force that man to take off his coat more quickly than you can."

"You're on," said the Sun. "You go first."

The North Wind blew a frigid blast at the man so that he pulled his coat even tighter to his body. Then the North Wind blew harder and harder so that ice showers fell upon the unfortunate man. His hands began to shake with the cold and his teeth rattled, but the poor fellow hugged his light coat even tighter. The man was not going to take off his coat.

"Now it's my turn," said the Sun.

The Sun came out from behind the cloud and shined his heat with a radiant glow.

At first the man stopped where he was. He looked up and smiled. Gradually his shivers and chattering teeth gave way to a more relaxed posture. Soon he decided to rest under the shade of a tree and he took off his coat.

Thus, it was that the Sun won the bet.

As a level-one example of fictive-narrative philosophy (the fable), the philosophical claim is boldly presented: "It is easier to get one's way with soft power (gentle persuasion) than with hard power (sheer force)." This claim is especially suited to fictive-narrative philosophy since it deals with a cluster of themes mentioned earlier (such as whether humans are basically good or bad or whether the best sort of motivation lies in carrots [incentives] or sticks [punitive behavior]).

State the Claim

The first step is to set out your understanding of the claim. For our purposes, let us suppose that you choose the claim that it is easier to get one's way with soft power than with hard power. (Obviously there are various alternative readings of the claim.)

Think About the Claim in Real-Life Contexts

The second step is to think about a real-life depiction of your understanding of the claim. Let us suppose that you think generally about the relation between soft and hard power in terms of contemporary international relations. This is currently a hot issue among those in power within the United States. Some say that if there is an unstable state in the world, the best solution is military intervention—such as the US interventions in Korea, Vietnam, and Iraq. Only force (hard power) can settle such instability. Others think that soft power can do a better job. For example, helping to build schools, hospitals, and roads and to develop the local economy of another nation might better solve that country's political instabilities than the threat or use of force against it.

Imagine a Narrative

The third step is to imagine a narrative to embody your vision of the claim. Initially, this would require thinking about your response at one of the three levels. Unlike the indirect response to direct discourse (above), where the recommendation was to stick to level one, in this case, it is easier to match the level of response to the level of fictive narrative given to you. If selection at hand is a level-one fictive philosophical narrative, such as Plato's "The Myth of the Charioteer" (included in this book), then the fictive response of level one might be best. If the selection is a level-two fictive philosophical narrative (such as the story "Aristotle the Outsider" in this book) or a third-level narrative (such as "The Queen and the Philosopher," also a story in this book), then a response at that level might be most appropriate (though, since level-three responses are so difficult, a level-two comment might work as well here).

Aesop's fable is at level one. Thus, the response might be easiest in this mode. A response to this narrative might depict a meeting of the US National Security Council as its members discuss intervention in Korea, Vietnam, or Iraq. You could create a fictional panel based on the real people involved in the actual events at the time, or you could create fictional characters. One might imagine, for example, a story that highlights a conflict between a hard-power advocate against a soft-power advocate in which the reasons for the various positions are set out and then some dramatic action involving the debate tilts to one side or the other. Again, for most students the level-one response will work best. Set out the argument within dialogue that is set in some sort of story context.

It is important to realize that this creative reaction mode of "storytelling" is not an "anything goes" moment. Narrative philosophy is just as rigorous as direct-deductive discourse. As the term progresses you should improve at both. The tools for evaluating your story when it is used to respond to another story are really the same as in the last section (a fictive-narrative response to a direct-deductive presentation). In general, the rubric for fictive-narrative philosophy is as follows.

Suggested Rubric for Evaluating Fictive-Narrative Philosophy

- Have you clearly chosen one of the three levels of fictive-narrative philosophy?
- Have you taken a recognizable pro or con position relative to the claim that you are evaluating (appropriate to that level)?
- Have you expressed your reasons in terms of the dialogue, action, and characterization?
- Does your effort work both as philosophy and narrative (relative to the chosen narrative level)?

A successful piece of fictive-narrative philosophy seeks to make a clear and nuanced claim through telling a story in which events and characters are credible, and it should demonstrate proficiency in Johnson's seven points.

■ READING AND DISCUSSION QUESTIONS

1. How does indirect narrative discourse work?
2. When is indirect narrative discourse appropriate?
3. Describe the step-by-step process for creating a work of fictive-narrative philosophy. Be sure to differentiate the three different levels.
4. How is the process of fictive-narrative philosophy different from direct logical discourse when one is evaluating a work of direct logical discourse or another work of fictive-narrative philosophy?

PART 2

ANCIENT AND MEDIEVAL PHILOSOPHY

Socrates answers crito by saying the
opinion of some men are to be regarded
while others aren't. He says they to follow the
opinion of one who has fear them or the opinion
of one who has understanding. He tells crito
they must not regard what many say to
of them but rather what one who has
understanding of just and unjust, you should
regard the opinion of the many about just and
unjust, good and evil, and honor + dishonor.

He spoke to the young ppl since they were
open to new things. When you write your
thoughts down, it was set in stone.

CHAPTER FOUR

Plato

Alfred North Whitehead, himself an eminent philosopher and mathematician, once suggested that European philosophy "consists of a series of footnotes to Plato." The founder of the Academy in Athens—the first institution of higher learning in the Western world—the Greek philosopher Plato (c. 428–c. 347 BCE) was a student of Socrates and, in turn, the mentor of Aristotle. In all but a couple of Plato's dialogues, the main character in the fictive narrative is Socrates, his teacher. The driving force of the presentation is a conversation between Socrates and one or more other characters (generally real people who lived in Greece—although not necessarily people whom Socrates might actually have confronted).

For Plato, the material world known to us through our senses is not the only fundamental reality. This is because of the constant changing of empirical objects. Plato believed that the only way to understand change is against a constant background of ideal Ideas or Forms. For example, all chairs are different from each other, but all embody, however imperfectly, an essence (that is, a Form, with capital F) of "chairness" within their individual, tangible forms (with lowercase f). Genuine knowledge can be gained only through the appreciation of such universal Forms, which exist in a realm beyond the sensory world.

THE CYNIC

Charles Johnson

The character of Plato tells the story of "The Cynic." Athens is still reeling from its disastrous defeat by the Spartan alliance, and Plato is particularly devastated by the city's execution of his mentor, Socrates. In his narration, he comments in passing, often with dismissive disparagement, on a number of philosophers of the day, including Thrasymachus, Protagoras, Parmenides, Heraclitus, Antisthenes, Democritus, Thales, and Anaximenes. Even Plato's own student, Aristotle, makes a cameo appearance in the story. But it is his encounter with Diogenes the Cynic (c. 412–323 BCE) that has the most impact on Plato. Renouncing all but the most meager of possessions, Diogenes lives a doglike life in the streets of Athens, which he wanders with a lantern, ostensibly seeking an honest man. Confronted by this provocatively unconventional thinker, Plato finds his very view of reality challenged.

> *"The ruler of the world is the*
> *Whirlwind, that has unseated Zeus."*
> —THE CLOUDS, ARISTOPHANES

If you listen to those who are wise, the people who defended my teacher at his trial before he was killed by the state, they will tell you that the golden days of our city were destroyed by the war. The Corinthians, who feared our expansionist policies and growing power, convinced the Spartans to make war against us. Our leader, Pericles,[1] knew we were stronger at sea than on shore. So he had all the inhabitants of Athenian territory in Attica huddle inside the fortifications of the city, which left the lands of the rich to be ravished by our enemies. But Pericles believed that after this sacrifice of land to the bellicose Spartans, our swift and deadly ships, *triremes* outfitted with three banks of oars, would wear them down in a war of attrition. His plan, this gamble, might have worked. But at the outset of the war, a plague fell upon Athens, laying waste to those crowded together in the city and, if that was not bad enough, Pericles himself died the following year. With his death, power in the Assembly was seized by demagogues like the young general Alcibiades,[2] who con-

---

1 **Pericles:** famous ruler of Athens at the height of their military glory against Asian armies.
2 **Alcibiades:** a passionate general in the Peloponnesian War (which Athens eventually lost against Sparta). He was also mentored by Socrates, Plato's teacher.

vinced the voters to abandon our defensive strategies and launch an attack on the city of Syracuse in faraway Sicily. This ill-advised invasion, this poorly planned military adventure, drained the manpower and treasure of the *polis,* our city-state. Within two years of the Sicilian expedition, "the hateful work of war," as Homer might put it, had wiped out our ships and ground forces. However, this was just the beginning of the spell of chaos cast upon us by the goddess Eris.[3]

The war dragged on for another ten years, dividing the population, feeding our disenchantment with civic life. Just as the chorus in a Sophoclean drama is powerless to stop the events leading to tragedy, so too, no one could stop the growing hatred of the poor for the rich, or the bitterness in those wealthy families who experienced catastrophe as they lost their crops year after year. The rich began to plot against the regime, against rule by the people, and against the Assembly, which had conducted the war like a dark comedy of miscalculations and decisions based on collective self-delusion.

When our defeat finally came, after a demoralizing twenty-seven years of conflict, everyone knew this was the end of the empire, that we had unleashed the furies, and entered a time of dangerous extremes, a long-prophesied Iron Age. Crime, fraud, and violence increased. Many Hellenes[4] started to feel that the gods like Zeus and Athena were mere fictions, or were helpless to affect our lives, and that the gossamer-thin foundation of laws and traditions our fathers and forbearers had lived by (especially our devotion to *sophrosyne* or moderation) were arbitrary. The faith in a moral order that unified us during our Golden Age was no longer possible. It seemed that overnight loyalty to our sea-girt city-state reverted back to family, tribe and clan, and a new breed of citizen was born. These were cold, calculating and egotistical men like the character Jason that Euripides created in *Medea.* They were devoted, not to civic duty, but instead to the immediate pleasures of food, drink, sex and, most important of all, power. These new men, who believed might was right, like Thrasymachus, saw "justice," "honesty," and "loyalty" as ideas created by and for the weak. Not too surprisingly, a new level of nastiness, incivility, and litigation entered our lives. Of these new men, Thucydides said, "The meaning of words had no longer the same relation to things, but was changed by them as they thought proper. Each man was strong only in the conviction that nothing was secure. Inferior intellects generally succeeded best. For, aware of their own deficiencies and feeling the capacities of their opponents, for whom they were no match in powers of speech and whose subtle wits were likely to anticipate them in contriving evil, they struck boldly at once."

Now, such new men needed new teachers, ones who were very different from the wonderful man who taught me. These teachers, foreigners, sprang up like Athena from the head of Zeus, came from places like Corinth and Ceos, were called Sophists, and

---

3 **Eris:** Greek goddess of discord and strife.
4 **Hellenes:** Greeks.

for a nice purse of drachmae,[5] they instructed the children of the rich in clever, honey-tongued rhetoric and perfumed lies aimed at appealing to the mob and swaying the members of the factious Assembly—prostitutes, my teacher called them, because he charged no fee. The most famous of these men was Protagoras, who argued that everyone knew things not as they are but only as they are in the moment of perception for *him*. "Man," he said, "is the measure of all things," and by this popular saying he meant nothing was objective, all we could have were opinions, and so each citizen was now his *own* law-giver. (And, as you know, opinions are like assholes—everybody has one.) In my youth, then, at this hour in history, in the wreckage of a spiritually damaged society, it came to pass that common, shared values had all but vanished, truth was seen as relative to each man, if not solipsistic, and nothing was universal anymore.

But the greatest, most unforgivable crime of my countrymen was, if you ask me, the killing of my teacher over his refusal to conform to the positions taken by different political parties. His accusers—Anytus, Meletus and Lycon—called him an atheist, a traitor, and a corruptor of youth. Then they brought him to trial, and I shall remember for all my days what he said in his defense: "Gentlemen, I am your grateful and devoted servant, but I owe a greater obedience to God than to you . . . I shall go saying, in my usual way, my good friend, you are an Athenian and belong to a city that is the greatest and most famous in the world for its wisdom and strength. Are you not ashamed that you give your attention to acquiring as much money as possible, and similarly with reputation and honor, and give no attention or thought to truth and understanding and the perfection of your soul?"

He could have fled the city, escaping injustice with the help of his students. Instead, and because he could not imagine living anywhere but Athens, he chose to drink the chill draught of hemlock.

To this very day, I regret that I could not be at my teacher's side when he died. That evening I was sick. But since his death, which wounded us all, I have done everything I can to honor him. Being one of his younger students, never his equal, I always feel like a son whose father has died too soon. Right when I was on the verge of maybe being mature enough to actually say something that might interest him. Sometimes I would see or hear something I wanted to share with him only to realize he was gone for the rest of *my* life. For years now I've carried on dialogues with him in my head, talking late at night into the darkness, saying aloud—perhaps too loud—all the things I wanted to tell him, apologizing for things I failed to say, often taking *his* part in our imaginary conversations until my five slaves, who are like family to me, started looking my way strangely. I didn't want anyone to think I had wandered in my wits, so I began quietly writing down these dialogues to free myself from the voices and questions in my head, adding more speakers in our fictitious conversations where his character is always the

---

5 **drachmae:** plural of drachma, a Greek currency.

voice of wisdom, which is how I want to remember him. Yet and still, his death left a scar on my soul, and a question that haunts me day and night: How can good men, like Socrates, survive in a broken, corrupt society?

There was one man who seemed as bedeviled by this dilemma as I was, but his response was so different from mine. I can't say we were on the same friendly terms as Damon and Pythias,[6] though sometimes he did feel like a brother, but one who infuriated me because he said my lectures at the Academy were long-winded and a waste of time. He was not, I confess, my only critic. My teacher's other students think my theories are all lunacy and error. They see my philosophy about eternal Ideas existing beyond the imperfections of this shadowy world as being nothing more than my cobbling together the positions of Heraclitus, who saw only difference in the world and denied identity, and Parmenides,[7] who saw identity and denied the existence of change. In their opinion, I've betrayed everything Socrates stood for. They positively hate my political view that only philosopher-kings should rule. Antisthenes has always been especially harsh toward me, treating me as if I was as cabbage-headed as one of the residents of Boeotia, perhaps because he, and not I, was present at Socrates' side when he passed away. Years ago, he had his own school before joining ours. In his teachings he rejected government, property, marriage, religion, and pure philosophy or metaphysics such as I was trying to do. Rather, he preached that plain, ordinary people could know all that was worth knowing, that an ordinary, everyday mind was enough. He taught in a building that served as a cemetery for dogs. Therefore, his pupils were called cynics (in other words "dog-like"), and among the most earthy, flamboyant and, I must say, scatological of his disciples was the ascetic Diogenes.

For an ascetic, he was shamelessly Dionysian,[8] and without an obol or lepton[9] to his name; but besides being Dionysian and shameless, Diogenes was a clown with hair like leaves and treebark, gnarled rootlike hands, and eyes like scars gouged into stone. He made a virtue of vulgarity, wore the worst clothing, ate the plainest porridge, slept on the ground or, as often as not, made his bed in a wine-cask, saying that by watching mice he had learned to adapt himself to any circumstance. Accordingly, he saw animals as his most trustworthy teachers, since their lives were natural, unselfconscious, and unspoiled by convention and hypocrisy. Like them, he was known for defecating, urinating, masturbating and rudely breaking wind in public. He even said we should have sex in the middle of the marketplace, for if the act was not indecent in private, we should

---

6 **Damon and Pythias:** young men legendary for their friendship.

7 **Heraclitus . . . Parmenides:** Heraclitus held the position that all empirical reality is changing. "You cannot step into the same river twice" was one of his aphorisms. Parmenides held the opposite view that everything is static and unchanging. Plato's philosophy of forms aspires to embrace both positions.

8 **Dionysian:** undisciplined, frenzied; after Dionysus, god of wine and the inspiration for human ecstasy.

9 **obol or lepton:** coins of small value.

not be ashamed to do it in public. Whenever he was praised for something, he said, "Oh shame, I must be doing something wrong!" Throughout Athens he was called The Dog, but to do him justice, there *was* a method in his madness. For example, his only possessions were his staff and a wooden bowl. But one afternoon Diogenes stumbled upon a boy using his hands to drink water from a stream. Happily, he tossed his bowl away, and from that day forward drank only with his bare hands.

Thus things stood in post-war Athens when one day The Dog decided to walk around the city holding a lighted lantern. He peered into all the stalls of the marketplace, peeked in brothels, as if he had lost something there, and when asked what he was doing, replied, "I'm looking for an honest man." His quest brought him to the Academy, where I was lecturing. As I placed several two-handled drinking cups before my students, I could from the corner of one eye see him listening, and scratching at dirt in his neck seams, and sticking his left hand under his robe into his armpit, then withdrawing it and sniffing his fingers to see if he needed a bath. I sighed, hoping he'd go away. I turned to my students and told them that while there were countless cups in the world, there was only one *idea* of a cup. This idea, the essence of cupness, was eternal; it came before all the individual cups in the world, and they all participated imperfectly in the immortal Form of cupness.

From the back of the room, Diogenes cleared his throat loudly.

"Excuse me," he said, "I can see the cup, but I don't see cupness *any*where."

"Well," I smiled at my students, "you have two good eyes with which to see the cup." I was not about to let him upstage me in my own class. Pausing, I tapped my forehead with my finger, "But it's obvious *you* don't have a good enough mind to comprehend cupness."

At that point, he sidled through my students, put down his lantern, and picked up one of the cylices.[10] He looked inside, then lifted his gaze to me. "Is this cup empty, Plato?"

"Why, yes, that's obvious."

"Then," he opened his eyes as wide as possible, which startled me because that was a favorite trick of my teacher, "where is the emptiness that comes before this empty cup?"

Right then my mind went cloudy. My eyes slipped out of focus for a second. I was wondering how to reply, disoriented even more by the scent of his meaty dog breath and rotten teeth. And then, Diogenes tapped my forehead with *his* finger, and said, "I believe you will find the emptiness is *here*." My students erupted with laughter, some of them even clapping when he, buffoon that he was, took a bow. (That boy from Stagira, Aristotle, who was always questioning me, and expressed the preposterous belief that the ideas must be *in* things, laughed until he was gasping for breath.) "I think your teacher's problem," he told them, "is that he'd like to run away from the messiness of the world, to disappear—*poof*!—into a realm of pure forms and beauty, where every-

---

10 **cylices:** plural of *cylix*, a shallow drinking cup.

thing has the order and perfection of mathematics. He's a mystic. And so—so dualistic! He actually wants certainty where there *is* none."

"What," I said, "is wrong with *that? Things* are terrible today! Everyone is suing everyone else. There's so much anger and hatred. No one trusts anyone anymore!"

Again, his eyes flew open, and he winked at my students, raising his shoulders in a shrug. "When have things *not* been terrible? What you don't see, my friend, is that there are only two ways to look at life. One, as if nothing is holy. The other, as if *every*thing is."

Oh, *that* stung.

All at once, the room was swimming, rushing toward me, then receding. I felt unsteady on my feet. In a matter of just a few moments, this stray dog had ruined my class. Now my students would always tap their heads and giggle when I tried to teach, especially that cocky young pup Aristotle. (I think he'd like to take my place if he could, but I know that will never happen.) I began to stutter, and I felt so embarrassed and overwhelmed by his wet canine smell that all I could say was, "In *my* opinion, only a fool would carry a lantern in the day time. Why don't you use it at night like a sensible man would?"

"As a night light?" He raised his eyebrows and bugged out his eyes again. "Thank you, Plato. I think I like that."

There was nothing for me to do except dismiss my students for the rest of the day, which The Dog had ruined. I pulled on my cape, and wandered through the marketplace until darkness came, without direction through the workmen, the temples of the gods, the traders selling their wares; among metics[11] and strangely tattooed nomads from the steppes who policed our polis; past the theater where old men prowled for young boys whose hair hung like hyacinth petals, and soldiers sang drinking songs, all the while cursing Diogenes under my breath, because the mangy cur was right. He was, whatever else, more Socratic than Socrates himself, as if the spirit of my teacher had been snatched from the Acherusian Lake, where souls wait to be reborn, and gone into *him* to chastise and correct me from beyond the grave, reminding me that I would always be just an insecure pupil intoxicated by ideas, one so shaken by a world without balance that I clung desperately to the crystalline purity and clear knowledge of numbers, the Apollonian exactitude and precision of abstract thought. Where my theories had denied the reality of our shattered world, he lapped up the illusion, like a dog indifferent to whether he was dining on a delicacy or his own ordure.

Tired, I finally decided to return home, having no idea how I could summon up the courage to face my students. And it was when I reached the center of town that I saw him again. He was still holding high that foolish lantern, and walking toward me with a wild splash of a smile on his face. I wanted to back away—I was certain he had fleas—or strike him a blow for humiliating me, but instead I held my ground, and said crisply, "Have you found what you're looking for yet?"

---

11 **metics:** resident noncitizens of the city-state.

"Perhaps," he said, and before I could step back, he lifted my chin with his fore-finger and thumb toward the night sky. "What do you see? Don't explain, *look*."

It was the first night of a full moon, but I hadn't noticed until now. Immediately, my mind started racing like that of a good student asked a question by his teacher. As if facing a test, I recalled that when Democritus tried to solve the mystery of the One and the Many, he said all things were composed of atoms, and Thales believed that everything was made of water, and Anaximenes claimed the world's diversity could be reduced to one substance, air. Oh, I could plaster a thousand interpretations on the overwhelmingly present and palpable orb above us, but at that moment something peculiar took place, and to this day I do not understand it. I looked and the plentitude of what I saw—the moon emerging from clouds like milk froth—could not be deciphered, and its opacity outstripped my speech. I was ambushed by its sensuous, singular, and savage beauty. Enraptured, I felt a shiver of desire (or love) rippling through my back from the force of its immediacy. For a second I was wholly unconscious of anyone beside me, or what was under my feet. As moonlight spilled abundantly from a bottomless sky, as I felt myself commingled with the seen, words failed me, my cherished opinions slipped away in the radiance of a primordial mystery that was as much me as it was the raw face of this full-orbed moon, a cipher so inexhaustible and ineffable it shimmered in my mind, surging to its margins, giving rise to a state of enchantment even as it seemed on the verge of vanishing, as all things do—*poleis*[12] and philosophical systems—into the pregnant emptiness Diogenes had asked me to explain. A sudden breeze extinguished the candle inside his lamp, leaving us enveloped by the enormity of night. There, with my vision unsealed, I felt only wonder, humility, and innocence, and for the first time I realized I did not have to understand, but only to *be*.

All I could do was swallow, a gulp that made The Dog grin.

"Good." He placed one piebald paw on my shoulder, as a brother might, or perhaps man's best friend. "For once you didn't dialogue it to death. I think I've found my honest man."

■ READING AND DISCUSSION QUESTIONS

1. In what ways is Plato's embrace of the theory of Forms a reaction to "the messi-ness of the world"—the decline of moral order and of shared values—following the defeat of Athens by Sparta?
2. Diogenes is a Cynic (from Greek *kynikos*, meaning "doglike"), so called because Cynics eschewed possessions and lived in the streets like dogs. How does Johnson reinforce the idea of Diogenes's doglike qualities throughout the story?
3. Why is Plato unable to answer Diogenes's question about "the emptiness that comes before this empty cup"? The form of a particular cup could participate in

---

12 *poleis*: plural of polis, the city-state.

the Form of cup, but is the case not different with emptiness? Emptiness is nothing. It is without form. Can there be a Form of nothing? Would that not make *nothing* into *something*? Comment.

4. Plato derides Diogenes for "lapp[ing] up the illusion" of the "shattered world" after Athens's defeat. In what ways is the world an "illusion" for Plato?

5. Diogenes tells Plato to *look* at, not explain, the night sky. Why? Is this related to the "nothing" in the cup? Is the sky a giant container (cup)? Comment.

6. What does Plato realize when observing the night sky with Diogenes?

■ FICTIVE-NARRATIVE PHILOSOPHY FEEDBACK

What claims are made in this story? Write them out in a bulleted list and include whether they are made through dialogue, dramatic action, or the presentation of the scene (including descriptive detail). One page. Then choose either a short direct-discourse response (according to the rules in Chapter 2) or a short fictive-narrative presentation (according to the rules in Chapter 3).

THE MYTH OF THE CHARIOTEER

Plato

Adapted from "Phaedrus," in *The Dialogues of Plato*, trans. B. Jowett, Vol. 1, 3rd ed. (1871; rpt. New York: Random House, 1892). *Note on the translation:* English words found in brackets are inserted by the translator to make better sense of the English rendering.

In "The Myth of the Charioteer," Plato depicts Socrates in conversation with his friend Phaedrus. Socrates expounds at length on the nature of the soul and the transmigration of a soul in the process of reincarnation, employing the allegory ("figure") of a charioteer who, driving a paired team of winged horses, strives to ascend to a view of the realm of reality—"the heaven which is above the heavens"—in order to gain true knowledge of "the colorless, formless, intangible essence, visible only to the mind, the pilot of the soul." Plato believes the soul has three parts: wisdom, spiritedness, and desire. Plato's narrator, Socrates, continues with his symbolic narrative to describe the actions of the soul in love.

The Nature of the Soul

Of the nature of the soul, though her true form be ever a theme of large and more than mortal discourse, let me speak briefly, and in a figure. And let the figure be composite—a pair of winged horses and a charioteer. Now, the winged horses and the charioteers of the gods are all of them noble and of noble descent, but those of other races are mixed; the human charioteer drives his in a pair; and one of them is noble and of noble breed, and the other is ignoble and of ignoble breed; and the driving of them of necessity gives a great deal of trouble to him.

I will endeavor to explain to you in what way the mortal differs from the immortal creature. The soul in her totality has the care of inanimate being everywhere and traverses the whole heaven in divers forms appearing—when perfect and fully winged she soars upward and orders the whole world; whereas the imperfect soul, losing her wings and drooping in her flight, at last settles on the solid ground—there, finding a home, she receives an earthly frame that appears to be self-moved but is really moved by her power; and this composition of soul and body is called a living and mortal creature. For immortal no such union can be reasonably believed to be; although fancy, neither having seen nor surely known the nature of God, may imagine an immortal creature having both a body and also a soul, which are united throughout all time. Let that, however, be as God wills and be spoken of acceptably to him. And now let us ask the reason the soul loses her wings!

The Realm of the Forms

The wing is the corporeal element that is most akin to the divine and by nature tends to soar aloft and carry that which gravitates downwards into the upper region, which is the habitation of the gods. The divine is Beauty, Wisdom, Goodness, and the like; and by these the wing of the soul is nourished and grows apace; but when fed upon evil and foulness and the opposite of good, it wastes and falls away. Zeus,[13] the mighty lord, holding the reins of a winged chariot, leads the way in heaven, ordering all and taking care of all; and there follows him the array of gods and demigods. When they go to banquet and festival, then they move up the steep to the top of the vault of heaven. The chariots of the gods in even poise, obeying the rein, glide rapidly; but the others labor, for the vicious steed goes heavily, weighing down the charioteer to the earth when his steed has not been thoroughly trained—and this is the hour of agony and extremest conflict for the soul. For the immortals, when they are at the end of their course, go forth and stand upon the outside of heaven, and the revolution of the spheres carries them round, and they behold the things beyond. But of the heaven, which is above the heavens, what earthly poet ever did or ever will sing worthily? It is such as I will describe; for I

must dare to speak the truth, when truth is my theme. There abides the very being with which true knowledge is concerned; the colorless, formless, intangible essence, visible only to mind, the pilot of the soul. The divine intelligence, being nurtured upon mind and pure knowledge, and the intelligence of every soul capable of receiving the food proper to it, rejoices at beholding reality and, once more gazing upon Truth, is replenished and made glad, until the revolution of the worlds brings her round again to the same place. In the revolution she beholds Justice, and Temperance, and Knowledge absolute, not in the form of generation or of relation, which men call existence, but Knowledge absolute in existence absolute; and beholding the other True Existences in like manner and feasting upon them, she passes down into the interior of the heavens and returns home; and there the charioteer putting up his horses at the stall gives them ambrosia to eat and nectar to drink.[14]

The Preparation of the Soul for Its Next Life on Earth

Such is the life of the gods; but of other souls, that which follows God best and is likest to him lifts the head of the charioteer into the outer world and is carried round in the revolution, troubled indeed by the steeds and with difficulty beholding True Being; while another only rises and falls, and sees, and again fails to see by reason of the unruliness of the steeds. The

---

13 **Zeus:** the king of the Greek gods.

14 **ambrosia . . . nectar:** food and drink of the gods.

rest of the souls are also longing after the upper world, and they all follow, but not being strong enough, they are carried round below the surface, plunging, treading on one another, each striving to be first; and there is confusion and perspiration and the extremity of effort; and many of them are lamed or have their wings broken through the ill driving of the charioteers; and all of them after a fruitless toil, not having attained to the mysteries of True Being, go away and feed upon opinion. The reason the souls exhibit this exceeding eagerness to behold the plain of Truth is that pasturage is found there, which is suited to the highest part of the soul; and the wing on which the soul soars is nourished with this.

And there is a law of Destiny that the soul that attains any vision of Truth in company with a god is preserved from harm until the next period, and if attaining always [this vision of truth] is always unharmed. But when she is unable to follow and fails to behold the Truth, and through some mishap sinks beneath the double load of forgetfulness and vice, and her wings fall from her and she drops to the ground, then the law ordains that this soul shall at her first birth pass not into any other animal but only into man; and the soul that has seen most of Truth shall come to the birth as a philosopher, or artist, or some musical and loving nature. Those who have seen Truth in the second degree shall be some righteous king or warrior chief. The soul that is of the third class shall be a politician, or economist, or trader. The fourth shall be a lover of gymnastic toils or a physician. The fifth shall lead the life of a prophet or hierophant.

To the sixth the character of a poet or some other imitative artist will be assigned; to the seventh the life of an artisan or husbandman; to the eighth that of a sophist or demagogue; to the ninth that of a tyrant. All these are states of probation, in which he who does righteously improves, and he who does unrighteously deteriorates his lot.

The Journey of Transmigrating Souls

Ten thousand years must elapse before the soul of each one can return to the place from whence she came, for she cannot grow her wings in less; only the soul of a philosopher, guileless and true, or the soul of a lover, who is not devoid of philosophy, may acquire wings in the third of the recurring periods of a thousand years. They who choose this life three times in succession have wings given them and go away at the end of three thousand years.

But the others receive judgment when they have completed their first life, and after the judgment they go, some of them to the houses of correction that are under the earth and are punished; others to some place in heaven whither they are lightly borne by justice, and there they live in a manner worthy of the life they led when in the form of men on earth. And at the end of the first thousand years, the good souls and also the evil souls both come to draw lots and choose their second life, and they may take any they please. The soul of a man may pass into the life of a beast or from the beast return again into the man. But the soul that has never seen the Truth will not pass into the human form. For a man must have intelligence of universals

(Forms) and be able to proceed from the many particulars of sense to one conception of reason—this is the recollection of those things that our soul once saw while following God—when regardless of that which we now call *being* she raised her head up toward the True Being. And therefore the mind of the philosopher alone has wings; and this is just, for he is always, according to the measure of his abilities, clinging in recollection to those things in which God abides and in beholding which He is what He is. And he who employs aright these memories is ever being initiated into perfect mysteries and alone becomes truly perfect. But as he forgets earthly interests and is rapt in the divine, the vulgar deem him mad and rebuke him; they do not see that he is inspired.

The Beautiful

This brings me to the whole point of the fourth and last kind of madness, which is imputed to him who, when he sees the beauty of earth, is transported with the recollection of the True Beauty; he would like to fly away, but he cannot; he is like a bird fluttering and looking upward and careless of the world below; and he is therefore thought to be mad. And I have shown this of all inspirations to be the noblest and highest and the offspring of the highest to him who has or shares in it, and he who loves the Beautiful is called a lover because he partakes of it. For, as has been already said, every soul of man has in the way of nature beheld True Being; this was the condition of her passing into the form of man. But all souls do not easily recall the things of the other world; they may have seen them for a short time only, or they may have been unfortunate in their earthly lot, and having had their hearts turned to unrighteousness through some corrupting influence, they may have lost the memory of the Holy Things that once they saw. Few only retain an adequate remembrance of them; and they, when they behold here any image of that other world, are rapt in amazement; but they are ignorant of what this rapture means because they do not clearly perceive. For there is no light of Justice or Temperance or any of the higher Ideas that are precious to souls in the earthly copies of them: they are seen through a glass dimly; and there are few who, going to the images, behold in them the Realities, and these only with difficulty. There was a time when with the rest of the happy band they saw Beauty shining in brightness—we philosophers following in the train of Zeus, others in company with other gods—and then we beheld the Beatific vision and were initiated into a mystery that may be truly called most blessed, celebrated by us in our state of innocence, before we had any experience of evils to come, when we were admitted to the sight of apparitions innocent and simple and calm and happy, which we beheld shining in pure light, pure ourselves and not yet enshrined in the living tomb that we carry about, now that we are imprisoned in the body, like an oyster in its shell. . . .

The Two Horses, the Charioteer, and Happiness

As I said at the beginning of this tale, I divided each soul into three—two horses and a charioteer—and one of the horses was good and the other bad: the division may remain, but I have not yet explained in what the goodness or badness of either consists, and to that I will proceed. The right-hand horse is upright and cleanly made; he has a lofty neck and an aquiline nose; his color is white and his eyes dark; he is a lover of honor and modesty and temperance and the follower of true glory; he needs no touch of the whip but is guided by word and admonition only. The other is a crooked lumbering animal, put together anyhow; he has a short, thick neck; he is flat faced and of a dark color, with gray eyes and of blood-red complexion, the mate of insolence and pride, shaggy around the ears and deaf, hardly yielding to whip and spur.

Now, when the charioteer beholds the vision of Love, and has his whole soul warmed through sense, and is full of the prickings and ticklings of desire, the obedient steed, then as always under the government of shame, refrains from leaping on the beloved; but the other, heedless of the pricks and of the blows of the whip, plunges and runs away, giving all manner of trouble to his companion and the charioteer, whom he forces to approach the beloved and to remember the joys of love. They at first indignantly oppose him and will not be urged on to do terrible and unlawful deeds; but at last, when he persists in plaguing them, they yield and agree to do as he bids them. And now they are at the spot and behold the flashing beauty of the beloved; when the charioteer sees it, his memory is carried to the True Beauty, whom he beholds in company with Modesty like an image placed upon a holy pedestal. He sees her, but he is afraid and falls backward in adoration and, by his fall, is compelled to pull back the reins with such violence as to bring both the steeds onto their haunches, the one willing and unresisting, the unruly one very unwilling; and when they have gone back a little, the one is overcome with shame and wonder, and his whole soul is bathed in perspiration; the other, when the pain, given him by the bridle and the fall, is over, having with difficulty taken breath, is full of wrath and reproaches, which he heaps upon the charioteer and his fellow steed, for want of courage and manhood, declaring that they have been false to their agreement and guilty of desertion. Again they refuse, and again he urges them on and will scarcely yield to their prayer that he wait until another time. When the appointed hour comes, they make as if they had forgotten, and he reminds them, fighting and neighing and dragging them on, until at length he, on the same thoughts intent, forces them to draw near again. And when they are near, he stoops his head, puts up his tail, and takes the bit in his teeth and pulls shamelessly. Then the charioteer is worse off than ever; he falls back like a racer at the barrier and, with a still more violent wrench, drags the bit out of the teeth of the wild steed and covers his abusive tongue and jaws with blood and forces his legs and haunches to the ground and punishes him sorely. And when this has happened several times and the villain has ceased from his wanton way, he is tamed and humbled and follows the will of the charioteer, and when he sees the beautiful one, he is ready to die of fear. And from that time forward, the soul of the lover follows the beloved in modesty and holy fear. . . . [His] happiness depends upon their [the horses] self-control. If the better elements of the soul that lead to order and philosophy prevail, then they pass their life here in happiness and harmony—masters of themselves and orderly—enslaving the vicious and emancipating the virtuous elements of the soul. When the end of life comes, they are light and winged for flight (having won the first of three rounds in these true Olympian Contests[15]). Nor can human discipline or divine inspiration confer on man any greater blessing than this.

---

15 **Olympian:** pertaining to Mount Olympus, where the Greek gods lived, and to the Olympic Games of ancient Greece, which began in the eighth century BCE and occurred every four years.

■ READING AND DISCUSSION QUESTIONS

1. The human charioteer drives one "noble" and one "ignoble" horse. What do the two horses represent?
2. What is the relation between soul and body?
3. What is the significance of wings?
4. In your own words, describe the realm of the Forms.
5. According to Plato (through the character of Socrates), souls are reborn. What happens to the soul of a righteous person?
6. The first degree of humankind consists of what kinds of people?
7. What distinguishes the different degrees of humankind?
8. Why does "the mind of the philosopher alone [have] wings"?
9. What is the role of the Form of Beauty?
10. In the presence of "the beloved," the "obedient steed" yields willingly to the charioteer's rein, but the "wild steed" pulls ahead "shamelessly." What do the behaviors of the two horses signify? How can this process be properly handled so that a person's soul might live in blessedness?

■ CLASS EXERCISES

A. *Direct logical discourse:* Using the tools found in Chapter 2, outline the argument from "The Myth of the Charioteer" about the relationship of the Forms to the different degrees of being human. Based on your assessment of one key premise, write a one-page argument about why you agree or disagree with the argument's conclusion.

B. *Fictive-narrative philosophy:* Using the tools found in Chapter 3, begin with a claim that relates to one of the reading and discussion questions above. Then, either rewrite the story with the same characters but evaluating more deeply the worldview tenets assumed in Plato's presentation or create a new story that applies these themes to our modern-day setting.

CRITO

Plato

From "Crito," *The Dialogues of Plato*, trans. B. Jowett, Vol. 1, 3rd ed. (1871; rpt. New York: Random House, 1892). *Note on the translation:* English words found in brackets are inserted by the translator to make better sense of the English rendering.

Plato's dialogue "Crito" begins with Socrates (c. 469–399 BCE) incarcerated in an Athenian prison, awaiting his imminent execution. The seventy-year-old Socrates was apparently caught up in the cynical politics of Athens in the bleak aftermath of the defeat of that city-state by Sparta and its allies in the Peloponnesian War (431–404 BCE). He was convicted on charges of rejecting the gods of the state religion and corrupting Athenian youth through his teachings. In Plato's dialogue, Socrates dismisses the many reasons his friend Crito advances for escaping, which Socrates could easily do by paying off the right people. Instead, he argues that the best course is to adhere to the law, even in the face of injustice and, indeed, death. Though "Crito" does not depict his death (see "Phaedo"), Socrates carried out his own execution by drinking hemlock.

SCENE: Socrates's prison

SOCRATES: Why have you come at this hour, Crito? It must be quite early?

CRITO: Yes, certainly.

SOC.: What is the exact time?

CR.: The dawn is breaking.

SOC.: I wonder that the keeper of the prison would let you in.

CR.: He knows me because I often come, Socrates; moreover, I have done him a kindness.

SOC.: And are you only just arrived?

CR.: No, I came some time ago.

SOC.: Then why did you sit and say nothing, instead of at once awakening me?

CR.: I should not have liked myself, Socrates, to be in such great trouble and unrest as you are—indeed I should not: I have been watching with amazement your peaceful slumbers; and for that reason I did not awake you, because I wished to minimize the pain. I have always thought you to be of a happy disposition; but never did I see anything like the easy, tranquil manner in which you bear this calamity.

SOC.: Why, Crito, when a man has reached my age he ought not to be repining at the approach of death.

CR.: And yet, other old men find themselves in similar misfortunes, and age does not prevent them from repining.

Soc.: That is true. But you have not told me why you come at this early hour.

Cr.: I come to bring you a message that is sad and painful—not, I believe, to yourself but to all of us who are your friends, and saddest of all to me.

Soc.: What? Has the ship come from Delos,[16] on the arrival of which I am to die?

Cr.: No, the ship has not actually arrived, but she will probably be here today, as persons who have come from Sunium tell me that they left her there; and therefore tomorrow, Socrates, will be the last day of your life.

Soc.: Very well, Crito; if such is the will of God, I am willing; but my belief is that there will be a delay of a day.

Cr.: Why do you think so?

Soc.: I will tell you. I am to die on the day after the arrival of the ship.

Cr.: Yes; that is what the authorities say.

Soc.: But I do not think that the ship will be here until tomorrow; this I infer from a dream that I had last night, or rather only just now, when you fortunately allowed me to sleep.

Cr.: And what was the nature of the dream?

Soc.: There appeared to me the likeness of a woman, fair and comely, clothed in bright raiment, who called to me and said, "O Socrates, the third day hence to fertile Phthia[17] shalt thou go."

Cr.: What a singular dream, Socrates!

Soc.: There can be no doubt about the meaning, Crito, I think.

Cr.: Yes, the meaning is only too clear. But, oh! my beloved Socrates, let me entreat you once more to take my advice and escape. For if you die not only shall I lose a friend who can never be replaced, but there is another evil: people who do not know you and me will believe that I might have saved you if I had been willing to give money, but that I did not care. Now, can there be a worse disgrace than this—that I should be thought to value money more than the life of a friend? For the many will not be persuaded that I wanted you to escape and that you refused.

Argument One:
Heeding the Voice of the Arête[18]

Soc.: But why, my dear Crito, should we care about the opinion of the many? Good men—and they are the only persons worth considering—will think of these things truly as they occurred.

Cr.: But you see, Socrates, that the opinion of the many must be regarded, for what is now happening shows that they can do the greatest evil to any one who has lost their good opinion.

Soc.: I only wish it were so, Crito, and that the many could do the greatest

---

16 **ship come from Delos:** Socrates's death was stalled until an Athenian delegation made an annual religious pilgrimage to the island of Delos. Executions were not permitted until the ship returned.

17 **Phthia:** literally, the home of Achilles, hero of *The Iliad*; metaphorically, death. The quotation is from *The Iliad* ix.363.

18 **Arête:** excellence or virtue. The question in this argument is whether popular opinion or the opinion of the few (the excellent or virtuous) is to be valued more.

evil; for then they would also be able to do the greatest good—and what a fine thing this would be! But in reality they can do neither; for they cannot make a man either wise or foolish; and whatever they do is the result of chance.

Cr.: Well, I will not dispute with you; but please tell me, Socrates, whether you are not acting out of regard for me and your other friends: are you not afraid that if you escape from prison we may get into trouble with the informers for having stolen you away and lose either the whole or a great part of our property, or that an even worse evil may happen to us? Now, if you fear on our account, be at ease; for in order to save you, we ought surely to run this, or even a greater, risk; be persuaded, then, and do as I say.

Soc.: Yes, Crito, that is one fear that you mention, but by no means the only one.

Cr.: Fear not—there are persons who are willing to get you out of prison at no great cost; and as for the informers, they are far from being exorbitant in their demands—a little money will satisfy them. My means, which are certainly ample, are at your service, and if you have a scruple about spending all mine, here are strangers who will give you the use of theirs; and one of them, Simmias the Theban, has brought a large sum of money for this very purpose; and Cebes and many others are prepared to spend their money in helping you to escape.

I say, therefore, do not hesitate on our account, and do not say, as you did

in the court, that you will have a difficulty in knowing what to do with yourself anywhere else. For men will love you in other places to which you may go and not in Athens only; there are friends of mine in Thessaly, if you like to go to them, who will value and protect you, and no Thessalian will give you any trouble. Nor can I think that you are at all justified, Socrates, in betraying your own life when you might be saved; in acting thus you are playing into the hands of your enemies, who are hurrying on your destruction.

And, further, I should say that you are deserting your own children; for you might bring them up and educate them; instead, you go away and leave them, and they will have to take their chance; and if they do not meet with the usual fate of orphans, there will be small thanks to you. No man should bring children into the world who is unwilling to persevere to the end in their nurture and education. But you appear to be choosing the easier part, not the better and manlier, which would have been more becoming of one who professes to care for virtue in all his actions, like yourself. And, indeed, I am ashamed not only of you but of us who are your friends, when I reflect that the whole business will be attributed entirely to our want of courage. The trial need never have come on or might have been managed differently; and this last act, or crowning folly, will seem to have occurred through our negligence and cowardice, who might have saved you, if we had been good for anything; and you might have saved yourself, for there was no difficulty at all. See now, Socrates, how sad and discreditable are the consequences, both to us and you.

Make up your mind then, or rather have your mind already made up, for the time of deliberation is over, and there is only one thing to be done, which must be done this very night and, if we delay at all, will be no longer practicable or possible; I beseech you therefore, Socrates, be persuaded by me, and do as I say.

Soc.: Dear Crito, your zeal is invaluable, if it is correct; but if wrong, the greater the zeal the greater the danger; and therefore we ought to consider whether I shall or shall not do as you say. For I am, and always have been, one of those natures that must be guided by reason, whatever the reason may be that upon reflection appears to me to be the best; and now that this chance has befallen me, I cannot repudiate my own words: the principles that I have hitherto honored and revered I still honor, and unless we can at once find other and better principles, I am certain not to agree with you; no, not even if the power of the multitude could inflict many more imprisonments, confiscations, and deaths, frightening us like children with hobgoblin terrors.

What will be the fairest way of considering the question? Shall I return to your old argument about the opinions of men?—we were saying that some of them are to be regarded and others not. Now, were we right in maintaining this before I was condemned? And has the argument that was once good

now proved to be talk for the sake of talking—mere childish nonsense? This is what I want to consider with your help, Crito—whether or not, under my present circumstances, the argument appears to be in any way different and is to be allowed by me or disallowed. That argument, which, as I believe, is maintained by many persons of authority, was to the effect, as I was saying, that the opinions of some men are to be regarded, and those of other men are not to be regarded. Now, you, Crito, are not going to die tomorrow—at least, there is no human probability of this—and therefore you are disinterested and not liable to be deceived by the circumstances in which you are placed. Tell me then whether I am right in saying that some opinions, and the opinions of some men only, are to be valued and that other opinions, and the opinions of other men, are not to be valued. I ask you whether I was right in maintaining this?

Cr.: Certainly.

Soc.: The good are to be regarded and not the bad?

Cr.: Yes.

Soc.: And the opinions of the wise are good, and the opinions of the unwise are evil?

Cr.: Certainly.

Soc.: And what was said about another matter? Is the pupil who devotes himself to the practice of gymnastics supposed to attend to the praise and blame and opinion of every man or of one man only—his physician or trainer, whoever he may be?

CR.: Of one man only.

Soc.: And he ought to fear the censure and welcome the praise of that one only and not of the many?

CR.: Clearly so.

Soc.: And he ought to act and train and eat and drink in the way that seems good to his single master who has understanding rather than according to the opinion of all other men put together?

CR.: True.

Soc.: And if he disobeys and disregards the opinion and approval of the one and regards the opinion of the many who have no understanding, will he not suffer evil?

CR.: Certainly he will.

Soc.: And what will the evil be, whither tending and what affecting, in the disobedient person?

CR.: Clearly, affecting the body; that is what is destroyed by the evil.

Soc.: Very good; and is not this true, Crito, of other things that we need not separately enumerate? In questions of just and unjust, fair and foul, good and evil, which are the subjects of our present consultation, ought we to follow the opinion of the many and to fear them or the opinion of the one man who has understanding? Ought we not to fear and reverence him more than all the rest of the world, and if we desert him shall we not destroy and injure that principle in us that may be assumed to be improved by justice and deteriorated by injustice—there is such a principle?

CR.: Certainly there is, Socrates.

Soc.: Take a parallel instance: if, acting under the advice of those who have no understanding, we destroy that which is improved by health and deteriorated by disease, would life be worth having? And that which has been destroyed is—the body?

CR.: Yes.

Soc.: Could we live, having an evil and corrupted body?

CR.: Certainly not.

Soc.: And will life be worth having if that higher part of man be destroyed that is improved by justice and depraved by injustice? Do we suppose that principle, whatever it may be in man, that has to do with justice and injustice to be inferior to the body?

CR.: Certainly not.

Soc.: More honorable than the body?

CR.: Far more.

Soc.: Then, my friend, we must not regard what the many say of us but what he, the one man who has understanding of just and unjust, will say and what the truth will say. And, therefore, you begin in error when you advise that we should regard the opinion of the many about just and unjust, good and evil, honorable and dishonorable.—"Well," some one will say, "but the many can kill us."

CR.: Yes, Socrates, that will clearly be the answer.

Soc.: And it is true, but still I find with surprise that the old argument is unshaken as ever. And I should like to know whether I may say the same of another proposition—that not life, but a good life, is to be chiefly valued?

CR.: Yes, that also remains unshaken.

Soc.: And a good life is equivalent to a just and honorable one—that holds also?

CR.: Yes, it does.

SOC.: From these premises I proceed to argue the question whether I ought or ought not try to escape without the consent of the Athenians: and if I am clearly right in escaping, then I will make the attempt; but if not, I will abstain. The other considerations that you mention, of money and loss of character and the duty of educating one's children, are, I fear, only the doctrines of the multitude, who would be as ready to restore people to life, if they were able, as they are to put them to death—and with as little reason. But now, since the argument has thus far prevailed, the only question that remains to be considered is whether we shall do rightly either in escaping or in suffering others to aid in our escape and paying them in money and thanks, or whether in reality we shall not do rightly; and if the latter, then death or any other calamity that may ensue on my remaining here must not be allowed to enter into the calculation.

CR.: I think that you are right, Socrates; how then shall we proceed?

Argument Two:
Abiding by the Laws of the State

SOC.: Let us consider the matter together, and either refute me if you can, and I will be convinced, or else cease, my dear friend, from repeating to me that I ought to escape against the wishes of the Athenians: for I highly value your attempts to persuade me to do so, but I may not be persuaded against my own better judgment. And now, please consider my first position, and try how you can best answer me.

CR.: I will.

SOC.: Are we to say that we are never intentionally to do wrong, or that in one way we ought and in another we ought not to do wrong, or is doing wrong always evil and dishonorable, as I was just now saying and as has already been acknowledged by us? Are all our former admissions, which were made within a few days, to be thrown away? And have we, at our age, been earnestly discoursing with one another all our life long only to discover that we are no better than children? Or, in spite of the opinion of the many, and in spite of consequences whether better or worse, shall we insist on the truth of what was then said, that injustice is always an evil and dishonor to him who acts unjustly? Shall we say so or not?

CR.: Yes.

SOC.: Then we must do no wrong?

CR.: Certainly not.

SOC.: Nor when injured injure in return, as the many imagine; for we must injure no one at all?

CR.: Clearly not.

SOC.: Again, Crito, may we do evil?

CR.: Surely not, Socrates.

SOC.: And what of doing evil in return for evil, which is the morality of the many—is that just or not?

CR.: Not just.

SOC.: For doing evil to another is the same as injuring him?

CR.: Very true.

SOC.: Then we ought not retaliate or render evil for evil to any one, whatever evil we may have suffered from him. But I would have you consider, Crito, whether you really mean what you are saying. For this opinion has never been held, and never will be held, by any considerable number of persons; and those who are agreed and those who are not agreed upon this point have no common ground and can only despise one another when they see how widely they differ. Tell me, then, whether you agree with and assent to my first principle, that neither injury nor retaliation nor warding off evil by evil is ever right. And shall that be the premise of our argument? Or do you decline and dissent from this? For so I have ever thought and continue to think; but if you are of another opinion, let me hear what you have to say. If, however, you remain of the same mind as formerly, I will proceed to the next step.

Cr.: You may proceed, for I have not changed my mind.

Soc.: Then I will go on to the next point, which may be put in the form of a question: ought a man do what he admits to be right, or ought he betray the right?

Cr.: He ought to do what he thinks right.

Soc.: But if this is true, what is the application? In leaving the prison against the will of the Athenians, do I wrong any? Or rather, do I not wrong those whom I ought least to wrong? Do I not desert the principles that were acknowledged by us to be just—what do you say?

Cr.: I cannot tell, Socrates, for I do not know.

Soc.: Then consider the matter in this way: imagine that I am about to run away from here, and the laws and the government come and interrogate me: "Tell us, Socrates," they say, "what are you about? Are you not going by an act of yours to overturn us—the laws and the whole state as far as you are concerned? Do you imagine that state can subsist and not be overthrown, in which the decisions of law have no power but are set aside and trampled upon by individuals?" What will be our answer, Crito, to these and like words? Any one, especially a rhetorician, will have a good deal to say on behalf of the law that requires a sentence to be carried out. He will argue that this law should not be set aside; and shall we reply, "Yes, but the state has injured us and given an unjust sentence." Suppose I say that?

Cr.: Very good, Socrates.

Soc.: "And was that our agreement with you?" the law would answer; "Or were you to abide by the sentence of the state?" And if I were to express my astonishment at their words, the law would probably add, "Answer, Socrates, instead of opening your eye—you are in the habit of asking and answering questions. Tell us, what complaint have you to make against us that justifies your attempt to destroy us and the state? In the first place did we not bring you into existence? Your father married your mother by our aid and begat you. Say whether you have any objection to urge against those of us who regulate marriage?" "None," I should reply. "Or against those of us who after birth regulate the nurture and education of children, in which you also were trained? Were not the laws, which have the charge of education, right in commanding your father to train you in music and gymnastics?" "Right," I should reply. "Well then, since you were brought into the world and nurtured and educated by us, can you deny in the first place that you are our child and slave, as your fathers were before you? And if this is true, you are not on equal terms with us; nor can you think that you have a right to do to us what we are doing to you. Would you have any right to strike or revile or do any other evil to your father or your master, if you had one, because you have been struck or reviled by him or received some other evil at his hands? You would not say this? And because we think right to destroy you, do you think that you have any right to destroy us in return, and your country as far as in you lies? Will you, O professor of true virtue, pretend that you are justified in this? Has a philosopher like you failed to discover that our country is more to be valued and higher and holier far than mother or father or any ancestor and more to be regarded in the eyes of the gods and of men of understanding? Also to be soothed and gently and reverently entreated when angry, even more than a father, and either to be persuaded, or if not persuaded, to be obeyed? And when we are punished by her, whether with imprisonment or stripes, the punishment is to be endured in silence, and if she leads us to wounds or death in battle, thither we follow as is right; neither may any one yield or retreat or leave his rank, but whether in battle or in a court of law or in any other place, he must do what his city and his country order him; or he must change their view of what is just. And if he may do no violence to his father or mother, much less may he do violence to his country." What answer shall we make to this, Crito? Do the laws speak truly, or do they not?

Cr.: I think that they do.

Soc.: Then the laws will say, "Consider, Socrates, if we are speaking truly that in your present attempt you are going to do us an injury. For, having brought you into the world, and nurtured and educated you, and given you and every other citizen a share in every good that we had to give, we further proclaim to any Athenian by the liberty that we allow him that if he does not like us when he has become of age and has seen the ways of the city and made our acquaintance, he may go where he pleases and take his goods with him. None of us laws will forbid him or interfere with him. Any one who does not like us and the city and who wants to emigrate to a colony or to any other city may go where he likes, retaining his property. But he who has experience of the manner in which we order justice and administer the state and still remains has entered into an implied contract that he will do as we command him. And he who disobeys us is, as we maintain, thrice wrong; first, because in disobeying us he is disobeying his parents; second, because we are the authors of his education; third, because he has made an agreement with us that he will duly obey our commands; and he neither obeys them nor convinces us that our commands are unjust; and we do not rudely impose them but give him the alternative of obeying or convincing us. That is what we offer, and he does neither.

"These are the sort of accusations to which, as we were saying, you, Socrates, will be exposed if you accomplish your intentions: you, above all other Athenians."

Suppose now I ask, why I rather than anybody else? They will justly retort that I above all other men have acknowledged the agreement. "There is clear proof," they will say, "Socrates, that we and the city were not displeasing to you. Of all Athenians you have been the most constant resident in the city, which, as you never leave, you may be supposed to love. For you never went out of the city either to see the games, except once when you went to the Isthmus, or to any other place unless when you were on military service; nor did you travel as other men do. Nor had you any curiosity to know other states or their laws: your affections did not go beyond us and our state; we were your special favorites, and you acquiesced in our government of you; and here in this city you begat your children, which is a proof of your satisfaction. Moreover, you might in the course of the trial, if you had liked, have fixed the penalty at banishment; the state which refuses to let you go now would have let you go then. But you pretended that you preferred death to exile and that you were not unwilling to die. And now you have forgotten these fine sentiments and pay no respect to us the laws, of whom you are the destroyer,

and are doing what only a miserable slave would do, running away and turning your back upon the compacts and agreements that you made as a citizen. And first of all answer this very question: are we right in saying that you agreed to be governed according to us in deed and not in word only? Is that true or not?"

How shall we answer, Crito? Must we not assent?

Cr.: We cannot help it, Socrates.

Soc.: Then will they not say, "You, Socrates, are breaking the covenants and agreements that you made with us at your leisure, not in any haste or under any compulsion or deception, but after you have had seventy years to think of them, during which time you were at liberty to leave the city if we were not to your mind or if our covenants appeared to you to be unfair. You had your choice and might have gone either to Lacedaemon or Crete, both of which states are often praised by you for their good government, or to some other Hellenic or foreign state. Whereas you, above all other Athenians, seemed to be so fond of the state, or, in other words, of us, her laws (and who would care about a state with no laws?), that you never stirred out of her; the halt, the blind, the maimed were not more stationary in her than you were. And now you run away and forsake your agreements. Not so, Socrates, if you will take our advice; do not make yourself ridiculous by escaping out of the city.

"For just consider, if you transgress and err in this sort of way, what good will you do either to yourself or to your friends? That your friends will be driven into exile and deprived of citizenship or will lose their property is tolerably certain; and you yourself, if you fly to one of the neighboring cities, as, for example, Thebes or Megara, both of which are well governed, will come to them as an enemy, Socrates, and their government will be against you, and all patriotic citizens will cast an evil eye upon you as a subverter of the laws, and you will confirm in the minds of the judges the justice of their own condemnation of you. For he who is a corrupter of the laws is more than likely to be a corrupter of the young and foolish portion of mankind. Will you then flee from well-ordered cities and virtuous men? And is existence worth having on these terms? Or will you go to them without shame and talk to them, Socrates? And what will you say to them? What you say here about virtue and justice and institutions and laws being the best things among men? Would that be decent of you? Surely not.

"But if you go away from well-governed states to Crito's friends in Thessaly, where there is great disorder and license, they will be charmed to hear the tale of your escape from prison, set off with ludicrous particulars of the manner in which you were wrapped in a goatskin or some other disguise and metamorphosed as the manner is of runaways; but will there be no one to remind you that in your old age you were not ashamed to violate the most sacred laws from a miserable desire for a little more life? Perhaps not, if you keep them in a temper; but if they are out of temper,

you will hear many degrading things. You will live, but how? As the flatterer of all men and the servant of all men. And doing what? Eating and drinking in Thessaly, having gone abroad in order that you may get a banquet. And where will be your fine sentiments about justice and virtue? Say that you wish to live for the sake of your children—to bring them up and educate them—will you take them into Thessaly and deprive them of Athenian citizenship? Is this the benefit that you will confer upon them? Or are you under the impression that they will be better cared for and educated here if you are still alive, although absent from them, for your friends will take care of them? Do you fancy that if you are an inhabitant of Thessaly, they will take care of them, and if you are an inhabitant of the other world, they will not take care of them? Nay, but if they who call themselves friends are good for anything, they will—to be sure they will.

"Listen, then, Socrates, to us who have brought you up. Think not of life and children first and of justice afterwards, but of justice first that you may be justified before the princes of the world below. For neither will you nor any that belong to you be happier or holier or juster in this life or happier in another if you do as Crito bids. Now you depart in innocence, a sufferer and not a doer of evil, a victim not of the laws but of men. But if you go forth, returning evil for evil and injury for injury, breaking the covenants and agreements that you have made with us and wronging those whom you ought least of all to wrong, that is to say, yourself, your friends, your country, and us, we shall be angry with you while you live, and our brethren, the laws in the world below, will receive you as an enemy; for they will know that you have done your best to destroy us. Listen, then, to us and not to Crito."

This, dear Crito, is the voice that I seem to hear murmuring in my ears, like the sound of the flute in the ears of the mystic. That voice, I say, is humming in my ears and prevents me from hearing any other. And I know that anything more that you may say will be vain. Yet speak if you have anything to say.

Cr.: I have nothing to say, Socrates.

Soc.: Leave me then, Crito, to fulfill the will of God and to follow whither he leads.

■ READING AND DISCUSSION QUESTIONS

1. Crito expresses concern that many will believe that he and his friends failed to exert themselves to save Socrates when they might have. How does Socrates respond?
2. According to Socrates, whose opinion should be regarded, and whose should not?
3. If leaving prison would violate the will of the Athenian people—that is, it would be against the law—Socrates declines to escape, although he will die if he stays. What are his reasons for remaining in prison, even though his escape might easily be arranged?
4. What arguments does Socrates imagine that "the law" might make against him were he to evade Athenian justice?
5. Socrates hypothesizes that he could have escaped to Thebes or Magara rather than accept the death penalty. Why does he assert, then, that those cities would have regarded him as "an enemy"?
6. Socrates also imagines that he might have fled to Thessaly, where he would have been welcomed. What reasons, then, does he give for why that would have been a wrong action to take?

■ CLASS EXERCISES

A. *Direct logical discourse:* Using the tools found in Chapter 2, outline the argument from the "Crito" that people have a duty to obey the laws of the state even when those laws are unjust. Based on your assessment of one key premise, write a one-page argument about why you agree or disagree with the argument's conclusion.

B. *Fictive-narrative philosophy:* Using the tools found in Chapter 3, begin with a claim that relates to the conclusion of either argument 1 or argument 2 and rewrite the story with the same characters but evaluating more deeply the worldview tenets assumed in Plato's presentation.

CHAPTER FIVE

Aristotle

Aristotle (384–322 BCE) was Plato's student and the mentor of Alexander the Great. Aristotle is credited for inventing formal logic, biology, and general science for the Western tradition. He may have written the first constitution for a state. His critical empiricism guides his contributions in other areas of philosophy. Unlike Plato, Aristotle thought that the abstract understanding of an empirical object was less real than the physical object itself. Aristotle was a Macedonian who lived a significant part of his life in Athens, a Greek city that did not especially like Macedonians (because of their political imperialism).

ARISTOTLE THE OUTSIDER*

Michael Boylan

In this story we confront Aristotle near the end of his life. His protector, Alexander, has just died. Aristotle does not want a repeat of the "Crito" in which the people of Athens kill a philosopher in their midst. Through flashbacks the story connects various aspects of Aristotle's life and philosophy as they come to bear upon these final moments.

Aristotle stood up and wiped his brow. His bronze, wrinkled skin and kinky, black, white-streaked, thinning, and receding hair glistened from the sun shooting through a break in the trees of Apollo's woods. It was almost the autumnal equinox, but the heat was nearly unbearable—even in the temple woods that bordered his school, the Lyceum (named after Apollo Lykeios, Apollo the wolf killer). He sat on a tree stump. His knees ached from all his famous walking. He used to love to walk. "Walk and talk" was his motto. Walking stimulated the mind and kept the body thin and fit. But the years had taken their toll on his knees. "Would I had been more moderate in my walking!" It was all well and good to say so now, but he used to love walking *so much.* But as he sat alone on a stump in the woods, he began to worry. Things had not been going so well in the past few weeks since news had come of Alexander's death. And then there was that damn poem. Aristotle shut his eyes to remember happier times.

"Aristotle, come here," cried his mother, Phaestis, from the porch at their Chalcian house near Stagiros (later called Stagira). It was a simple, yet well-appointed, house—an abode fit for Nicomachus, the court physician to King Amyntas. His mother spoke in the Ionian dialect famous for the way its speakers enunciate consonants. Sometimes his father, the doctor (who also spoke Ionian), even sent out trails of spit as he tried to make everything perfectly clear.

"Aristotle!"

The boy reluctantly obeyed. He had been watching insects hatch out of some animal dung. It just happened. It was like a miracle how the insects came forth. He wanted to know more.

"Aristotle!!"

He had to react—though he didn't want to.

* I would like to thank Anthony Preus for his helpful comments on the story. I also dedicate the eulogy sonnet to him.

"Aristotle, what is the meaning of this?"

The boy put on his "nothing face," the one that did not betray emotion. He knew what his mother was about to say. He had to think quickly.

When he came to his mother, she held up the carcass of a wolf wrapped in a bloody piece of tarp. Aristotle strode forward and collected the carcass gently in his hands and held it to his chest. "I didn't kill it mother."

"Why not? Wolves are the terror of us all. They write about it in stories."

"This animal I found dead, and I wanted to look at it more carefully. I wanted to see what wolves were like."

"What can you tell from this? The body is mangled beyond recognition."

"I know that it isn't a very good specimen. I've had to use a lot of imagination. Next time, I'll talk to the trappers before the body is spoiled by the scavengers."

"Stupid boy! That is not an occupation fitting for your station. Your father's an important man. You carry yourself like a scum boy or those murderous barbarian Persians. Do you know your blood, child?"

"I'm sorry mother. I was just curious." Then his mother cuffed Aristotle on the side of his head. His ears rang. It made him dizzy. But he still held the wolf.

His mother made her exit.

Then Aristotle knelt down. He took out his knife and sliced up the carcass further. The one organ that had always intrigued him the most was the heart. Unfortunately, this specimen's heart was gone. Aristotle had observed in other animal bodies that there were differences among various animal hearts. The boy always felt an almost reverent awe when he carefully cut open what he felt was the center of life itself. He sat and stared at the mangled carcass for a while until the setting sun told him he'd better wash up and help his mother with the evening meal. Soon it would be his birthday. It was good to be on his best behavior so he might start the autumn right.

His birthday was a success! His father took him to King Amyntas's court where he met a boy, the youngest in the royal line, named Philip. Philip was a skinny kid whose sharp elbows often found their place in Aristotle's ribs or face as the older boy pushed his way in front of his playmate when they were engaged in sport. The games weren't played fairly, but that didn't bother Philip. He wasn't about *fair*; he was about winning—even if at the end, his buddy Aristotle was nursing a bloody nose.

One day they were playing a quiet game of recognizing Homeric passages and completing them. Aristotle had proposed one that stumped his playmate. Philip excused himself and ran to his tutor to gain the answer surreptitiously and the win. Unfortunately for Philip, the tutor didn't know the answer either! Philip came back and suggested they play another game. Aristotle smiled. He saw through it all. But he was a prudent boy. He knew that Philip could whip him in a fight, so if he were to get on with this bully-cheat, he'd have to protect himself with what he did best.

The happiest day of his youth was his twelfth birthday, when his father took him to his court surgery. The suite of rooms was rather sparse. The rough-cut stonewalls gave a strength to the quarters. In the main room the floor was slanted so that liquids might proceed downward to a drain to the outside. In the center of the room were various circular stone outcroppings that served as chairs. There was also a red-colored, marble table whose surface was polished like a mirror. His father had his patients lie down there for various treatments. It was where his father practiced animal dissection.

Aristotle followed timidly behind his father. He had no idea what to expect. His father sat him down on one of the stone stools. Then Nicomachus turned and walked to a cabinet at the far end of the room. It was made of rose-colored wood and badly chipped. Aristotle watched with some trepidation as his father made his selection of implements from the cabinet, turned, and smiled in a foreign way. Nicomachus then proceeded toward his son with two knives in his hand (one large and one small). Why was he smiling like that? Aristotle didn't want to consider his darkest fears.

"Aristotle," his father began. "Today on your birthday, I will initiate you into the first level of the guild of Asclepiad—named after the physician Asclepios of Homeric renown." His father set the knives down on the table, walked over to Aristotle, and took him by the hand to walk outside.

At the far end of the yard was a pen of animals. Nicomachus took his son there and told him to pick out a baby pig. Aristotle did so and carried it back to the surgery. There Nicomachus took the blunt handle of the knife and struck the pig on the head, rendering the animal unconscious. Then he sliced the animal's throat.

"Aristotle, get me that bucket over there."

The boy complied. The father massaged the dead body so that it would continue to bleed. Soon the carcass ceased to bleed and his father made an incision down the belly with the small knife.

"The pig, my boy, is very similar to us all. This is how my teacher taught me dissection. Today, I will teach you. It is the first step in the initiation to the guild of Asclepiad." Nicomachus pointed with his knife. "Here is the esophagus where food goes in order to make blood. It goes to the stomach and then to the liver and finally back to the heart. In the heart the final concoction occurs, and the blood is sent out to the body to be used via the pipes, or *phlebes*, that go from the heart."

"What happens then, father?"

"Why, it gets used up, of course. Blood is nourishment. Sometimes it also has divine *ichor*,[1] but that's another birthday."

The time was divided between his father's discourses and Aristotle's own investigations with the knife. At the end of the day, as the light began to fade, his father wiped his bloody hands on a rag and then grasped Aristotle about the shoulders. "My son, today you became a man. Today you showed me that you, too, could be a physician and follow in the footsteps of your father."

Aristotle looked up to his father. He was never closer to him than at that moment.

---

1 *ichor*: the blood of the gods.

Soon afterwards Aristotle's father died. However, other Hippocratic families assisted Aristotle in his medical training. For five years he went through the motions of learning the craft of medicine. But medicine just wasn't theoretical enough for him. Aristotle's interests were broader. He convinced his mother to let him study at Plato's Academy in Athens. She agreed but gave him this admonition: "Be careful of the Athenians and the Spartans. The Athenians think they know it all, while the Spartans think they are the most powerful. Both of them are wrong. Keep to yourself. You are not one of them, and they will never let you forget that."

The first years at the Academy were heady. Aristotle loved the combination of work, study, and fellowship. Athens was vibrant. It was so different from Chalcis and his mother's home. At first Aristotle tried to write dramatic dialogues in the manner of his teacher. He tried to provide a twist by dividing his narratives into those like tragedy and others like comedy. One day in his eighth year at the school, he was summoned to talk with Plato.

Plato was sitting on an open-air bench on the porch before the garden. He sported a long, square beard. It gave him an aura of gravitas. There was no room on the bench for Aristotle, so he had to stand. The younger man's angle was such that he looked directly into the setting sun. The light hurt his eyes.

"I've heard that you've begun writing plays," said the head of the Academy.

Aristotle squinted and then looked downward. "Yes, sir."

"Most likely you are doing this in imitation of me."

Aristotle continued to look downward. "Yes, sir."

Plato then froze his face and began breathing hard. "You dunderhead! Did you ever attend my lecture on the evils of imitative art?"

"Yes, sir."

"Then did you remember how I denigrated writing tragedies—and especially comedies, with their wretched bawdy meters?"

"Yes, sir."

"Well, get over it, boy! If you want to write narratives that carefully craft direct argument as part of the dialogue, then fine. You'll be my heir. You've a lot of potential, Aristotle. I really mean it. But if you persist in trying to write pathetic drama that actually could be produced on stage to popular taste, then I've got something to say to you, boy. You'll never make it. You will not be on the tongues of those who appreciate fine intellect."

"Yes, sir." Aristotle's body was now telling him he had to move slightly as his frozen joints predicted that he'd soon fall.

Plato looked at his student and pursed his lips. Then he grimaced and shook his head. "I don't know about you, Aristotle. You're quick enough, really. But you don't really know how to fit in. There's something about you that is *foreign*—not that I hate foreigners. Hey, some of my best friends are foreigners, like Dion of Syracuse. You know there has always been an international flavor to the Academy. What I'm talking about is something different. I think that there is something *different* about you. And that's not generally something in your favor." Then Plato got up to leave. First, he wiped his nose, and then he cocked his head and inhaled as if he were about to say something else but had thought better of it. Plato turned and walked away, then stopped and turned back. "Especially the comedies. You've got to burn them, or someone else will."

Aristotle was upset. He went to his friend, Isocrates the rhetorician, who ran a competing school at the Lyceum. Isocrates liked to engage in strange physical postures. He told the assembly that it was to straighten his spine (which was slightly bent). Thus, he often would find a place away from the porch and venture into the garden and sit akimbo thinking about an argument.

"He said *that* to *you*?" Isocrates was a homely man, but he used his features well to express whatever he was feeling.

Aristotle nodded.

"Well, you know, you are his little darling."

Aristotle cocked his head.

"I don't mean it in that way. I mean that he respects you."

Aristotle sighed.

"You take your own stance. You don't just parrot him. That takes balls, Aristotle."

"But what about my plays?"

Isocrates reached out and touched Aristotle on the shoulder. "Your plays are just fine, Aristotle. But you'll never be Sophocles. You're too smart for that. If people knew what you thought about apart from the plays, then you'd be at the top of the heap. But here, Plato is right. The people, the hoi polloi, aren't up for it. They only want a good time. Go to the tragedy and get home for some whoopie with their wives." Then Isocrates looked Aristotle right in the eyes. "Aristotle, after one of your plays, they'd have to go home and have a rhetorical *discourse* with their wives."

Aristotle smiled.

"Hey, Aristotle, that's not what people want! Get real, man."

When Plato died, Aristotle was traveling for Philip. This was due to Demosthenes and his crew, who were whipping up anti-Macedonian hate in Athens. Things looked sketchy. Aristotle took the opportunity discretely to visit Philip.

Aristotle was not made Plato's successor (despite being the favorite among the other students). Aristotle, near the end of Plato's life, had more people listening to him than did the master. He had more students. But Aristotle was very pluralistic in his approach: from the stage to the cage (with the animals he was constantly observing). Thus, in one way, it was no surprise that Plato's nephew, Speusippus, succeeded him as head of the Academy. On the one hand, it marked a turn in the shared community worldview away from Aristotle's pluralism toward a mathematical depiction of philosophy. Aristotle found the reduction of philosophy to mathematics problematic. On the other hand, the school building was Plato's own property, and Speusippus was in Plato's will. It made practical sense as well.

It was time for something new. Aristotle accepted an invitation to join a former student, Hermeias, who was gathering a platonic circle about him in Assos in Mysia, near Troy. Hermeias was the ruler, having risen from the lowest stratum of society. This didn't suit the privileged Athenians very well. Aristotle's movements were noted and recorded by the cup and suck types. It was lucky for Aristotle that Philip was one of the most powerful men on earth.

Aristotle spent three years in this environment. He was in heaven. During this time, he created an encyclopedic series of written observations on nature. It was just like his childhood—only this time there was no nagging mother calling. But another woman poked her head into his reverie.

He was sitting on a rocky beach at low tide looking at the animals scurrying back to their element. From behind, a woman and a man approached. It was late afternoon.

"Do you believe me now," said the woman. The man was emotionless.

"I do now, sis. You have to admit that it seemed a bit bizarre. This guy, who Hermeias said is the equal of Plato, is sitting on the beach playing with the lobsters."

"He is an agent of Philip, you know," said the woman.

"He seems to be connected to just about everybody," replied the brother.

Pythias took her brother's arm and gave it a squeeze. "Go and talk to him."

The brother laughed slightly and then did as he was told. The result was an invitation to dinner that led to a courtship consummated in marriage and the birth of a daughter whom Aristotle dutifully named after his mother.

It was a short marriage. Pythias caught a disease from her travels with her husband to Lesbos to study animals. Aristotle left little Phaestis, his daughter, with uncle Hermeias and sojourned to his mother's house, where he stayed for a time. He met another woman, Herpyllis, who bore him a son. Aristotle named him Nicomachus after his father.

Next, Aristotle hooked up in Lesbos with his younger colleague, Theophrastus, who had attended many of Aristotle's lectures. They shared a keen interest in natural philosophy, unlike many of the mathematically oriented sect who ruled the Academy.

"Bum break on the Scholarch spot at the Academy, man," began Theophrastus when they finally sat down. "I mean *you* are the one everyone respects. And you've stayed put for five years. You've paid your dues. But it's their loss. Why don't you just stay here with me and set up a school based upon natural philosophy. The past few weeks we've spent together have been great."

Aristotle raised his hand and grasped his friend's shoulder. "You know I wouldn't have given it another thought if the Scholarch were based upon merit. But to lose something due to inside maneuvering and Plato's will—I don't know. It is not my idea of the way philosophy should be handled. It's just that clique of mathematicians who live in their own world and think that they dirty their hands by studying nature."

"I wish they'd read Heraclitus. As you taught me, he said about the kitchen, 'There are gods even here.'"

"Yeah."

Theophrastus smiled. "If there are gods in the slaughter house, where all kinds of nastiness reside, then you can bet there are gods in nature! You said there was no contradiction in systematic thinking and natural experimentation. That system you invented, the syllogism, is really far better than math for presenting the truths of nature."

"Well, it's a good theory. I still have to work out the kinks. You know, sometimes I think it goes too quickly. But then it is meant to be exact: how does the middle attach to the extremes? It focuses the mind to a single inference. But it is not sufficient. It is a mode of presentation. It is posterior to my theory of natural discovery. I haven't really worked that out very well yet. But there's time left. You know I've always said that. My mother was the one who always liked to create a sense of urgency. But my nature is to lie back a bit and wait until things sort themselves out in my mind."

Then Theophrastus got up and paced about. "And what a mind, too."

Aristotle smiled.

"No, I mean it. I know that being Macedonian is a chain around your neck. They hate Philip. The Athenians are just so narrow-minded. You've tried to be one of them. You even suggested a league of Hellenic nations that could create world peace. But they are so involved with their bloodlines that an outsider really doesn't stand much of a chance. I like your name for them: the cup and suck club. They drink together and suck up to the gentry."

"Well, Plato was well connected," said Aristotle looking down.

"Yes," said Theophrastus, stopping in his pacing.

Aristotle looked up again and saw his friend against the setting sun. The light transformed the other's head into a black disk. It was almost as though his head were a planet eclipsing the solar circle.

Then Theophrastus went and sat right next to his teacher. "You could go back to Philip."

"Oh, I have. I've been doing some business for him of late to keep the wolf away. We were childhood pals you know. Lately, he's been sending me letters asking me to teach his son, Alexander."

"Why don't you accept?"

"I don't know. I'm seriously considering it. Sometimes Philip scares me a little. I'm not sure how close I want to be to him." Aristotle grimaced and then looked up at the angle of the sun. "Right now I'm not thinking of anything. Let's go look at lobsters and crabs while there's still sunlight."

Theophrastus smiled. "Terrific! I'd like to see for myself what you told me about lobster claws."

Aristotle gave his friend a pat on the shoulder as they made their way to the sea.

He spent the rest of the year on Lesbos before deciding to travel back to the court of Philip and tutor Alexander. After only a few years with his charge, Aristotle thought he had failed. Alexander was very channeled in the way he thought about things. In the absence of Philip, Alexander became regent, and the experience was heady. Aristotle became more of an advisor than a teacher.

When Aristotle talked with his friend Theophrastus again, the story was different. They met on the outskirts of Athens. Things were tense since Philip had died and Alexander had begun his military campaign. Alexander had marched south to squelch the uprising and destroyed Thebes. This bold action caused various city-states, including Athens, to sue for treaties. As a favor to Aristotle, Alexander made it a condition of the peace that Aristotle be allowed to open a school in Athens, something that, as an outsider, he wouldn't otherwise have been able to do.

"So, what did you teach this guy, Alexander?"

"I don't know what you mean. You know how I teach? You've heard my lectures."

"But this guy is going crazy in his conquests. He's already outperformed his father."

"Alexander does what it takes to win. I could never teach him ethics. I tried going over a treatise I've been developing on politics. It will use the community ethos but be practically sensitive to what a state needs to do to survive through the role of citizenship."

"But Alexander is your protector. We all know about the gold he's sent you."

"Yes, the gold. I don't dismiss it, but I most appreciate the rare animals he also sends. It's better when they are alive, but even if I get them dead, then I can cut them up."

"You never cut up live creatures, do you?"

"No way. It doesn't have anything to do with religion. It's just that if nature does nothing in vain, then who am I to mess with it for the vanity of my own personal curiosity?"

"But we eat animals."

"Yes, but that's different. We kill them for food just like they kill other animals for food. But no other animal kills to satisfy curiosity. That just isn't right."

"Hey, but what about plants?" asked Theophrastus putting his hand on Aristotle's shoulder.

Aristotle smiled. He reciprocated and put his hand also on Theophrastus's shoulder. "I think you're safe there, my friend. Plants have only one soul, you know."

"Yes, much safer. No plants, by nature, desire to know."

Aristotle smiled. "Yes, you always like that lecture. I intend to expand it further to a full treatise some day. There is always time, you know."

"Yes, I know. But I'm more concerned about eating live things than you are," laughed Theophrastus.

Alexander died in the middle of June. It was now September. The old poem that Aristotle had written years before as a eulogy came to haunt him. It was thought to be an excessively Macedonian way of thinking and, by extension, very unpatriotic to Athens. The problematic lines were[2]

> O virtue, toilsome for the generation of mortals to achieve,
> The fairest prize that life can win . . .
> Such courage dost thou implant in the mind, imperishable,
> Better than gold, dearer than parents or soft-eyed sleep . . .
> For the sake of thy dear form the nursling of Atarneus [that is, Hermeias],
> Too, was bereft of the light of the sun.

---

2 These two translations come from R. D. Hicks, *Diogenes Laertius: Lives of Eminent Philosophers* (London: Heinemann, 1925), I, v.

People thought that Aristotle had overdone it. He was showing this tyrant too much respect and in so doing forsaking Athens. Theocritus of Chios summed up one form of attack against Aristotle:

To Hermeias, the eunuch, the slave withal of Eubulus, an empty monument was raised by empty-witted Aristotle, who by constraint of a lawless appetite chose to dwell at the mouth of the Borborus [muddy stream] rather than in the Academy.

Aristotle's *thymos*[3] was with the Macedonians. This usurping kingdom—first with Philip and then with his son, Alexander—threatened the Athenian self-image. With this baggage of prejudice, Aristotle was only able to open his school (Isocrates's old academy, which once had been used to train wrestlers) with the help of Alexander in the Treaty of Athens. The very fact of Aristotle's return to Athens attracted quite a crowd. In the mornings he would walk amid the same woods Socrates once haunted and discuss esoteric philosophical issues, hence the name "Peripatetic" for his school— though some say the term came earlier when his pupil Alexander was recovering from an illness and Aristotle walked him to health while he gave him his lessons. In the afternoon, he would discourse on more general exoteric matters with a larger audience. Because Alexander continued to reverence his former tutor with periodic sums of money and specimens from his conquests, Aristotle was able to accumulate a large number of manuscripts and created a library, one of the finest in the world. He instituted his own classification scheme, which the library in Alexandria later imitated.

During this time he solidified all his notes into formal lectures, which he regularly delivered to his larger audiences. The contrast with his teacher, Plato, was critical. Whereas Plato believed in a holistic composite of all knowledge, Aristotle thought that each separate area should be discussed by itself. In many ways this was exactly what his teacher had done—for example, in his lecture called "Timaeus." But others forgot about this and wanted to emphasize Aristotle's differences—with the implication that Aristotle was a failure.

And here he was sitting in the woods feeling the heat. It was almost the autumnal equinox, his birthday. It should be cooling off a bit, but it wasn't. With Alexander's death in June, his last vestige of Macedonian protection (not to mention money) had come to an end. The Athenians were a mercurial lot. They'd love you one day and kill you the next.

Eurymedon denounced Aristotle for not holding the gods in honor. He claimed that Aristotle was an impious heretic. This was not good news.

Aristotle wanted to talk to his friend Theophrastus. He wanted so much for everything to work out. But his mind was buzzing. It was just like Plato had said about his mentor, Socrates. He remembered Plato's animated voice and how he elongated the *eta* so that it almost sounded like two letters instead of one.

---

3 *thymos:* spirited or emotional.

"And then Meletis and Anytus decided that Socrates was a liability." Plato moved to his left and began moving his mouth without talking. "The Peloponnesian War had been lost because of the accommodation to democratic inefficiency. Everyone had an opinion! Why didn't they trust the committee appointed to deal with the war?"

Plato threw his hands in the air. He gathered himself and strode forward. "Look, those bozos were frustrated. They didn't know what to do. Athens was in a funk, and the vacuum of power sought a scapegoat."

The students began to murmur. "What does the populace, the hoi polloi, want most when there is a call for a scapegoat?"

No one answered.

"Come on! Are you a bunch of ninnies? Tell me what you think!"

No one answered. There were some sounds of people shifting about.

Plato shut his eyes, then opened them again with a vicious stare. "They choose an easy target: just what the stupid populace loves to hate—impiety."

This time groans of anger punctuated the murmurs.

"That's right, the political dunces play the rhetorical religious card every time. It's a sure winner for the hoi polloi. Kill the heretic bastard! Forget how he's served the state in war and peace. He's a goddamn atheist, and he has to pay for it."

One young student sitting at the back yelled, "No!!"

Plato clenched his fists together and pumped them above his head. "That's right. That's what we all should have said, me included. We just didn't know he'd go through with it. We thought he'd leave Athens. Everyone wanted him to leave Athens."

And then Plato seemed to lose energy. His voice became almost a whisper. "It was a travesty." And then the scion's chest heaved almost as one's does for a lost wife. The room was deathly quiet.

The scene was emblazoned on Aristotle's mind. He arose, bolt upright. "They're not going to try me on trumped up charges. I will not allow the Athenians to sin twice against Philosophy." And with that he gathered his things and left the city once again for his mother's Chalcian residence.

In a year Aristotle was dead.

A fictional eulogy poem for Aristotle (from the point of view of Theophrastus):

> All your life they saw you as merely Macedonian:
> A people hated by Athens for their military prowess
> (Especially keen in the city-state of losers)
> You endured preferment of legacy, power, and position.
> And yet you continued—in the face of intimidation.
> Your nonbiological works were largely composed
> In the city that forced you to be: an Outsider.
> In a city that should have taken you to its bosom.

And yet you so admired the legal system of Athens
That you voluntarily made it central to your *Ethics*.
And then your vision of the role of being a citizen
Was derived from what you experienced in Athens
It was a crucial part of your *Politics*—and yet this very
State denied *you* citizenship: to be an equal in the city you loved!

■ READING AND DISCUSSION QUESTIONS

1. What is the significance of the wolf in the early scene with Aristotle's mother?
2. What worldviews and behaviors do Philip and Aristotle display as children? How are they significant?
3. On his twelfth birthday Aristotle is initiated into medicine by his father. Why did Aristotle not become a physician? How would his life have been different? Do your parents ever pressure you to take up a particular career?
4. Why was Plato angry that Aristotle was writing imitative art? Is Plato's position reasonable? How would society be different if we accepted Plato's position on imitative art?
5. Plato believed that all knowledge was a whole to be studied as such. Aristotle believed in categorizing particular types of knowledge to be studied separately. What are the advantages and disadvantages of each approach?
6. When Plato died, Aristotle left Athens. Why? Should he not have stayed as Socrates did? Is the argument for staying or leaving any different after Alexander's death?
7. Why was Aristotle's connection with Hermeias problematic?
8. How did Aristotle's mentoring of Alexander affect Aristotle's life?
9. What characteristics of Aristotle made Theophrastus admire him? What is unique about the friendship between a teacher and his student? How does it differ from other friendships?

■ FICTIVE-NARRATIVE PHILOSOPHY FEEDBACK

What claims are made in this story? Write them out in a bulleted list and include whether they are made through dialogue, dramatic action, or the presentation of the scene (including descriptive detail). One page. Then choose either a short direct-discourse response (according to the rules in Chapter 2) or a short fictive-narrative presentation (according to the rules in Chapter 3).

ON THE SOUL

Aristotle

Adapted from Aristotle's *De Anima*, trans. J. A. Smith (Oxford: Oxford University Press, 1910). *Note on the translation:* English words found in brackets are inserted by the translator to make better sense of the English rendering.

In this selection Aristotle offers a series of short, carefully constructed, direct logical arguments about the nature and activity of the soul. Here, "soul" is a very robust concept that embraces a wide variety of characteristics, such as "rationality," "imagination," "perception," "nutrition," and "the power of movement."

What Is Soul?

Holding as we do that, while knowledge of any kind is a thing to be honored and prized, one kind of it may, either by reason of its greater exactness or of a higher dignity and greater wonderfulness in its objects, be more honorable and precious than another, on both accounts we should naturally be led to place in the front rank the study of the soul. The knowledge of the soul[4] admittedly contributes greatly to the advance of truth in general and, above all, to our understanding of Nature, for the soul is in some sense the principle of animal life.[5] Our aim is to grasp and understand, first, its essential nature and, second, its properties; of these some are thought to be affections proper to the soul itself, while others are considered to attach to the animal owing to the presence within it of soul.

To attain any assured knowledge about the soul is one of the most difficult things in the world. As the form of question that here presents itself (namely, the question, What is it?) recurs in other fields, it might be supposed that there is some single method of inquiry applicable to all objects whose essential nature we are endeavoring to ascertain (as there *is* for derived properties the single method of demonstration); in that case what we should have to seek

---

4 **soul,** or "psyche," in this context is better understood as the English word "mind." In other contexts it can refer to other powers of the body, such as the abilities of locomotion, sensation, and nutrition.

5 **the principle of animal life:** "soul" (or "psyche") in this second context is the principle of life for plants, animals, and humans by focusing upon unique functions.

for would be this unique method. But if there is no such single and general method for solving the question of essence, our task becomes still more difficult; in the case of each different subject we shall have to determine the appropriate process of investigation. If to this there be a clear answer (for example, that the process is demonstration or division or some other known method), difficulties and hesitations still beset us—with what facts shall we begin the inquiry? For the facts that form the starting points in different subjects must be different, as, for example, in the case of numbers and surfaces.

Can the Mind Be Separated from the Body?

A further problem presented by the affections of soul is this: are they all affections of the complex of body and soul, or is there any one among them peculiar to the soul by itself? To determine this is indispensable but difficult. If we consider the majority of them, there seems to be no case in which the soul can act or be acted upon without involving the body (for example, anger, courage, appetite, and sensation generally). Thinking seems the most probable exception; but if this too proves to be a form of imagination or to be impossible without imagination, it too requires a body as a condition of its existence. If there is any way of acting or being acted upon proper to soul, soul will be capable of separate existence; if there is none, its separate existence is impossible. In the latter case, it will be like what is straight, which has many properties arising from the straightness in it (for example, that of touching a bronze

sphere at a point), though straightness divorced from the other constituents of the straight thing cannot touch it in this way; it cannot be so divorced at all since it is always found in a body. It therefore seems that all the affections of soul involve a body—passion, gentleness, fear, pity, courage, joy, loving, and hating; in all these there is a concurrent affection of the body. In support of this we may point to the fact that, while sometimes on the occasion of violent and striking occurrences there is no excitement or fear felt, on others faint and feeble stimulations produce these emotions, namely, when the body is already in a state of tension resembling its condition when we are angry. Here is a still clearer case: in the absence of any external cause of terror, we find ourselves experiencing the feelings of a man in terror. From all this it is obvious that the affections of soul are enmattered formulable essences.

The Mind and Sensations

Smell and its object are much less easy to determine than what we have hitherto discussed; the distinguishing characteristic of the object of smell is less obvious than those of sound or color. The ground of this is that our power of smell is less discriminating and in general inferior to that of many species of animals; men have a poor sense of smell, and our apprehension of its proper objects is inseparably bound up with, and so confused by, pleasure and pain, which shows that in us the organ is inaccurate. It is probable that there is a parallel failure in the perception of color by animals that have hard eyes: probably they discriminate differences of color only by the presence or absence of what excites fear, and it is probably thus that human beings distinguish smells. It seems that there is an analogy between smell and taste and that the species of tastes run parallel to those of smells—the only difference being that our sense of taste is more discriminating than our sense of smell because the former is a modification of touch, which reaches in man the maximum of discriminative accuracy. While in respect of all the other senses we fall below many species of animals, in respect of touch we far excel all other species in exactness of discrimination. That is why man is the most intelligent of all animals. This is confirmed by the fact that it is to differences in the organ of touch and to nothing else that the differences between man and man in respect of natural endowment are due; men whose flesh is hard are ill endowed by nature; men whose flesh is soft are well endowed.

Thinking, Discriminating, and Perceiving

[Next, we will examine] thinking, discriminating, and perceiving. Thinking, both speculative and practical, is regarded as akin to a form of perceiving; for in the one as well as the other the soul discriminates and is cognizant of something which *is*. Indeed, the ancients go so far as to identify thinking and perceiving; for example, Empedocles says, "For 'tis in respect of what is present that man's wit is increased," and, again, "whence it befalls them from time to time to think diverse thoughts," and Homer's phrase "For suchlike is man's mind" means the same. They

all look upon thinking as a bodily process like perceiving and hold that like is *known* as well as *perceived* by like, as I explained at the beginning of our discussion. Yet, they ought at the same time to have accounted for error also; for it is more intimately connected with animal existence, and the soul continues longer in the state of error than in that of truth. They cannot escape the dilemma: either (1) whatever seems is true (and there are some who accept this), or (2) error is contact with the unlike; for that is the opposite of the knowing of like by like.

But it is a received principle that error as well as knowledge in respect to contraries is one and the same.

That perceiving and practical thinking are not identical is therefore obvious, for the former is universal in the animal world; the latter is found in only a small division of it. Further, speculative thinking is also distinct from perceiving—I mean that in which we find rightness and wrongness—rightness in prudence, knowledge, true opinion, and wrongness in their opposites; for perception of the special objects of sense is always free from error and is found in all animals, while it is possible to think falsely as well as truly, and thought is found only where there is discourse of reason as well as sensibility. For imagination is different from either perceiving or discursive thinking, though it is not found without sensation, or judgment without it [imagination]. That this activity is not the same kind of thinking as judgment is obvious. For imagining lies within our own power whenever we wish (for example, we can call up a picture, as in the practice of mnemonics by the use of mental images), but in forming opinions we are not free: we cannot escape the alternative of falsehood or truth. Further, when we think something to be fearful or threatening, emotion is immediately produced, and so too with what is encouraging; but when we merely imagine we remain as unaffected as persons who are looking at a painting of some dreadful or encouraging scene. Again, within the field of judgment itself we find varieties—knowledge, opinion, prudence, and their opposites; of the differences between these I must speak elsewhere.

Thinking, Imagination, and Judgment

Thinking is different from perceiving and is held to be in part imagination, in part judgment: we must therefore first mark off the sphere of imagination and then speak of judgment. If, then, imagination is that in virtue of which an image arises for us, excluding metaphorical uses of the term, is it a single faculty or disposition relative to images, in virtue of which we discriminate and are either in error or not? The faculties in virtue of which we do this are sense, opinion, science, and intelligence.

That imagination is not sense is clear from the following considerations: (1) Sense is either a faculty or an activity (for example, sight or seeing): imagination takes place in the absence of both, as, for example, in dreams. (2) Again, sense is always present, imagination not. If actual imagination and actual sensation were the same, imagination would be found in all the brutes: this is held not to be the case; for example, it is not found in ants or bees or grubs. (3) Again, sensations are always true; imaginations are for the most part false. (4) Once more, even in ordi-

nary speech, we do not, when sense functions precisely with regard to its object, say that we imagine it to be a man, but rather when there is some failure of accuracy in its exercise. And (5), as we were saying before, visions appear to us even when our eyes are shut. Neither is imagination *any* of the things that are never in error: for example, knowledge or intelligence, for imagination may be false.

It remains therefore to see if it is opinion, for opinion may be either true or false.

But opinion involves belief (for without belief in what we opine, we cannot have an opinion), and in the brutes though we often find imagination, we never find belief. Further, every opinion is accompanied by belief, belief by conviction, and conviction by discourse of reason, while in some of the brutes we find imagination, without discourse of reason. It is clear then that imagination cannot, again, be (1) opinion *plus* sensation, or (2) opinion mediated by sensation, or (3) a blend of opinion and sensation; this is impossible both for these reasons and because the content of the supposed opinion cannot be different from that of the sensation (I mean that imagination must be the blending of the perception of white with the opinion that it is white: it could scarcely be a blend of the opinion that it is good with the perception that it is white): to imagine is therefore (on this view) identical with the thinking of exactly the same as what one in the strictest sense perceives. But what we imagine is sometimes false though our contemporaneous judgment about it is true; for example, we imagine the sun to be a foot in diameter though we are convinced that it is larger than the inhabited part of the earth, and the following dilemma presents itself. Either (a) while the fact has not changed and the observer has neither forgotten nor lost belief in the true opinion that he had, that opinion has disappeared, or (b) if he retains it, then his opinion is at once true and false. A true opinion, however, becomes false only when the fact alters without being noticed.

Imagination is therefore neither any one of the states enumerated nor compounded out of them.

But because when one thing has been set in motion, another thing may be moved by it, and imagination is held to be a movement and to be impossible without sensation (that is, to occur in beings that are percipient and to have for its content what can be perceived), and because movement may be produced by actual sensation and that movement is necessarily similar in character to the sensation itself, this movement must be (1) necessarily (a) incapable of existing apart from sensation, and (b) incapable of existing except when we perceive, (2) such that in virtue of its possession, that in which it is found may present various phenomena both active and passive, and (3) such that it may be either true or false.

The reason of the last characteristic is as follows. Perception (1) of the special objects of sense is never in error or admits the least possible amount of falsehood. (2) That of the concomitance of the objects concomitant with the sensible qualities comes next: in this case certainly we may be deceived; for while the perception that there is white before us cannot be false, the perception that what is white is this or that may be false. (3) Third comes the perception of the universal attributes that accompany the concomitant objects to which the special sensibles attach (I mean, for exam-

ple, of movement and magnitude); it is in respect of these that the greatest amount of sense-illusion is possible.

The motion that is due to the activity of sense in these three modes of its exercise will differ from the activity of sense: (1) the first kind of derived motion is free from error while the sensation is present; (2) and (3) the others may be erroneous whether it is present or absent, especially when the object of perception is far off. If, then, imagination presents no other features than those enumerated and is what we have described, imagination must be a movement resulting from an actual exercise of a power of sense.

As sight is the most highly developed sense, the name *phantasia* ("imagination") has been formed from *phaos* ("light") because it is not possible to see without light.

And because imaginations remain in the organs of sense and resemble sensations, animals in their actions are largely guided by them, some (that is, the brutes) because of the nonexistence in them of mind, others (that is, men) because of the temporary eclipse in them of mind by feeling or disease or sleep.

About imagination, what it is and why it exists, let so much suffice.

Rational Thought

Turning now to the part of the soul with which the soul knows and thinks (whether this is separable from the others in definition only or spatially as well), we have to inquire (1) what differentiates this part, and (2) how thinking can take place.

If thinking is like perceiving, it must be either a process in which the soul is acted upon by what is capable of being thought or a process different from but analogous to that. The thinking part of the soul must therefore be, while impassible, capable of receiving the form of an object; that is, it must be potentially identical in character with its object without being the object. Mind must be related to what is thinkable, as sense is to what is sensible.

Therefore, since everything is a possible object of thought, mind in order, as Anaxagoras says, to dominate, that is, to know, must be pure from all admixture; for the copresence of what is alien to its nature is a hindrance and a block; it follows that it, too, like the sensitive part, can have no nature of its own, other than that of having a certain capacity. Thus, that in the soul that is called mind (by mind I mean that whereby the soul thinks and judges) is, before it thinks, not actually any real thing. For this reason it cannot reasonably be regarded as blended with the body; if so, it would acquire some quality (for example, warmth or cold) or even have an organ like the sensitive faculty: as it is, it has none. It was a good idea to call the soul "the place of forms," though (1) this description holds only of the intellective soul, and (2) even this is the forms only potentially, not actually.

Observation of the sense organs and their employment reveals a distinction between the impassibility of the sensitive and that of the intellective faculty. After strong stimulation of a sense, we are less able to exercise it than before, as, for example, in the case of a loud sound, we cannot hear easily immediately after, or in the case of a bright color or a powerful odor, we cannot see or smell, but in the case of mind, thought about an object that is highly intelligible renders it more and not less able afterwards to think objects that are less intelligible: the reason is that while the faculty of sensation is dependent upon the body, *mind is separable from it.*

Once the mind has become each set of its possible objects, as a man of science[6] has, when this phrase is used of one who is actually a man of science (this happens when he is now able to exercise the power on his own initiative), its condition is still one of potentiality, but in a different sense from the potentiality that preceded the acquisition of knowledge by learning or discovery: the mind, too, is then able to think *itself.*

Form and Matter

Since we can distinguish between a spatial magnitude and what it is to be such, and between water and what it is to be water, and so in many other cases (though not in all, for in certain cases the thing and its form are identical), flesh and what it is to be flesh are discriminated either by different faculties or by the same faculty in two different states: for flesh necessarily involves matter and is like what is snubnosed, a *this* in a this. Now, it is by means of the sensitive faculty that we discriminate the hot and the cold, that is, the factors

---

6 **science:** in this context, "science" means exact knowledge rather than our modern understanding of critical empiricism.

that combined in a certain ratio constitute flesh: the essential character of flesh is apprehended by something different either wholly separate from the sensitive faculty or related to it as a bent line to the same line when it has been straightened out.

Again, in the case of abstract objects, what is straight is analogous to what is snub-nosed; for it necessarily implies a continuum as its matter; its constitutive essence is different, if we may distinguish between straightness and what is straight: let us take it to be twoness. It must be apprehended, therefore, by a different power or by the same power in a different state. To sum up, in so far as the realities it knows are capable of being separated from their matter, so it is also with the powers of mind.

The Knower and the Known

The problem might be suggested: if thinking is a passive affection, then if mind is simple and impassible and has nothing in common with anything else, as Anaxagoras says, how can it come to think at all? For interaction between two factors is held to require a precedent community of nature between the factors. Again, it might be asked, is mind a possible object of thought to itself? For if mind is thinkable per se and what is thinkable is in kind one and the same, then either (a) mind will belong to everything, or (b) mind will contain some element common to it with all other realities that makes them all thinkable.

1. Have not we already disposed of the difficulty about interaction involving a common element, when we said that mind is in a sense potentially whatever is thinkable, though actually it is nothing until it has thought? What it thinks must be in it just as characters may be said to be on a writing tablet on which as yet nothing actually stands written: this is exactly what happens with mind.

2. Mind is itself thinkable in exactly the same way as its objects are. For (a) in the case of objects that involve no matter, what thinks and what is thought are identical, for speculative knowledge and its object are identical. (Why mind is not always thinking, we must consider later.) (b) In the case of those that contain matter, each of the objects of thought is only potentially present. It follows that while *they* will not have mind in them (for mind is a potentiality of them only in so far as they are capable of being disengaged from matter), mind may yet be thinkable.

Summary

Let us now summarize our results about soul and repeat that the Soul is in a way all existing things; for existing things are either sensible or thinkable, and knowledge is in a way what is knowable, and sensation is in a way what is sensible: in *what* way we must inquire.

Knowledge and sensation are divided to correspond with the realities, potential knowledge and sensation answering to potentialities, and actual knowledge and sensation to actualities. Within the soul the faculties of knowledge and sensation are *potentially* these objects, the one what is knowable, the other what is sensible. They must be either the things themselves or their forms. The former alternative is, of course, impossible: it is not the stone that is present in the soul but its form.

It follows that the soul is analogous to the hand, for as the hand is a tool of tools, so the mind is the form of forms and sense the form of sensible things.

Since, according to common agreement, there is nothing outside and separate in existence from sensible spatial magnitudes, the objects of thought are in the sensible forms, namely, both the abstract objects and all the states and affections of sensible things. Hence, (1) no one can learn or understand anything in the absence of sense, and (2) when the mind is actively aware of anything, it is necessarily aware of it along with an image, for images are like sensuous contents except in that they contain no matter.

Imagination is different from assertion and denial, for what is true or false involves a synthesis of concepts. In what will the primary concepts differ from images? Must we not say that neither these nor even our other concepts are images, though they necessarily involve them?

The soul of animals is characterized by two faculties: (a) the faculty of discrimination that is the work of thought and sense, and (b) the faculty of originating local movement. Sense and mind we have now sufficiently examined. Let us next consider what it is in the soul that originates movement. Is it a single part of the soul, separate either spatially or in definition? Or is it the soul as a whole? If it is a part, is that part different from those usually distinguished or already mentioned by us, or is it one of them? The problem at once presents itself, in what sense we are to speak of parts of the soul or how many we should distinguish. For in a sense there is an infinity of parts: it is not enough to distinguish, with some thinkers, the calculative, the passionate, and the desiderative, or with others the rational and the irrational; for if we take the dividing lines followed by these thinkers, we shall find parts far more distinctly separated from one another than these, namely, those we have just mentioned: (1) the *nutritive*, which belongs both to plants and to all animals, and (2) the *sensitive*, which cannot easily be classed as either irrational or rational; further (3) the *imaginative*, which is, in its being, different from all, while it is very hard to say with which of the others it is the same or not the same, supposing we determine to posit *separate* parts in the soul; and lastly (4) the *appetitive,* which would seem to be distinct both in definition and in power from all hitherto enumerated.

It is absurd to break up the last-mentioned faculty: as these thinkers do, for wish is found in the calculative part and desire and passion in the irrational; and if the soul is tripartite,[7] appetite will be found in all three parts.

---

7 **tripartite:** consisting of three parts: wisdom, spiritedness, and appetite or desire. Plato's tripartite soul depicts appetite as being a separate part.

■ READING AND DISCUSSION QUESTIONS

1. Aristotle uses the same word, "soul" *(psyche)*, to refer to the human mind, animal sensation and locomotion, and plant nutrition. Humans have all three powers of the soul. The other life forms are more limited. How does this definition of soul as an active power color the way you understand Nature?

2. To properly define something, Aristotle suggests that we answer the functional question, What is it? Look again at question 1. From the information there, what is the essence of soul for Aristotle?

3. Does Aristotle believe the mind can be separable from the body? (How would this answer affect religions that believe in the possibility of a life after death?) Are other senses of soul separable from the body—such as the nutritive soul?

4. Aristotle says that though human sense organs are inferior to those of other animals, humans excel over animals in exactness of discrimination. What does he mean by this?

5. Those who hold that thinking is identical to perceiving fall prey to a logical dilemma: either (1) whatever seems is true, or (2) error is contact with the unlike. What is the force of this dilemma when considering the power of "discrimination"?

6. What is the power of the imagination, and how does it impact thinking? Can imagination be false? Can knowledge be false?

7. Describe the genesis of imagination.

8. Does the mind blend with the objects of thought? How is the rational soul a "place of forms"?

9. How should we recognize the roles of form and matter when contemplating a snub nose (as Socrates reputedly had)?

10. If intellectual activity were merely a passive reception, how would this affect the relationship between the knower and the known?

■ CLASS EXERCISES

A. *Direct logical discourse:* Using the tools found in Chapter 2, pick out one of the subsections from Aristotle and outline the argument contained within. Based on your assessment of one key premise, write a one-page argument about why you agree or disagree with the argument's conclusion.

B. *Fictive-narrative philosophy:* Using the tools found in Chapter 3, begin with a claim from the reading questions above and structure a narrative based on a fictional class discussion of that question between two or three students with different opinions. Make sure the claims are defended using the techniques of either "show" (via the dramatic action) or "tell" (via the content of the structured dialogue). Three pages.

CHAPTER SIX

Buddha

Siddhartha Gautama, the Buddha, lived circa 563 to 483 BCE in Lumbini (now Nepal near the Indian border). The city is at the foothills of the Himalayas, where Siddhartha lived until the age of twenty-nine. As his father was a king, Siddhartha was destined for a life of luxury. When he was twenty-nine, he ventured out and was disturbed to see the sick, aged, and suffering that contrasted greatly with his own life. Further excursions reinforced this reality. Moved by these events, he decided to overcome these scourges by becoming an ascetic. Siddhartha escaped his surroundings, and this was the beginning of a journey that eventually led to his Enlightenment.

PRINCE OF THE ASCETICS

Charles Johnson

This is a story about the awakening of Siddhartha Gautama. It is told by a narrator, Mahanama, who with his four brothers is seeking the peace and wisdom of the Atma (true self). The quest of the brothers is contrasted with that of a twenty-nine-year-old powerful sadhu,[1] who was gaining attention after his crossing of the river Anoma. For six years they choose this stranger as their spiritual leader when something unusual happens!

<hr>

रूपं शुन्यता शुन्यतैव रूपं

"Form is emptiness, emptiness is form."
The Prajñā Pāramitā Hridaya Sūtra

Once upon a time, my companions and I lived in the forest near the village of Uruvela on the banks of the Nairanjana River. We were known far and wide as five men who had forsaken worldly affairs in order to devote ourselves completely to the life of the spirit. For thousands of years in our country, this has been the accepted way for the Four Stages of Life. First, to spend the spring of one's youth as a dedicated student; the summer as a busy householder using whatever wealth he has acquired to help others; the fall as an ascetic who renounces all duties at age fifty and retires into the forest; and the goal of the winter season is to experience the peace and wisdom found only in the Atma [or Self] which permeates all parts of the world as moisture seeps through sand. My brothers in this noble Fourth Stage of tranquility, which we had just entered, were Kodananna, Bhadiya, Vappa, and Assajii. We had once been family men, members of the Vaishya [trader] caste,[2] but now owned no possessions. We lived, as was right, in poverty and detachment. We wore simple yellow robes and fasted often. Wheresoever we walked, always in single file, Vappa, a small man with a snoutlike nose, took the lead, sweeping the ground before us with a twig-broom so we would not crush

<hr>

1 **sadhu:** in Hinduism a mystic and ascetic who is also often a wandering soul dedicated to achieving liberation through meditation.

2 **caste:** the Hindu caste system consists of four Varnas: Brahmins (teachers, scholars, priests), Kshatriyas (kings and warriors), Vaishyas (merchants, traders, landlords), and Shudras (working class people in nonpolluting jobs). Those not in the caste system are foreigners or untouchables.

any living creatures too small to see. When we did not leave our ashram[3] to make alms-rounds for food in Uruvela, we satisfied our hunger with fruit, but not taken off trees; rather we gathered whatever had fallen to the ground. Each day we wrote the Sanskrit word *ahum* or "I" on the back of our hands so that we rarely went but a few moments without seeing it and remembering to inquire into the Self as the source of all things. People throughout the kingdom of Magadha affectionately called us *Bapu* [or father] because they knew that we had just begun the difficult path described in the *Vedas* and *Upanishads*.[4] The scriptures say that a fast mind is a sick mind. But we, my brothers and I, were slowly taming the wild horses of our thoughts, learning the four kinds of yoga, banishing the ego, that toadstool that grows out of consciousness, and freeing ourselves from the twin illusions of pleasure and pain.

But one day it came to pass that as we made our monthly rounds in the summer-gilded village, begging for alms, the merchants and women all looked the other way when we arrived. When Assajii asked them what was wrong, they apologized. With their palms upturned, each explained how he had already given his monthly offering to a stunning young swami, a *mahatma*, a powerful *sadhu*[5] who was only twenty-nine years old and had recently crossed the River Anoma, which divided our kingdom from the land of the Shakya tribe. They said just being in his presence for a few moments brought immeasurable peace and joy. And if that were not shocking enough, some were calling him *Munisha*, "Prince of the Ascetics."

"How can this be?" My heart gave a slight thump. "Surely you don't mean that."

A portly merchant, Dakma was his name, who was shaped like a pigeon, with bright rings on his fingers, puffed at me, "Oh, but he *is* such. We have never seen his like before. You—*all* of you—can learn a thing or two from him. I tell you, Mahanama, if you are not careful, he will put you five lazybones out of business."

"Lazybones? You call *us* lazybones?"

"As your friend, I tell you, this young man gives new meaning to the words sacrifice and self-control."

Needless to say, none of this rested happily on my ears. Let it be understood that I, Mahanama, am not the sort of man who is easily swayed, but whatever serenity I had felt after my morning meditation was now gone, and suddenly my mind was capricious, like a restless monkey stung by a scorpion, drunk, and possessed by a demon all at the same time.

"This *sadhu*," I asked, helplessly, "where might we find him?"

Sujata, the unmarried daughter of a householder, with kind, moonlike eyes, stepped forward. "He lives at the edge of the forest by the river where the banyan trees grow. I

---

3 **ashram:** hermitage.

4 ***Vedas*** and ***Upanishads*:** Hindu holy wisdom

5 **swami . . . *mahatma* . . . *sadhu*:** honorific titles for holy men.

have never seen *any* man so beautiful. Everyone loves him. I feel I could follow him anywhere . . . ”

Now I was in a mental fog. There was a dull pounding in my right temple as we trekked forthwith at a fast pace back into the forest. Vappa was sweeping his twig-broom so furiously—he was as angry and upset as I was—that billowing clouds of dust rose up around us, and we must have looked, for all the world, like a herd of enraged, stampeding elephants. Soon enough we tracked down the brash young man responsible for our alms bowls being empty.

To my surprise, and yet somehow not to my surprise, the villagers had not lied. We found him meditating naked, except for a garland of beads, in a diagonal shaft of leaf-filtered light from the banyan tree above him. Straightaway, I saw that his posture in meditation was perfect, his head tilted down just so, leaving only enough space that an egg could be inserted between his chin and throat. He was twenty years younger than me, no older than one of my sons, his body gaunt and defined, his face angular, framed by a bell of black hair. He looked up when we approached, introduced ourselves, and pressed him to explain how he could have the nerve to install himself in *our* forest. In a sad, heavy way he exhaled, holding me with eyes that seemed melancholy, and said:

“I seek a refuge from suffering.”

“Who,” asked Bhadiya, cocking his head to one side, “are your teachers? What credentials do you have?”

“I have studied briefly with the hermit Bhagava. Then with lāra Kālāma and Udraka Rāmaputra, who taught me mastery of the third and fourth stages of meditation. But,” he sighed, “neither intellectual knowledge nor yogic skills has yet led me to the liberation I am seeking.”

I felt humbled right down to my heels. Those two venerated teachers were among the greatest sages in all India. Compared to *them*, my own guru long ago was but a neophyte on the path.

Twilight was coming on as he spoke, the blue air darkening to purple the four corners of the sky. A whiff of twilight even tinctured the shadows as he unfurled what I surmised was a bald-faced lie, a fairy tale, a bedtime story so fantastic only a child could believe it. Until a year ago, he said, he had been a prince whose loving father, Shuddodana, had sheltered him from the painful, hard and ugly things of the world. The palace in which he was raised, with its parks, lakes and perfectly tended gardens, gave you a glimpse of what the homes of the gods must look like. He was raised to be a warrior of the Shakya tribe, had a hundred raven-haired concubines of almost catastrophic beauty, and ate food so fine and sumptuous even its rich aroma was enough to sate a man’s hunger. He said he would have continued this voluptuous life of pleasure and privilege, for he had all that this world could offer, but one day while he and his charioteer Channa were out riding, he saw a man old and decrepit. On a different day he saw a man severely stricken with illness. On the third day he saw a corpse being carried away for cremation. And when he recognized that this fate awaited *him*, he could not be consoled. All satisfaction with the fleeting pleasures of his cloistered life in the palace left him. But then, on a fourth trip, he saw a wandering holy man whose equanimity in the face of the instability and impermanence of all things told him that *this* was the life he must pursue. And so he left home, abandoning his beautiful wife Yoshodhara, and their newborn son Rahula, and found his lonely way to our forest.

Once he had breathed these words, my companions begged to become his disciples. Kodananna even went as far as to proclaim that if all the scriptures for a holy life were lost, we could reconstruct them from just this one devoted ascetic's daily life. He had seduced them with his sincerity for truth-seeking. I, Mahanama, decided to remain with my brothers, but, to be frank, I had great misgivings about this man. He came from the Kshatriya caste of royalty. Therefore he was, socially, one *varna* [or caste] above us, and I had never met a member of royalty who wasn't smug and insensitive to others. Could only *I* see his imperfections and personal failures? How could he justify leaving his wife and son? I mean, he was not yet fifty, but he had forsaken his responsibilities as a householder. True enough, his family was well taken care of during his absence, because he was a pampered, upper-caste rich boy, someone who'd never missed a meal in his life but now was slumming among the poor, who could shave his waist-long beard, his wild hair, take a bath and return to his father's palace if one day the pain and rigor of our discipline became disagreeable. I, Mahanama, have never had an easy life. To achieve even the simplest things, I had to undergo a thousand troubles, to struggle and know disappointment. I think it was then, God help me, that I began to hate *every* little thing about him: the way he walked and talked and smiled, his polished, courtly gestures, his refined habits, his honeyed tongue, his upper-caste education, none of which he could hide. The long and short of it was that I was no longer myself. Although I consented to study with him, just to see what he knew, I longed, so help me, to see him fail. To slip or make a mistake. Just *once*, that's all I was asking for.

And I *did* get my wish, though not exactly as I'd expected.

To do him justice, I must say our new teacher was dedicated, and more dangerous than anyone knew. He was determined to surpass all previous ascetics. I guess he was still a warrior of the Shakya tribe, but instead of vanquishing others all his efforts were aimed at conquering himself. Day after day he practiced burning thoughts of desire from his mind and tried to empty himself of all sensations. Night after night he prayed for a freedom that had no name, touching the eighty-six sandalwood beads on his *mala*[6] for each mantra he whispered in the cold of night, or in rough, pouring rain. Seldom did he talk to us, believing that speech was the great-grandson of truth. Nevertheless, I spied on him, because at my age I was not sure any teacher could be trusted. None could meet our every expectation. None I had known was whole or perfect.

---

6 **mala:** beads are used to count prayers or mantras. Today, they generally have 19, 21, 27, or 108 beads. Most commonly they are made of wood.

Accordingly, I critically scrutinized everything he did and did not do. And what struck me most was this: it was as if he saw his body, which he had indulged with all the pleasures known to man, as an enemy, an obstacle to his realization of the highest truth, and so it must be punished and deprived. He slept on a bed of thorns. Often he held his breath for a great long time until the pain was so severe he fainted. Week after week he practiced these fanatical austerities, reducing himself to skin bone and fixed idea. My companions and I frequently collapsed from exhaustion and fell behind. But he kept on. Perhaps he was trying to achieve great merit, or atone for leaving his family, or for being a fool who threw away a tangible kingdom he could touch and see for an intangible fantasy of perfection that no one had ever seen. Many times we thought he was suicidal, particularly on the night he made us all sleep among the dead in the charnel grounds, where the air shook with insects, just outside Uruvela. During our first years with him he would eat a single jujube fruit, sesame seeds, and take a little rice on banana leaves. But as the years wore on, he—being radical, a revolutionary—rejected even that, sustaining himself on water and one grain of rice a day. Then he ate nothing at all.

By the morning of December seventh, in our sixth year with him, he had fallen on evil days, made so weakened, so frail, so wretched he could barely walk without placing one skeletal hand on Bhadiya's shoulder and the other on mine. At age thirty-five, his eyes resembled burnt holes in a blanket. Like a dog was how he smelled. His bones creaked, and his head looked chewed up by rats, the obsidian hair that once pooled round his face falling from his scalp in brittle patches.

"Mahanama," he said. There were tears standing in his eyes. "You and the others should not have followed me. Or believed so faithfully in what I was doing. My life in the palace was wrong. This is wrong too."

The hot blast of his death breath, rancid because his teeth had begun to decay, made me twist my head to one side. "There must be . . ." he closed his eyes to help his words along, "some Way between the extremes I have experienced."

I kept silent. He sounded vague, vaporish.

And then he said, more to himself than to me, "Wisdom is caught, not taught."

Before I could answer he hobbled away, like an old, old man, to bathe, then sit by himself under a banyan tree. I believe he went that far away so we could not hear him weep. This tree, I should point out, was one the superstitious villagers believed possessed a deity. As luck would have it, the lovely Sujata, with her servant girl, came there often to pray that she would one day find a husband belonging to her caste and have a son by him. From where we stood, my brothers and I could see her approaching, stepping gingerly to avoid deer pellets and bird droppings and, if my eyes did not deceive me, she, not recognizing him in his fallen state, thought our teacher was the tree's deity. Sujata placed before him a golden bowl of milk-porridge. To my great delight, he hungrily ate it.

I felt buoyant, and thought, *Gotcha.*

Vappa's mouth hung open in disbelief. Bhadiya's mouth snapped shut. Kodananna rubbed his knuckles in his eyes. They all knew moral authority rested on moral consistency. Assajii shook his head and cried out, "This woman's beauty, the delights of food, and the sensual cravings tormenting his heart are just too much for him to resist. Soon he will be drinking, lying, stealing, gambling, killing animals to satisfy his appetite, and sleeping with other men's wives. Agh, he can teach us nothing."

Disgusted, we left, moving a short distance away from him in the forest, our intention being to travel the hundred miles to the spiritual center of Sarnath in search of a better guru. My brothers talked about him like he had a tail. And while I cackled and gloated for a time over the grand failure of our golden boy, saying, "See, I *told* you so," that night I could not sleep for thinking about him. He was alone again, his flesh wasted away, his mind most likely splintered by madness. I pitied him. I pitied all of us, for now it was clear that no man or woman would ever truly be free from selfishness, anger, hatred, greed, and the chronic hypnosis that is the human condition. Shortly after midnight, beneath a day-old moon in a dark sky, I rose while the others slept and crept back to where we had left him.

He was gone, no longer by the banyan tree. Up above, a thin, rain-threaded breeze loosed a whirlwind of dead leaves. It felt as if a storm was on its way, the sky swollen with pressure. And then, as I turned to leave, seeking shelter, I saw faintly a liminal figure seated on kusha grass at the eastern side of a bodhi tree, strengthened by the bowl of rice-milk he had taken, and apparently determined not to rise ever again if freedom still eluded him. I felt my face stretch. I wondered if I had gone without food so long that I was hallucinating, for I sensed a peculiar density in the darkness, and the numinous air around him seemed to swirl with wispy phantoms. I heard a devilish voice—perhaps his own, disguised—demanding that he stop, which he would not do. Was he totally mad and talking to himself? I could not say. But for three watches of the night he sat, wind wheeling round his head, its sound in the trees like rushing water, and once I heard him murmur, "At last I have found and defeated you, *ahumkara*, I-Maker."

At daybreak, everything in the forest was quiet, the tree bark bloated by rain, and he sat, as if he'd just come from a chrysalis, in muted, early morning light, the air full of moisture. Cautiously, I approached him, the twenty-fifth Buddha, knowing that something new and marvelous had happened in the forest that night. Instead of going where the path might lead, he had gone instead where there was no path and left a trail for all of us. I asked him:

"Are you a god now?"

Quietly, he made answer. "No."

"Well, are you an angel?"

"No."

"Then what are you?"

"Awake."[7]

---

7 **"Are you a god now?"** . . . **"Awake":** these six lines of dialogue are from the spiritual teachings of the late, great Eknath Easwaran.

That much I could see. He had discovered his middle way. It made me laugh. These rich kids had all the luck. I knew my brothers and I would again become his disciples, but this time, after six long years, we'd finally be able to eat a decent meal.

■ READING AND DISCUSSION QUESTIONS

1. What are the four stages of life in the Hindu tradition according to the narrator?
2. What stage are the five brothers seeking? How is the path of Siddhartha different?
3. What is the significance of the caste of the brothers? How do they view Siddhartha's caste?
4. What dynamic tensions are to be found in the title "Prince of the Ascetics"?
5. Why were the intellectual skills of meditation and yoga not enough for Siddhartha?
6. Mahanama describes Siddhartha as displaying sincerity for truth seeking and being a sort of warrior. What might it mean to be a warrior for truth?
7. What is meant by the phrase "Wisdom is caught, not taught"?
8. Mahanama is skeptical of Siddhartha when he first meets him and then after Siddhartha drinks the milk-porridge. What are the sources of each moment of skepticism, and how are they resolved?
9. What is meant by the notion of defeating the I-Maker? How does the middle way make this attainable?
10. Nirvana is sometimes called "enlightenment," but here it is referred to as being "awake." What is the difference between these two definitions, and how does "awakening" work in the ending of the story?

■ FICTIVE-NARRATIVE PHILOSOPHY FEEDBACK

What claims are made in this story? Write them out in a bulleted list and include whether they are made through dialogue, dramatic action, or the presentation of the scene (including descriptive detail). One page. Then choose either a short direct-discourse response (according to the rules in Chapter 2) or a short fictive-narrative presentation (according to the rules in Chapter 3).

DHAMMAPADA

Siddhartha Gautama, the Buddha

From *Dhammapada,* trans. F. Max Müller (Oxford: Oxford University Press, 1881). *Note on the translation:* English words found in brackets are inserted by the translator to make better sense of the English rendering.

The Dhammapada *is one of the best-known texts of the Theravada canon and is ascribed to Siddhartha, the Buddha. It comprises twenty-six chapters and 423 verses. Below are excerpts from thirteen chapters. Try to check off chapters that give advice on how to live well and those that might relate to the Four Noble Truths: Sarvam Duhkha—all is suffering; Trishna—desire is the cause of suffering; Nirvana—the extinction of desire liberates one from suffering; and Madhyamarga—the direction to follow is the Eightfold Path (a. right understanding, b. right thoughts, c. right speech, d. right conduct, e. right livelihood, f. right effort, g. right mindfulness, and h. right concentration).*

Chapter I: The Twin Verses

1. All that we are is the result of what we have thought: it is founded on our thoughts; it is made up of our thoughts. If a man speaks or acts with an evil thought, pain follows him, as the wheel follows the foot of the ox that draws the carriage.

2. All that we are is the result of what we have thought: it is founded on our thoughts; it is made up of our thoughts. If a man speaks or acts with a pure thought, happiness follows him, like a shadow that never leaves him.

3. "He abused me; he beat me; he defeated me; he robbed me"—in those who harbor such thoughts, hatred will never cease.

4. "He abused me; he beat me; he defeated me; he robbed me"—in those who do not harbor such thoughts hatred will cease.

5. For hatred does not cease by hatred at any time: hatred ceases by love; this is an old rule.

6. The world does not know that we must all come to an end here—but those who know it, their quarrels cease at once.

7. He who lives looking for pleasures only, his senses uncontrolled, immoderate in his food, idle, and weak, Mara [the tempter] will certainly overthrow him, as the wind throws down a weak tree.

8. He who lives without looking for pleasures, his senses well controlled, moderate in his food, faithful and

strong, him Mara will certainly not overthrow, any more than the wind throws down a rocky mountain.

19. The thoughtless man, even if he can recite a large portion [of the law] but is not a doer of it, has no share in the priesthood but is like a cowherd counting the cows of others.

20. The follower of the law, even if he can recite only a small portion [of the law] but, having forsaken passion and hatred and foolishness, possesses true knowledge and serenity of mind, he, caring for nothing in this world or that to come, has indeed a share in the priesthood.

Chapter II: On Earnestness

21. Earnestness is the path of immortality [Nirvana], thoughtlessness the path of death. Those who are in earnest do not die; those who are thoughtless are as if dead already.

22. Those who are advanced in earnestness, having understood this clearly, delight in earnestness and rejoice in the knowledge of the Ariyas [the elect].

23. These wise people, meditative, steady, always possessed of strong powers, attain to Nirvana, the highest happiness.

Chapter IV: Flowers

44. Who shall overcome this earth, and the world of Yama [the lord of the departed], and the world of the gods? Who shall find out the plainly shown path of virtue, as a clever man finds out the [right] flower?

45. The disciple will overcome the earth, and the world of Yama, and the world of the gods. The disciple will find out the plainly shown path of virtue, as a clever man finds out the [right] flower.

46. He who knows that this body is like froth and has learnt that it is as unsubstantial as a mirage will break the flower-pointed arrow of Mara and never see the king of death.

47. Death carries off a man who is gathering flowers and whose mind is distracted, as a flood carries off a sleeping village.

48. Death subdues a man who is gathering flowers and whose mind is distracted before he is satiated in his pleasures.

58, As on a heap of rubbish cast upon
59. the highway the lily will grow full of sweet perfume and delight, thus the disciple of the truly enlightened Buddha shines forth by his knowledge among those who are like rubbish, among the people that walk in darkness.

Chapter VI: The Wise Man

85. Few are there among men who arrive at the other shore [become Arhats]; the other people here run up and down the shore.

86. But those who, when the law has been well preached to them, follow

the law will pass across the dominion of death, however difficult to overcome.

87, 88.
A wise man should leave the dark state [of ordinary life] and follow the bright state [of the Bhikshu]. After going from his home to a homeless state, he should in his retirement look for enjoyment where there seemed to be no enjoyment. Leaving all pleasures behind and calling nothing his own the wise man should purge himself from all the troubles of the mind.

Chapter VII: The Venerable [Arhat]

90. There is no suffering for him who has finished his journey and abandoned grief, who has freed himself on all sides and thrown off all fetters.

91. They depart with their thoughts well collected; they are not happy in their abode; like swans who have left their lake, they leave their house and home.

92. Men who have no riches, who live on recognized food, who have perceived void and unconditioned freedom [Nirvana], their path is difficult to understand, like that of birds in the air.

93. He whose appetites are stilled, who is not absorbed in enjoyment, who has perceived void and unconditioned freedom [Nirvana], his path is difficult to understand, like that of birds in the air.

94. The gods even envy him whose senses, like horses well broken in by the driver, have been subdued, who is free from pride and free from appetites.

95. Such a one who does his duty is tolerant like the earth, like Indra's bolt[8]; he is like a lake without mud; no new births are in store for him.

Chapter X: Punishment

129. All men tremble at punishment; all men fear death; remember that you are like unto them and do not kill or cause slaughter.

130. All men tremble at punishment; all men love life; remember that thou art like unto them and do not kill or cause slaughter.

131. He who seeking his own happiness punishes or kills beings who also long for happiness will not find happiness after death.

132. He who seeking his own happiness does not punish or kill beings who also long for happiness will find happiness after death.

133. Do not speak harshly to anybody; those who are spoken to will answer thee in the same way. Angry speech is painful; blows for blows will touch thee.

134. If, like a shattered metal plate [gong], thou utter not, then thou hast reached Nirvana; contention is not known to thee.

---

8 **Indra's bolt:** the thunderbolt of Indra, king of the gods.

Chapter XI: Old Age

146. How is there laughter, how is there joy, as this world is always burning? Why do you not seek a light, ye who are surrounded by darkness?

147. Look at this dressed-up lump, covered with wounds, joined together, sickly, full of many thoughts, which has no strength, no hold!

148. This body is wasted, full of sickness, and frail; this heap of corruption breaks to pieces; life indeed ends in death.

149. Those white bones, like gourds thrown away in the autumn, what pleasure is there in looking at them?

150. After a stronghold has been made of the bones, it is covered with flesh and blood, and there dwell in it old age and death, pride and deceit.

151. The brilliant chariots of kings are destroyed, the body also approaches destruction, but the virtue of good people never approaches destruction—thus do the good say to the good.

152. A man who has learnt little grows old like an ox; his flesh grows, but his knowledge does not grow.

153, Looking for the maker of this tab-
154. ernacle, I shall have to run through a course of many births, so long as I do not find [him], and painful is birth again and again. But now, maker of the tabernacle, thou hast been seen; thou shall not make up this tabernacle again. All thy rafters are broken, thy ridge pole is sundered; the mind, approaching the Eternal [Visankhara, Nirvana], has attained to the extinction of all desires.

155. Men who have not observed proper discipline and have not gained treasure in their youth perish like old herons in a lake without fish.

156. Men who have not observed proper discipline and have not gained treasure in their youth lie, like broken bows, sighing after the past.

Chapter XII: Self

157. If a man hold himself dear, let him watch himself carefully; during one at least out of the three watches, a wise man should be watchful.

158. Let each man direct himself first to what is proper; then let him teach others; thus a wise man will not suffer.

159. If a man makes himself as he teaches others to be, then, being himself well subdued, he may subdue [others]; one's own self is indeed difficult to subdue.

160. Self is the lord of self; who else could be the lord? With self well subdued, a man finds a lord such as few can find.

Chapter XIII: The World

167. Do not follow the evil law! Do not live on in thoughtlessness! Do not follow false doctrine! Be not a friend of the world.

168. Rouse thyself! Do not be idle! Follow the law of virtue! The virtuous rest in bliss in this world and in the next.

169. Follow the law of virtue; do not follow that of sin. The virtuous rest in bliss in this world and in the next.

170. Look upon the world as a bubble; look upon it as a mirage: the king of death does not see him who thus looks down upon the world.

171. Come, look at this glittering world, like unto a royal chariot; the foolish are immersed in it, but the wise do not touch it.

Chapter XIV: The Buddha [The Awakened]

179. He whose conquest is not conquered again, into whose conquest no one in this world enters, by what track can you lead him, the Awakened, the Omniscient, the trackless?

180. He whom no desire with its snares and poisons can lead astray, by what track can you lead him, the Awakened, the Omniscient, the trackless?

181. Even the gods envy those who are awakened and not forgetful, who are given to meditation, who are wise, and who delight in the repose of retirement [from the world].

182. Difficult [to obtain] is the conception of men; difficult is the life of mortals; difficult is the hearing of the True Law; difficult is the birth of the Awakened [the attainment of Buddhahood].

183. Not to commit any sin, to do good, and to purify one's mind,

that is the teaching of [all] the Awakened.

184. The Awakened call patience the highest penance, long suffering the highest Nirvana; for he is not an anchorite[9] [*pravragita*] who strikes others; he is not an ascetic [*sramana*] who insults others.

185. Not to blame, not to strike, to live restrained under the law, to be moderate in eating, to sleep and sit alone, and to dwell on the highest thoughts—this is the teaching of the Awakened.

186. There is no satisfying lusts, even by a shower of gold pieces; he who knows that lusts have a short taste and cause pain, he is wise.

187. Even in heavenly pleasures he finds no satisfaction; the disciple who is fully awakened delights only in the destruction of all desires.

188. Men, driven by fear, go to many a refuge, to mountains and forests, to groves and sacred trees.

189. But that is not a safe refuge; that is not the best refuge; a man is not delivered from all pains after having gone to that refuge.

190. He who takes refuge with Buddha, the Law [Dharma], and the Church [Sangha]: he who, with clear understanding, sees the four holy truths—

191. Namely pain, the origin of pain, the destruction of pain, and the eightfold holy way that leads to the quieting of pain—

192. That is the safe refuge; that is the best refuge; having gone to that

---

9 **anchorite:** religious hermit.

refuge, a man is delivered from all pain.

193. A supernatural person [a Buddha] is not easily found; he is not born everywhere. Wherever such a sage is born, that race prospers.

Chapter XX: The Way

273. The best of ways is the eightfold; the best of truths, the four words; the best of virtues, passionlessness; the best of men, he who has eyes to see.

274. This is the way; there is no other that leads to the purifying of intelligence. Go on this way! Everything else is the deceit of Mara [the tempter].

275. If you go on this way, you will make an end of pain! The way was preached by me, when I had understood the removal of the thorns [in the flesh].

276. You yourself must make an effort. The Tathagatas [Buddhas] are only preachers. The thoughtful who enter the way are freed from the bondage of Mara.

277. "All created things perish"; he who knows and sees this becomes passive in pain; this is the way to purity.

278. "All created things are grief and pain"; he who knows and sees this becomes passive in pain; this is the way that leads to purity.

279. "All forms are unreal"; he who knows and sees this becomes passive in pain; this is the way that leads to purity.

Chapter XXIV: Thirst

334. The thirst of a thoughtless man grows like a creeper; he runs from life to life, like a monkey seeking fruit in the forest.

348. Give up what is before, give up what is behind, give up what is in the middle, when thou goest to the other shore of existence; if thy mind is altogether free, thou wilt not again enter into birth and decay.

351. He who has reached the consummation, who does not tremble, who is without thirst and without sin, he has broken all the thorns of life: this will be his last body.

352. He who is without thirst and without affection, who understands the words and their interpretation, who knows the order of letters [those that are before and that are after], he has received his last body; he is called the great sage, the great man.

353. "I have conquered all; I know all; in all conditions of life I am free from taint; I have left all, and through the destruction of thirst I am free; having learnt myself, whom shall I teach?"

369. O Bhikshu, empty this boat! If emptied, it will go quickly; having cut off passion and hatred, thou wilt go to Nirvana.

370. Cut off the five [senses]; leave the five; rise above the five. A Bhikshu, who has escaped from the five fetters, he is called Oghatinna, "saved from the flood."

371. Meditate, O Bhikshu, and be not heedless! Do not direct thy thought to what gives pleasure, that thou mayest not for thy heedlessness have to swallow the iron ball [in hell] and that thou mayest not cry out when burning, "This is pain."

Chapter XXVI:
The Brahmana [Arhat][10]

383. Stop the stream valiantly; drive away the desires, O Brahmana! When you have understood the destruction of all that was made, you will understand that which was not made.

384. If the Brahmana has reached the other shore in both laws [in restraint and contemplation], all bonds vanish from him who has obtained knowledge.

385. He for whom there is neither this nor that shore, nor both, him, the fearless and unshackled, I call indeed a Brahmana.

414. Him I call indeed a Brahmana who has traversed this miry road, the impassable world and its vanity, who has gone through and reached the other shore, is thoughtful, guileless, free from doubts, free from attachment and content.

415. Him I call indeed a Brahmana who in this world, leaving all desires, travels about without a home and in whom all concupiscence[11] is extinct.

416. Him I call indeed a Brahmana who, leaving all longings, travels about without a home and in whom all covetousness is extinct.

420. Him I call indeed a Brahmana whose path the gods do not know, nor spirits [*Gandharvas*], nor men, whose passions are extinct, and who is an Arhat ["venerable"].

421. Him I call indeed a Brahmana who calls nothing his own, whether it be before, behind, or between, who is poor and free from the love of the world.

422. Him I call indeed a Brahmana, the manly, the noble, the hero, the great sage, the conqueror, the impassible, the accomplished, the awakened.

423. Him I call indeed a Brahmana who knows his former abodes, who sees heaven and hell, has reached the end of births, is perfect in knowledge, a sage, and whose perfections are all perfect.

---

10 **Brahmana (Arhat):** spiritual practitioners who have achieved the state of nirvana, or freedom from suffering.

11 **concupiscence:** refers in this context to sexual desire.

■ **READING AND DISCUSSION QUESTIONS**

1. What sort of life does the *Dhammapada* promote?
2. Which chapter(s) strike you as promoting a different personal worldview than you now possess? What about those chapters is most significant (cite specific verses)? How does the discourse work?
3. Which chapter(s) strike you as reaffirming your personal worldview? What about those chapters is most significant (cite specific verses)? How does the discourse work?
4. Which chapter(s) present the clearest case of indirect discourse (fictive-narrative philosophy)? What claim is being made?
5. Which chapter(s) present the clearest case of direct logical argument? What claim is being made?

■ **CLASS EXERCISES**

A. *Direct logical discourse:* Using the tools found in Chapter 2, outline one of the arguments from one chapter of the *Dhammapada* about an insight into how to live one's life or what is real. Using your answer to reading and discussion question 5, recreate the argument. Then, based on your assessment of one key premise of the argument you have reconstructed, write a one-page argument about why you agree or disagree with the argument's conclusion.

B. *Fictive-narrative philosophy:* Using the tools found in Chapter 3, begin with a claim that relates to reading and discussion question 4. Then, create a modern-day story about people or situations familiar to you that makes the logical claim you have identified. Three pages.

CHAPTER SEVEN

Aquinas

*T*homas Aquinas (1225–1274) was a philosopher and theologian. He effectively used the new translations of Aristotle into Latin to create a very naturalistic philosophical system that owes much to Aristotle. Aquinas created commentaries on Aristotle (interpreting him directly) and incorporated many ethical, logical, and metaphysical distinctions in his master work, Summa Theologica. In that work (a small selection of which is provided below), he displayed an ability to combine philosophy and theology so as to initiate a tradition that grounded philosophical claims in (at the very least) rationally plausible arguments. The Summa Theologica *and his other great work, the* Summa contra gentiles, *changed the face of medieval philosophy and the rationally based theology of Catholicism.*

THE MURDER OF THOMAS AQUINAS[*]

Michael Boylan

This story is a fanciful reconstruction of Aquinas's death based on known facts and a novel interpretation of them. Aquinas was born at Roccasecca in a hilltop castle. The great Benedictine abbey of Monte Cassino, where Aquinas began his studies, was within sight. Later, Aquinas was transferred to the University of Naples, where he learned about the Dominicans, a recently founded mendicant order. Aquinas became a Dominican over the objections of his family. He eventually went north to study with Albert the Great in Cologne, then became a master and filled one of the Dominican chairs at the University of Paris for three years. Then trouble began about whether he was an Averroist or an unorthodox Aristotelian (both heretical positions)—these were serious charges that, if proved, might result in his excommunication (expulsion from the Roman Catholic Church). For the next ten years, Aquinas had to defend his position against his enemies. In 1274, on his way to the Council of Lyon, he fell ill and died on March 7 in the Cistercian abbey at Fossanova, twenty kilometers from his birthplace. He was on his way to a meeting that would discuss whether there would be another crusade to the Holy Land. Certain vested interest groups advocated another crusade, particularly the Knights Templar. In the story, Aquinas's aunt, Countess Ceccano, is investigating the circumstances of her nephew's death.

There was a chill in the early morning March air. The ides were approaching. The light was dim. Two men in plain Cistercian robes were standing with the mayor in front of a form clad in a simple Dominican habit. The brothers were both slight in stature: one short and the other of medium height. Their robes seemed an almost penitential burden for their meager frames. The mayor, in contrast, was rather rotund and brightly dressed. He sported a thick black moustache. His clothes fit tightly around his tummy and ample posterior.

They stood in silence. The brothers seemed content with stillness, while the mayor bounced around on the balls of his feet. The rough-hewn gray-brown stones that formed the walls of the Cistercian abbey at Fossanova were dank with wet and mold.

---

[*] *This story is a work of fiction. It is based on various real occurrences, but it should not be read as a factual history.*

The short clerics began chain coughing when they were interrupted by a convoy of men dressed as servants as a fine woman made her way forward.

The mayor became very agitated. He gathered himself and said, "My Countess Ceccano, what a great honor." The brothers murmured their assent without making eye contact with the middle-aged dowager.

The countess, dressed in a lavish, full-figured black dress that complimented her appearance, stepped forward to look at the form of her nephew. Her first response was to place her hand upon her headscarf, cross herself, and then make a fist in the air that she brought to her breast.

The mayor stopped bouncing and began to tremble.

The countess turned her head toward the men about her and asked, "What do you plan to do about this?"

The mayor looked at the monks. The monks looked at the mayor. Their eyes froze and then shot to the floor. Then, suddenly, they turned up again to the countess. The smaller monk broke the silence. "There will be a memorial mass, of course."

The countess's eyes rolled up to the heavens and then back to these men in front of her. "What are you talking about, you fools! Of course there'll be a memorial mass. You'd give a memorial mass for a gardener who died tending the grounds. Do you know who is lying here? This man's a saint of God!" The blood vessels in the countess's forehead rose to prominence.

"Of course we have heard of your nephew. They say he has lectured and written many scholarly things. His comments on Peter of Lombard are well regarded."

"Do you know any of the positions of my nephew?"

The two monks fidgeted. The smaller friar began to bite his fingernails, but it was the mayor who bounced forward. "I talked to a man named Bonaventure once who said he knew your nephew. The man was in awe of Thomas."

The countess started to pace back and forth. Then she circled the slab that held her nephew. When she stopped she put her hands defiantly to her waist. "When I asked you what you were going to do, I meant, what are you going to do about the death of my nephew. He was a prominent man on the way to a conference that will change history. He was murdered."

There was an audible gasp. The short monk's legs began to buckle. The medium-sized man couldn't catch his brother so that the little man fell to the floor, hitting his head on the slab that held Aquinas. There was an immediate deluge of blood. The mayor ran out the door.

After much commotion, it was the servants who saved the short monk's life. The countess looked knowingly at the little man and exited the scene.

"When you say that your nephew was murdered, what do you base this upon?" The questioner was an emissary of the bishop. In most conversations, an emissary of the bishop would instill fear and trembling. But Countess Francesca Ceccano made and broke bishops. She had little regard for their emissaries except as they served her purposes.

"Well, what do we normally base such an accusation upon?" The countess was a tall, full-figured lady who still retained a vestige of her youthful beauty. She was nobody's fool, and now the lines on her face showed determination.

"I would not know." This is the first time he'd ever interviewed royalty.

"What is your name?" demanded the countess as she squinted her eyes at the skinny knave before her.

"Luigi, my countess." He tried to pull at his hair, but his head was shaved.

"Haven't been long in orders?"

"No, my countess." Luigi put down his pen as it was dripping on his robe.

"Well, look here Luigi. There is a saying that the only way to get things done is to speak to a decision maker. If you want to take my statement in writing, please tell Bishop Benedict to make an appointment with me personally."

Luigi struggled to get his effects together but kicked over his writing box. The countess stood up and retired.

"So, what's all this about murder?" asked the count as he and his wife sat on their castle balcony, which had a grand view of the countryside. A wind blew up in the mountains so that the white hair on the side of the count's head rose up to magnify his presence. Like Thomas's brothers, he had some experience with Emperor Frederick's military at the highest levels (including the Teutonic Knights). He knew how things worked in the Holy Roman Empire: the politics and the intrigues. Since the balance of power was in the south of Italy and Sicily, the count was geographically situated to intercept messengers and the like.

A servant brought them wine, bread, and olive oil. The count dismissed the tiny vassal with a shake of his right hand while grabbing some bread to dip with his left.

"You know I'm as well-bred as you are," stated the countess. "In fact, there are some things people will tell a woman that they will not tell a man."

The count laughed and dropped his piece of bread, staining his clothes with drops of olive oil.

"You laugh?" queried the countess.

"Yes, I laugh. Your nephew, the little scholar—"

"Thomas. His name is—or *was*—Thomas. He was also well born."

"But he didn't follow his family's wishes for his vocation."

"That's not the point now."

"What is the point?"

"He was murdered."

"Why?"

"Ah, that's what I want to discuss with you before the bishop arrives."

"The bishop's coming *here*? Why? What have you done, Francesca?" The count now took to downing a glass of wine and then spitting on his hands and grooming his flyaway hair.

"Don't worry. He won't attack us. Unless I'm wrong, his enemies aren't ours—in this case." The countess allowed herself a smile of accomplishment. It was as if the wind were her ally during the exchange. Her coiffure hair was in place, and she knew where the conversation was going.

"What are you talking about? You don't really believe this murder stuff, do you?" The count uttered these words as he looked away to his lands. He saw a rustic old man leading a flock of sheep across his pastures. He smiled and then turned back to his wife.

"Well, darling, I'm sure you couldn't imagine a cleric without position of bishop or above being worth thinking about. But let me tell you this. My nephew, Thomas, was an unpredictable man. You couldn't frame him. You couldn't depend upon his knuckling under to authority. I mean, look at his life.

"He was taken with Dominic—I mean, *really*. This was a rather intellectual road to take. The traditional paths of sinecure would have led him to be a Benedictine (like his brother). The Benedictines had an abbey very close in Monte Cassino. Life would have been easy, but Thomas rejected it. Why? Beats me. I sure didn't follow *his* way. I married *you*!"

The old Count smiled and drank another glass of wine. His gaze went again to the flock of sheep slowly making their way across the field near the stream that marked the end of his lands.

"The family tried to get him to follow reason even to the point of kidnapping him for a couple of years. The things they did to turn that boy's head are not fit for general conversation."

"A woman?"

The countess smiled. "And not just any woman."

The count turned and looked again over the plains. It was a beautiful countryside. The land was bounteous such that the count made out handsomely on the rents. It was so good that they gave the Church a double portion without feeling any pain. It also bought some influence.

"Well, finally the family relented, and he became a Dominican and studied with the top philosopher in the world, Albert the Great, who called him the 'dumb ox' because Thomas was modest and didn't try to impress people. But Albert later called him his brightest student."

"That guy was on the other side of the Rhine," said the count as he poured another glass. It was early spring, so the birds were making quite a noise. The air was thickening slightly with the smells of new life. It was still almost a month to Easter.

"Yes, but soon they got him to Paris. What a place that was in the early fifties. They really cared about their theology."

"But there was some unpleasantness then, eh?"

"You know there was: a battle between the city and the university. It got bloody, but the university prevailed."

"Too bad," said the count. "You know I don't really trust those university priests. They can't be controlled."

This time it was the countess's turn to pour herself a glass and dip some bread into the precious oil. "Praise to the Lord for those who will not be controlled," said Francesca.

The count almost dropped his glass. These were words he didn't like to hear.

"As far as I'm concerned, there are several groups that would have liked to see my Thomas dead. Let me go over these with you so that we can plan a response."

"I don't promise a response," said the count.

"Well, if you don't, I know other people. I still have family."

"Go on. Who are the suspects?"

"First, you must remember that in Paris Thomas was against the double truth of the Averroists." Francesca put down her glass and pointed in the air with her index finger.

"Stop right there. Who are the Averroists? Sounds pagan to me."

"Averroes was an Islamic commentator on Greek philosophy. He showed the way that it might become the theology for Islam."

"What do I care about paganism?"

"Look, you married an educated wife—not because it thrilled you but because my family would give you a large dowry. Now, remember, the dowry purse is tied by strings that can be pulled shut if you don't respect me."

"My butterfly, I have always respected you. I just don't go in too much for all this foolishness."

"You mean philosophy. Well, you and most men can call it foolish, but you'll never meet a woman at any station of life who is not a philosopher. It's the only way we can get by."

"Oh, come on. We have a castle and servants—"

"You really don't get it. But now is not the time. Listen to me. The simple fact is that the Averroists put forth a 'double truth' doctrine in that there are truths of philosophy that are false in theology."

"So what?"

"Well, don't you see? It creates all sorts of problems. Since living in the world is under philosophy, while salvation is under theology, a person could possibly pursue contradictory paths."

"So what?" The count finished the bottle of wine and rang the bell for another to be brought forward.

"Are you playing with me? If most people live under natural philosophy and that is divorced from theology, then there is no real place for the Church in our lives."

"So what?"

Francesca was taken aback. "That is rather cynical even for you."

The count took that as a compliment.

"Say, I'm getting tired. I think I'll take a nap," said the count, getting up. His head turned instinctively toward the herd of sheep. They were halfway across the stream bordering his property and heading for the other side. He dropped his wine glass onto the stone floor. "That man's stealing my sheep! I trust these peasants, and look how they re-pay me."

This time it was the countess's turn for ennui. "What are a few sheep?"

"No, that guy's stealing my sheep. Enrico, come here! Saddle up my horse immediately!"

When the bishop came to call, he brought a retinue, including three scribes who would simultaneously take dictation so that mistakes might be ferreted out. This practice was only employed on important occasions. They met in the chapel of the castle.

Bishop Benedict, a very young man, was handsome and vigorous. Francesca thought that he looked a bit like an attack dog—only human.

"You know that you have leveled serious charges," began the bishop. He was dressed casually, wearing only his copse and skull headpiece.[1]

The countess nodded. She was one of three people who had put this man in his post, and he knew it.

"From where I sit, there are really only three possible suspects," began the countess. She was also dressed simply in a slim, black dress. She wore no jewelry, and her hair was tied back by her dark brown scarf. As she began to speak, she looked sharply to the right eye of the bishop. She lifted up the palm of her right hand as she continued. "The first suspect comes from Thomas's enemies in the academy. You know that he was a very original thinker. He was able to acquire a mandate for William of Moerbeke to translate the works of Aristotle into Latin. This was a big deal. The Spanish versions of Aristotle only fueled the Averroists and their associated heresies. Most of Aristotle only resided in the hands of the Moslems. And we well know that we haven't had very good relations with them recently."

The bishop sat up straight and put his knees together. His scribes looked to his eminence to see whether they should be copying this. The bishop nodded.

"Getting copies of legitimate manuscripts was a miracle in itself (at least one of three). There were many, like the Franciscans, who didn't think that Greek philosophy should be studied. They thought that it would lead to the heresy of Averroism."

The bishop cleared his throat.

"So, in one fell swoop, my nephew embraced Greek philosophy, argued that reason and faith should be one and not separate, and put forth a unique reading of all the common objections to claims of dogma and doctrine. It was beautiful. He did the impossible—a second miracle."

The bishop faked a smile. It was then that he realized how dim the light was in the castle chapel. The stone walls were cut smooth and mortared clean. He looked up: the ceiling was timbered with dark beams, strong and unbent, but at the edges spiders seemed to be congregating. Quickly the bishop fixed his eyes back on the countess, who was achieving full form.

---

1 **copse and skull headpiece:** the headgear worn by a bishop of the Roman Catholic Church.

"But there were those who wanted to excommunicate Thomas for his writings. They thought he was too bold, too much intrigued with natural philosophy." Francesca sat back and gestured toward the ceiling.

"Well, I've heard as much," replied Benedict.

"You only hear things from others. I know. I helped put you where you are today, and don't you forget it."

The bishop frowned. He had no good word to say. Above the spiders calculated, and a scout was sent forth.

Then, Francesca put both of her hands to her mouth, kissed them, and spread them out. At that moment she became aware of a spider that was lowering itself from the ceiling in the general direction of the bishop. She didn't comment. "Look, unlike my husband, the count, I don't distrust the academics—I adore them. Would that I had been born a man!"

The bishop signaled to the scribes not to include those words.

"At any rate, I don't think anyone in Paris is involved with my nephew's murder—though he upset a lot of people there."

"Including the pope," put Benedict.

"Not really. I don't think that the pope ever really wanted to excommunicate Thomas. That's a bunch of foolishness built up by his enemies." The spider was smoothly lowering itself. "Then there are those who opposed his charter to form a new stadium generale in Naples."

"Of course. I know all about that. Quite irregular, if you ask me."

"Well, I didn't know about it until very recently (when I began my investigation). But just like those intemperate academic dunderheads in Paris, there arose in Naples a series of false complaints. Well, I say that there is such a thing as venting spleen, and there is another thing that is murder. They are two different species, as my Thomas used to say."

"So, what's the end to all of this?" Benedict was getting a bit peeved. He began fidgeting with the fastening of his copse.

"The coup de grâce concerns his last activity of life. This had nothing to do with his ability to unite faith and reason, or to solve the most common objections to the Sentences, or to make the faith more concrete and consonant with the latest discoveries in science—none of this, which was his life work, was as important as his last mission of life as a key delegate to the Council of Lyon."

"Ah, yes, the Council of Lyon." The bishop smiled.

"You know what is on the agenda?"

"Well, I wasn't invited."

"I should say not. But let me tell you. You know we have a Teutonic Knight in our family." All of a sudden the spider stopped its descent. It was time to get away from here. This bit of news visibly shook the bishop. He gestured to the scribes to stop writing all together.

"When you say the Teutonic Knights, you mean some time ago, don't you, when they were engaged in the Crusades?"

"When I say the Teutonic Knights, I mean as recently as a week ago when I received this message." The lady Francesca drew out a letter from her bosom. She lifted it high and then replaced it.

The bishop almost got out of his chair to retrieve the note but then sat back again.

"On May first, one month after Easter Sunday, and before Ascension, the leaders of the Church will discuss whether we will undertake a massive crusade," pronounced Francesca formally.

"Of course, there are other issues on the agenda," began Benedict.

"Like unifying the Church. Yes, you are right. It is on the agenda. But what about this possible foray might get my nephew killed? It is that he was a man of peace."

"And the Teutonic Knights didn't like this?"

"No. The Teutonic Knights and Knights Hospitaller are fine with this. The iron in the fire is the Knights Templar."

With the utterance of these words, the bishop visibly blanched. He slumped in his chair, and the spider disappeared.

"You know that my nephew defied Jacques de Molay?"

"I know nothing of these matters," muttered Bishop Benedict. He began biting his nails and rubbing his bishop's ring on his nose.

"Well, I do. And I need accountability, or else I'm going above your head. I can do it, and so can my husband. I have chosen to talk to you because I put you where you are, and I believe you to be an honest man."

The Bishop cringed. He didn't know what to say.

Francesca reached out her hand and touched the bishop's hand. The gesture calmed him. He looked in his benefactor's eyes with credence. "Tell me what you want me to do."

The countess retained her posture, leaning toward the bishop and reaching out to put her hand atop his ring. "Let me tell you. After the fall of Jerusalem twenty-five years ago, the Knights Templar split with the other two orders of holy knights. They have used their massive income and their bases in Ruad and Acre in the Holy Land to create a presence by which they can get money from both sides. The worst possible situation for them is world peace. This is really what the Khwarezmi[2] also despise. When there is continual war, a sense of urgency arises so that everyday peasants who strive to live off the land owned by others can be surtaxed to support a war far away that they have been told is critical to their security."

"You are a cynic, aren't you?"

"I was taught by my nephew, a saint of God, through long letters containing copies of Moerbeke's translations of Aristotle and my nephew's brilliant way of showing how these truths can be applied to our modern era."

"You are an unusual woman."

---

2 **Khwarezmi:** Sunni Moslems who survived the demise of their empire (from modern Turkey to Iran) in 1220 but still maintained influence in the region.

Francesca laughed. "That is not the issue. What is pertinent is that my nephew had proven his moral integrity. First, he was captured by his family to dissuade him from joining the order of Dominic. Second, they tried to seduce him to get something on him. Third, he was improperly situated in the unpleasantness in Paris. Fourth, his designs for the future were the subject of controversy."

"What of his advocacy of Greek philosophy and his denial of double truth?"

"Ah, that would be enough to have him killed, except that scholars don't operate that way. They are very mean of speech, but they don't really act on their words. Actually, they don't really act on anything—but that's another matter."

"So, you say it's Jacques de Molay and the Templars who had your nephew murdered?"

"Yes. The Council of Lyons is considering giving them a preeminent role in a new crusade campaign."

"But another crusade at this time would be ridiculous!"

"Of course, but special interests want to keep the war thing going. But Thomas was against all of this. Did you read his writings on the proper moral conditions for war? Or his distinction between the 'obligation for self-defense' and the 'permission for self-defense'?"

The Bishop looked down. "I am not really a scholar, Countess."

"I know that, but I also know that you are a man of character. Otherwise I wouldn't have put you into your job."

Again the bishop grimaced. At the top of the rafters various other spiders dropped down slightly.

"Well, I will appeal to your moral character. You must depend upon me for the facts of the case and the theoretical grounding. When we are talking about the murder of a saint of God, no one should lie."

The bishop opened his mouth but did not speak. The spiders dropped another foot.

"Here's what I want you to do. We must act before the Council of Lyons. We must debunk the theory that Thomas hit his head on a tree branch while riding to Lyons. We must also debunk the theory that Thomas simply collapsed on the road while walking. I know for a fact that he wasn't walking. Then, we must concentrate upon Jacques de Molay's minion, Dietrich, a renegade from the Teutonic Knights. I have several witnesses who will testify that he was in this region just before Thomas was due to leave."

"So what?"

"Well, if Thomas was a man of peace who wanted the Crusades shut down and peaceful negotiations undertaken with the Moslems (as he instigated once before through his project with Moerbeke), then who would have been the most dangerous man at the forthcoming conference?"

"Thomas?"

"Now you see my meaning. Thomas could have stopped the Crusades movement and transitioned into a peaceful interaction with the Moslems as he had before. Everyone might share Jerusalem. We don't need to kill for it. The killing industry gets rich while propagating lies to get everyone worried. When they see an obstacle, they react with force. The Templars murdered Thomas Aquinas because they knew he would turn the Council of Lyon into a conference for peace. Peace is a dangerous idea. The wealthy and entrenched fear it. Jacques de Molay saw this clearly and ordered the murder of my nephew."

Bishop Benedict didn't have anything good to say.

"Will you use your powers to investigate these claims? Only you can do it."

"And only a woman would ask that I do it."

"Commit now. I need to know."

The bishop got up and walked about the room. He came back and ate the olives and grapes on the table. He didn't drink the wine. He went to the window and looked over the landscape. There were fewer sheep than usual according to his understanding of the diocese.

Then he turned and said, "Yes, I will investigate this. Your claims are plausible, and in the spirit of your nephew, plausibility is the threshold to accepting truth."

Francesca leaped up and hugged the bishop. He looked her in the eyes and then left without saying anything further.

On April 2, 1274, one day after Easter, the young bishop was found poisoned in the rectory. On May 11, 1274, the Council of Lyon created special secret protocols that covertly extended the Crusades indefinitely under the direction of the Templars. Because the mission was covert, to this day there are no existing records of this event, except within the secret vaults of the Knights Templar.

■ READING AND DISCUSSION QUESTIONS

1. Look up on the Internet the Dominican Order of the Roman Catholic Church (and their founder Dominic) and the Benedictines (and their founder Benedict). Based on your research, why do you think Aquinas chose to be a Dominican?
2. Look on the Internet for information concerning the hierarchy of the Roman Catholic Church. Place the following in an organizational chart: nun, monk, parish priest, bishop, archbishop, cardinal, pope.
3. How did the culture of the times constrain Countess Ceccano, Aquinas's aunt, in her fictive investigation?
4. Look up on the Internet "Peter of Lombard." Why was he important in medieval European philosophy?
5. Look up on the Internet "the Crusades." What were they? When did they occur? How many of them were there? Who won and who lost?
6. Look up on the Internet "the Knights Templar," "the Teutonic Knights," and "the Knights Hospitaller." What did they have to do with the Crusades? What rumors have been associated with each over the years?
7. Look up on the Internet "Averroes." Who was he? What was his doctrine of double truth? Why was Aquinas implicated in this? What was the result?

8. What was the Council of Lyons?
9. Hypothetically, who would have gained by the murder of Thomas Aquinas?

■ FICTIVE-NARRATIVE PHILOSOPHY FEEDBACK

What claims are made in this story? Write them out in a bulleted list and include whether they are made through dialogue, dramatic action, or the presentation of the scene (including descriptive detail). One page. Then choose either a short direct-discourse response (according to the rules in Chapter 2) or a short fictive-narrative presentation (according to the rules in Chapter 3).

SUMMA THEOLOGICA: "ON THE NATURAL LAW"

Thomas Aquinas

Adapted and translated by Michael Boylan from *Summa Theologica* (Rome: Typographia Forzani, 1894), I–II, q93, a2; q93, a3; q94, a4. *Note on the translation:* English words found in brackets are inserted by the translator to make better sense of the English rendering.

One of the most widely influential parts of the Summa Theologica *is Aquinas's writing on natural law, which has been used to justify universal standards of conduct that apply to all cultures and times. Some of the judges at the Nüremberg trials (of Nazi war criminals following World War II) said later that they had been influenced by the natural law tradition pioneered by Thomas Aquinas.*

This rendition of the Summa eliminates the questions-and-answers section that is often very esoteric and requires more facility in medieval philosophy. Instead, the "key distinctions" have been put together to render the essence of Aquinas's position: (a) the natural law is the same for all people, and (b) the natural law cannot be changed.

Augustine[3] says that knowledge of eternal law is universally imprinted by nature. My view is this: we can know substance in two ways: (a) through itself (per se), and (b) through its effects (which are attributed to that entity); for example, one may not see the sun in its substance [or he'd go blind], but he might know it by its heat. Therefore, it is reasonable to say that no one can have per se knowledge of the eternal law itself—except God and the elect of God (who apprehend God's essence). But all other humans know analogically as a reflection varying by the more and less. This is because all knowledge of truth is a reflection of, and a participation in, eternal law. The eternal law is characterized by eternal truth just as Augustine says.

All humans know something about truth—at least concerning the common principles of the natural law. In other aspects of truth they partake more or less [according to their aptitude and application]. In this way they know the eternal law to a greater or lesser extent.

---

3 **Augustine:** Saint Augustine of Hippo (354–430 CE).

Augustine says that the temporal law is only just and lawful inasmuch as it reflects the eternal law. My view is this: the eternal law prescribes a plan directing purposive action. Now, in every [natural event] there are primary movers and secondary movers. The latter derive their efficacy from the former. This is the same in government: the king directs his [barons] who in turn direct their [vassals]. In this way a state's purposive action flows from the king through his lesser administrators. This is also true in art [within the art guild]. The master of the guild directs other craftsmen, from the journeymen to the apprentices (who work with their hands).

Because the ultimate civil plan is in the control of the chief governor, all lesser administrators must follow the chief governor [so long as] these plans are in tune with the eternal law. It should be noted that the activities of the bureaucracy may concern statutes that are in addition to the eternal law (the standard of right reason). Therefore, in as much as any [proper] statute [no matter how lowly] participates in right reason, it can be said to be [remotely] derived from the eternal law. This is what Augustine meant when he said that in the temporal law justice derives from participation in the eternal law.

Isidore[4] asserts that the natural law is common to all nations. My view is this: man is inclined to the natural law. This includes all objects to which man is rationally drawn and guides his action in the world. [Aristotle] in the *Physics* says that there are two sorts of predication: (a) generic, and (b) specific. This corresponds to the distinction between theoretical and practical reason. Theoretical reason deals with that which cannot be otherwise [that is, necessary deductive conclusions] about universals. Practical reason deals with the realm of the contingent: human action. This means that when we make a transition from the universal principles common to many species, the application to the particular often encounters less exactness. Thus, according to theoretical reason, truth is common to all in the same way—including principles and their applications (though this truth via its conclusions is not universally known—only the principles themselves are known by all).

In matters of human action, truth is disputed in particular actual applications (though the common principles may be accepted and general notions of application are accepted). Thus, it is evident that regarding common accepted principles (either theoretical or practical), the normative force is the same for everyone and known by all. But the dictums of theoretical reason are not known by all (though they are true for all). For example, it is true for all that the sum of the interior angles of a triangle is equal to that of two right angles (180°), but it is not known by all.

In practical reason, conclusions [of moral arguments] are neither necessarily true nor known by all. For example, generally it is the case that goods entrusted to someone's care should be returned to their owner. In the majority of cases this maxim holds. However, it may be the case that to do so would be injurious—such as returning arms to someone so that he might fight against his country. This possibility is not salvaged if one legalistically creates a

4 **Isidore:** Saint Isidore of Seville (c. 560–636).

fine-tuned contract that tries to specify all possible situations. (In fact the more practical parameters are added, the greater the chance of confusion and failure.)

Therefore, we must conclude that the natural law is the primary accepted common principle. It is the same for all concerning knowledge and application. But regarding particular cases, it is only binding in the majority of cases (as we have just argued). This is because there are excep-

tions—[such as the case with the arms]. There may also be instances [in which the normal deliberative processes are perverted due] to the condition of ignorance, such as when the agent is overcome by passion or the ignorance engendered via an evil habit [such as drunkenness] or an evil [genetic or natural] disposition. For example, at one time among the early peoples in Germany, theft was considered permissible (according to Julius Caesar).

■ READING AND DISCUSSION QUESTIONS

1. What does it mean to have per se knowledge versus knowledge obtained through effects visually obtained? Give an everyday example.
2. How is eternal law different from natural law for Aquinas?
3. Why is purposive action important to Aquinas?
4. How would the concept of primary and secondary movers be interpreted in a modern industrial democracy?
5. Why does Aquinas believe that humans are inclined to the natural law? What does he mean by this?
6. What does the distinction between theoretical and practical reason mean? What aspects of your own life are governed by theoretical and practical reason?
7. What is the relationship between universals and particulars? Why does Aquinas say that in life we begin with particulars? Give an example.
8. Why are the conclusions of direct logical arguments concerning practical reason not necessary? (Hint: pull up on the Internet a social-advice column. Do you always agree with the recommendations of the writer? Why or why not?)
9. What common principles of action do you feel all people agree upon?

■ CLASS EXERCISES

A. *Direct logical discourse:* Using the tools found in Chapter 2, outline the argument from the *Summa* on natural law, using the reading questions as a point of departure. Based on your assessment of one key premise, write a one-page argument about why you agree or disagree with the argument's conclusion,

B. *Fictive-narrative philosophy:* Using the tools found in Chapter 3, begin with a claim that relates to the reading and discussion questions above. Then create a modern-day story about people or situations familiar to you that makes the logical claim you have identified. Three pages.

MIDTERM PROJECT

A. *Direct logical discourse:* Expanding on one of your previous direct-discourse evaluations, reexamine two premises in the reconstructed argument in order to write either a pro or a con response to the argument's conclusion, based on your assessment of the two key premises. Be sure to show that you understand what the opposite side might say against your argument and counter-refute the hypothetical objector. Five pages.

B. *Fictive-narrative philosophy:* Expand on one of your previous narratives (a different one from the argument examined in "A"). In this expanded version, strive for greater development of characters, scene, and/or dramatic action. To help keep you on track, use your previous responses to the pertinent "Fictive-Narrative Philosophy Feedback" section. Four pages.

PART 3

MODERN AND CONTEMPORARY PHILOSOPHY

Cogito ego sum
two realms of reality, mind and
physical substances, interacted with
each other in the pineal gland.

CHAPTER EIGHT

Descartes

René Descartes (1596–1650) is sometimes credited with ushering in the modern age of philosophy and mathematics. In philosophy, he employed a method that required radical skepticism of the fundamental starting points of knowledge. This priority made epistemology (the study of what we can properly know) a prerequisite for metaphysics (the study of what things properly exist, ontology, and their ordering, cosmology). Prior to Descartes, the medieval philosophers had limited their skepticism to narrow points of conceptual analysis having to do with the truth of particular premises in a direct logical argument. Descartes called into question the very starting point of the whole endeavor.

In mathematics Descartes flipped the medieval worldview of seeing geometry as more primary than arithmetic. Through the development of analytic geometry, all geometric figures could be described via equations in algebra via a four-quadrant system, later called the Cartesian coordinate system. Descartes is thus a major figure in both philosophy and mathematics.

THE QUEEN AND THE PHILOSOPHER[*]

Charles Johnson

In 1649, Queen Christina of Sweden became interested in Descartes's work and pre-vailed upon him to come to Stockholm. This Scandinavian sovereign was a true renais-sance character. Strong-willed and vigorous, she insisted that Descartes should teach her philosophy at five in the morning. This unphilosophic hour of rising at dead of night in a Swedish winter was more than Descartes could endure. He took ill and died in Febru-ary 1650.

—BERTRAND RUSSELL, WISDOM OF THE WEST

Years and years agone, I cautioned Meister Descartes about this dangerous, young woman, the notorious Queen Christina and, to his credit, he *did* heed my monitions the first time she sent one of her warships to fetch him to Sweden. I mean, didn't he have enough troubles already? She wanted him to serve as her personal tutor in philos-ophy and mathematics. At the time, we were living not too uncomfortably in Holland on an estate twenty miles north of Amsterdam. The master enjoyed performing his daily meditations in a study shaped like an octagon, and this overlooked a beautiful garden, the sight of which brought him a feeling of serenity—his meditations were, of course, always in the afternoons or evenings, because all his life he was in the habit of sleeping ten hours a day and never rising before noon. I, Gustav Schulter, his valet and secretary who knew my place in this world and was not likely to rise above it, was at Descartes's side when he politely declined Queen Christina's invitation for him to join her court. He gave the admiral of her warship a letter that praised the Queen's beauty, her likeness to God, and he requested, regretfully, that she forgive his inability at the moment to bask "in the sunbeams of her glorious presence."

If matters had ended there—if, for example, she had given up and set her sights in-stead on Francis Bacon or Galileo as trophies to be installed in the Swedish court for her amusement, all would have gone well, I believe, for the father of modern philosophy. However, 22-year-old Christina was not to be denied. She sent a *second* ship from Sweden to bring her Descartes. Was this a highborn hijacking? An aristocratic body-snatching? Call his capture what you will. My master, whose cup-hilt rapier once held at bay a gang

---

[*] *Significant biographical research in this story is drawn from Paul Strathern's superb little book* Descartes in 90 Minutes *(Chicago: Ivan R. Dee, 1996).*

of buccaneers—devils, one and all—intent upon robbing him of his fine garments, was defeated. One does not decline when royalty comes calling *twice.* So in October, 1649, and after our friends said, "Goodbye and God's speed," we began our exodus and exile from Holland, sailing for Stockholm—and straight into the most nightmarish, cautionary tale (or *conte philosophique*) any metaphysician has ever known.

During our passage through the Baltic Sea, as our vessel swung lazily from side to side on the grayslick waters, I very much wondered at his acquiescence to the whim of a willful monarch said to prefer her art collection to the welfare of her people. He was fifty-three that fall, twice her age, and though he still cut a sartorial if strange figure, you would not have guessed from his guise the depths of his genius. In stature, he was small, with a gigantic head, and more than enough Gallic nose for two or three Parisians. If you squinted, blurring his image a bit, he looked rather like a magpie or a crow that decided one day to become a man, but only got half-way. His voice was frail. As his valet, I knew him to be a good Catholic, a solitary, a selfish, an unmarried and at times a highly eccentric man. For example, he told me that on November 11, 1619, he took to living inside a stove during an especially harsh winter in Bavaria. But it was there—inside his stove (or, as some claim, his stove-heated room)—that he experienced a Platonic vision of the world portrayed entirely in terms of the eternal beauty of mathematics. This mystical moment directed him inward, to his suspending all his beliefs and systematically doubting the existence of *every*thing—the world, God, his perceptions—until he could find something so apodictic and certain that even the Almighty, if he was an Evil Deceiver, could not fool him about it. That certainty, said my master, was the thinking self. His *cogito ergo sum*—"I think, therefore I am"—became the most oft-quoted sentence in (and the foundation of) Western philosophy, and from this single brick of rationalism he rebuilt a mechanistic world, dividing it into mind substances (*res cogitans*) and physical substances (*res extentias*), with a benevolent God standing above it all, insuring that the innate ideas he had implanted within us were true. His bifurcation of phenomena into Mind and Matter—into two separate "truths," as it were—was a politically shrewd compromise that left men of science in our time free to explore things material, and men of the cloth free to hold forth on things *im*material, such as the soul, that Ghost in the Machine. (For example, in the master's philosophy, animals were merely machines controlled by external stimuli.) So yes, Descartes carved out a space in the ruins of medieval scholasticism for science to progress. Just the same, his *Meditations*, and his methods, still ignited controversy across the European continent. The Jesuits sensed his systematic doubt would be their undoing. The president of Holland's most esteemed university condemned him as an atheist, and the Calvinists in the Netherlands accused him of heresy. I know little of these things, being only a humble valet, but I gathered that once you get famous, you can count on getting famous problems.

Notwithstanding his misgivings about Queen Christina and moving to Sweden, I suspect he saw her offer in terms of his present troubles with the Church. She hoped the founder of analytic geometry, the creator of Cartesian coordinates, and the man who revolutionized optics by discovering the law of refraction, would help her create in her country an Academy of Sciences that would rival anything in Paris. Christina planned to make him a naturalized Swedish citizen, bring him into the Swedish aristocracy, and give him an estate on German lands she had conquered. Unless I am beguiled by the master's Evil Deceiver, Descartes saw her proposal as almost too good to be true—she would, he imagined, save him from his enemies in the Church, and among other philosophers, who were amplifying their opposition to his ideas.

As things turned out, her proposal—like so many in this life—*was* too good to be true. Descartes once said he wrote his *Meditations* in an autobiographical style to make it accessible to women. Maybe he succeeded too well, for Queen Christina not only understood his philosophical musings, but she saw his blunders as well. In every respect, she was magnific. Before Christina was born, astrologers predicted she would be a boy, and at first everyone thought King Gustavus Adolphus did have a son because she came into the world with a caul covering her pelvis. Forasmuch as the king had no male heirs, her father ordered that Christina was to be raised and trained as a prince. She was easily the homeliest woman in all Christendom and only stood five-feet tall in her slippers. But this "Queen of Sweden, of the Goths, and the Wends" was vigorously athletic, tough as an armadillo, disciplined, crisp and efficient, and spent twelve hours a day, six days a week, at sports and her studies. Christina wrote and spoke five languages. Her favorite activities were riding and hunting bears. She never slept more than five hours a night. Like a well-trained soldier, she took little food, was contemptuous of extremes of heat and cold, and she expected the same Spartan behavior from everyone around her. Not too surprisingly, she refused to marry and it was rumored that she liked girls, specifically a young countess new to her court named Ebba Sparre. "It is necessary to try to *surpass* one's self always," Christina was fond of saying, "This occupation ought to last as long as life." She also was famous for saying, "I myself find it much less difficult to strangle a man than to fear him."

I must confess that I, Gustav, not being a bold man, *did* fear this galloping *Ubermensch*[1] of a queen. There was no question that Descartes was fond of her. In public conversations he praised her for being "The Philosopher Queen," and in private talks with me called her his "Viking Amazon"; she called *him* whatever she pleased.

On the day we arrived he was feasted with *smörgåsbord, snaps,* and *glögg,*[2] and lavishly honored by her court, as was appropriate for a luminary such as himself. But then Christina dropped her first royal slipper. After granting him permission to see her only twice, she informed Descartes that she was busy with affairs of state and could not begin her lessons with him for at least six weeks. During that time, she said, he should productively occupy himself with writing a ballet in verse to commemorate her role in

---

1 *Übermensch*: superman.

2 *smörgåsbord, snaps,* **and** *glögg*: a buffet meal, liquor, and spiced wine.

the Peace of Westphalia, which concluded the Thirty Year's War. Besides all this, she ordered him to compose a comedy in five acts and draw up the statutes for a Swedish Academy of Arts and Sciences.

So, as I say, Descartes was not happy about this delay, but it couldn't be helped. To these time-wasting chores he dutifully applied himself as, saints preserve us, a cold, dark winter set in—the worst winter in sixty years—and turned Stockholm into a hyperborean cavern buried beneath a hundred kinds of snow, with ice forming in your hair if you were outside for but a few moments. The temperature fell well below zero. My master seemed to keep a cold. "By heaven, Gustav, my old friend," he said through clogged-up sinuses, "it seems to me that men's thoughts freeze here during the winter, just as does the water. Our brains *are*, you know, eighty percent liquid."

Anon, he came to see how cruel, how unforgiving was this northern climate. And also how wickedly devious Queen Christina could be when after six weeks she dropped her *second* royal slipper. She knew—as *every*one knew—that erenow Descartes slept until noon. Christina, on the other hand, was out of bed each day at 4 a.m. She wanted her lessons in philosophy and mathematics three times a week at the wee hour of 5 a.m. in the unheated library of her royal palace, with all the windows thrown open. Perhaps she felt her regimen of defying refrigeration, of being indifferent to discomfort, would help Descartes to "surpass himself always."

In truth, it had the opposite effect, and for the first time I began to suspect she was in league with the Devil. For two difficult weeks I helped the master out of bed at 3 a.m. It was, I must say, like trying to bring Lazarus back to life. I filled his shivering, sleep-deprived body with hot tea; I helped him out of his nightshirt and into his black coat, knee breeches, and thick woolen scarf. I guided Descartes through his elaborate, French toiletries, then I drove him in a sleigh over the frost-surfaced, sleety ground thither to her castle, the air raw and stinging my lungs, and with him all the while sneezing and coughing and shivering as if he might shake himself apart.

There, just outside her frigid, wind-swept library lined on all sides with books, Descartes trembled. As the Queen bade him enter, he shook off a sudden wave of drowsiness and his cold-stiffened fingers brought forth from his valise the pages of the statues he'd written for her Academy. In a voice still phlegmed by sleep, he said, "Your Highness, I hope these pages will please you."

"For your sake, I hope they do." Christina was lively, even playful at this godforsaken hour. Spread out on a long table before the Queen were my master's books. A thin wind through the windows changed the room's pressure, and all at once my left ear felt stopped up, my right had a ringing sound, and my toes felt like knots of wood. So please don't think poorly of me if my memory of this tutorial appears sketchy. Reaching back, I do remember her saying, "But there is something in your published writing that troubles me. You say that Mind and Matter are separate substances. But if my soul *wills* my left hand to rise"—as she said this Christina gave the air a swipe with the back of her hand—"it remains a mystery how the immaterial will can affect my material body."

Descartes' teeth chattered loudly. His steamy breath rolled out: "Your Majesty, it is my belief that the interaction of the soul and body occurs in the pineal gland, where—"

"Just a moment! Don't speak! *Stop*!"

The master pulled up short, his mouth snapping shut, and he let his gaze fall to where his feet felt cemented to the floor.

"Do you have *evidence* for this?" she asked.

"Well, not exactly . . . "

"Oh, poo, then the idea is preposterous, isn't it?" Christina put her head back. "Why *there*? Why not in the kidneys? Or the stomach?"

No one had pointed out this problem to him until now, or at least not so forcefully. My master, in a mental fog, tried to answer; his mouth opened, but no sound was forthcoming, as if his thoughts had glaciated. I suffer you then to see this almost Siberian chamber in the middle of a Scandinavian winter as the inner circle of a Hell perfectly designed for slugabed René Descartes.

The Ice Queen smiled and sat back in her chair.

"Do you see my problem, dear? For want of a better phrase, I would call it a 'mind-body problem,' an unnecessary and silly dualism that *you've* created. And this theory of yours about animals being machines is a delicious piece of sophistry! My goodness, I never saw my *clock* making babies!"

Particles of snow drifted inside and settled on Descartes' books. Weaving from the paralytic chill, he blew hot breath into his hands until they heated a little, briefly defrosting himself long enough to say, "Your Highness, *every*thing I've written logically follows if you begin, as I did, with systematic doubt."

The Queen rolled her head to the left, and raised her right eyebrow. "But your *Meditations* are not at all systematic, and they are fatally flawed."

His voice slipped a scale. "They *are*?"

"Forgive me if I speak frankly, for I'm not the world famous philosopher *you* are, but I boast a knowledge of many things, as every monarch should." She looked at him steadily, as she might a bear she had just cornered. "If you stop doubting everything when you reach your own thoughts of doubt, you *can't* just say, 'I think, therefore I am,' because all you can be truly *certain* of at that moment is that thought is going on. You've assumed and added a self, an *I*, that is not *given*—only presupposed—in that experience."

My master looked sacked and empty. His frost-bitten limbs were stiff and mechanical like the fantastic animals that populated his philosophy. "I think . . . I need more time . . . to consider this, your Majesty."

"*Do* consider, it," she said. "Be advised I would like a good answer when we meet again two days from now."

That next tutorial was not destined to be. The master never completely thawed. He came down with pneumonia, and seven days after his lesson with the Queen he first slipped into delirium, then on February 11, 1650, a coma from which he never emerged.

His body was buried near the Queen's estate in a small Catholic cemetery for unbaptized children. And how did I, Gustav, feel now that my master was gone? Whoever is wise and has observed these things must conclude that every original thinker would do well to fear too much attention from the High and Mighty. I wanted to go home and cry into my wife's bosom for awhile. But I didn't have a wife. Eventually, I did return to Germany, with Christina's unanswered questions still shimmering in my mind. And even now, late at night when I try unsuccessfully to sleep and look back on those bone-chilling months, I find myself unable to decide if the Queen was a brief footnote in Meister Descartes' history, or if he, poor soul, was simply a footnote in hers.

■ READING AND DISCUSSION QUESTIONS

1. Queen Christina was twenty-two years old and the monarch of Sweden. What is the significance of her age and her gender to the story (remember the culture she was living in)?
2. What can be understood about Descartes getting inside of an oven?
3. Why were the Jesuits and Calvinists afraid of Descartes? Was this perceived threat a part of his reason for going to Sweden?
4. Why did Christina say, "It is necessary to surpass oneself always"? Do you believe this is true? What would the acceptance of this do to one's personal worldview?
5. What do you make of the first tasks Christina assigned to Descartes (the first slipper)?
6. Why did Christina want her philosophy lessons to begin at 5 a.m. (the second slipper)?
7. What is your evaluation of Christina's questions concerning Descartes's metaphysical theory of dualism?
8. Christina is called the ice queen. What is the significance of this?
9. What is your evaluation of Christina's critique of the "I think; therefore, I am" argument?
10. Why was Descartes buried in a cemetery for unbaptized children?

■ FICTIVE-NARRATIVE PHILOSOPHY FEEDBACK

What claims are made in this story? Write them out in a bulleted list and include whether they are made through dialogue, dramatic action, or the presentation of the scene (including descriptive detail). One page. Then choose either a short direct-discourse response (according to the rules in Chapter 2) or a short fictive-narrative presentation (according to the rules in Chapter 3).

FINDING A FOUNDATION FOR KNOWLEDGE

René Descartes

Adapted from René Descartes, *Meditations on First Philosophy,* trans. Elizabeth S. Haldane and G. R. T. Ross, in *The Philosophical Writings of Descartes,* vol. 1 (1911; rpt. Cambridge: Cambridge University Press, 1931). *Note on the translation:* English words found in brackets are inserted by the translator to make better sense of the English rendering.

The Meditations on First Philosophy *is one of Descartes's most popular works. In* Meditation I *he attempts to prove that minimum epistemological assumptions (assumptions about how we know) require us only to accept indubitable logical processes of thinking and that all else is subjected to radical doubt. In* Meditation II *he argues that whether or not there is a Great Deceiver, the subject can be certain of his own existence. The second key argument of* Meditation II *concerns Descartes's theory of dualism in which his analysis of candle wax leads him to conclude that bodies are better known by the understanding than by the senses.*

Meditation I

Of the things which may be brought within the sphere of the doubtful

It is now some years since I detected how many were the false beliefs that I had from my earliest youth admitted as true and how doubtful was everything I had since constructed on this basis; and from that time I was convinced that I must once and for all seriously undertake to rid myself of all the opinions that I had formerly accepted and commence to build anew from the foundation if I wanted to establish any firm and permanent structure in the sciences. But as this enterprise appeared to be a very great one, I waited until I had attained an age so mature that I could not hope that at any later date I should be better fitted to execute my design. This reason caused me to delay so long that I should feel that I was doing wrong were I to occupy in deliberation the time that yet remains to me for action. Today, then, since very opportunely for the plan I have in view I have delivered my mind from every care [and am happily agitated by no passions] and since I have procured for myself an assured leisure in a peaceable retirement, I shall at last seriously and freely address myself to the general upheaval of all my former opinions.

Now, for this object it is not necessary that I should show that all of these are false—I shall perhaps never arrive at this end. But inasmuch as reason already persuades me that I ought no less carefully to withhold my assent from matters that are not entirely certain and indubitable than from those that appear to me manifestly to be false, if I am able to find in each one some reason to doubt, this will suffice to justify my rejecting the whole. And for that end it will not be requisite that I should examine each in particular, which would be an endless undertaking; for owing to the fact that the destruction of the foundations of necessity brings with it the downfall of the rest of the edifice, I shall only in the first place attack those principles upon which all my former opinions rested.

All that up to the present time I have accepted as most true and certain I have learned either from the senses or through the senses; but it is sometimes proved to me that these senses are deceptive, and it is wiser not to trust entirely to any thing by which we have once been deceived.

But it may be that although the senses sometimes deceive us concerning things that are hardly perceptible or very far away, there are yet many others to be met with as to which we cannot reasonably have any doubt, although we recognize them by their means. For example, there is the fact that I am here, seated by the fire, attired in a dressing gown, having this paper in my hands and other similar matters. And how could I deny that these hands and this body are mine, were it not perhaps that I compare myself to certain persons, devoid of sense, whose cerebella are so troubled and clouded by the violent vapors of black bile[3] that they constantly assure us that they think they are kings when they are really quite poor, or that they are clothed in purple when they are really without covering, or who imagine that they have an earthenware head or are nothing but pumpkins or are made of glass. But they are mad, and I should not be any the less insane were I to follow examples so extravagant.

At the same time I must remember that I am a man; consequently I am in the habit of sleeping and in my dreams representing to myself the same things or sometimes even less probable things than do those who are insane in their waking moments. How often has it happened to me that in the night I dreamed that I found myself in this particular place, that I was dressed and seated near the fire, whilst in reality I was lying undressed in bed! At this moment it does indeed seem to me that it is with eyes awake that I am looking at this paper; that this head that I move is not asleep, that it is deliberately and of set purpose that I extend my hand and perceive it; what happens in sleep appears neither so clear nor so distinct as all this. But in thinking this over, I remind myself that on many occasions I have in sleep been deceived by similar illusions, and in dwelling carefully on this reflection, I see so manifestly that there

---

3 **black bile:** refers to the four-humors theory originated by the Hippocratic writers and systematized by Galen. The last version of the Galenic theory listed the four humors as blood, phlegm, yellow bile, and black bile. Each was associated with a particular power. Good health was the result of maintaining the moderate expression of each.

are no certain indications by which we may clearly distinguish wakefulness from sleep that I am lost in astonishment. And my astonishment is such that it is almost capable of persuading me that I now dream.

Now, let us assume that we are asleep and that all these particulars (for example, that we open our eyes, shake our head, extend our hands, and so on) are but false delusions; and let us reflect that possibly neither our hands nor our whole body are such as they appear to us to be. At the same time we must at least confess that the things represented to us in sleep are like painted representations that can only have been formed as the counterparts of something real and true; in this way those general things at least (that is, eyes, a head, hands, and a whole body) are not imaginary things but things really existent. For, as a matter of fact, painters, even when they study with the greatest skill to represent sirens and satyrs by forms the most strange and extraordinary, cannot give them natures that are entirely new but merely make a certain medley of the members of different animals; or if their imagination is extravagant enough to invent something so novel that nothing similar has ever before been seen, and then their work represents a thing purely fictitious and absolutely false, it is certain all the same that the colors of which this is composed are necessarily real. And for the same reason, although these general things, to wit, [a body], eyes, a head, hands, and such like, may be imaginary, we are bound at the same time to confess that there are at least some other objects yet more simple and more universal that are real and true; and of these just in the same way as with

certain real colors, all these images of things that dwell in our thoughts, whether true and real or false and fantastic, are formed.

To such a class of things pertains corporeal nature in general and its extension, the figure of extended things, their quantity or magnitude and number, as also the place in which they are, the time that measures their duration, and so on.

That is possibly why our reasoning is not unjust when we conclude from this that physics, astronomy, medicine, and all other sciences that have as their end the consideration of composite things are very dubious and uncertain; but that arithmetic, geometry, and other sciences of that kind that only treat of very simple and very general things, without taking great trouble to ascertain whether they are actually existent or not, contain some measure of certainty and an element of the indubitable. For whether I am awake or asleep, two and three together always form five, and the square can never have more than four sides, and it does not seem possible that truths so clear and apparent can be suspected of any falsity [or uncertainty].

Nevertheless I have long had fixed in my mind the belief that an all-powerful God exists by whom I have been created such as I am. But how do I know that He has not brought it to pass that there is no earth, no heaven, no extended body, no magnitude, no place, and that [I nevertheless possess the perceptions of all these things], which seem to me to exist just exactly as I now see them? And, besides, as I sometimes imagine that others deceive themselves in the things that they think they know best, how do I know that I am not deceived every time I add two and three, or count the sides of a square, or judge of things yet simpler, if anything simpler can be imagined? But possibly God has not desired that I should be thus deceived, for He is said to be supremely good. If, however, it is contrary to His goodness to have made me such that I constantly deceive myself, it would also appear to be contrary to His goodness to permit me to be sometimes deceived, and nevertheless I cannot doubt that He does permit this.

There may indeed be those who would prefer to deny the existence of a God so powerful rather than believe that all other things are uncertain. But let us not oppose them for the present and grant that all that is here said of a God is a fable; nevertheless in whatever way they suppose that I have arrived at the state of being that I have reached—whether they attribute it to fate or to accident or make out that it is by a continual succession of antecedents or by some other method—since to err and deceive oneself is a defect, it is clear that the greater will be the probability of my being so imperfect as to deceive myself ever, as is the author to whom they assign my origin the less powerful. To these reasons I have certainly nothing to reply, but at the end I feel constrained to confess that there is nothing in all that I formerly believed to be true of which I cannot in some measure doubt, and that not merely through want of thought or through levity but for reasons that are very powerful and maturely considered, so that henceforth I ought not the less carefully to refrain from giving credence to these opinions than to that which is manifestly false, if I desire to arrive at any certainty [in the sciences].

But it is not sufficient to have made these remarks; we must also be careful to keep them in mind. For these ancient and commonly held opinions still revert frequently to my mind, long and familiar custom having given them the right to occupy my mind against my inclination and rendered them almost masters of my belief; nor will I ever lose the habit of deferring to them or of placing my confidence in them, so long as I consider them as they really are, that is, opinions in some measure doubtful, as I have just shown, and at the same time highly probable, so that there is much more reason to believe in them than to deny them. That is why I consider that I shall not be acting amiss if, taking of set purpose a contrary belief, I allow myself to be deceived and for a certain time pretend that all these opinions are entirely false and imaginary, until at last, having thus balanced my former prejudices with my latter [so that they cannot divert my opinions more to one side than to the other], my judgment will no longer be dominated by bad usage or turned away from the right knowledge of the truth. For I am assured that there can be neither peril nor error in this course and that I cannot at present yield too much to distrust, since I am not considering the question of action but only of knowledge.

I shall then suppose not that God who is supremely good and the fountain of truth, but some evil genius not less powerful than deceitful has employed his whole energies in deceiving me; I shall consider that the heavens, the earth, colors, figures, sound, and all other external things are naught but the illusions and dreams of which this genius has availed himself in order to lay traps for my credulity; I shall consider myself as having no hands, no eyes, no flesh, no blood, nor any senses, yet falsely believing myself to possess all these things; I shall remain obstinately attached to this idea, and if by this means it is not in my power to arrive at the knowledge of any truth, I may at least do what is in my power [that is, suspend my judgment] and with firm purpose avoid giving credence to any false thing or being imposed upon by this arch deceiver, however powerful and deceptive he may be. But this task is a laborious one, and insensibly a certain lassitude leads me into the course of my ordinary life. And just as a captive who in sleep enjoys an imaginary liberty, when he begins to suspect that his liberty is but a dream, fears to awaken and conspires with these agreeable illusions that the deception may be prolonged, so insensibly of my own accord I fall back into my former opinions, and I dread awakening from this slumber, lest the laborious wakefulness that would follow the tranquility of this repose should have to be spent not in daylight but in the excessive darkness of the difficulties that have just been discussed.

Meditation II

Of the nature of the human mind and that it is more easily known than the body

Argument One

The meditation of yesterday filled my mind with so many doubts that it is no longer in my power to forget them. And yet, I do not see in what manner I can resolve them; and just as if I had all of a sudden fallen into very deep water, I am so disconcerted that I can neither make certain of setting my feet on the bottom nor swim and so support myself on the surface. I shall nevertheless make an effort and follow anew the same path as that on which I yesterday entered (that is, I shall proceed by setting aside all that in which the least doubt could be supposed to exist, just as if I had discovered that it was absolutely false); and I shall ever follow in this road until I have met with something that is certain or at least, if I can do nothing else, until I have learned for certain that there is nothing in the world that is certain. Archimedes,[4] in order that he might draw the terrestrial globe out of its place and transport it elsewhere, demanded only that one point should be fixed and immoveable; in the same way I shall have the right to conceive high hopes if I am happy enough to discover one thing only that is certain and indubitable.

I suppose, then, that all the things that I see are false; I persuade myself that nothing has ever existed of all that my fallacious memory represents to me. I consider that I possess no senses; I imagine that body, figure, extension, movement, and place are but the fictions of my mind. What, then, can be esteemed as true? Perhaps nothing at all, unless that there is nothing in the world that is certain.

But how can I know there is not something different from those things that I

4 **Archimedes:** Syracusan mathematician and inventor (c. 287–c. 212 BCE), who legendarily claimed he could move the earth with a lever, if given a very firm place to stand and a fixed point that he could use as a fulcrum.

have just considered, of which one cannot have the slightest doubt? Is there not some God, or some other being by whatever name we call it, who puts these reflections into my mind? That is not necessary for is it not possible that I am capable of producing them myself? I, myself, am I not at least something? But I have already denied that I had senses and body. Yet, I hesitate, for what follows from that? Am I so dependent on body and senses that I cannot exist without these? But I was persuaded that there was nothing in all the world, that there was no heaven, no earth, that there were no minds nor any bodies: was I not then likewise persuaded that I did not exist? Not at all; of a surety I myself did exist since I persuaded myself of something [or merely because I thought of something]. But there is some deceiver or other, very powerful and very cunning, who ever employs his ingenuity in deceiving me. Then, without doubt, I exist also if he deceives me, and let him deceive me as much as he will, he can never cause me to be nothing so long as I think that I am something. So, after having reflected well and carefully examined all things, we must come to the definite conclusion that this proposition—I am; I exist—is necessarily true each time I pronounce it or mentally conceive it.

Argument Two

But I do not yet know clearly enough what I am, I who am certain that I am; hence, I must be careful to see that I do not imprudently take some other object in place of myself and thus that I do not

go astray in respect of this knowledge that I hold to be the most certain and most evident of all that I have formerly learned. That is why I shall now consider anew what I believed myself to be before I embarked upon these last reflections; and of my former opinions I shall withdraw all that might even in a small degree be invalidated by the reasons I have just brought forward in order that there may be nothing at all left beyond what is absolutely certain and indubitable.

What then did I formerly believe myself to be? Undoubtedly I believed myself to be a man. But what is a man? Shall I say a reasonable animal? Certainly not, for then I should have to inquire what an animal is and what is reasonable; thus, from a single question I should insensibly fall into an infinitude of others more difficult; and I should not wish to waste the little time and leisure remaining to me in trying to unravel subtleties like these. But I shall rather stop here to consider the thoughts that of themselves spring up in my mind and were not inspired by anything beyond my own nature alone when I applied myself to the consideration of my being. In the first place, then, I considered myself as having a face, hands, arms, and all that system of members composed of bones and flesh as seen in a corpse that I designated by the name of "body." In addition to this I considered that I was nourished, that I walked, that I felt, and that I thought, and I referred all these actions to the soul; but I did not stop to consider what the soul was, or if I did stop, I imagined that it was something extremely rare and subtle, like a wind, a flame, or an ether, which was spread throughout my grosser parts. As to body I had no manner of doubt about its nature but thought I had a very clear knowledge of it; and if I had desired to explain it according to the notions that I had then formed of it, I should have described it thus: by the body I understand all that which can be defined by a certain figure; something that can be confined in a certain place and can fill a given space in such a way that every other body will be excluded from it; that can be perceived either by touch, or by sight, or by hearing, or by taste, or by smell, that can be moved in many ways not, in truth, by itself but by something that is foreign to it, by which it is touched [and from which it receives impressions]. For to have the power of self-movement, as also of feeling or of thinking, I did not consider to appertain to the nature of body; on the contrary, I was rather astonished to find that faculties similar to them existed in some bodies.

But what am I, now that I suppose that there is a certain genius that is extremely powerful and, if I may say so, malicious, who employs all his powers in deceiving me? Can I affirm that I possess the least of all those things that I have just said pertain to the nature of body? I pause to consider, I revolve all these things in my mind, and I find none of which I can say that it pertains to me. It would be tedious to stop to enumerate them. Let us pass to the attributes of soul and see if there is any one that is in me? What of nutrition or walking [the first mentioned]? But if it is so that I have no body, it is also true that I can neither walk nor take nourishment. Another attribute is sensation. But one cannot feel without body, and besides I have thought I perceived many things during sleep that I recognized in my waking moments as not having been experienced at all. What of thinking? I find here that thought is an attribute that belongs to me; it alone cannot be separated from me. I am; I exist; that is certain. But how often? Just when I think; for it might possibly be the case if I ceased entirely to think that I should likewise cease altogether to exist. I do not now admit anything that is not necessarily true: to speak accurately, I am not more than a thing that thinks, that is to say, a mind or a soul, or an understanding, or a reason, which are terms whose significance was formerly unknown to me. I am, however, a real thing and really exist, but what thing? I have answered: a thing that thinks.

And what more? I shall exercise my imagination [in order to see if I am not something more]. I am not a collection of members that we call the human body: I am not a subtle air distributed through these members; I am not a wind, a fire, a vapor, a breath, or anything at all that I can imagine or conceive because I have assumed that all these were nothing. Without changing that supposition I find that I only leave myself certain of the fact that I am somewhat. But perhaps it is true that these same things that I supposed were nonexistent because they are unknown to me are really not different from the self that I know. I am not sure about this and shall not dispute about it now; I can only give judgment on things that are known to me. I know that I exist, and I inquire what I am, I whom I know to exist. But it is very certain that the knowledge of my existence taken in its precise significance does not depend on things whose existence is not yet known to me; consequently it does not depend on those that I can feign in imagination. And, indeed, the very term *feign* in imagination proves to me my error, for I really do this if I image myself a something, since to imagine is nothing other than to contemplate the figure or image of a corporeal thing. But I already know for certain that I am and that it may be that all these images and, speaking generally, all things that relate to the nature of body are nothing but dreams [and chimeras]. For this reason, I see clearly that I have as little reason to say, "I shall stimulate my imagination in order to know more distinctly what I am," than to say, "I am now awake, and I perceive somewhat that is real and true; but because I do not yet perceive it distinctly enough, I shall go to sleep of express purpose so that my dreams may represent the perception with greatest truth and evidence." And, thus, I know for certain that nothing of all that I can understand by means of my imagination belongs to this knowledge I have of myself and that it is necessary to recall the mind from this mode of thought with the utmost diligence in order that it may be able to know its own nature with perfect distinctness.

But what, then, am I? A thing that thinks. What is a thing that thinks? It is a thing that doubts, understands, [conceives,] affirms, denies, wills, and refuses and that also imagines and feels.

Certainly it is no small matter if all these things pertain to my nature. But why should they not so pertain? Am I not that being who now doubts nearly everything, who nevertheless understands certain things, who affirms that one only is true, who denies all the others, who desires to know more, who is averse to being deceived, who imagines many things, sometimes indeed despite his will, and who perceives many likewise, as by the intervention of the bodily organs? Is there nothing in all this that is as true as it is certain that I exist, even though I should always sleep and though he who has given me being employed all his ingenuity in deceiving me? Is there likewise any one of these attributes that can be distinguished from my thought or might be said to be separate from myself? For it is so evident of itself that it is I who doubts, who understands, and who desires that there is no reason here to add anything to explain it. And I have certainly the power of imagining likewise, for although it may happen (as I formerly supposed) that none of the things that I imagine are true, nevertheless this power of imagining does not cease to be really in use, and it forms part of my thought. Finally, I am the same who feels, that is to say, who perceives certain things, as by the organs of sense, since in truth I see light, I hear noise, I feel heat. But it will be said that these phenomena are false and that I am dreaming. Let it be so; still, it is at least quite certain that it seems to me that I see light, that I hear noise, and that I feel heat. That cannot be false; properly speaking it is what is in me called feeling and, used in this precise sense, is no other thing than thinking.

From this time I begin to know what I am with a little more clarity and distinction than before; nevertheless it still seems to me, and I cannot prevent myself from thinking, that corporeal things, whose images are framed by thought and that are tested by the senses, are much more distinctly known than that obscure part of me that does not come under the imagination. Although really it is very strange to say that I know and understand more distinctly these things whose existence seems to me dubious, that are unknown to me, and that do not belong to me than I do others of the truth of which I am convinced, that are known to me, and that pertain to my real nature—in a word, than myself. But I see clearly how the case stands: my mind loves to wander and cannot yet suffer itself to be retained within the just limits of truth. Very good; let us once more give it the freest rein so that when afterwards we seize the proper occasion for pulling up, it may the more easily be regulated and controlled.

Let us begin by considering the commonest matters, those that we believe to be the most distinctly comprehended, to wit, the bodies that we touch and see; not indeed bodies in general, for these general ideas are usually a little more confused, but let us consider one body in particular. Let us take, for example, this piece of wax: it has been taken quite freshly from the hive, and it has not yet lost the sweetness of the honey that it contains; it still retains somewhat of the odor of the flowers from which it has been culled; its color, its figure, its size are apparent; it is hard, cold, and easily handled, and if you strike it with the finger, it will emit a sound. Finally, all the things that are requisite to cause us distinctly to recognize a body are met with in it. But notice that while I speak and approach the fire, what remained of the taste is exhaled, the smell evaporates, the color alters, the figure is

destroyed, and the size increases; it becomes liquid, it heats—scarcely can one handle it—and when one strikes it, no sound is emitted. Does the same wax remain after this change? We must confess that it remains; none would judge otherwise. What then did I know so distinctly in this piece of wax? It could certainly be nothing of all that the senses brought to my notice since all these things that fall under taste, smell, sight, touch, and hearing are found to be changed, and yet the same wax remains.

Perhaps it was what I now think, namely, that this wax was not that sweetness of honey, nor that agreeable scent of flowers, nor that particular whiteness, nor that figure, nor that sound, but simply a body that a little while before appeared to me as perceptible under these forms and is now perceptible under others. But what, precisely, is it that I imagine when I form such conceptions? Let us attentively consider this, and abstracting from all that does not belong to the wax, let us see what remains. Certainly nothing remains excepting a certain extended thing that is flexible and movable. But what is the meaning of flexible and movable? Is it not that I imagine that this piece of wax being round is capable of becoming square and of passing from a square to a triangular figure? No, certainly it is not that, since I imagine it admits of an infinitude of similar changes, and I nevertheless do not know how to compass the infinitude by my imagination, and consequently this conception that I have of the wax is not brought about by the faculty of imagination. What now is this extension? Is it not also unknown? For it becomes greater when the wax is melted, greater when it is boiled, and greater still when the heat increases; and I should not conceive [clearly] according to truth what wax is, if I did not think that even this piece that we are considering is capable of receiving more variations in extension than I have ever imagined. We must then grant that I could not even understand through the imagination what this piece of wax is and that it is my mind alone that perceives it. I say this piece of wax in particular, for as to wax in general it is yet clearer. But what is this piece of wax that cannot be understood excepting by the [understanding or the] mind. It is certainly the same that I see, touch, and imagine, and finally it is the same that I have always believed it to be from the beginning. But what must be observed particularly is that its perception is neither an act of vision, nor of touch, nor of imagination, and has never been such although it may have appeared formerly to be so, but only an intuition of the mind, which may be imperfect and confused as it was formerly or clear and distinct as it is at present, according as my attention is more or less directed to the elements that are found in it and of which it is composed.

Yet, in the meantime I am greatly astonished when I consider [the great feebleness of mind] and its proneness to fall [insensibly] into error; for although without giving expression to my thoughts I consider all this in my own mind, words often impede me, and I am almost deceived by the terms of ordinary language. For we say that we see the same wax, if it is present, and not that we simply judge that it is the same from its having the same color and figure. From this I should conclude that I knew the wax by means of vision and not simply by the intuition of the mind; unless by chance I remember that, when looking from a window and saying I see men who pass in the street, I really do not see them but infer that what I see is men, just as I say that I see wax. And yet, what do I see from the window but hats and coats, which may cover automatic machines? Yet I judge these to be men. And similarly solely by the faculty of judgment that rests in my mind, I comprehend that which I believed I saw with my eyes.

A man who makes it his aim to raise his knowledge above the common should be ashamed to derive the occasion for doubting from the forms of speech invented by the vulgar; I prefer to pass on and consider whether I had a more evident and perfect conception of what the wax was when I first perceived it and when I believed I knew it by means of the external senses or at least by the common sense as it is called, that is to say, by the imaginative faculty, or whether my present conception is clearer now that I have most carefully examined what it is and in what way it can be known. It would certainly be absurd to doubt this. For what in this first perception was distinct? What was there that might not as well have been perceived by any of the animals? But when I distinguish the wax from its external forms, and when, just as if I had taken from it its vestments, I consider it quite naked, it is certain that although some error may still be found in my judgment, I can nevertheless not perceive it thus without a human mind.

But finally, what shall I say of this mind, that is, of myself, for up to this point, I do not admit in myself anything but mind? What then, do I, who seem to perceive this piece of wax so distinctly, now know myself, not only with much more truth and certainty but also with much more distinctness and clearness? For if I judge that the wax is or exists from the fact that I see it, it certainly follows much more clearly that I am or that I exist myself from the fact that I see it. For it may be that what I see is not really wax; it may also be that I do not possess eyes with which to see anything; but it cannot be that when I see, or (for I no longer take account of the distinction) when I think I see, I myself who think am naught. So, if I judge that the wax exists from the fact that I touch it, the same thing will follow, to wit, that I am; and if I judge that my imagination or some other cause, whatever it is, persuades me that the wax exists, I shall still conclude the same. And what I have here remarked of wax may be applied to all other things that are external to me [and are met with outside of me]. And further, if the [notion or] perception of wax has seemed to me clearer and more distinct, not only after the sight or the touch but also after many other causes have rendered it quite manifest to me, with how much more [evidence] and distinctness must it be said that I now know myself, since all the reasons that contribute to the knowledge of wax or any other body whatever are yet better proofs of the nature of my mind! And so many other things in the mind itself may contribute to the elucidation of its nature that those that depend on body, such as these just mentioned, hardly merit being taken into account.

But finally, here I am, having insensibly reverted to the point I desired, for since it is now manifest to me that even bodies are not properly speaking known by the senses or by the faculty of imagination but by the understanding only, and since they are not known from the fact that they are seen or touched but only because they are understood, I see clearly that there is nothing that is easier for me to know than my mind. But because it is difficult to rid oneself so promptly of an opinion to which one was accustomed for so long, it will be well that I should halt a little at this point so that by the length of my meditation, I may more deeply imprint on my memory this new knowledge.

■ READING AND DISCUSSION QUESTIONS

1. In Meditation I, Descartes talks about constructing a sound building, which is a metaphor for his knowledge. What does such a metaphor convey to the reader? Are there ways in which gaining knowledge is unlike fashioning a building?

2. In Meditation I, Descartes describes various ways that one might be deceived. Think for a moment about deception: where is the source of human error? Write down a few examples of when you were in error and try to analyze the source of this error.

3. In Meditation I Descartes declares, "Arithmetic, geometry, and other sciences of that kind that only treat of very simple and very general things, without taking

great trouble to ascertain whether they are actually existent or not, contain some measure of certainty and an element of the indubitable." Why should arithmetic and geometry be more certain than sense impressions?

4. In Argument One of Meditation II, Descartes posits the possible existence of an Evil Deceiver. Sketch out just how you think such an evil genius might affect the subject trying to properly ground his knowledge claims. Sketch out a brief scene.
5. In Argument One of Meditation II, Descartes suggests that thinking about one's own thinking proves that there is a subject doing the thinking. Write a short dialogue between a supporter and a detractor to this argument.
6. In Argument Two of Meditation II, Descartes claims that the physical qualities of wax change when a beeswax candle drips wax, yet we still understand the wax to be the same wax. Do you think that this proves there is an essence of wax that supersedes the physical properties of wax? Is this like Plato's Forms?

■ CLASS EXERCISES

A. *Direct logical discourse:* Using the tools found in Chapter 2, outline one of the arguments from Meditation I or Meditation II discussed in the questions above. Based on your assessment of one key premise, write a one-page argument about why you agree or disagree with the argument's conclusion.

B. *Fictive-narrative philosophy:* Using the tools found in Chapter 3, begin with a claim that relates to the reading and discussion questions above. Then create a modern-day story about people or situations familiar to you that makes the logical claim you have identified. Three pages.

Kant believed there are 2 independent
sources in metaphysics: empirical & rational.
He felt there was a relationship empirical
and rational structures of the mind.
use of cat example as proof.

"What is true and what is reality".

when we assume we add our
interpretation to the reality

many obstacles would come your way
to alter your plans but new + better things
will come your way. "new man"

CHAPTER NINE

Kant

Immanuel Kant famously begins the introduction to his Critique of Pure Reason, *"There can be no doubt that all our knowledge begins with experience . . . but though all our knowledge begins with experience, it does not follow that it all arises out of experience."*[1] *This quotation from the second edition of the first* Critique *displays a critical Kant who wants to find a way to integrate questions of epistemology and metaphysics. This is in contrast to the precritical Kant who followed rationalist metaphysicians in constructing systems describing "what is" and "how it is organized."*

----

1 Immanuel Kant, *Critique of Pure Reason*, trans. Norman Kemp Smith (New York: St. Martins, 1929): B-1.

KANT AWAKENED*

Michael Boylan

This story catches Kant at his "tipping moment" from his precritical phase to his critical philosophy, when he literally and figuratively "wakes up." The opening scene includes various basic impressions of time and space. Kant considers these. He has not yet written his critical works, but he is troubled. Then he has a dinner party with a colleague who appreciates his existent dogmatic works. But all of us (philosophers and aspiring philosophers) are allowed to change our minds.

It was a bright April day. The light of the morning dawn pierced through a small hole in the shade and played upon the sleeping figure's closed eyelid. At first the man stirred, trying to avoid the light, but then one eye opened. It was inevitable. He had to discern the source and then observe it.

Immanuel opened his left eye. He was lying on his right side. Initially, his attention focused on the hole in the shade, but then it broadened to the widening band that interacted with the dust as it made its way to the far side of his bedroom. The light hit the oaken floor, creating a rhombus with the short side near. His gaze lifted to the armoire against the wall and then back to his washbasin. The dark wood of the washbasin contrasted sharply with the white porcelain bowl and the chipped white bedpan beneath. The scene was rather flat—much like a painting.

Then Kant opened his right eye. All of a sudden the scene was different. The light seemed less intense. The armoire jutted out from the wall. The brass knobs jumped forward from the walnut veneer. Large tear-shaped drops of water stood ready atop the washbasin.

Normally, this would be the time to spring up and face the world. But not today. Today was different. Today, he would stop and observe again. He tried looking from his right eye. Again, there were differences. The shape of the rhombus on the floor altered—both in form and in position.

A fly buzzed about and landed on his nose. The two creatures eyed each other. Kant was curious. How did the fly view the room? Then he heard the scuttling of a mouse. There were always a few mice in the house. Hilda, his cat, was getting on in years—yet she had always been a good mouser.

---

* *Some of the background material for this fictional story comes from Manfred Kuehn,* Kant: A Biography *(Cambridge: Cambridge University Press, 2001).*

How did Hilda and the mice see the room? Could there be an objective room in space if so many creatures might have a different point of view? Of course, Aristotle taught that there was a *scala naturae* (a hierarchical scale of nature) in which the inputs of humans trumped all others. This came from Aristotle. Aristotle was an important guy, no matter what the thinkers of the Aufklärung (Enlightenment) asserted—or so said the celebrated Christian Wolff.

Still, the whole thing bothered Immanuel. As a man of small stature, he knew that many had misjudged him. What was it about perception that gave it some credence to the eye? Where do mistakes come from? He again shut his right eye. Even though everything was flatter, it wasn't completely a plane. It wasn't two-dimensional Euclidean space. It was still three dimensional, but in what way? And who says? And based on what claims?

Clearly there were the features of the room to which he gave more stature on the basis of his privileged two-eyed account. This trumped the perceptions of the fly and of the mouse—whatever their experience might be.

Then there was the *sequential* nature of the enterprise. He began observing the tear in the shade. That created certain expectations in him about the source of light. Might it have been different if he had begun with the washbasin or the bedpan? Was the ordering all that important? And did the ordering depend on him? Could he change the ordering in his mind?

Kant abruptly sat up. He thought about his awakening experience, and it troubled him.

The day was Friday, April 15, 1771. In one week he'd be forty-seven. As was his custom, he had dinner guests on Friday. He had chosen this family's invitation for a week before his birthday because he knew that things didn't always go smoothly when they came over. Diedrick Halle was a very dominating figure and a former student of Wolff. Sometimes everything was fine, but then there were those other occasions in which he got into a flurry. Halle's temper was notorious. On his walk, Kant determined to prethink all the possible arguments Diedrick might bring up.

It was a pleasant day for a walk, but Immanuel was not a mere fair-weather perambulator. He believed in regular habits. They were good for the mind and for the constitution. When he was on his walk, it seemed that he was in a different world. He began with purposeless enjoyment of the flowers of spring that were out in fine display. Soon he would transfer to topics he had considered on his last walk. This special interval had a reality all its own as internal conversations continued across time and space as days ran into and out of each other.

The doorbell rang. Kant wasn't yet ready. A last-minute decision to change his tie caused him to rush upstairs. The Halles weren't due until 7:30, but they were always a little early. But this seemed earlier than usual! He wished his Austrian clock had chimes on the quarter hour. He heard Martin Lampe, his faithful servant, get the door. He started down the stairs with his tie crooked.

"Diedrick," began Immanuel with a glance to his clock. It was 7:17.

The tall, robust man with his elegantly receding hairline was all smiles as he ushered his wife and son in ahead of him. "Immanuel, old man, sorry to be early, but I schedule things so well—don't you know—that I'm frequently early." Then Diedrick laughed hardily as Lampe took the outer wraps of Frieda Halle and their son, Wolf. Diedrick hardly ever wore an outer coat. He claimed his mind heated his body just fine, thank you.

"Please come in to the parlor and have a seat. Lampe will bring you some beer and a few tasty bits."

Kant descended the last stair for a well-choreographed entrance with Diedrick and Frieda sliding forward on his invitation toward the room to his right. Orders for refreshments had been made, and all seemed in order—that is, except for the young eight-year-old son of Diedrick, Wolf. Kant kept a keen eye on the boy. He knew this sort of child from his days as a tutor. The sallow-complexioned, skinny boy had captured Hilda, Kant's cat. The young scalawag was seated against the wall with the cat in his arms and tormenting it by pulling its tail. The cat was twisting about and scraping the boy's arm with its claws. Then the boy did something that made the cat spring away and into the kitchen.

Frieda, a short and sickly woman, ran to her child. "Wolf, are you all right?" she said lifting the boy's arm, which had been scratched through his white shirt and was now bleeding slightly.

Diedrick moved to his wife and son and told them to excuse themselves and freshen up. Immanuel had tilted his head in order that he might hear the repercussions of all these happenings in the kitchen—where his Hilda had fled.

One thing that I regret is how often people forget that they are connected to others. This connection requires a kind of sympathy. As he walked the day after the dinner, Kant wondered why events had occurred as they had. Could it have gone differently?

"You must forgive *mein Klein Lausbub*[2]—he's such a rascal," said Diedrick as the two men sipped a strong Baltic beer.

"Oh, don't trouble yourself over it," replied Kant as he set down his drink and played with his tie. "Things often get askew."

Diedrick chuckled as Lampe brought in some nibble foods. Diedrick helped himself to a goodly portion.

Kant only took two small pieces. He raised his eyebrow as if to see where the wife and child were.

"What I can't understand is that I hear you are backing away from your Inaugural Lecture. I mean, I thought I knew you to be a Wolffian: a man who took Leibniz and made him better. But now I hear that you're having second thoughts." Halle leaned forward toward his host. "Tell me it isn't so!"

---

2 *mein Klein Lausbub*: an affectionate expression equivalent to calling someone a little rascal or a little scamp.

"Well, Diedrick, I'm not so sure I'm changing everything. I'm just thinking about refining a few points." Kant offered to refill Diedrick's glass. "You know, when you're done with that, I have some new Mosel wine that just recently came to me from the west. Perhaps you'd like some?"

Diedrick smiled, then finished his beer as he recounted the various lectures he'd been invited to give during the last six months. When he was done, Kant took a glass and poured some Mosel wine imported from the Rhineland country. He motioned to Diedrick, who took up a glass so that Kant could politely pour him one as well.

The two men lifted their glasses and sipped the light, sweet nectar.

"Look, Immanuel, I'm not here to be your shepherd, but as one of Wolff's most famous students, I think I have an obligation to keep the tradition pure."

Kant chuckled and set down his glass. The evening light was starting to fade as the rays slanting through the wavy glass windows suffused the room less intensely.

"We can get through this efficiently," began Diedrick.

"Quite. I love efficiency."

"Rather, old chap."

"So, let's begin."

"In your Inaugural Lecture and previous writings you seemed to agree that metaphysics is first philosophy. Do you now deny this?"

"No, but I may be amending how I understand metaphysics."

Humph. Diedrick cleared his throat. "Do you still agree that metaphysics begins with rigorous definitions and that these a priori posits form the conceptual foundation for all that is to follow? Do you still agree that this rational construct conditions the way we view the world and that it follows deductively on the model of mathematics?"

"In a way, yes. But look, I'm no longer so sure that there are two independent sources: empirical and rational. I think that there is some sort of complicated relationship between the empirical input and the rational structures of the mind."

Diedrick downed his glass at a gulp and took the rest of the finger food. "Bosh! If there are two realities, then there must be two sources of knowledge. To try to integrate them is a fool's game." The larger man sighed and poured himself another glass of wine.

"I'm not so sure, Diedrick. I've been reading a Scottish writer, David Hume, and he suggests a course that would imply that the paradigm I've been working with is flawed."

"Flawed?" Halle began to laugh. "I've never heard of the fellow. You say his name is Hume? Has he done anything in mathematics or natural philosophy?"

"Well, I don't know. I just received this translated piece of a book that was originally published in England. It rather interested me."

"Look, aside from that usurper Newton, can you name for me any other Englishman who can do higher mathematics?"

"Really, Diedrick—" began Kant when Frieda and Wolf returned.

Immanuel rose and offered them chairs. The boy's sleeve had a few holes in it, but the spots of blood had been washed out. The mother looked tired, and the boy looked sullen.

Kant began to offer these two latecomers some food, but it was all gone. The host started to call for Lampe, when the servant magically appeared and declared, "Gentlemen, dinner is served."

Kant smiled and motioned to his guests to retire to the small dining room.

The fare began with beet soup with bread.

"I hear that you are fond of music, Frau Halle," began Kant.

Frieda blushed. She was slight and very pale, rather more Russian than German.

"What sort of music do you most like?" continued Immanuel with a genuine smile.

Diedrick answered for his wife. "Frieda is rather popular in her tastes. She likes Standfuss and Scholtze and their ilk. Not classical, of course."

Frieda put on a smile that resembled a grimace.

Kant took another drink of wine. The group followed suit. Then the smaller philosopher turned to the child. "And then how are your studies progressing, Wolf?" At that moment Lampe reappeared with another bottle and poured more wine.

The boy seemed very uncomfortable with the question. Frieda, sitting next to her son, put her hand on his head and gave it a pat. "Wolf is rather shy, Herr Professor. He is not used to speaking at the dinner table in our house."

"I'm very sorry to make him uncomfortable, Frau Halle," returned the smaller philosopher.

"We feel that the way to mold the character of a young person is to instill strict discipline at an early age," Diedrick said. "Attention and silence are virtues designed to do just that."

Kant tilted his head. "Ah, much like my Pietist parents."

Now it was Diedrick's turn to put on a forced smile. "Well, just like you, I began that way. But following my teacher—"

Lampe was clearing the soup plates and bringing on the main course: pork schnitzel cooked with egg in a mushroom sauce.

"This looks delicious," blurted Frieda.

Diedrick shot a glance at his wife that silenced her. Wolf began licking his lips.

Lampe filled the glasses, and the dinner was begun.

After a bit of academic gossip, Diedrick asked again, "If I may return to our talk in the study, Immanuel, I would be curious to know what you think about the necessary a priori concepts that make experience possible—such as 'cause and effect.'"

"Well, you know, as I started to say—"

The entrance of his cat, Hilda, interrupted Kant. The black-and-white animal strode forth like the queen of the realm. She paused in her parade for a moment to walk between the legs of the smaller philosopher, rubbing her fur and arched tail against his right leg. Then Hilda moved toward the outside of the table when she stopped. She looked up and viewed the boy, Wolf. There, she froze momentarily when suddenly she cocked her head and raced into the other room.

Diedrick laughed hardily. "I guess the young rascal scared her!"

All at the table laughed—except for Kant, who was watching Hilda's journey.

"Excuse me," he said getting up suddenly and moving to the other room. The whole party looked at each other and, taking their cue from Diedrick, and followed him.

At the far corner of the next room was Hilda. She had just killed a mouse. Kant applauded her and then turned to Diedrick. "You see she was after a mouse after all."

Diedrick replied, "How queer! I could have sworn that—"

"I knew it wasn't Wolf," Frieda said. "That was just a misunderstanding."

Everyone nodded and returned to the table.

Why didn't you say to them then that this was the perfect instance of mistaken causation? That big bore was only interested in browbeating you into submission. He thinks he's so fine: such a wide-ranging reputation that he's known from the Ruhr to Bavaria to Warsaw. Who am I to confront such a luminary? I who never venture from my provincial realm and my mid-afternoon walks along the river.

When the *Apfelkuchen*[3] came everyone was happy. Frieda told the group how she had been testing several recipes and thought this was the best. Even Wolf seemed serene as he gulped down the sweet.

Diedrick wiped his mouth and declared, "You know Frieda's right. The status of a recipe is much like mathematics and natural philosophy. You have a plan of necessary principles that you impose upon the world to make it intelligible. As our luminary Christian Wolff has said, metaphysics is a demonstrative a priori science that fills out Leibniz's Principle of Sufficient Reason. You said as much, too, in your Inaugural Lecture, Herr Professor."

"Yes, I know. You came to the lecture. I appreciated that. It showed friendship."

"Of course, old man, you've paid your dues in full. But back to our topic of conversation, if I may?"

Kant waved him on with a hand gesture.

"Well, I wanted to get back to that issue of cause and effect."

Kant twisted his head. "Well, in the example of the cat—"

"Damn the cat!" Diedrick said with some force and thumped the table with his fist.

I should have stopped him right there.

"Darling!" interjected Frieda putting her hand on her husband's arm. Wolf was grinning.

"That shows nothing, Immanuel. Look, there are two cases. In case one, it is my son, Wolf, who caused your cat Hilda to flee due to his roughhousing with her earlier. In case two, it is the presence of the mouse that caused the cat to scamper away. In either situation, there is a clear and necessary cause that can completely and univocally account for the cat's behavior. Could anyone disagree?"

"And what if the cat just decided to run at that very moment and then saw the mouse?" put Kant as he signaled Lampe to bring the coffee.

---

3 *Apfelkuchen*: apple cake.

"Then that's case three. It changes nothing."

"There are no uncaused events because that would violate Leibniz's Principle of Sufficient Reason?"

"Quite."

"But what if the connection between cause and effect were not necessary but only contingent?"

"Why would that ever occur? It doesn't matter how many alternate cases you provide, they simply become case *n*."

"And how do we *know* this?"

"Why from our rigorous definitions, of course. You've said as much yourself. I've heard you."

The coffee came. Kant was careful about ordering the beans himself and mixing them. He took pride in his blending. "Well, I'm not so sure about this," he said as they all took a cup of coffee. Diedrick smiled as if he were the victor. Most philosophers picture themselves in imaginary jousts with their opponents. The thrill of victory is one to be savored over a steaming hot cup of exotic coffee!

———————

It had hung over his head all night: the Inaugural Lecture. For this reason, he took a copy of the program with him on his walk. He had to get things straight in his mind. He agreed with much of what Dietrich had said, but the mix just wasn't right. Was he, Kant, changing his opinion? How much had his head been turned by Hume's skeptical naturalism?

It's not easy to argue when you are fiddling with many of the ways you view the world. Personal worldview alteration is a complicated endeavor—especially for a careful philosopher like Kant. He came to a bridge where he stopped and opened the program again. It had been a turning point in his life. It meant real professional work. No more tutoring of kids and odd jobs.

How proud he was when he delivered his exposition. Why was it that now he felt extreme ambivalence about the whole thing? Kant leaned over the bridge railing. He was in rapture over the sound of the river beneath the bridge on its way to the sea. What a mysterious force a river was. On the opposite bank were the final tulips of spring: red, yellow, and white.

Then there was a sudden forceful gust of cold air. It was not uncommon for there to be cold air in April. The gust startled him, and he lost grip of his program. The piece of paper flew from his hands, danced about in the powerful flow of air, and lazily swirled into the rushing stream flowing to the sea.

Immanuel Kant watched the piece of paper rush away. He took a deep breath. It invigorated him. He was a new man: it was time to go back home and get to work.

■ READING AND DISCUSSION QUESTIONS

1. When Kant is in bed he looks about his room and describes it as a painting. In what way is a painting like space? In what way is it different? What caused the aberration in sensation?

2. When Kant has both eyes open, the space changes. Which space experience is correct? What does "correct" mean here?

3. On this day time is also different for Kant. When he meets the fly, the philosopher wonders about the fly's experience of the room (along with the mouse's and his cat's). How can we rank various sorts of sensory experience? Is the scale of nature the answer? Why or why not?

4. How does the sequential ordering of perception alter our judgment of the result? Are such orderings in a subject's power? What does this tell us about the place of time in our perceptual experience?

5. Go to the Internet and look up Christian Wolff. If Kant's awakening indicates a change in his thinking, then how does Wolff represent the old Kant?

6. Kant muses on human connection. Do you think that Diedrick, his wife, Frieda, or their son, Wolf, would ever have such a conjecture? Why or why not?

7. Diedrick believes that metaphysics is detached from epistemology much as conventional mathematics. Are rationalism and empiricism at war here? What is at stake?

8. What are the dynamics of the Halle family? Do you think that this family's worldview will be likely to encourage the sort of skepticism that René Descartes endorsed?

9. When Hilda, the cat, enters and exits the room, the Halles mistake the cause. What about their philosophical worldview might incline the Halles to other mistakes concerning causation? Evaluate the ensuing discussion.

10. Evaluate the scene where Kant stands on the bridge. How do the various symbols reflect the changes he is going through?

■ FICTIVE-NARRATIVE PHILOSOPHY FEEDBACK

What claims are made in this story? Write them out in a bulleted list and include whether they are made through dialogue, dramatic action, or the presentation of the scene (including descriptive detail). One page. Then choose either a short direct-discourse response (according to the rules in Chapter 2) or a short fictive-narrative presentation (according to the rules in Chapter 3).

ON GEOMETRICAL METHOD AND THE METHOD OF METAPHYSICS

Gottfried Wilhelm Freiherr von Leibniz

Adapted from *Discourse on Metaphysics*, ed. Albert R. Chandler, trans. George Montgomery (1902) (LaSalle, IL: Open Court, 1924). *Note on the translation:* English words found in brackets are inserted by the translator to make better sense of the English rendering.

Gottfried Wilhelm Freiherr von Leibniz (1646–1716) was a gifted German thinker in several fields, including mathematics (he coinvented a form of calculus), physics, logic, and philosophy. Leibniz's full metaphysical system consists of only God and principles of bare individuation called "monads." It is a mathematically appealing system that prompted Alfred North Whitehead (another philosopher-mathematician) to modify it in his book Process and Reality, *which stood as cornerstone of process philosophy and theology. Within the artificial constructs of Leibniz's comprehensive, mathematically styled system, all commonly understood concepts, such as causation, space, time, and the physical world, are redefined. Leibniz stands as a paradigm of the so-called rationalist Enlightenment thinker.*

This text samples several of Leibniz's key notions: the axiomatic method (from geometry), how the Principle of Sufficient Reason stands alongside the Principle of Noncontradiction in grounding logic, the predicate-in-subject theory, and modalities of necessity. For specific guidance on technical terms, the reader is encouraged to look to the footnotes for further explication. Leibniz and his follower Christian Wolff provide a dramatic backdrop for David Hume and Kant to follow.

On Geometrical Method and Its Application

It is laudable to wish to apply the geometrical method to metaphysical matters, but we must admit that until now it has rarely been done with success. Monsieur Descartes himself, with all his undeniably great skill, never had less success than when he attempted it in one of his Replies to Objections.[4] For it is easier to be successful in mathematics, where numbers,

---

4 **Replies to Objections:** in his *Meditations* (1641), French philosopher and mathematician René Descartes (1596–1650) included objections to his arguments from leading thinkers along with his replies to those objections.

diagrams, and calculations make up for the hidden defects of words; in metaphysics, where we lack such aids (at least in usual matters of reasoning), that lack must be compensated for by a rigorous form of reasoning and exact definitions of terms; but we see neither there. . . . As everything in geometry can be explained by calculation with numbers and also by an analysis of the spatial situation— although certain problems are more easily solved by the first of these two methods and others by the second—in the same way I find there are diverse ways of considering phenomena. Everything can be explained by efficient and final causes,[5] but whatever concerns reasonable substances (the minds of men) is more naturally explained by the consideration of ends, whereas other substances (bodies) are better explained by efficient causes.

The Principle of Sufficient Reason

All other developments depend on the principle that the whole is greater than the part, as everything Euclid established in his *Elements*[6] with the sole aid of addition and subtraction; on the other hand, the determination of the resultant *conatus* of two forces (equal but acting in different directions) depends on a principle of higher rank: *nothing happens without a reason.* The consequences of this principle are that we must avoid unstable changes as much as possible, that between contraries the middle term should be selected, that we may add what we please to a term provided no other term is harmed by doing so; and still many other consequences are important in political science. . . . This most noble Principle of Sufficient Reason is the apex of rationality in motion. . . .[7]

The Two Truths Grounding All Knowledge

There are two first principles of all reasoning, the principle of contradiction . . . and the principle that a reason must be given, that is, that every true proposition that is not known per se [in or through itself] has an a priori proof[8] or that a

---

5 **efficient and . . . final causes:** based on Aristotle's theory of the four causes. The efficient cause brings something to be due to the motions of the matter involved. The material cause brings something to be through the material properties of the objects. The formal cause brings something to be due to the essence of the constituent objects. The final cause is the purpose for the sake of which some outcome comes to be.

6 **Euclid . . . *Elements*:** Euclid (flourished about 300 BCE), Greek mathematician called the Father of Geometry for his *Elements*, a book of rigorous mathematical proofs.

7 **rationality of motion:** refers to the conjecture that there are independent laws of nature that cover all natural events that are identically constructed. In other words, there is no randomness to natural events. This principle of physics was still a matter of debate at the time.

8 **a priori proof:** a proof based solely on deductions that are independent of experience, such as 3 + 4 = 7. They are called a priori because they come from posits that are accepted prior to any experience. The opposite sort of proposition is a posteriori and is derived from sense experience, literally *from out of experience.*

reason can be given for every truth, or, as is commonly said, that nothing happens without a cause (the Principle of Sufficient Reason). Arithmetic and geometry do not need this principle, but physics and mechanics do, and Archimedes[9] employed it. . . .

Theory of Truth

In demonstration I use two principles, of which one is that what implies a contradiction is false, the other is that a reason can be given for every truth (which is not identical or immediate), that is, that the notion of the predicate is always expressly or implicitly contained in the notion of its subject[10] and that this holds good no less in extrinsic than in intrinsic denominations,[11] no less in contingent than in necessary truths. [12] . . .

[This can be shown by reference to Julius Caesar.] For if some individual could complete the whole demonstration and so prove this connection of the subject (which is Caesar) with the predicate (which is his successful enterprise [winning the battle of Pharsalus, etc.]), he would then be able to demonstrate that the future dictatorship of Caesar had its roots within him—why he resolved to cross the Rubicon[13] rather than stop, and why he won rather than lost the battle at Pharsalus.[14]

The demonstration of this predicate of Caesar (that he resolved to cross the Rubicon) is not as absolute as those of numbers or of geometry,[15] but it presupposes the series of things that God has chosen freely

---

9 **Archimedes:** Archimedes of Syracuse (c. 287–c. 212 BCE), Greek mathematician, engineer, and inventor.

10 **predicate . . . subject:** Leibniz's *predicate-in-subject* posit is important to his construction of his monad theory (his comprehensive metaphysical system). This is how it works: truth is said to be a proposition in which the predicate is contained within the subject. Kant called such propositions "analytic." An example would be "All bachelors are unmarried males." If one knows either the subject or the predicate, then one has the other half as well. In this case, Leibniz is inclined to begin with the predicate, such as "unmarried males." Thus, if one understands the predicate, then he already has the subject, "bachelors," as well.

11 **extrinsic . . . intrinsic denominations:** *intrinsic* propositions and demonstrations deal with predicates that attach to the subject necessarily—that is, they cannot be otherwise. *Extrinsic* propositions and demonstrations can be otherwise, and the predicates accidentally attach themselves to a subject. Leibniz is a little fuzzy on this, as per his predicate-in-subject formulation, see footnote 16.

12 **contingent . . . necessary truths:** *necessary truths* connect to intrinsic predication in such a way that they cannot be doubted, while *contingent truths* connect to extrinsic predication such that the outcome may or may not be doubted.

13 **Caesar . . . Rubicon:** the roman general Julius Caesar (100–44 BCE) faced a choice: remain north of the Rubicon River with his army to preserve peace, or cross the river and precipitate civil war. He chose to cross, and defeated Pompey the Great at the battle of Pharsalus.

14 Because of a break in the text, Michael Boylan has added this similar selection from Leibniz's *Discourse on Metaphysics*, section 13.

15 **not as absolute as . . . geometry:** this is a rather controversial point. In his predicate-in-subject theory that the proposition "A is A" (the postulate of identity), Leibniz says that the predicate is

and that is founded on the first free decree of God, namely, to do always what is most perfect, and on the decree that God has made (in consequence of the first) with regard to human nature that man will always do (though freely) what appears best. Now every truth that is founded on decrees of this kind is contingent, although it is certain. . . . All contingent propositions have reasons for being as they are rather than otherwise, or (what is the same thing) they have a priori proofs of their truth that render them certain and show that the connection of subject and predicate in these propositions has its foundation in the nature of the one and the other; but they do not have demonstrations of necessity since these reasons are only founded on the principle of contingency, or of the existence of things, that is, on what is or appears the best among several equally possible things. . . .

Modalities of Necessity

As there is an infinity of possible worlds,[16] there is also an infinity of laws, some proper to one, others to another, and each possible individual of any world contains in its own notion the laws of its world. I think you will concede that not everything possible exists. But when this is admitted, it follows that it is not from absolute necessity but from some other reason (as good, order, perfection) that some possibles obtain existence rather than others.

---

contained within the subject via a relation of identity. This could mean that the connection between the predicate and subject in all intrinsic propositions is such that they connect necessarily. Some have suggested that this might mean that Caesar must have crossed the Rubicon. If this extension were correct, then free will would be obliterated. But Leibniz denies this by parsing further the nature of predicate-in-subject connections in cases of extrinsic predication leading to contingent truths.

16 **an infinity of possible worlds:** Leibniz put forth the notion of possible worlds (as did Henry More in Cambridge). If one not only considers necessity from the standpoint of earth as we know it now but extends it around the galaxy and to other dimensions, then a stronger sense of necessity emerges. In thinking about this, it is important to note the power of Galileo and his telescope in bringing such possible thought constructs to people's minds. This move is also important in constructing the ambitious monadology.

■ READING AND DISCUSSION QUESTIONS

1. If metaphysics aspires to explore what objects exist, how they exist, and how they are arranged, then how can axiomatic geometry [Euclid] aid us in this endeavor?
2. What is the Principle of Sufficient Reason? How does it affect the worldview of a scientist?
3. The Principle of Noncontradiction says that you cannot have the conjunction of opposites at the same time: for example, you cannot be pregnant and not pregnant at the same time. There is no such state as "a little pregnant." Aristotle sets

this as the cornerstone of logic. Now Leibniz puts the Principle of Sufficient Reason alongside it. Do you agree with him on its fundamental nature?

4. Give an example of Leibniz's predicate-in-subject approach and then evaluate how well you think it describes the truth of predication.

5. Think about other worlds (universes or dimensions). What common truths that you accept now might be false there? Are there any truths that you believe cannot change? Why?

■ CLASS EXERCISES

A. *Direct logical discourse:* Using the tools found in Chapter 2, outline the argument from one of the sections. Based on your assessment of one key premise, write a one-page argument about why you agree or disagree with the argument's conclusion.

B. *Fictive-narrative philosophy:* Using the tools found in Chapter 3, begin with a claim that relates to the reading and discussion questions above. Then create a modern-day story about people or situations familiar to you that makes the logical claim you have identified. Three pages.

THREE TYPES OF HUMAN KNOWLEDGE: HISTORY, PHILOSOPHY, AND MATHEMATICS

Christian Wolff

Adapted from Christian Wolff, *Preliminary Discourse on Philosophy in General*, trans. Richard J. Blackwell (Indianapolis: Bobbs-Merrill, 1963), 3–14. *Note on the translation:* English words found in brackets are inserted by the translator to make better sense of the English rendering.

Christian Wolff (1679–1754) was a German philosopher who historically came between Leibniz and Kant. In his preface to the Critique of Pure Reason, *Kant calls Wolff the greatest of the dogmatic philosophers. Kant also refers to him as the "celebrated Wolff." Wolff, like Leibniz (and others of the period), believed that mathematics and axiomatic geometry offered a methodological model of how philosophy should proceed.*

Wolff's philosophy (like Leibniz's) seeks the certainty and necessity of mathematics as it fashions a metaphysical account. Wolff in fact taught more courses in mathematics than he did philosophy. He was one of the first professors in Germany to teach calculus and was responsible for bringing the German mathematical curriculum up to a modern standard. He was also interested in making philosophy relevant to a wider audience (which began from his publishing much of his work in German rather than Latin). On the divisions of knowledge, Wolff parsed two major categories: common (or natural) knowledge and scientific (exact) knowledge. Scientific (exact) knowledge is in turn divided into historical, philosophical, and mathematical categories. The following excerpt discusses the categories of this higher form of human knowledge.

The Three Sorts of Direct Knowledge[17]

1. By means of the senses we know things that are and occur in the material world. And the mind is conscious of the changes that occur within itself. No one is ignorant of this. Let one merely direct one's attention to one's self.

Led by the senses, we know that animals, vegetables, and minerals exist; the sun rises and sets; man who is guided by

---

17 **Three Sorts of Direct Knowledge:** for Wolff there are three sorts of knowledge that can be known directly: (a) our own personal existence, (b) the existence of a material world outside of us, and (c) our certainty about our knowledge of a and b (compare with item 20 below).

reason is the least powerful of the beasts; the soul can remember the past; what is unknown is not desired.

2. We are not now investigating how far the senses can penetrate in their knowledge of things that are and occur in the material world or of whether the soul is conscious of all the things that occur within it. These problems will be treated elsewhere. For the present it is sufficient to point out that knowledge acquired by the senses and by attention to ourselves cannot be called into doubt. We do not here belabor the limits of this knowledge, for this would be of no use in the present discussion.

Historical Knowledge

3. Knowledge of those things that are and occur either in the material world or in immaterial substances is called history.

For example, historical knowledge is possessed by him who knows from experience that the sun rises in the morning and sets in the evening, that at the beginning of spring the buds of trees blossom forth, that animals are propagated by generation, that we desire nothing except under the aspect of good.

4. Things that are or occur possess a reason from which it is understood why they are or occur. The truth of this statement is clear from examples, assuming that we provide sufficient attention and the required acumen.

For example, a rainbow is not produced unless the rays of the sun fall upon water droplets arranged according to a definite law. Rain does not fall unless the heavens are covered with clouds and the condition of the air is conducive for the generation of rain. The mind does not desire a given object unless it has judged it to be good. The mind desires only the good because it perceives pleasure in the good.

5. I will not at this time explain the previous statement more clearly; nor will I prove its universality.[18] We will investigate this matter more carefully elsewhere. Here it is sufficient if we affirm only what agrees with experience. Nor is it possible to present contrary examples of things that completely lack a reason. I do not deny that examples can be given where the reason is hidden. But at least I do deny that there are examples in which it can be clearly shown that no reason is present. Nor is it our task here to prove the universality of what has been asserted. It is sufficient that everyone ought to concede that there are very many cases in which the truth of the previous assertion is evident. Nor do we hold that the reason of things that are or occur is completely known by us, except where we have produced the reason for all to see. Therefore, for our present purposes it makes no difference whether the universality of what has been asserted is accepted or called into doubt or completely rejected. We are

---

18 **nor will I prove its universality:** Wolff believes in a sort of intuitionism akin to what Euclid appealed to in the creation of his axiomatic geometry. One begins with the acceptance of fundamental posits (called postulates) and then proceeds along with an intuited rule of inference to prove various theorems. Such is the mathematically based methodology of the time.

proposing no qualifications regarding our knowledge of reasons.

Philosophical Knowledge

6. The knowledge of the reason [why] of things that are or occur is called philosophy.[19]

For example, he has philosophical knowledge of the motion of the water in a riverbed who can explain in an intelligible way how this motion depends on the slope of the bottom and on the pressure from the higher water that the lower water sustains. Also, he has philosophical knowledge of appetition[20] who can show the reason why the desire for a given object arises from the knowledge of the object.

7. Philosophical knowledge differs from historical knowledge. The latter consists in the bare knowledge of the fact (#3). The former progresses further and exhibits the reason of the fact so that it be understood why something of this sort could occur (#6). Who, indeed, does not see a great difference here? Bare knowledge of the fact and knowledge of the reason of that fact are by no means the same thing.

For example, it is one thing to know that water flows in the bed of a river, and it is quite another thing to know that this occurs because of the slope of the bottom and because of the pressure that the lower water sustains from the higher. The first states the fact; the second contains the reason of the fact.

8. He who knows the reason of a fact that is alleged by another man has historical knowledge of the philosophical knowledge of another. For he who knows the reason of a fact alleged by another man knows what that man's philosophical knowledge is in the given case (#6). Now the philosophical knowledge of another man is a fact. Therefore, he knows a fact about another man, and consequently he has historical knowledge of the philosophical knowledge of that other man.

For example, a man knows that Isaac Newton[21] said that the cause of the elliptical motion of the primary planets and comets around the sun and of the secondary planets around the primary—for example, the satellite of Jupiter around Jupiter, the satellite of Saturn around Saturn, and the moon around the earth—is

---

19 **knowledge of the reason . . . philosophy:** for Wolff, the "reason why" is merely a logical exercise and not a subject of critical empiricism. It harkens back to Book One of Aristotle's *Posterior Analytics* in which he examines why stars twinkle. Option A is that stars twinkle because they are far away; option B says that the stars are far away because they twinkle. Aristotle opts for option A because he thinks there is a purer sense of logical causation. In other words, in option A we can imagine star *x* that does not twinkle but would when moved sufficiently far away from the center of the universe, Earth. This is the sort of causal formula that Wolff seeks to bring about.

20 **appetition:** desire; seeking or longing for.

21 **Isaac Newton:** Sir Isaac Newton (1643–1727), English mathematician, physicist, and astronomer. Wolff was one of the first teachers of Newton's calculus in Germany.

an impressed force and the force of gravity by which they are moved either toward the sun as a center or toward a primary planet as a center. Such a man has historical knowledge of the philosophical knowledge of a great man concerning the motion of the planets and comets. For he knows a fact, namely, what Newton thought concerning the physical causes of the elliptical motion of the planets and comets.

9. If one does not know how to demonstrate that the reason alleged by another for a fact is indeed the reason of that fact, then he lacks philosophical knowledge of the fact. He only knows that a certain reason for a fact has been alleged by another. He does not know why this is the reason of the fact, and thus it must be said that he does not know the reason. And who would doubt that in this case he lacks philosophical knowledge (#6)?

For example, let there be someone who knows that Newton held that the cause of the elliptical motion of the primary planets around the sun and of the secondary planets around the primary planets is the impressed force and gravity of the primary planets toward the sun as a center and of the secondary planets toward the primary planets. Unless he can distinctly explain how circular, and especially elliptical, motion arises from an impressed force and gravity toward the center of the body about which a revolution takes place, and thus can demonstrate that the planets are moved by an impressed force and are turned away from rectilinear motion by the force of gravity, he does not possess philosophical knowledge of celestial motions.

10. Historical knowledge provides the foundation for philosophical knowledge insofar as experience establishes those things from which the reason can be given for other things that are and occur or can occur. Things that are established by experience are known by historical knowledge (#3). And if from this you discover the reason of other things that are and occur, you have built up philosophical knowledge (#6). Therefore, history is the foundation of philosophical knowledge.

For example, let there be someone who knows from experiments that air has both weight and elasticity, although he does not know the cause of its weight and elasticity. From this he discovers the reason for the ascent of water in pumps and in artificial fountains, for example, the fountain of Hero.[22] Such a person has historical knowledge of the weight and elasticity of air. Upon this he builds philosophical knowledge of water ascending in pumps and flowing from fountains.

11. Hence, it is clear that historical knowledge must not be neglected by one who aspires to philosophy. History should precede and be constantly joined with philosophy. For when historical knowledge provides the foundation for philosophy (#10), only those things that truly exist and occur are admitted as possible (#3). And thus philosophical knowledge, which is built upon history, depends upon a firm and unshaken foundation. Therefore, who would deny that one who as-

---

22 **fountain of Hero:** a fountain that runs on water and air pressure, invented by Hero (or Heron) of Alexandria (c. 10–70 CE).

pires to philosophical knowledge ought to work on this foundation? Hence, history must precede philosophy and be constantly joined with it, lest a firm foundation be absent.

12. Although we have given in the foregoing (#10) only examples from physics, nevertheless what we have said above (#11) applies to all the other types of knowledge. In the abstract disciplines, such as first philosophy, the fundamental notions must be derived from experience, which establishes historical knowledge (#3). Moral and civil philosophy also seek principles. Even mathematics presupposes historical knowledge from which it derives some axioms and the notion of its object. This is my view concerning pure mathematics. In regard to mixed mathematics the same thing is more abundantly clear. Thus, although we have carefully distinguished historical knowledge from philosophy (#3, #6), lest we confuse them (#7), nevertheless we have not depreciated or condemned history (#11). Rather we have determined the proper value of both. Indeed, there is for us throughout all philosophy a holy marriage of both. Not only do we ascribe to the use of historical knowledge in philosophy, but we also defend its utility in life. Both of these points are discovered by experience. The reason for them will be explained when we discuss the use of logic.

13. Whatever is finite possesses a determinate quantity. The truth of this statement is clear from examples; we need only give sufficient attention. And the reason for this is not difficult to see. Insofar as something is finite, it can be increased and decreased. And insofar as it can be increased or decreased, quantity should be attributed to it. Hence, determinate quantity must be attributed to whatever is finite insofar as it is finite.

For example, the heat of the midday sun is not the same all year round in the same place; nor is it the same at the same time at diverse latitudes. From the winter to the summer solstice, it increases, and for the same reason it decreases from the summer to the winter solstice. Therefore, on any day of the year the midday sun possesses a determinate degree of heat that either increases or decreases from the heat of another day by an assignable quantity (such that from a knowledge of the degrees the difference can be clearly assigned). Water flows in the bed of a river with a determinate velocity, which is decreased in a less inclined artificial channel through which the water is forced by a wheel and is increased when the water runs over a precipice. Similarly a planet that revolves about the sun is at a determinate distance from the sun at every point of its orbit. The impressed force, upon which the planet depends to move through a tangent at that point, is of a determinate degree or produces a determinate velocity. Likewise, the centripetal force, by which the planet is turned away from rectilinear motion, is of a determinate degree. The same thing is to be found in immaterial things. Attention in different men differs by degrees. One man's attention is greater; another's is smaller. One man can sustain his attention in conceiving and working out a long demonstration; another man's attention is exhausted by a shorter demonstration. Who does not know that there are various degrees of virtue and vice for a diversity of subjects?

Mathematical Knowledge

14. Knowledge of the quantity of things is called mathematics.

For example, he has mathematical knowledge of the heat of the midday sun who knows its quantity. He perceives the ratio or proportion of the heat on given days. For example, he compares the heat of the midday sun at the summer solstice with the heat of the midday sun at the winter solstice, and he concludes that the former is so many times greater than the latter. Similarly he has mathematical knowledge of the motion of a river who knows how a determinate degree of velocity, by which water flows through a riverbed, is produced by the slope of the bottom and by the depth of the water. He has mathematical knowledge of the motion of a planet in orbit who can clearly explain how at a given point of the orbit or at a given distance from the sun, the velocity of the planet depends on the quantity of the impressed and centripetal force, and how from the action of this double force on the planet an elliptical figure is produced in the orbit. He has mathematical knowledge of attention who perceives the ratio or proportion between the attention required by a longer demonstration and that which is sufficient for a shorter demonstration.

15. He who knows the quantity of a thing that is assigned by someone else has historical knowledge of that other man's mathematical knowledge. For he who knows what quantity another assigns to a finite thing knows a fact about that other man. And since history is knowledge of the fact (#3), and mathematics is knowledge of quantity (#14), he who only knows the quantity of a thing that is assigned by another merely has historical knowledge of the other's mathematical knowledge.

For example, Newton demonstrated the quantity of the centripetal force of the planets revolving elliptically around the sun and their velocity at any given point of the orbit.[23] He who knows how much centripetal force and velocity Newton designated for a planet at a given point of the orbit or at a given distance from the sun has historical knowledge of Newton's mathematical knowledge of the motion of the planets.

16. If one can demonstrate the quantity assigned to a thing by another, then he as well as the other has mathematical knowledge of that thing. For he who can demonstrate the quantity of a thing knows the quantity of that thing and therefore has mathematical knowledge of the thing (#14). And although another assigned that quantity first, and hence had prior mathematical knowledge of the thing (#14), this does not affect the later knowledge. For the difference that he seeks is not from an extrinsic principle but is intrinsic to the thing.

For example, let there be someone who can demonstrate, either with Newton's

---

23 **Newton demonstrated . . . orbit:** before calculus, natural science could not quantify in theory. This third stage of scientific knowledge was emerging during the era in which Wolff lived. It marked a historical change in how one might explain causes. Wolff was quick to see this and set it forward to a broad audience.

proof or with another proof, the quantity of the centripetal force and the velocity of a planet revolving elliptically around the sun at a given distance from the sun. Both this man and Newton have mathematical knowledge of the elliptical motion of the planets. The knowledge itself is not affected by the fact that Newton had it first.

17. Mathematical knowledge differs from both historical and philosophical knowledge. For history rests in the bare knowledge of the fact (#3). In philosophy we discover the reason of things that are or can be (#6). And in mathematics we determine the quantities that are present in things. It is one thing to know the fact, another thing to perceive the reason of the fact, and still another thing to determine the quantity of things.

Examples clearly illustrate this difference. He who knows that the heat of the midday sun sometimes increases and sometimes decreases has historical knowledge. He who knows that a greater degree of heat depends on a greater density of the rays striking a plane and on a less oblique angle of incidence has philosophical knowledge. And he who can determine the density of the rays and the size of the angle, and hence the degree of heat, has mathematical knowledge. It is indeed clear that the determination of the density of the rays, the size of the angle, and the consequent degree of heat is different from the simple knowledge that the heat of the midday sun is greater at one time than at another. It is no less clear that such a determination also

differs from a knowledge of the cause of a greater or lesser degree of heat. The same thing is clear from the other examples that we have previously used.

18. Sometimes historical knowledge and sometimes philosophical knowledge provides the foundation for mathematical knowledge. This fact is proven by examples. It is not our task to explain here why this can occur and when the one and when the other applies.

My treatise entitled *Optici* [*Optics*, 1741] in the *Catoptrica* provides mathematical knowledge of the reflected vision produced by mirrors.[24] It establishes propositions concerning the process of reflection and the place of the image that are derived from observation and must be treated as axioms; for example, the angle of reflection is equal to the angle of incidence, and the place of the image is the intersection of the reflected rays with the perpendicular. However, there is very little interest in why the angle of reflection is equal to the angle of incidence and in why the image appears at the intersection of the reflected rays with the perpendicular. And astronomers derive mathematical knowledge of celestial motions from observation independently of the physical causes involved. In forming a mathematical theory of the motion of heavy things, Galileo[25] did not treat the cause of this motion. Rather he was satisfied by the fact that the cause of gravity, whatever it might be, acts on a heavy body in the same way at any distance from the center of the earth. But

---

24 **knowledge of mirrors:** Wolff shows here that he is putting his theory into practice. It is part of Wolff's emphasis of making philosophy relevant to the world in which he lived.

25 **Galileo:** Galileo Galilei (1564–1642), Italian astronomer and physicist.

he who tries to establish mathematical knowledge of the varying heat of the midday sun ought to know the causes of this variation (#17). In the *Elementa aerometriae* [*Elements of Aerometry*, 1709] I have shown how mathematics is applied to experiments when the causes are not yet known and how effects are proportionate to the power of their causes. Hence, there are examples that illustrate both cases.[26]

19. There can be historical knowledge of mathematical truths. For things that are demonstrated by mathematical principles, especially in mixed mathematics, can also be seen to be so by experiments.[27] Therefore, those who teach the truth of mathematical theorems by appealing to experience provide true historical knowledge of these theorems (#3), even though they might be ignorant of the mathematical demonstrations (#16).

In pure mathematics, corresponding to these experiments are the numerical examples, which illustrate the theorems, and the mechanical examination of the figures that are constructed next to the proposed theorems. Those who neglect the demonstrations and are satisfied with these examples have only historical knowledge of mathematical truths.

Common and Secret Historical Knowledge

20. The facts of nature are sometimes so hidden that they do not spontaneously present themselves to one who is attentive. The truth of this statement is not unknown by those who have become so versed in the sciences that they are not satisfied with what they already know and thus investigate the way in which the principles are established.

For example, the light of the sun by nature comprises different rays or lights. But this fact is not at all evident. It does not offer itself spontaneously to one who contemplates the light of the sun. Nor is it known without hesitation from experiments on illuminated objects. Indeed it must be demonstrated that the light of the sun is composite by means of the circumstances of the experiment, which makes this fact perceptible to sight. It must be proven with special demonstrations that the lights from which the light of the sun is composed are both simple and heterogeneous. Many experiments and other knowledge from history, philosophy, and mathematics are required in order that what should be proven here can be proven with clarity. All of this is quite apparent in Newton's *Optics*,[28] where this hidden fact of nature was revealed for us. The same is also to be seen throughout the whole of experimental philosophy. Astronomy also sheds light for us on this argument. And when we treat psychology and moral philosophy, further examples will occur.

21. While some facts of nature are hidden (#20), others are so apparent (#1) that they require only attention and, of course,

---

26 **examples illustrate both cases:** another example of Wolff making philosophy relevant to the times.

27 **mixed mathematics:** in today's parlance, this might be rendered as either "experimental science" or "engineering."

28 **Newton's *Optics*:** Isaac Newton published his experiments on light and colors in his *Opticks* (1704).

some acumen. The hidden facts must be brought to light by skilled investigators, and even then they are not known unless reason gives its assistance to the senses. As a result we distinguish between common and secret historical knowledge. The former is a knowledge of the facts of nature, including rational nature, which are apparent. The latter is a knowledge of the facts of nature, including rational nature, which are hidden.

I add the phrase "including rational nature" to emphasize that the facts of nature also include those things that occur in finite, immaterial substances, as for example our own minds. These are objects of historical knowledge no less than things that happen in the material world (#3). For examples of common historical knowledge, see #3, and for examples of secret historical knowledge, see #20.

22. Common historical knowledge is the lowest grade of human knowledge. For historical knowledge is acquired by the senses attending to things that actually are or occur (#1, #3). Hence, it does not presuppose any prior knowledge from which as premises it ought to deduce a great labyrinth of proofs. Therefore, there is no type of knowledge that is inferior to common historical knowledge.

23. And thus the reason is clear why vulgar knowledge and knowledge of things that we use in life and of many other things is historical. For with vulgar knowledge we go no further than those things that we first notice by means of the senses. And if we happen to know the reasons and causes of things because they are apparent

to the senses, nevertheless we do not distinctly perceive how the one thing can be the cause of the other or how this or that occurs because of this reason. Examples confirm what we have said.

For example, everyone knows that water boils on a fire because they have seen this occur many times. But they do not know why the water boils; indeed very few ever even think about this. And although the heat of the fire is the cause of the boiling, this vulgar knowledge is only historical. For the mere notion that an effect arises from the conjunction of two things is quite different from a distinct explanation of how the effect can occur. And thus this is not philosophical knowledge (#3, #6).

24. Art often reduces secret historical knowledge to common historical knowledge. The operations of art and also experiments often bring to light facts of nature that otherwise would be hidden. Hence it makes no difference to the knower whether nature presents things to the senses or whether art provides the senses with things that otherwise would escape their notice. With the help supplied by art, only attention and acumen are needed to arrive at the contents of both secret and common historical knowledge. Therefore, by means of art, secret knowledge is reduced to common knowledge.

For example, the art of fusing metals exhibits to the observer the hidden properties and effects of fire. Experiments that use pneumatic pumps reveal the hidden properties and effects of air. Examples are given by Emanuel Swedenborg,[29] assessor

---

29 **Emanuel Swedenborg:** Swedish scientist (1688–1772).

of the metallurgical faculty in Sweden, in his *Nova observata circa ferrum et ignem*[30] and *Observationes miscellaneae circa res naturales*.[31] In the former work, he relates how heat was applied to carbon for ten or twelve days after the carbon had been shielded on every side. Although no spark of fire appeared in the carbon, the mass of the carbon was decreased to one-tenth its original size by the heat. However, over an open forge, after about a quarter or half-hour, fire and flames erupted spontaneously, as it were, and covered the surface. A piece of carbon that was not well burnt in a crack of the wall was hung by itself and began to burn when in free contact with the air. The flames were very volatile and circled around as if licking the surface of the carbon, without any spark appearing in the carbon.

Confirmation of Philosophical Knowledge

25. Hence, it follows that philosophy would be helped if phenomena observed in the workshops of craftsmen and elsewhere in the arts (for example, in rural economy) were collected and accurately described. For such things constitute a part of secret historical knowledge (#21) that cannot be obtained otherwise by the senses (#24). And thus, they provide a foundation for philosophical knowledge that otherwise we would lack (#10).

26. If one knows by reason that something can occur, and by experimentation he observes that this does occur, then he confirms philosophical knowledge with history. For he who knows by reason that something can occur has philosophical knowledge (#6). And he who observes that this same thing does occur has historical knowledge (#3). Therefore, since that which he knows by reason can occur is observed as actually occurring, historical knowledge agrees with philosophical knowledge. Since one cannot doubt whether that which is observed actually to occur can occur, this historical knowledge is placed beyond all chance of doubt, and the philosophical knowledge is clearly confirmed by the historical knowledge.

Hence, the reason is clear why we must constantly join historical and philosophical knowledge (#12), even though they are not the same, as we have explained above (#11).

27. If the quantity of an effect is shown to be proportionate to the power of the cause, then philosophical knowledge acquires complete certitude from mathematics. For he who proves that the quantity of an effect is proportionate to the power of the cause has mathematical knowledge (#14). And he who knows the cause of an effect has philosophical knowledge (#6). Hence, if it can be demonstrated that the quantity of an effect does not exceed the power of the cause to which we attribute it, then mathematical knowledge agrees with philosophical knowledge. And since an effect cannot more evidently proceed from a cause than where the quantity of

---

30 *Nova . . . ignem*: *New Observations on Iron and Fire.*
31 *Observationes . . . naturales*: *Miscellaneous Observations on Natural Things.*

the effect is equal to the power of the cause, philosophical knowledge acquires complete certitude from mathematics.

In the preface to the *Elementa aerometriae*, which I first published in 1709, I have already warned that the certitude of physical knowledge depends in many ways on mathematics. And in order that I might give visible proof, I wrote out these mathematical elements for physics, which applies mathematics to experiments. Later in my *Hydraulica matheseos* [Hydraulic *Mechanics*, a part of his *Mathematical Elements of the Universe*, 1741], I have applied them to the elements of the universe because of their considerable usefulness.

28. Hence, it follows that mathematical knowledge must be joined to philosophy if you desire the highest possible certitude.

For this reason we also grant a place in philosophy to mathematical knowledge, even though we have distinguished it from philosophy (#17). For we hold that nothing is more important than certitude.

■ READING AND DISCUSSION QUESTIONS

1. For Wolff what are the three sorts of direct knowledge? How is this different from secret or obscure knowledge?
2. Wolff contends that sense impressions cannot be called into doubt. Contrast this position to Descartes in the *Meditations*. Who is right and why?
3. Wolff thinks that history is the apprehension of some fact. Do you think that bare apprehension of a fact is possible? Can we put our worldview away and be mere mechanical recording machines?
4. Wolff says that popular acceptance is not a benchmark of truth. How is this position similar to the first argument in the "Crito"?
5. Philosophical knowledge is the reason for a fact. Wolff cites Isaac Newton as an example. Newton's reasoning is largely a priori and based on mathematics. What are the strengths and weaknesses of this approach?
6. Mathematical knowledge reveals quantities. Should this sort of knowledge be prior or posterior to philosophical knowledge? What is at stake?
7. How does Wolff think that art can bring people to secret (obscure) knowledge?

■ CLASS EXERCISES

A. *Direct logical discourse:* Using the tools found in Chapter 2, outline the argument from one of the sections above. Based on your assessment of one key premise, write a one-page argument about why you agree or disagree with the argument's conclusion.

B. *Fictive-narrative philosophy:* Using the tools found in Chapter 3, begin with a claim that relates to the reading and discussion questions above. Then create a modern-day story about people or situations familiar to you that makes the logical claim you have identified. Three pages.

OF THE ACADEMICAL OR SKEPTICAL PHILOSOPHY

David Hume

Adapted from David Hume, *An Enquiry Concerning Human Understanding* (London: A. Millar, 1748).

David Hume (1711–1776) is generally considered to be a major philosopher in the Western tradition. He broke onto the scene early with his ambitious Treatise on Human Nature *(1739–1740). He also wrote influential works on social contract theory, ethics, and economics. His six-volume* History of England *was very popular in his time. Hume is best known for his brand of mitigated skeptical empiricism. He is generally grouped with John Locke and Bishop Berkeley as one of the three great British empiricists of the age.*

In this selection Hume makes two general arguments. In parts 1 to 3, his principal claim is against modern (Descartes) and ancient (Pyrrhus) radical skepticism. Hume's claim in this regard is that only limited, mitigated skepticism can be useful. The second major claim concerns the grounds of justified intellectual belief. Hume argues that only intellectual belief based on reasoning about quantity and number or experimental fact is justifiable.

Part I: Argument Against Cartesian Doubt

There is not a greater number of philosophical reasonings displayed upon any subject than those that prove the existence of a Deity and refute the fallacies of atheists; and yet the most religious philosophers still dispute whether any man can be so blinded as to be a speculative atheist. How shall we reconcile these contradictions? The knights errant, who wandered about to clear the world of dragons and giants, never entertained the least doubt with regard to the existence of these monsters.

The skeptic is another enemy of religion, who naturally provokes the indignation of all divines and graver philosophers, though it is certain that no man ever met with any such absurd creature or conversed with a man who had no opinion or principle concerning any subject, either of action or speculation. This begets a very natural question: what is meant by a skeptic? And how far it is possible to push these philosophical principles of doubt and uncertainty?

There is a species of skepticism *antecedent* to all study and philosophy that is much inculcated by Descartes[32] and others as a sovereign preservative against error and precipitate judgment. It recommends a universal doubt, not only of all our former opinions and principles but also of our very faculties—of whose veracity, say they, we must assure ourselves by a chain of reasoning deduced from some original principle that cannot possibly be fallacious or deceitful. But neither is there any such original principle, which has a prerogative above others, that are self-evident and convincing; [nor,] if there were, could we advance a step beyond it but by the use of those very faculties of which we are supposed to be already diffident. The Cartesian[33] doubt, therefore, were it ever possible to be attained by any human creature (as it plainly is not) would be entirely incurable, and no reasoning could ever bring us to a state of assurance and conviction upon any subject.

It must, however, be confessed that this species of skepticism, when more moderate, may be understood in a very reasonable sense and is a necessary preparative to the study of philosophy by preserving a proper impartiality in our judgments and weaning our mind from all those prejudices that we may have imbibed from education or rash opinion. To begin with clear and self-evident principles, to advance by timorous and sure steps, to review frequently our conclusions and examine accurately all their consequences—though by these means we shall make both a slow and a short progress in our systems—are the only methods by which we can ever hope to reach truth and attain a proper stability and certainty in our determinations.

There is another species of skepticism *consequent* to science and enquiry, when men are supposed to have discovered either the absolute fallaciousness of their mental faculties or their unfitness to reach any fixed determination in all those curious subjects of speculation about which they are commonly employed. Even our very senses are brought into dispute by a certain species of philosophers, and the maxims of common life are subjected to the same doubt as the most profound principles or conclusions of metaphysics and theology. As these paradoxical tenets (if they may be called tenets) are to be met with in some philosophers, and the refutation of them in several, they naturally excite our curiosity and make us enquire into the arguments on which they may be founded.

I need not insist upon the more trite topics employed by the skeptics in all ages against the evidence of sense, such as those derived from the imperfection and fallaciousness of our organs, on numberless occasions; the crooked appearance of an oar in water; the various aspects of objects according to their different distances; the double images that arise from the pressing one eye; with many other appearances of a like nature. These skeptical topics, indeed, are only sufficient to prove that the senses alone are not implicitly to be depended on, but that we must correct their evidence by

---

32 **Descartes:** René Descartes (1596–1650), French philosopher and mathematician.
33 **Cartesian:** pertaining to Descartes.

reason and by considerations derived from the nature of the medium, the distance of the object, and the disposition of the organ, in order to render them, within their sphere, the proper criteria of truth and falsehood. Other more profound arguments against the senses admit not of so easy a solution.

It seems evident that men are carried by a natural instinct or prepossession to repose faith in their senses and that without any reasoning, or even almost before the use of reason, we always suppose an external universe, which depends not on our perception but would exist though we and every sensible creature were absent or annihilated. Even the animal creations are governed by a like opinion and preserve this belief of external objects in all their thoughts, designs, and actions.

It seems also evident that, when men follow this blind and powerful instinct of nature, they always suppose the very images presented by the senses to be the external objects and never entertain any suspicion that the one are nothing but representations of the other. This very table, which we see as white and feel as hard, is believed to exist, independent of our perception, and to be something external to our mind, which perceives it. Our presence bestows not being on it; our absence does not annihilate it. It preserves its existence uniform and entire, independent of the situation of intelligent beings who perceive or contemplate it.

But this universal and primary opinion of all men is soon destroyed by the slightest philosophy, which teaches us that nothing can ever be present to the mind but an image or perception and that the senses are only the inlets through which these images are conveyed, without being able to produce any immediate intercourse between the mind and the object. The table, which we see, seems to diminish as we remove farther from it. But the real table, which exists independent of us, suffers no alteration. It was, therefore, nothing but its image that was present to the mind. These are the obvious dictates of reason, and no man, who reflects, ever doubted that the existences—which we consider, when we say *this house* and *that tree*—are nothing but perceptions in the mind and fleeting copies or representations of other existences, which remain uniform and independent.

So far, then, are we necessitated by reasoning to contradict or depart from the primary instincts of nature and to embrace a new system with regard to the evidence of our senses. But here philosophy finds herself extremely embarrassed when she would justify this new system and obviate the cavils and objections of the skeptics. She can no longer plead the infallible and irresistible instinct of nature, for that led us to a quite different system, which is acknowledged fallible and even erroneous. And to justify this pretended philosophical system by a chain of clear and convincing argument, or even any appearance of argument, exceeds the power of all human capacity.

By what argument can it be proved that the perceptions of the mind must be caused by external objects, entirely different from them, though resembling them (if that be possible) and could not arise either from the energy of the mind itself, or from the suggestion of some invisible and unknown spirit, or from some other cause still more unknown to us? It is acknowledged that, in fact, many of these perceptions arise not from anything external, as in dreams, madness, and other diseases. And nothing can be more inexplicable than the manner in which body should so operate upon mind as ever to convey an image of itself to a substance, supposed of so different and even contrary a nature.

It is a question of fact whether the perceptions of the senses be produced by external objects resembling them. How shall this question be determined? By experience, surely, as all other questions of a like nature. But here experience is, and must be, entirely silent. The mind has never anything present to it but the perceptions and cannot possibly reach any experience of their connection with objects. The supposition of such a connection is, therefore, without any foundation in reasoning.

To have recourse to the veracity of the supreme Being in order to prove the veracity of our senses is surely making a very unexpected circuit. If his veracity were at all concerned in this matter, our senses would be entirely infallible because it is not possible that he can ever deceive. Not to mention that if the external world be once called in question, we shall be at a loss to find arguments by which we may prove the existence of that Being or any of his attributes.

This is a topic, therefore, in which the profounder and more philosophical skeptics will always triumph, when they endeavor to introduce a universal doubt into all subjects of human knowledge and enquiry. Do you follow the instincts and propensities of nature, may they say, in assenting to the veracity of sense? But these lead you to believe that the very perception or sensible image is the external object. Do you disclaim this principle in order to embrace a more rational opinion, that the perceptions are only representations of something external? You here depart from your natural propensities and more obvious sentiments and yet are not able to satisfy your reason, which can never find any convincing argument from experience to prove that the perceptions are connected with any external objects.

There is another skeptical topic of a like nature, derived from the most profound philosophy, which might merit our attention, were it requisite to dive so deep in order to discover arguments and reasonings that can so little serve to any serious purpose. It is universally allowed by modern enquirers that all the sensible qualities of objects—such as hard, soft, hot, cold, white, black, etc.—are merely secondary and exist not in the objects themselves but are perceptions of the mind, without any external archetype or model that they represent. If this be allowed with regard to secondary qualities, it must also follow with regard to the supposed primary qualities of extension[34] and solidity; nor can the latter be any more entitled to that denomination than the former. The idea of extension is entirely acquired from the senses of sight and feeling, and if all the qualities, perceived by the senses, be in the mind, not in the object, the same conclusion

---

34 **extension:** the property of occupying space.

must reach the idea of extension, which is wholly dependent on the sensible ideas or the ideas of secondary qualities. Nothing can save us from this conclusion but the asserting that the ideas of those primary qualities are attained by *abstraction*, an opinion, which, if we examine it accurately, we shall find to be unintelligible and even absurd. An extension that is neither tangible nor visible cannot possibly be conceived. And a tangible or visible extension that is neither hard nor soft, black nor white, is equally beyond the reach of human conception. Let any man try to conceive a triangle in general that is neither isosceles nor scalene,[35] nor has any particular length or proportion of sides, and he will soon perceive the absurdity of all the scholastic notions with regard to abstraction and general ideas.

Thus, the first philosophical objection to the evidence of sense or to the opinion of external existence consists in this: that such an opinion, if rested on natural instinct, is contrary to reason and, if referred to reason, is contrary to natural instinct, and at the same time carries no rational evidence with it to convince an impartial enquirer. The second objection goes farther and represents this opinion as contrary to reason, at least if it be a principle of reason that all sensible qualities are in the mind, not in the object. Bereave matter of all its intelligible qualities, both primary and secondary, and you in a manner annihilate it and leave only a certain unknown, inexplicable *something* as the cause of our perceptions—a notion so

imperfect that no skeptic will think it worthwhile to contend against it.

Part II: The Futility of Excessive Skepticism (Pyrrhonism)

It may seem a very extravagant attempt of the skeptics to destroy *reason* by argument and ratiocination, yet is this the grand scope of all their enquiries and disputes. They endeavor to find objections both to our abstract reasonings and to those that regard matter of fact and existence.

The chief objection against all *abstract* reasonings is derived from the ideas of space and time—ideas that, in common life and to a careless view, are very clear and intelligible, but when they pass through the scrutiny of the profound sciences (and they are the chief object of these sciences) afford principles that seem full of absurdity and contradiction. No priestly dogmas, invented on purpose to tame and subdue the rebellious reason of mankind, ever shocked common sense more than the doctrine of the infinite divisibility of extension, with its consequences, as they are pompously displayed by all geometricians and metaphysicians with a kind of triumph and exultation. A real quantity, infinitely less than any finite quantity, containing quantities infinitely less than itself, and so on ad infinitum[36]—this is an edifice so bold and prodigious that it is too weighty for any pretended demonstration to support, because it shocks the clearest and most natural principles of human reason. But what renders the matter more extraordinary is

---

35 **isosceles . . . scalene:** triangles with two equal sides (isosceles) or no equal sides (scalene).
36 **ad infinitum:** to infinity.

that these seemingly absurd opinions are supported by a chain of reasoning, the clearest and most natural; nor is it possible for us to allow the premises without admitting the consequences.

Nothing can be more convincing and satisfactory than all the conclusions concerning the properties of circles and triangles, and yet, when these are once received, how can we deny that the angle of contact between a circle and its tangent is infinitely less than any rectilinear angle, that as you may increase the diameter of the circle in infinitum, this angle of contact becomes still less, even in infinitum, and that the angle of contact between other curves and their tangents may be infinitely less than those between any circle and its tangent, and so on, in infinitum? The demonstration of these principles seems as unexceptionable as that which proves the three angles of a triangle to be equal to two right ones, though the latter opinion be natural and easy, and the former big with contradiction and absurdity. Reason here seems to be thrown into a kind of amazement and suspense, which, without the suggestions of any skeptic, gives her a diffidence of herself and of the ground on which she treads. She sees a full light that illuminates certain places, but that light borders upon the most profound darkness. And between these she is so dazzled and confounded that she scarcely can pronounce with certainty and assurance concerning any one object.

The absurdity of these bold determinations of the abstract sciences seems to become, if possible, still more palpable with regard to time than extension. An infinite number of real parts of time, passing in succession and exhausted one after another, appears so evident a contradiction that no man, one should think, whose judgment is not corrupted instead of being improved by the sciences, would ever be able to admit of it.

Yet, still reason must remain restless and unquiet, even with regard to that skepticism to which she is driven by these seeming absurdities and contradictions. How any clear, distinct idea can contain circumstances contradictory to itself or to any other clear, distinct idea is absolutely incomprehensible and is, perhaps, as absurd as any proposition that can be formed. So that nothing can be more skeptical or more full of doubt and hesitation than this skepticism itself, which arises from some of the paradoxical conclusions of geometry or the science of quantity.

The skeptical objections to *moral* evidence, or to the reasonings concerning matter of fact, are either *popular* or *philosophical*. The popular objections are derived from the natural weakness of human understanding; the contradictory opinions that have been entertained in different ages and nations; the variations of our judgment in sickness and health, youth and old age, prosperity and adversity; the perpetual contradiction of each particular man's opinions and sentiments; with many other topics of that kind. It is needless to insist farther on this head. These objections are but weak. For as in common life we reason every moment concerning fact and existence and cannot possibly subsist without continually employing this species of argument, any popular objections derived from thence must be insufficient to destroy that evidence. The great subverter of

Pyrrhonism [excessive skepticism][37] or the excessive principles of skepticism is action, and employment, and the occupations of common life. These principles may flourish and triumph in the schools, where it is, indeed, difficult if not impossible to refute them. But as soon as they leave the shade and by the presence of the real objects that actuate our passions and sentiments are put in opposition to the more powerful principles of our nature, they vanish like smoke and leave the most determined skeptic in the same condition as other mortals.

The skeptic, therefore, had better keep within his proper sphere and display those *philosophical* objections that arise from more profound researches. Here, he seems to have ample matter of triumph, while he justly insists that all our evidence for any matter of fact that lies beyond the testimony of sense or memory is derived entirely from the relation of cause and effect; that we have no other idea of this relation than that of two objects that have been frequently conjoined together; that we have no argument to convince us that objects that have, in our experience, been frequently conjoined will likewise, in other instances, be conjoined in the same manner; and that nothing leads us to this inference but custom or a certain instinct of our nature, which it is indeed difficult to resist but, like other instincts, may be fallacious

and deceitful. While the skeptic insists upon these topics, he shows his force, or rather, indeed, his own and our weakness, and seems, for the time at least, to destroy all assurance and conviction. These arguments might be displayed at greater length if any durable good or benefit to society could ever be expected to result from them.

For here is the chief and most confounding objection to *excessive* skepticism: that no durable good can ever result from it while it remains in its full force and vigor. We need only ask such a skeptic *what his meaning is and what he proposes by all these curious researches.* He is immediately at a loss and knows not what to answer. A Copernican or Ptolemaic,[38] who supports each his different system of astronomy, may hope to produce a conviction that will remain constant and durable with his audience. A Stoic or Epicurean[39] displays principles that may not only be durable but have an effect on conduct and behavior. But a Pyrrhonian cannot expect that his philosophy will have any constant influence on the mind, or if it had, that its influence would be beneficial to society. On the contrary, he must acknowledge, if he will acknowledge anything, that all human life must perish, were his principles universally and steadily to prevail. All discourse, all action would immediately cease, and men remain in a total lethargy, till the

---

37 **excessive skepticism:** this sort of skepticism is attributed to the ancient Greek Pyrrhus (360–270 BCE). He was part of a school of ancient thinkers who often used this approach in medicine against the Dogmatics.

38 **Copernican or Ptolemaic:** Nicolaus Copernicus (1473–1543) set out a radical new sun-centered conception of the solar system that altered the earth-centered conception of the universe advanced by Roman Egyptian astronomer Ptolemy (c. 90–c. 168 CE).

39 **Stoic or Epicurean:** adherent of the philosophy of self-control, especially over the emotions (Stoicism), or of seeking moderate pleasure and avoiding pain (Epicureanism).

necessities of nature, unsatisfied, put an end to their miserable existence. It is true; so fatal an event is very little to be dreaded. Nature is always too strong for principle. And though a Pyrrhonian may throw himself or others into a momentary amazement and confusion by his profound reasonings, the first and most trivial event in life will put to flight all his doubts and scruples and leave him the same, in every point of action and speculation, with the philosophers of every other sect or with those who never concerned themselves in any philosophical researches. When he awakes from his dream, he will be the first to join in the laugh against himself and to confess that all his objections are mere amusement and can have no other tendency than to show the whimsical condition of mankind, who must act and reason and believe—though they are not able, by their most diligent enquiry, to satisfy themselves concerning the foundation of these operations or to remove the objections that may be raised against them.

Part III: Mitigated Skepticism

There is, indeed, a more *mitigated* skepticism, or *academical* philosophy, which may be both durable and useful and may in part be the result of this Pyrrhonism, or *excessive* skepticism, when its undistinguished doubts are, in some measure, corrected by common sense and reflection. The greater part of mankind are naturally apt to be affirmative and dogmatical in their opinions, and while they see objects only on one side and have no idea of any counterpoising argument, they throw themselves precipitately into the principles to which they are inclined; nor have

they any indulgence for those who entertain opposite sentiments. To hesitate or balance perplexes their understanding, checks their passion, and suspends their action. They are, therefore, impatient till they escape from a state which to them is so uneasy, and they think that they can never remove themselves far enough from it by the violence of their affirmations and obstinacy of their belief.

But could such dogmatical reasoners become sensible of the strange infirmities of human understanding, even in its most perfect state, and when most accurate and cautious in its determinations, such a reflection would naturally inspire them with more modesty and reserve and diminish their fond opinion of themselves and their prejudice against antagonists. The illiterate may reflect on the disposition of the learned, who, amid all the advantages of study and reflection, are commonly still diffident in their determinations. And if any of the learned be inclined from their natural temper to haughtiness and obstinacy, a small tincture of Pyrrhonism might abate their pride by showing them that the few advantages that they may have attained over their fellows are but inconsiderable, if compared with the universal perplexity and confusion that is inherent in human nature. In general, there is a degree of doubt and caution and modesty that in all kinds of scrutiny and decision ought forever to accompany a just reasoner.

Another species of *mitigated* skepticism that may be of advantage to mankind and may be the natural result of the Pyrrhonian doubts and scruples is the limitation of our enquiries to such subjects as are best adapted to the narrow capacity of human understanding. The *imagination* of man is naturally sublime, delighted with whatever is remote and extraordinary and running without control into the most distant parts of space and time in order to avoid the objects that custom has rendered too familiar to it. A correct *judgment* observes a contrary method and, avoiding all distant and high enquiries, confines itself to common life and to such subjects as fall under daily practice and experience, leaving the more sublime topics to the embellishment of poets and orators or to the arts of priests and politicians. To bring us to so salutary a determination, nothing can be more serviceable than to be once thoroughly convinced of the force of the Pyrrhonian doubt and of the impossibility that anything but the strong power of natural instinct could free us from it. Those who have a propensity to philosophy will still continue their researches because they reflect that, besides the immediate pleasure attending such an occupation, philosophical decisions are nothing but the reflections of common life, methodized and corrected. But they will never be tempted to go beyond common life so long as they consider the imperfection of those faculties that they employ, their narrow reach, and their inaccurate operations. While we cannot give a satisfactory reason for why we believe, after a thousand experiments, that a stone will fall or fire burn, can we ever satisfy ourselves concerning any determination that we may form with regard to the origin of worlds and the situation of nature, from and to eternity?

This narrow limitation, indeed, of our enquiries is, in every respect, so reasonable that it suffices to make the slightest examination into the natural powers of the human mind and to compare them with their objects, in order to recommend it to us. We shall then find what are the proper subjects of science and enquiry.

Part IV:
Justified Intellectual Belief

It seems to me that the only objects of the abstract sciences or of demonstration are quantity and number and that all attempts to extend this more perfect species of knowledge beyond these bounds are mere sophistry and illusion. As the component parts of quantity and number are entirely similar, their relations become intricate and involved, and nothing can be more curious, as well as useful, than to trace by a variety of mediums their equality or inequality, through their different appearances. But as all other ideas are clearly distinct and different from each other, we can never advance farther by our utmost scrutiny than to observe this diversity and, by an obvious reflection, pronounce one thing not to be another. Or if there be any difficulty in these decisions, it proceeds entirely from the undeterminate meaning of words, which is corrected by juster definitions. That *the square of the hypotenuse is equal to the squares of the other two sides*[40] cannot be known, let the terms be ever so exactly

---

40 **the square . . . other two sides:** the theorem by Greek mathematician Pythagoras (c. 580–c. 500 BCE) that the squared length of the side (the hypotenuse) opposite the right angle in a triangle equals the sum of the squared lengths of the other two sides.

defined, without a train of reasoning and enquiry. But to convince us of this proposition, *that where there is no property, there can be no injustice,*[41] it is only necessary to define the terms and explain injustice to be a violation of property. This proposition is, indeed, nothing but a more imperfect definition. It is the same case with all those pretended syllogistic reasonings that may be found in every other branch of learning, except the sciences of quantity and number; and these may safely, I think, be pronounced the only proper objects of knowledge and demonstration.

All other enquiries of men regard only matter of fact and existence, and these are evidently incapable of demonstration. Whatever *is* may *not be.* No negation of a fact can involve a contradiction. The non-existence of any being, without exception, is as clear and distinct an idea as its existence. The proposition that affirms it not to be, however false, is no less conceivable and intelligible than that which affirms it to be. The case is different with the sciences, properly so called. Every proposition that is not true is there confused and unintelligible. That the cube root of sixty-four is equal to the half of ten is a false proposition and can never be distinctly conceived. But that Caesar, or the angel Gabriel, or any being never existed may be a false proposition but still is perfectly conceivable and implies no contradiction.

The existence, therefore, of any being can only be proved by arguments from its cause or its effect—and these arguments are founded entirely on experience. If we reason a priori, anything may appear able to produce anything. The falling of a pebble may, for aught we know, extinguish the sun, or the wish of a man control the planets in their orbits. It is only experience that teaches us the nature and bounds of cause and effect and enables us to infer the existence of one object from that of another. Such is the foundation of moral reasoning, which forms the greater part of human knowledge and is the source of all human action and behavior.

Moral reasonings are either concerning particular or general facts. All deliberations in life regard the former, as also all disquisitions in history, chronology, geography, and astronomy.

The sciences, which treat of general facts, are politics, natural philosophy, physics, chemistry, and so on, where the qualities, causes, and effects of a whole species of objects are enquired into.

Divinity or theology, as it proves the existence of a Deity and the immortality of souls, is composed partly of reasonings concerning particular [facts], partly concerning general facts. It has a foundation in *reason* so far as it is supported by experience. But its best and most solid foundation is *faith* and divine revelation.

Morals and criticism are not so properly objects of the Understanding as of taste and sentiment. Beauty, whether moral or natural, is felt more properly than perceived. Or if we reason concerning it and endeavor to fix its standard, we regard a

---

41 **that where . . . no injustice:** paraphrased from *An Essay Concerning Human Understanding* (1690) by English philosopher John Locke (1632–1704).

new fact, to wit: the general taste of mankind, or some such fact, which may be the object of reasoning and enquiry.

When we run over libraries, persuaded of these principles, what havoc must we make? If we take in our hand any volume—of divinity or school metaphysics, for instance—let us ask, *Does it contain any abstract reasoning concerning quantity or number?* No. *Does it contain any experimental reasoning concerning matter of fact and existence?* No. Commit it then to the flames, for it can contain nothing but sophistry and illusion.

■ READING AND DISCUSSION QUESTIONS

1. What does Hume find problematic with antecedent Cartesian skepticism?
2. What does Hume find problematic with consequent skepticism? How would this sort of skepticism undercut empiricism?
3. Hume wants to treat sense impressions as fundamental givens. Is brute sensory fact possible? What might an objector say?
4. Descartes offers two proofs for the existence of God in order to prove the veracity of our senses (if there is a God who is good, then why would he trick us with defective senses). Hume thinks such an argument is "an unexpected circuit." What does Hume mean by this? Set out the claim from Hume's point of view.
5. What is problematic about the following sentence: "Pyrrhus argues, 'All knowledge claims are false.'"?
6. What is problematic about a radical skeptic arguing against the truth of a mathematical proof?
7. What is mitigated skepticism, and why does Hume think it is superior to the forms of radical skepticism?
8. What are the two legitimate sources of intellectual belief?
9. What sources are bogus pretenders to justifying intellectual belief? Why are they bogus?

■ CLASS EXERCISES

A. *Direct logical discourse:* Using the tools found in Chapter 2, outline either the argument from parts 1 to 3 in favor of mitigated skepticism against radical skepticism or the argument from part 4 that intellectual belief should be based on either reasoning about quantity and number or experimental fact. Based on your assessment of one key premise, write a one-page argument about why you agree or disagree with the argument's conclusion.

B. *Fictive-narrative philosophy:* Using the tools found in Chapter 3, begin with a claim that relates to the reading and discussion questions above. Then create a modern-day story about people or situations familiar to you that makes the logical claim you have identified. Three pages.

THE POSSIBILITY OF METAPHYSICS

Immanuel Kant

Adapted from Paul Carus, *Kant's Prolegomena [to any Future Metaphysics]* (Chicago: Open Court, 1902). *Note on the translation:* English words found in brackets are inserted by the translator to make better sense of the English rendering.

Immanuel Kant (1724–1804) is one of the most important philosophers in the Western tradition. Kant's works touched widely on many aspects of philosophy, including episte-mology, metaphysics, ethics, and aesthetics. In his "critical" turn, Kant wants to accept the criticisms against dogmatic metaphysics and then to offer a new way to understand metaphysics in the light of the epistemological turn of Enlightenment thinkers—especially David Hume.

In this selection from the Prolegomena to any Future Metaphysics, *Kant tries to re-define the discipline via the introduction of several key terms. We begin with the form of a proposition. A proposition is analytic when the meaning of the predicate term is con-tained within the meaning of the subject term. Thus, in the proposition "All bachelors are unmarried males," the meaning of the subject term, "bachelor," contains within it the meaning of the predicate term, "unmarried male." Because of this property, analytic propositions do not tell us anything new in the transition from subject to predicate. Syn-thetic propositions operate differently. In this case the predicate term expands upon the subject term and gives us new information about the world. In the proposition "The boiling point of water at sea level is 100 °C," the subject term is defined by its chemical composition only (H_2O) but is silent on other properties—thus, knowing that this liquid boils at 100 °C expands the knowledge of the subject term and gives us further informa-tion about the world.*

A priori and a posteriori have already been defined as referring to propositions that are justified via data that are arrived at before experience (such as mathematics) or after experience (such as testing the boiling point of water). Before Kant, it was agreed that there were analytic a priori propositions (the propositions of mathematics and the dog-matic philosophers) and synthetic a posteriori propositions (the propositions of natural science). Kant's novel contribution is the synthetic a priori proposition (a proposition that is not derived from experience yet expands the range of the predicate term such that it applies to our experience in the world). If he's successful, this is a move toward critical metaphysics.

Hume's Rejection of A Priori Cause and Effect

Hume started from a single but important concept in metaphysics, namely, that of cause and effect (including its derivatives force and action, etc.). He challenges *reason*, which pretends to have given birth to this idea from herself, to answer him by what right she thinks anything to be so constituted, that if that thing be posited, something else also must necessarily be posited, for this is the meaning of the concept of cause.

He demonstrated irrefutably that it was perfectly impossible for *reason* to think a priori and by means of concepts a combination involving necessity. We cannot at all see why, in consequence of the existence of one thing [an effect], another [a cause] must necessarily exist or how the concept of such a combination can arise a priori. Hence, he inferred that *reason* was altogether deluded with reference to this concept, which she erroneously considered as one of her children, whereas in reality it was nothing but a bastard of *imagination*, impregnated by experience, which subsumed certain representations under the Law of Association[42] and mistook the subjective necessity of habit for an objective necessity arising from insight. Hence, he inferred that reason had no power to think such combinations, even generally, be-cause her concepts would then be purely fictitious and all her pretended a priori cognitions nothing but common experiences marked with a false stamp. In plain language there is not, and cannot be, any such thing as metaphysics at all.

However hasty and mistaken Hume's conclusion may appear, it was at least founded upon investigation, and this investigation deserved the concentrated attention of the brighter spirits of his day as well as determined efforts on their part to discover, if possible, a happier solution of the problem in the sense proposed by him, all of which would have speedily resulted in a complete reform of the science.

But Hume suffered the usual misfortune of metaphysicians, of not being understood. It is positively painful to see how utterly his opponents, Reid, Oswald, Beattie, and lastly Priestley,[43] missed the point of the problem; for while they were ever taking for granted that which he doubted and demonstrating with zeal and often with impudence that which he never thought of doubting, they so misconstrued his valuable suggestion that everything remained in its old condition, as if nothing had happened.

Common Sense and Critical Reason

The question was not whether the concept of cause was right, useful, and even indis-

---

42 **Law of Association:** Hume argues that a more reasonable account is the constant conjunction of two events under a law of association instead of assuming a mechanical necessity between cause and effect.

43 **Reid . . . Priestley:** Scottish philosophers Thomas Reid (1710–1796), John Oswald (c. 1760–1793), and James Beattie (1735–1803) and British scientist and theologian Joseph Priestley (1733–1804).

pensable for our knowledge of nature, for this Hume had never doubted; but whether that concept could be thought by reason a priori and, consequently, whether it possessed an inner truth, independent of all experience, implying a wider application than merely to the objects of experience. This was Hume's problem. It was a question concerning the *origin*, not concerning the *indispensable need* of the concept. Were the former decided, the conditions of the use and the sphere of its valid application would have been determined as a matter of course.

But to satisfy the conditions of the problem, the opponents of the great thinker should have penetrated very deeply into the nature of reason, so far as it is concerned with pure thinking—a task that did not suit them. They found a more convenient method of being defiant without any insight, namely, the appeal to *common sense.* It is indeed a great gift of God to possess right, or (as they now call it) plain common sense. But this common sense must be shown practically, by well-considered and reasonable thoughts and words, not by appealing to it as an oracle, when no rational justification can be advanced. To appeal to common sense, when insight and science fail, and no sooner—this is one of the subtle discoveries of modern times, by means of which the most superficial ranter can safely enter the lists with the most thorough thinker and hold his own. But as long as a particle of insight remains, no one would think of having recourse to this subterfuge. For what is it but an appeal to the opinion of the multitude, of whose applause the philosopher is ashamed, while the popular charlatan glories and confides in it?

I should think that Hume might fairly have laid as much claim to common sense as Beattie, and in addition to a critical reason (such as the latter did not possess), which keeps common sense in check and prevents it from speculating or, if speculations are under discussion, restrains the desire to decide because it cannot satisfy itself concerning its own arguments. By this means alone can common sense remain sound. Chisels and hammers may suffice to work a piece of wood, but for steel engraving we require an engraver's needle. Thus, common sense and speculative understanding are each serviceable in their own way, the former in judgments that apply immediately to experience, the latter when we judge universally from mere concepts, as in metaphysics, where sound common sense, so called in spite of the inapplicability of the word, has no right to judge at all.

Kant's Debt to Hume

I openly confess, the suggestion of David Hume was the very thing that many years ago first interrupted my dogmatic slumber and gave my investigations in the field of speculative philosophy quite a new direction. I was far from following him in the conclusions at which he arrived by regarding not the whole of his problem but a part, which by itself can give us no information. If we start from a well-founded but undeveloped thought that another has bequeathed to us, we may well hope by continued reflection to advance farther than the acute man to whom we owe the first spark of light.

I therefore first tried whether Hume's objection could not be put into a general form and soon found that the concept of the connection of cause and effect was by no means the only idea by which the Understanding thinks the connection of things a priori, but rather that metaphysics consists altogether of such connections. I sought to ascertain their number, and when I had satisfactorily succeeded in this by starting from a single principle, I proceeded to the deduction of these concepts, which I was now certain were not deduced from experience, as Hume had apprehended, but sprang from the pure understanding. This deduction (which seemed impossible to my acute predecessor, which had never even occurred to anyone else, though no one had hesitated to use the concepts without investigating the basis of their objective validity) was the most difficult task ever undertaken in the service of metaphysics; and the worst was that metaphysics, such as it then existed, could not assist me in the least, because this deduction alone can render metaphysics possible. But as soon as I had succeeded in solving Hume's problem not merely in a particular case but with respect to the whole faculty of pure reason, I could proceed safely, though slowly, to determine the whole sphere of pure reason completely and from general principles, in its circumference as well as in its contents. This was required for metaphysics in order to construct its system according to a reliable method. . . .

Is Metaphysics at All Possible?

Were a metaphysics that could maintain its place as a science[44] really in existence, could we say, here is metaphysics, learn it, and it will convince you irresistibly and irrevocably of its truth? This question would be useless, and there would only remain that other question (which would rather be a test of our acuteness than a proof of the existence of the thing itself): "How is the science possible, and how does reason come to attain it?"

But human reason has not been so fortunate in this case. There is no single book to which you can point, as you do to Euclid,[45] and say, "This is metaphysics; here you may find the noblest objects of this science, the knowledge of a highest Being, and of a future existence, proved from principles of pure reason." We can be shown indeed many judgments, demonstrably certain, and never questioned, but these are all analytical and rather concern the materials and the scaffolding for metaphysics than the extension of knowledge, which is our proper object in studying it (§ 2).

Even supposing you produce synthetical judgments (such as the Law of Sufficient Reason,[46] which you have never proved, as you ought to, from pure reason a priori, though we gladly concede its truth), you lapse when they come to be employed for your principal object, into such doubtful assertions, that in all ages

---

44 **science:** in this context means exact knowledge. Here Kant is asking whether metaphysics can yield exact knowledge.

45 **Euclid:** Euclid of Alexandria (flourished 300 BCE), author of *Elements*, a book of rigorous mathematical proofs that defined the field of geometry for two thousand years.

46 **Law of Sufficient Reason:** see the Leibniz selection in this chapter.

one metaphysics has contradicted another, either in its assertions or their proofs, and thus has itself destroyed its own claim to lasting assent. Nay, the very attempts to set up such a science are the main cause of the early appearance of skepticism, a mental attitude in which reason treats itself with such violence that it could never have arisen save from complete despair of ever satisfying our most important aspirations.

For long before men began to inquire into nature methodically, they consulted abstract reason, which had to some extent been exercised by means of ordinary experience; for reason is ever present, while laws of nature must usually be discovered with labor. So metaphysics floated to the surface, like foam, which dissolved the moment it was scooped off. But immediately there appeared a new supply on the surface, to be ever eagerly gathered up by some, while others, instead of seeking in the depths the cause of the phenomenon, thought they showed their wisdom by ridiculing the idle labor of their neighbors.

The essential and distinguishing feature of pure mathematical cognition among all other a priori cognitions is that it cannot at all proceed from concepts but only by means of the construction of concepts.[47] As therefore in its judgments it must pro-

ceed beyond the concept to that which its corresponding visualization (*Anschauung*) contains, these judgments neither can, nor ought to, arise analytically, by dissecting the concept, but are all synthetical.

The Essential Subject of Metaphysics

I cannot refrain from pointing out the disadvantage resulting to philosophy from the neglect of this easy and apparently insignificant observation. Hume being prompted (a task worthy of a philosopher) to cast his eye over the whole field of a priori cognitions in which human understanding claims such mighty possessions heedlessly severed from it a whole, and indeed its most valuable, province, namely, pure mathematics; for he thought its nature, or, so to speak, the state-constitution of this empire, depended on totally different principles, namely, on the Law of Contradiction alone.[48] And although he did not divide judgments in this manner formally and universally as I have done here, what he said was equivalent to this: that mathematics contains only analytical, but metaphysics synthetical, a priori judgments. In this, however, he was greatly mistaken, and the mistake had a decidedly injurious effect upon his whole conception. . . . How

---

47 **construction of concepts:** this is what Kant calls a *transcendental argument*. This sort of argument constructs what is necessary to allow experience to occur. Because the object of a transcendental argument must be before experience, it is a priori. Because the outcome of the argument permits the subject to experience the world, it is also *synthetic* (it gives information in the predicate term that is beyond the subject term and applies to the world). Thus, the transcendental argument requires the application of Kant's novel synthetic a priori proposition.

48 **Law of Contradiction:** this law (also known as the Law of Noncontradiction) means that one cannot assert some proposition and its logical opposite at the same time in the same way; for example, one cannot be both pregnant and nonpregnant at the same time.

are synthetic propositions a priori possible? For the sake of popularity I have above expressed this problem somewhat differently, as an inquiry into purely rational cognition, which I could do for once without detriment to the desired comprehension, because, as we have only to do here with metaphysics and its sources, the reader will, I hope, after the foregoing remarks, keep in mind that when we speak of purely rational cognition, we do not mean analytical but synthetical cognition.

Metaphysics stands or falls with the solution of this problem: its very existence depends upon it. Let any one make metaphysical assertions with ever so much plausibility, let him overwhelm us with conclusions, if he has not previously proved able to answer this question satisfactorily, I have a right to say, "This is all vain baseless philosophy and false wisdom." You speak through pure reason and claim, as it were, to create cognitions a priori by not only dissecting given concepts but also by asserting connections that do not rest upon the law of contradiction and that you believe you conceive quite independently of all experience; how do you arrive at this, and how will you justify your pretensions? An appeal to the consent of the common sense of mankind cannot be allowed; for that is a witness whose authority depends merely upon rumor. . . .

All metaphysicians are therefore solemnly and legally suspended from their occupations till they shall have answered in a satisfactory manner the question, "How are synthetic cognitions a priori possible?" For the answer contains the only credentials that they must show when they have

anything to offer in the name of pure reason. But if they do not possess these credentials, they can expect nothing else of reasonable people, who have been deceived so often, than to be dismissed without further ado. . . .

The Form of Our Sensory Intuitions

If our intuition [that is, our sense experience] were perforce of such a nature as to represent things as they are in themselves, there would not be any intuition a priori, but intuition would be always empirical. For I can only know what is contained in the object in itself when it is present and given to me. It is indeed even then incomprehensible how the visualizing (*Anschauung*) of a present thing should make me know this thing as it is in itself, as its properties cannot migrate into my faculty of representation. But even granting this possibility, a visualizing of that sort would not take place a priori, that is, before the object were presented to me; for without this latter fact, no reason of a relation between my representation and the object can be imagined, unless it depend upon a direct inspiration.

Therefore, in one way only can my intuition (*Anschauung*) anticipate the actuality of the object and be a cognition a priori, namely, if my intuition contains nothing but the form of sensibility, antedating in my subjectivity all the actual impressions through which I am affected by objects. For that objects of sense can only be intuited according to this form of sensibility I can know a priori. Hence, it follows that propositions, which concern this form of sensuous intuition only, are possible and valid for objects of the senses; conversely, intuitions that are possible a priori can never concern any other things than objects of our senses.

Accordingly, it is only the form of sensuous intuition by which we can intuit things a priori, but by which we can know objects only as they *appear* to us (to our senses), not as they are in themselves; and this assumption is absolutely necessary if synthetical propositions a priori be granted as possible or if, in case they actually occur, their possibility is to be comprehended and determined beforehand.

Now, the intuitions that pure mathematics lays at the foundation of all its cognitions and judgments, which appear at once apodeictic[49] and necessary, are space and time. For mathematics must first have all its concepts in intuition and pure mathematics in pure intuition; that is, it must construct them. If it proceeded in any other way, it would be impossible to make any headway, for mathematics proceeds not analytically by dissection of concepts but synthetically, and if pure intuition be wanting, there is nothing in which the matter for synthetical judgments a priori can be given. Geometry is based on the pure intuition of space. Arithmetic accomplishes its concept of number by the successive addition of units in time; and pure mechanics especially cannot attain its concepts of motion without employing the representation of time. Both representations, however, are only intuitions; for if we omit from the empirical intuitions of bodies and their alterations (motion) everything empirical, or belonging to sensation, space and time lie a priori at the basis of the empirical. Hence, they can never be omitted, but at the same time, by their being pure intuitions a priori, they prove that they are mere forms of our sensibility, which must precede all empirical intuition, or perception of actual objects, and conformably to which objects can be known a priori, but only as they appear to us.

The problem of the present section is therefore solved. Pure mathematics, as synthetical cognition a priori, is only possible by referring to no other objects than those of the senses. At the basis of their empirical intuition lies a pure intuition (of space and of time), which is a priori. This is possible because the latter intuition is nothing but the mere form of sensibility, which precedes the actual appearance of the objects, in that it, in fact, makes them possible. . . .

Kant's Solution to the Problem of Metaphysics

Empirical judgments, so far as they have objective validity, are judgments of experience, but those that are only subjectively valid, I name mere judgments of perception. The latter require no pure concept of the Understanding but only the logical connection of perception in a thinking subject. But the former always require, besides the representation of the sensuous intuition, particular *concepts originally begotten in the Understanding*, which produce

---

49 **apodeictic:** pertaining to predication or conclusions considered to be necessary—it cannot be otherwise.

the objective validity of the judgment of experience.

All our judgments are at first merely judgments of perception; they hold good only for us (that is, for our subject), and we do not till afterwards give them a new reference (to an object), and desire that they shall always hold good for us and in the same way for everybody else; for when a judgment agrees with an object, all judgments concerning the same object must likewise agree among themselves, and thus the objective validity of the judgment of experience signifies nothing else than its necessary universality of application. And conversely when we have reason to consider a judgment necessarily universal (which never depends upon perception but upon the pure concept of the Understanding under which the perception is subsumed), we must consider it objective also, that is, that it expresses not merely a reference of our perception to a subject but a quality of the object. For there would be no reason for the judgments of other men necessarily agreeing with mine if it were not the unity of the object to which they all refer and with which they accord; hence, they must all agree with one another.

Therefore, objective validity and necessary universality (for everybody) are equivalent terms, and though we do not know the object in itself, yet when we consider a judgment as universal and also necessary, we understand it to have objective validity. By this judgment we cognize the object (though it remains unknown as it is in itself) by the universal and necessary connection of the given perceptions. As this is the case with all objects of sense, judgments of experience take their objective validity not from the immediate cognition of the object (which is impossible) but from the condition of universal validity in empirical judgments, which, as already said, never rests upon empirical or, in short, sensuous conditions but upon a pure concept of the Understanding. The object always remains unknown in itself; but when by the concept of the Understanding the connection of the representations of the object, which are given to our sensibility, is determined as universally valid, the object is determined by this relation, and it is the judgment that is objective.

To illustrate the matter: when we say, "The room is warm, sugar sweet, and wormwood bitter," we have only subjectively valid judgments. I do not at all expect that I or any other person shall always find it as I now do; each of these sentences only expresses a relation of two sensations to the same subject, to myself, and that only in my present state of perception; consequently they are not valid of the object. Such are judgments of perception. Judgments of experience are of quite a different nature. What experience teaches me under certain circumstances, it must always teach me and everybody; and its validity is not limited to the subject nor to its state at a particular time. Hence, I pronounce all such judgments as being objectively valid. For instance, when I say the air is elastic, this judgment is as yet a judgment of perception only—I do nothing but refer two of my sensations to one another. But, if I would have it called a judgment of experience, I require this connection to stand under a condition, which makes it universally valid. I desire therefore that I and everybody else should always connect necessarily the same perceptions under the same circumstances.

We must consequently analyze experience in order to see what *is* contained in this product of the senses and of the Understanding and how the judgment of experience itself is possible. The foundation is the intuition of which I become conscious (that is, perception, or *perceptio*), which pertains merely to the senses. But in the next place, there are acts of judging (which belong only to the Understanding). But this judging may be twofold—first, I may merely compare perceptions and connect them in a particular state of my consciousness; or, secondly, I may connect them in consciousness generally. The former judgment is merely a judgment of perception and of subjective validity only: it is merely a connection of perceptions in my mental state, without reference to the object. Hence, it is not, as is commonly imagined, enough for experience to compare perceptions and to connect them in consciousness through judgment; there arises no universality and necessity for which alone judgments can become objectively valid and be called experience.

Quite another judgment therefore is required before perception can become experience. The given intuition must be subsumed under a concept, which determines the form of judging in general relatively to the intuition, connects its empirical consciousness in consciousness generally, and thereby procures universal validity for empirical judgments. A concept of this nature is a pure a priori concept of the Understanding, which does nothing but determine for an intuition the general way in which it can be used for judgments. Let the concept be that of cause, then it determines the intuition, which is subsumed under it, for example, that of air, relative to judgments in general, namely, the concept of air serves with regard to its expansion in the relation of antecedent to consequent in a hypothetical judgment. The concept of cause accordingly is a pure concept of the Understanding, which is totally disparate from all possible perception and only serves to determine the representation subsumed under it, relatively to judgments in general, and so to make a universally valid judgment possible.

Before, therefore, a judgment of perception can become a judgment of experience, it is requisite that the perception should be subsumed under some such a concept of the Understanding; for instance, air ranks under the concept of causes, which determines our judgment about it in regard to its expansion as hypothetical. Thereby, the expansion of the air is represented not as merely belonging to the perception of the air in my present state or in several states of mine, or in the state of perception of others, but as belonging to it necessarily. The judgment "The air is elastic" becomes universally valid and a judgment of experience only by certain judgments preceding it, which subsume the intuition of air under the concept of cause and effect: and they thereby determine the perceptions not merely as regards one another in me but relatively to the form of judging in general, which is here hypothetical, and in this way they render the empirical judgment universally valid.

If all our synthetical judgments are analyzed so far as they are objectively valid, it will be found that they never consist of mere intuitions connected only (as is commonly believed) by comparison into a judgment, but that they would be impossible were not a pure concept of the Understanding superadded to the concepts abstracted from intuition, under which concept these latter are subsumed, and in this manner only combined into an objectively valid judgment. Even the judgments of pure mathematics in their simplest axioms are not exempt from this condition. The principle "A straight line is the shortest between two points" presupposes that the line is subsumed under the concept of quantity, which certainly is no mere intuition but has its seat in the Understanding alone and serves to determine the intuition (of the line) with regard to the judgments that may be made about it, relatively to their quantity, that is, to plurality (as *judicia plurativa*). For under them it is understood that in a given intuition there is contained a plurality of homogenous parts.

To prove, then, the possibility of experience so far as it rests upon pure concepts of the Understanding a priori, we must first represent what belongs to judgments in general and the various functions of the Understanding in a complete table. For the pure concepts of the Understanding must run parallel to these functions, as such concepts are nothing more than concepts of intuitions in general, so far as these are determined by one or other of these functions of judging, in themselves, that is, necessarily and universally. Hereby also the a priori principles of the possibility of all experience, as of an objectively valid empirical cognition, will be precisely determined. For they are nothing but propositions by which all perception is

(under certain universal conditions of intuition) subsumed under those pure concepts of the Understanding.

In order to comprise the whole matter in one idea, it is first necessary to remind the reader that we are discussing not the origin of experience but of that which lies in experience. The former pertains to empirical psychology and would even then never be adequately explained without the latter, which belongs to the Critique of cognition and particularly of the Understanding.

Experience consists of intuitions, which belong to the sensibility, and of judgments, which are entirely a work of the Understanding. But the judgments, which the Understanding forms alone from sensuous intuitions, are far from being judgments of experience. For in the one case the judgment connects only the perceptions as they are given in the sensuous intuition, while in the other the judgments must express what experience in general, and not what the mere perception (which possesses only subjective validity), contains. The judgment of experience must therefore add to the sensuous intuition and its logical connection in a judgment (after it has been rendered universal by comparison) something that determines the synthetical judgment as necessary and therefore as universally valid. This can be nothing else than that concept that represents the intuition as determined in itself with regard to one form of judgment rather than another, namely, a concept of that synthetical unity of intuitions that can only be represented by a given logical function of judgments.

The sum of the matter is this: the business of the senses is to intuit—that of the Understanding is to think. But thinking is uniting representations in one conscious-

--- **Logical Table of Judgments** ---

1. *As to quantity*	2. *As to quality*
Universal Particular Singular	Affirmative Negative Infinite
3. *As to relation*	4. *As to modality*
Categorical Hypothetical Disjunctive	Problematical Assertorical Apodeictical

--- **Transcendental Table of the Pure Concepts of the Understanding** ---

1. *As to quantity*	2. *As to quality*
Unity (the measure) Plurality (the quantity) Totality (the whole)	Reality Negation Limitation
3. *As to relation*	4. *As to modality*
Substance Cause Community	Possibility Existence Necessity

--- **Pure Physiological Table of the Universal Principles of the Science of Nature** ---

1. Axioms of intuition	2. Anticipations of perception
3. Analogies of experience	4. Postulates of empirical thinking generally

ness. This union originates either merely relative to the subject and is accidental and subjective, or it is absolute and is necessary or objective. The union of representations in one consciousness is judgment. Thinking therefore is the same as judging, or referring representations to judgments in general. Hence, judgments are either merely subjective, when representations are referred to a consciousness in one subject only and united in it, or objective, when they are united in a consciousness generally, that is, necessarily. The logical functions of all judgments are but various modes of uniting representations in consciousness. But if they serve for concepts, they are concepts of their necessary union in a consciousness and, so, principles of objectively valid judgments. This union in a consciousness is either analytical, by identity, or synthetical, by the combination and addition of various representations one to another. Experience consists in the synthetical connection of phenomena (perceptions) in consciousness, so far as this connection is necessary. Hence, the pure concepts of the Understanding are those under which all perceptions must be subsumed ere they can serve for judgments of experience, in which the synthetical unity of the perceptions is represented as necessary and universally valid.

Judgments, when considered merely as the condition of the union of given representations in a consciousness, are rules. These rules, so far as they represent the union as necessary, are rules a priori and, so far as they cannot be deduced from higher rules, are fundamental principles.

But in regard to the possibility of all experience, merely in relation to the form of thinking in it, no conditions of judgments of experience are higher than those which bring the phenomena, according to the various forms of their intuition, under pure concepts of the Understanding, and render the empirical judgment objectively valid. These concepts are therefore the a priori principles of possible experience.

The principles of possible experience are then at the same time universal laws of nature, which can be cognized a priori. And thus the problem in our second question, "How is the pure science of nature possible?" is solved. For the system that is required for the form of a science is to be met with in perfection here, because, beyond the above-mentioned formal conditions of all judgments in general offered in logic, no others are possible, and these constitute a logical system. The concepts grounded thereupon, which contain the a priori conditions of all synthetical and necessary judgments, accordingly constitute a transcendental system. Finally, the principles, by means of which all phenomena are subsumed under these concepts, constitute a physical system, that is, a system of nature, which precedes all empirical cognition of nature, makes it even possible, and hence may in strictness be denominated the universal and pure science of nature.

■ READING AND DISCUSSION QUESTIONS

1. Kant concurs with Hume that a priori reason cannot originate an inner truth about causation in our experience that is necessary. Instead, we must content ourselves with the constant conjunction of antecedent and consequent that Kant calls the Law of Association. Why is this an important point? What would Wolff or Leibniz say?

2. How does Kant think others mistake Hume's point on causation?

3. What does Kant say is his debt to Hume?

4. Kant asks whether metaphysics can still be a science even if we accept Hume's general concerns on causation. What does Kant mean by this question?

5. What is Kant's criticism of Leibniz's principle or law of sufficient reason?

6. Explain what Kant means when he says that mathematical cognition does not proceed a priori from concepts but must be constructed in a process analogous to visualization.

7. Explain what a synthetic a priori proposition is and why these propositions are essential to Kant's project to redefine metaphysics.

8. When we visualize a cat running (or any physical object), what forms are presupposed in our act of visualizing? How are the intuitions of time and space involved?

9. What is a judgment of experience? What does the Logical Table of Judgments tell us about a judgment's formal structure?

10. The understanding is the power to think by uniting representations into one consciousness. The union of representations constitutes a judgment. How is this complicated model different from Wolff's and Leibniz's simple power of reason? What are the consequences of these differences?

11. Sketch out briefly how Kant thinks he has defended metaphysics. Did he succeed?

■ CLASS EXERCISES

A. *Direct logical discourse:* Using the tools found in Chapter 2, outline the argument from one of the sections. Based on your assessment of one key premise, write a one-page argument about why you agree or disagree with the argument's conclusion.

B. *Fictive-narrative philosophy:* Using the tools found in Chapter 3, begin with a claim that relates to the reading and discussion questions above. Then create a modern-day story about people or situations familiar to you that makes the logical claim you have identified. Three pages.

For each according to ability, to
each according to need

CHAPTER TEN

Marx

*K*arl Marx (1818–1883) was trained as a philosopher. His early works are philosophical. Later, along with Friedrich Engels, his work took a practical turn and advocated the political/ economic system of revolutionary communism. This adaptation of his philosophy to a practical account was, at its height, the most dominant ideology in the world (quite an achievement).

    One of Marx's key concepts is historical materialism. Under this account social systems flourish or flounder according to their impact upon human productive power. Marx believed that history would progress through a series of stages that would end in communism. He believed that various economic systems (such as capitalism) had internal flaws or contradictions that would lead to their eventual collapse. Marx also had an interesting relationship with the writings of G. W. F. Hegel. Marx used different parts of Hegel's methodology but generally with a much different objective. For example, right-wing Hegelians took the Philosophy of Right *as a conservative doctrine that erected a caution sign in front of social change. Marx was a revolutionary. Hegel created an idealistic theory of "spirit" in history that Marx turned upside down into a history dominated by materialism rather than spirit. Also, Marx changed Hegel's key notion of dialectic. Dialectic as defined in* Hegel's Logic *concerns a process whereby one begins with a thesis that in order to be understood implies its logical complement—here called the antithesis. Both the thesis and antithesis in the initial stage, or moment of dialectic, are flawed due to their abstract nature. As one bounces back and forth trying to satisfy the need for concrete particularity, a concrete universal between the poles is gradually formed. This dynamic process Hegel called the dialectic. Marx mounted a revision of Hegel's dialectical methodology by emphasizing a positive progression rather than a back-and-forth.*

A GAME OF CHESS IN PARIS*

Michael Boylan

This story captures a significant moment in the life of Karl Marx: when he puts aside his philosophical idealism in favor of Engels's more pragmatic political approach. The two really did meet on or about this time in the Café de la Régence near the Tuileries. This café really did sport chess tables and was a popular hang out for chess enthusiasts. Whether Marx and Engels actually played chess and (if they did) the nature of the match are matters of fictive speculation.

Karl Marx was heading to the Café de la Régence near the Tuileries Gardens. He was walking along the Quai des Tuileries with the garden to his left and the Seine to his right toward the Louvre (now a decaying art museum). It was August, and it was hot. The Seine smelled, and flies were buzzing about the rotting decay of summer.

Marx wore a white cotton shirt with a soiled, wrinkled bright red cravat and tattered gray waistcoat that was missing a button.[†] His sleeves were stained at the armpits. He thrust his hands deeply into the pockets of his thin, light gray trousers, which were shiny at the knees. A rolled-up newspaper stuck out of his back pocket. His hair was a bit kinky and askew. He sported a dark brown moustache that had not been trimmed for a week.

When he got to the café cum chess establishment, he was amazed at the number of people already there. It was only 1 p.m., but the place was three-quarters full with people at chess tables and regular tables and with a busy contingent in the back playing pool.

---

* *In creating this fictive account, I wish to acknowledge Francis Wheen,* Karl Marx: A Life *(New York: W. W. Norton, 2000), esp., ch. 3 (p. 75 passim); Friedrich Engels, "When I Visited Marx in Paris in the Summer of 1844 . . . ," from* On the History of the Communist League, *translated in* The Cologne Communist Trial *(1885; rpt. London: Lawrence and Wishart, 1971); "Ueber den Ateil von Marx und Engels an der Politischen bewegung zur Vorbereitung der Revonlutionvon 1848,"* Zeitschrift fuer Geschichtswissenschaft *7, no. 5 (1959): 1028–1064; Neil J. Smelser,* Karl Marx: On Society and Social Change *(Chicago: University of Chicago Press, 1973), x ff.; Patrice Higonnet,* Paris: Capital of the World, *trans. Arthur Goldmammer (Cambridge, MA: Harvard University Press, 2002), 65ff; and Saul K. Padover,* Karl Marx: An Intimate Biography *(New York: McGraw-Hill, 1978), 183ff. These provided some of the material upon which this story is based.*

† *I wish to thank Annette Ames for her professional costume advice.*

190

Karl stepped up and was met by a very tiny, thin man with jet-black straight hair that was combed down with grease. The man wore a white shirt, black trousers, and a white waist apron. Around his neck was a black-and-white checked scarf tied to the side.

"S'il vous plaît, monsieur, do you want a regular or a chess table?"

Karl thought a moment and then said, "A chess table, naturellement monsieur. My friend and I want amusement."

The waiter smiled and walked Karl to a table on the sidewalk: one of the last sidewalk tables left. "Would you like some wine, coffee, or a little food?" inquired the man with the slicked-down hair.

"Sure, a glass of wine would be fine. When my friend comes, bring a bottle with some bread and cheese—and some chess pieces, of course."

"What sort of wine?"

"What is your cheapest?"

"Cotês du Rhone—the new stuff."

"Exactly."

The waiter retired.

Karl leaned back in his wrought iron chair. The metal loops that formed its back cut into his shoulder blades. He decided to unwrap the newspaper he had been carrying in his pant pocket and to light up a cigar. He was in Paris to meet his friend Friedrich Engels, who was staying over for a week or so. Marx was always late, but Engels was even later. Marx began reading his paper.

He hadn't been reading long before his friend arrived.

"What trash are you reading there, Karl? *Der Rheinishche Zeitung*? Give me a break. I hear it's being edited by a real hack!"

Karl glanced up at his friend and blew a mouthful of smoke at him. "Friedrich, you got to get some class in order to read a paper like this—Young Hegelians,[1] don't you know. Not the tired old man I'm sure you're used to reading." Then Karl stood up and shook his friend's hand and offered him a seat. Friedrich nodded and put his charcoal summer frock coat with its shiny gold buttons and stylish sharp-waist cutaway over the back of the chair. He wore a new dark red cravat that was accented by a waistcoat of maroon brocade.

"Where are the chess pieces?"

"Well, you can bring your own or you can rent them for a bit more on the bill."

"And did you bring some pieces?" asked Engels.

"Hell, no. I put it on your tab. You can afford it."

"I don't know if I can afford *you,*" Engels said as he took out a cigar of his own.

The waiter came by with a glass of wine that Karl offered to his friend, who took it.

---

1 **Young Hegelians:** intellectuals who, after the death of German philosopher Georg Wilhelm Friedrich Hegel (1770–1831), mounted radical criticisms of the Prussian religious and political order.

"Very nice of you, old thing," put Engels as he exhaled some smoke of his own and took a sip of wine. Then he made a face. "Very young, isn't it?"

"Trying to save you some money," replied Karl.

"Let's be clear on when it is time to economize. I'm getting something else."

Friedrich reordered the lunch with a proper Bordeaux.

After the small talk, Friedrich brought up Manchester. "You know that after our talk I found that there is a lot of interest in Feuerbach[2] and his critique of Hegel and of Christianity."

Then the food, wine, and chess pieces came. Marx put out his cigar and slipped the stub into his pocket. With his left hand he picked up a piece of bread as his friend poured the wine. Karl paused with the bread at his lips as he spied a comely young lady attired in a long blue and purple striped silk day dress that flattered her thin figure by smocking in the front and back from her waist just high enough to accent her young bosom. She wore a bonnet of gold with black piping that blocked the view of most of her face—leaving only a teasing glimpse of her elegant nose and chin. Around her neck was tied a thin yellow ribbon. Her hands sported thin white gloves. In her left hand she held an embroidered linen handkerchief from Belgium. An older woman, in a full skirt of green and white plaid silk taffeta with scalloped edges, accompanied the young siren. The lines of the matron reminded one of the letter *A*. Was it the beauty's mother? About the matron's head was a large rounded bonnet with curled red ribbons bouncing about. A full orange ribbon was tied in a bow around her neck. Both women carried their parasols carelessly to the side. The pair sauntered leisurely past the café. Friedrich looked too. When the pair had passed, the younger, Engels, lifted his eyebrows. "Beautiful women in Paris, eh Karl?"

The twenty-six-year-old newspaper editor smiled and took a bite of his bread. "You know, I'm still developing my ideas on this. On the one hand you have Bauer,[3] who thinks that Judaism is a barrier to emancipation. That's a bunch of crap. On the other hand, I think that organized religion is rather anthropocentric—don't you?"

"I think organized religion is a pile of shit!" replied Engels.

"Much too gross. You know there is such a thing as 'the thought itself.' In philosophy we often talk about this. The thought itself is only intelligible as it is embodied within a given culture at a certain moment in history."

"There you go with your highfalutin philosophy again. If there is one thing I'd like to be able to do, it's to rid you of this bourgeois philosophy."

"Socrates, Democritus, and Epicurus[4] were not bourgeois."

"There you go with your book learning again." Engels took a big piece of cheese and put it on the bread and ate the whole thing in one mouthful. Then he washed it down with an entire glass of wine.

---

2 **Feuerbach:** Ludwig Feuerbach (1804–1872), German philosopher.

3 **Bauer:** Bruno Bauer (1809–1882), German philosopher and theologian.

4 **Socrates, Democritus, and Epicurus:** Greek philosophers.

"Hey, you think that the school of hard knocks is the only way to learn, so be it," began Karl, "but let's play a little game just now as we continue our conversation. I'm sure that you'll see that there are some advantages to book learning. Maybe you'll change your mind."

Engels smiled and started setting up the white pieces as his own.

Marx grimaced.

The game began simply enough. The moves would have been rapid fire except for the conversation. "You know, Friedrich, you do me wrong to accuse me of being with the bourgeois in my education. Did you not read the article that I published by Max Stirner[5] titled 'The False Principles of Our Education' in which he advocates a model extending practical education, on a general scale, against our current model of the elite, considering abstract esoteric questions within the confines of a rarefied domain of ahistorical philosophy of ideas?"

"Well, you're the philosopher," said Engels as he moved his queen's knight to queen two. "But you were going there so mechanically, I don't think you noticed that on my third move I left my queen's knight's pawn without protection."

"Oh, really? I don't know. I was thinking about a plan I have to get you."

"The game has just begun."

The waiter brought them some more food and another bottle of wine. "I don't know what you have against the university, Friedrich." Karl found himself surprisingly hungry. He began to fashion a plan of attack in the chess game. He would get out his bishops and knights and gain control of the center. Then his opponent would see the elegance of his superior position and backtrack until Karl had won his point.

"Well, you know I've had some issues with my father," began Friedrich carefully studying the board. "But let me tell you that on one account we are in complete accord: each one of us has to make his own way in the world from the bottom up. That's why I took a crap job in his company after secondary school so that I could see things the way everyone else does. It gave me a street-smart education—what my father used to call 'the school of experience.'"

Karl looked at the board and moved his bishop to queen two. He always regarded openings as rather deductive. Something about this attracted him. The center of the board was neutralized, and he only had to get his other bishop out on the side and then pinch the king from the extremes while the light infantry rode up the middle and created utter chaos. Karl believed that if one had a deductive view of the realm of play, victory was inevitable.

"Well, I think that one thing we can agree upon is our criticism of Hegel," put Karl after his move.

"Well, yes and no. The chap was way off with his theory of the controlling force of *Geist*[6] in human history. We can replace *Geist* with modern science and economics and

---

5 **Max Stirner:** German philosopher Johann Kaspar Stirner (1806–1856), better known as Max Stirner.

6 **Geist:** here refers to a controlling spirit in human history.

rid ourselves of that bunch of nonsense. But I have been taken by some of Hegel's dialectical stances—like the master-slave dialectic."

Marx murmured soft assent.

Then Engels castled, reversing the position of the king and the rook.

"You know, I think you're engaging in a dialectic of your own just now on the chessboard. I could do the same, and many might applaud me, but I see my dialectic as somewhat different." Karl had his plan for the center of the board, and he didn't want to be taken offtrack.

Engels showed his hand, encouraging Marx to continue. Karl obliged. "Well, you see, I think (like you) that our friend Hegel got some things right though he also got a lot wrong."

Engels smiled and picked up the last piece of cheese as he moved a pawn to king four. Marx immediately took his pawn.

"The logically necessary character of dialectic reveals the progressive nature of human alienation. Hegel began this methodology in the introduction to the *Phenomenologie der Geist*. He set out several dialectical moments—some of which signified alienation."

"But social-political *alienation* was not a real problem for Herr Hegel because of the *Geist*."

"True, but that's getting ahead of ourselves. First, let's deal with alienation." Marx reached for some cheese, but the bowl was empty. He looked up to his friend, who presented a flat smile that appeared exaggerated by Friedrich's overgrown moustache. Karl grimaced back and picked up the last piece of bread. Then Friedrich poured the last glass of wine.

"You see?" began Karl. "But again we are going too quickly. This is something that I've been working on lately. My thesis is this: there are four progressive dialectical moments in alienation (to use Hegel's language) among the workingmen. The first is alienation from the product. When a skilled artisan creates something, a part of him resides in the artifact."

"Do you call a bolt of cloth produced in a textile mill an artifact?" Engels asked as he moved his king's rook toward the middle.

"Well, things aren't always what they seem, are they. Here you're building up an arsenal in the back center, while I have my light brigade out front. To have a satisfying job, a person has to take pride in what he or she produces—even if it is only a bolt of cloth in your father's factories."

"Please, argumentum ad hominem[7] does not suit you." The waiter came by to see if they wanted anything else, but Friedrich waved him away.

---

7 **argumentum ad hominem:** "argument against the man," a reply to an argument that evades the substance of the argument by instead raising questions about the person advancing it.

"No need to get huffy. It's just that people should feel pride in what they produce. They should recognize that part of who they are is in that product. When it is taken away in a mechanical fashion, they become alienated from that product."

Engels shrugged his shoulders and moved his king's rook to queen one. Marx didn't fully see the significance of this move.

"The next moment of alienation follows dialectically from the first. Once they are alienated from their work, then they become alienated from the activity of work itself, which is arduous and unpleasant."

"Anything can seem unpleasant."

"But, don't you see? If you're connected to your product, then the unpleasantness of your work doesn't matter. It's all part of an expression of self."

"All right. Your move."

Marx moved as he continued, "When one's outlet for individuality is squelched through the abolition of these primary relationships to product and its production, then one's very individuality is at risk. One's pride in his unique dignity as a person may float away—leading to another level of dialectical alienation."

Engels took out another cigar and lit it before moving his pawn to queen's rook four. Marx immediately jumped on this and took Engels's bishop. This put Marx in the lead very slightly.

"But cannot we expect more of our working men?" said Engels taking the first full puff of his newly lit cigar.

"I think we expect a lot from our workers, but then they expect more from themselves. But it is hardly fair to get down on them when they are mechanically driven to the third dialectical moment of their alienation of themselves from their very humanity." Marx leaned over the table and screwed up his face. There was sweat on his brow that he did not attempt to mop away. One drop fell upon the crown of his king.

Engels smiled and took another puff on his cigar. Though he wore a necktie, he seemed to be in a different temperature zone. There were no beads of sweat on his forehead. "So, you are improving on Herr Hegel with three dialectical moments of alienation that arise from work in our present manifestation of *Geist*?"

"*Geist* has nothing to do with it, and you know it. We're talking about *der dialektische Materialismus*. Materialism takes the place of spirit. It's all that science can prove." Marx sat back and wiped his brow. He felt rather proud of his little speech. Engels nodded, and they each exchanged a few moves on the chessboard.

Then Marx paused. "You know I haven't finished."

"I rather guessed as much," replied Engels. "But you're almost finished, right?"

Marx pursed his lips and moved again on the chessboard. "There is a fourth moment in the dialectic of alienation. It is an alienation from others. This gives the bourgeoisie the power to manipulate because the worker becomes isolated as the relation of exchange replaces the natural human satisfaction of reciprocity based on human need. In many ways this fourth and last form of alienation is the most insidious of all. This is because it takes from the worker his ability to help his neighbor and his power to change his own lot. It's rather a divide-and-conquer strategy—much like those American pamphleteers talked about in their own revolutionary struggle: Thomas Paine, John Adams,[8] and the like."

"You've read those?"

Marx nodded.

"Do you really think that there is something to be learned there?"

Marx nodded.

"No wonder you're so smart with all that book learning. It's all beyond a dunderhead like me." Engels then moved his bishop to bishop six: check.

"This doesn't look good," said Marx. "How did you get all your rooks down here? Is it a medieval crusade, goddamnit?"

"Play it out, Herr Philosopher," said Friedrich finishing his cigar. "Maybe you'll find a way to change it all through your four levels of alienation in dialectical materialism?"

Marx moved his king to bishop one. But the end was inevitable. There was nothing to be done. The power of the rooks—sometimes called castles because of what they represent—was too much. Three moves later Karl resigned. He was defeated by the most powerful forces on the board (save for the royalty). His early ideals about holding the center of the board through mechanical matching of his opponent proved futile even though they were technically correct. Who could have faulted him? But then he didn't castle when he could have. But he had been oblivious to the infiltration of the powerful rooks. These *c-rooks* used their capitalist influence to systematically infiltrate his design and bring about his downfall. Perhaps he'd underestimated the necessity of power properly applied to achieve the desired end?

Karl looked up and shook Friedrich's hand. "Say, why don't we go over to the park next door and sit under a tree to cool off. This game has given me some new ideas!"

Friedrich nodded, and the two walked forward into a week of conversation and contemplation that would change history.

■ NOTE

After having read this story, some intrepid souls may want to recreate the game that is used to situate this story. The game is based upon an early effort by Edward Lasker who

---

8 **Thomas Paine, John Adams:** Paine (1737–1809), American pamphleteer whose *Common Sense* (1776) helped galvanize pro-independence sentiment; Adams (1735–1826), American Founding Father and second president of the United States.

recounts it in *Chess Secrets I Learned from the Masters* (New York: David McKay Company, 1951), p. 31ff. The game goes like this (bolded moves indicate what I take to be key moments in the game):

White (Engels)-Black (Marx)/ 1. N-KB3—PQ4/ 2. P-Q4—N-KB3/ 3. B-B4—P-B4/ 4. P-K3—P-K3/ 5. P-B3—N-B3/ **6. QN-Q2—B-Q2**/ 7. B-Q3—B-K2/ **8. O-O—R-QB1**/ 9. PxP—BxP/ **10. P-K4—PxP**/ 11. NxP—NxN/ 12. BxN—Q-N3/ 13. Q-K2—N-K2/ **14. KR-Q1—B-N4**/ 15. Q-Q2—N-N3/ **16. P-QR4—NxB**/ 17. PxB—Q-B2/ 18. P-QN4—B-K2/ 19. RxP—R-Q1/ **20. B-B6 check—K-B1**/ 21. Q-B2—P-KN3/ 22. RxP—Q-B-1/ 23. RxR check—Marx resigns.

I suggest replaying this game with a classmate and discussing the positions on the board—especially after the bolded moves—in light of the action that is occurring in the story. How do the two reinforce each other?

■ READING AND DISCUSSION QUESTIONS

1. Go to the Internet and research who Marx and Engels were and how communism began. How is socialism different from communism?
2. What did you make of the coincidence of a chess café located near the country's greatest art museum? Is chess an art or a science?
3. Why was Marx sweating while Engels was not? Why is this significant to the story?
4. In general, how does the metaphor of a chess game relate to the topic of conversation?
5. Who was wealthier, Marx or Engels? How does this affect the dynamics of the scene and the conversation?
6. When the subject of religion comes up, the two men react differently. What does this tell us about their approaches? Is Marx really bourgeois?
7. What about Marx's basic approach to the chess game dooms him to lose to an opponent like Engels? How is this reflected in their later relationship?
8. How is Marx's account of alienation not in the Hegelian dialectic style? What is Marx's concern?

■ FICTIVE-NARRATIVE PHILOSOPHY FEEDBACK

What claims are made in this story? Write them out in a bulleted list and include whether they are made through dialogue, dramatic action, or the presentation of the scene (including descriptive detail). One page. Then choose either a short direct-discourse response (according to the rules in Chapter 2) or a short fictive-narrative presentation (according to the rules in Chapter 3).

PREFACE

G. W. F. Hegel

Adapted from G. W. F. Hegel, *The Phenomenology of Mind*, trans. J. B. Baillie (London: G. Allen & Unwin, 1931), 107–111.* *Note on the translation:* English words found in brackets are inserted by the translator to make better sense of the English rendering.

Georg Wilhelm Friedrich Hegel (1770–1831), considered by many to be one of the most influential philosophers of the nineteenth century, created a comprehensive system of logic, epistemology, metaphysics, and ethics (including social and political ethics) that influenced other key philosophers, such as Karl Marx and Martin Heidegger (who even wrote a commentary upon the phenomenology of spirit). Hegel makes a clean break from the critical empiricism of Immanuel Kant to an intricate idealism based on the subject. In the following selections, three of Hegel's most famous presentations lay out important aspects of his philosophical point of view.

In this first passage, from the preface to his Phenomenology of Mind, *Hegel sets out an idealistic theory of epistemology and metaphysics that relies on his dynamic dialectical method (which adds onto the presentation of a problem one layer at a time). Hegel is keen to separate himself from Kant and connect to the pre-Aristotelian Greek philosophers. He believes that Kant is too abstract (in Hegel's vocabulary, Kant stops at the first dialectical moment). One moves away from empty formalism by establishing determinate identity through a dialectic that incorporates concrete identity.*

In everyday life the mind finds its content in different kinds of knowledge, experiences of various sorts, concrete facts of sense, thoughts, too, and principles, and, in general, in whatever lies ready to hand, or passes for a solid stable entity, or real being. The mind follows wherever this leads, sometimes interrupting the connection by an unrestrained caprice in dealing with the content, and takes up the attitude of determining and handling it in quite an external fashion. It runs the content back to some touchstone of certainty or other, even though it be but the feeling of the moment; and conviction is satisfied if it reaches some familiar resting place.

---

* This text is also translated under the title The Phenomenology of Spirit *(according to how one wishes to translate the German word* Geist*).*

But when the necessity of the notion banishes from its realm the loose procedure of the *raisonnements* ("reasonings") of conversation, as well as the pedantic style of scientific pomposity, its place, as we have already mentioned, must not be taken by the disconnected utterance of presageful surmise and inspiration and the arbitrary caprice of prophetic utterance; for this does not merely despise that particular form of scientific procedure but condemns scientific procedure altogether.

Kant's Empty Formalism

Now that the triplicity,[9] adopted in the system of Kant—a method rediscovered, to begin with, by instinctive insight but left lifeless and uncomprehended—has been raised to its significance as an absolute method, true form is thereby set up in its true content, and the conception of science has come to light. But the use this form has been put to in certain quarters has no right to the name of science. For we see it there reduced to a lifeless schema, to nothing better than a mere shadow, and scientific organization to a synoptic table. This formalism thinks it has comprehended and expressed the nature and life of a given form when it proclaims a determination of the schema to be its predicate. The predicate may be subjectivity or objectivity, or again magnetism, electricity, and so on, contraction or expansion, East or West, and such like—a form of predication that can be multiplied indefinitely because, according to this way of working, each determination, each mode, can be applied as a form or schematic element in the case of every other, and each will thankfully perform the same service for any other. With a circle of reciprocities of this sort, it is impossible to make out what the real fact in question is, or what the one or the other is. We find there sometimes constituents of sense picked up from ordinary intuition, determinate elements that, to be sure, should mean something else than they say; at other times what is inherently significant, namely, pure determinations of thought—like subject, object, substance, cause, universality, etc.—these are applied just as uncritically and unreflectingly as in everyday life, are used much as people employ the terms strong and weak, expansion and contraction. As a result, that type of metaphysics is as unscientific as those ideas of sense.

Instead of the inner activity and self-movement of its own actual life, such a simple determination of direct intuition (*Anschauung*)—which means here sense knowledge—is predicated in accordance with a superficial analogy, and this external and empty application of the formula is called "construction." The same thing happens here, however, as in the case of

---

9 **triplicity:** Hegel alludes here to Kant's categories of thesis, antithesis, and synthesis, which are set out in Kant's "Transcendental Dialectic" (the last major section of the *Critique of Pure Reason*). It should be noted that Hegel's own "triple method" of dialectic is more dynamic and interactive than Kant's, which merely sets out opposing theses (such as whether the universe has a beginning or not) and then forges a compromise. On a surface level these seem to be similar, but they operate differently: static (Kant) versus dynamic (Hegel).

every kind of formalism. A man's head must be indeed dull if he could not in a quarter of an hour get up the theory that there are enervating (weakening), innervating (stimulating), and indirectly enervating diseases and as many cures, and who could not in as short a time be turned from being a man who works by rule of thumb into a theoretical physician.

Formalism in the case of speculative philosophy of nature (*Naturphilosophie*) takes the shape of teaching that understanding is electricity, animals are nitrogen, or equivalent to South or North and so on. When it does this, whether as badly as it is here expressed or even concocted with more terminology, such forceful procedure brings and holds together elements to all appearance far removed from one another; the violence done to stable inert sense elements by connecting them in this way, confers on them merely the semblance of a conceptual unity and spares itself the trouble of doing what is after all the important thing—expressing the notion itself, the meaning that underlies sense ideas. All this sort of thing may strike anyone who has no experience with admiration and wonder. He may be awed by the profound genius he thinks it displays and be delighted at the happy ingenuity of such characterizations since they fill the place of the abstract notion with something tangible and sensuous and so make it more pleasing; and he may congratulate himself on feeling an instinctive mental affinity for that glorious way of proceeding. The trick of wisdom of that sort is as quickly acquired as it is easy to practice. Its repetition, when once it is familiar, becomes as boring as the repetition of any bit of sleight of hand once we see through it.

The instrument for producing this monotonous formalism is no more difficult to handle than the palette of a painter on which lie only two colors, say red and green, the former for coloring the surface when we want a historical piece, the latter when we want a bit of landscape. It would be difficult to settle which is greater in all this, the agreeable ease with which everything in heaven and earth and under the earth is plastered with that botch of color or the conceit that prides itself on the excellence of its means for every conceivable purpose; the one lends support to the other. What results from the use of this method of sticking on to everything in heaven and earth, to every kind of shape and form, natural and spiritual, the pair of determinations from the general schema, and filing everything in this manner, is no less than an "account as clear as noonday"[10] of the organized whole of the universe. It is, that is to say, a synoptic index, like a skeleton with tickets stuck all over it or like the rows of boxes kept shut and labeled in a grocer's stall, and is as intelligible as either the one or the other. It has lost hold of the living nature of concrete fact; just as in the former case we have merely dry bones with flesh and blood all gone, and in the latter, there is shut away in those boxes something equally lifeless too. We have already remarked that the final outcome of this style of thinking is, at the same time, to paint entirely in one kind of

---

10 **"account as clear as noonday":** from Johann Gottlieb Fichte's "Sonnenklarer Bericht an das Publikum über das eigentliche Wesden der neuesten Philosophie."

color; for it turns with contempt from the distinctions in the schematic table, looks on them as belonging to the activity of mere reflection, and lets them drop out of sight in the void of the absolute, and there reinstates pure identity, pure formless whiteness. Such uniformity of coloring in the schema with its lifeless determinations, this absolute identity, and the transition from one to the other—these are the *one* as well as the other, the expression of inert lifeless understanding, and equally an external process of knowledge.

Not only can what is excellent not escape the fate of being thus devitalized and despiritualized and excoriated of seeing its skin paraded about by lifeless knowledge and the conceit such knowledge engenders, but such a fate lets us realize the power the "excellent" exercises over the heart (*Gemüth*), if not over the mind (*Geist*). Moreover, we recognize thereby, too, the constructive unfolding into universality and determinateness of form that marks the complete attainment of excellence and alone makes it possible that this universality can be turned to superficial uses.

The Notion of Determinate Identity

Science can become an organic system only by the inherent life of the notion.[11] In science the determinateness,[12] which was taken from the schema and stuck onto existing facts in external fashion, is the self-directing inner soul of the concrete content. The movement of what is partly consists in becoming another to itself and thus developing explicitly into its own immanent content; partly, again, it takes this evolved content, this existence it assumes, back into itself, that is, makes *itself* into a moment, and reduces itself to simple determinateness. In the first stage of the process negativity lies in the function of distinguishing and establishing existence; in this latter return into self, negativity consists in the bringing about of determinate simplicity. It is in this way that the content shows its specific characteristic not to be received from something else and stuck on externally; the content gives itself this determinate characteristic, appoints itself of its own initiative to the rank of a moment and to a place in the whole. The pigeon-holing process of understanding retains for itself the necessity and the notion controlling the content, that which constitutes the concrete element, the actuality and living process of the subject matter that it labels. Or rather, understanding does not retain this for itself; on the contrary, understanding fails to know it. For if it had as much insight as that, it would surely show that it had. It is not even aware of the need for such insight; if it were, it would drop its schematizing process or, at least, would no longer be satisfied to know by way of a mere table of contents. A table of contents is all that understanding gives; the content itself it does not furnish at all.

If the specific determination (say even one like magnetism) is one that in itself is concrete or actual, it all the same gets

---

11 **notion:** *Begriff;* a concept or the way something is understood. This is an important term for Hegel.

12 **determinateness:** to be determinate is to be *necessary*, in other words, it cannot be otherwise. Compare Kant's use of *apodeictic*.

degraded into something lifeless and inert since it is merely predicated of another existing entity and not known as an immanent living principle of this existence; nor is there any comprehension of how in this entity its intrinsic and peculiar way of expressing and producing itself takes effect. This, the very kernel of the matter, formal understanding leaves to others to add later on. Instead of making its way into the inherent content of the matter in hand, understanding always takes a survey of the whole and assumes a position above the particular existence about which it is speaking; that is, it does not see it at all.

True scientific knowledge, on the contrary, demands abandonment to the very life of the object or, which means the same thing, claims to have before it the inner necessity controlling the object and to express this only. Steeping itself in its object, it forgets to take that general survey, which is merely a turning of knowledge away from the content back into itself. But being sunk into the material in hand and following the course that such material takes, true knowledge returns back into itself, yet not before the content in its fullness is taken into itself, is reduced to the simplicity of being a determinate characteristic, drops to the level of being one aspect of an existing entity, and passes over into its higher truth. By this process, the whole as such, surveying its entire content, itself emerges out of the wealth wherein its process of reflection seemed to be lost.

In general, in virtue of the principle that substance is implicitly and in itself subject, all content makes its reflection into itself in its own special way. The subsistence or substance[13] of anything that exists is its self-identity, for its want of identity, or oneness with itself, would be its dissolution. But self-identity is pure abstraction, and this is just thinking. When I say quality, I state simple determinateness; by means of its quality one existence is distinguished from another or is an "existence"; it is for itself, something on its own account, or subsists with itself because of this simple characteristic. But by doing so it is essentially thought.

Here we find contained the principle that Being is thought: here is exercised that insight which usually tends to deviate from the ordinary nonconceptual way of speaking of the identity of thought and being. In virtue, further, of the fact that subsistence on the part of what exists is self-identity or pure abstraction, it is the abstraction of itself from itself, in other words, is itself its own want of identity with itself and dissolution—its own proper inwardness and retraction into self—its process of becoming.

Owing to the nature that being thus has, and so far as what is has this nature from the point of view of knowledge, this thinking is not an activity that treats the content as something alien and external; it is not reflection into self away from the content. Science is not that kind of idealism that stepped into the place of the dog-

---

13 **subsistence or substance:** the point here is that substance must contain a principle of enduring over time in order to be able to say that it subsists. This is an important question for all idealistic theories since they originate within the subject.

matism of mere assertion and took the shape of a dogmatism of mere assurance, the dogmatism of mere self-certainty. Rather, since knowledge sees the content go back into its own proper inner nature, the activity of knowledge is absorbed in that content—for it (the activity) is the immanent self of the content—and is also at the same time returned into itself, for this activity is pure self-identity in otherness. In this way the knowing activity is the artful device that, while seeming to refrain from activity, looks on and watches how specific determinateness with its concrete life, just where it believes it is working out its own self-preservation and its own private interest, is, in point of fact, doing the very opposite, is doing what brings about its own dissolution and makes itself a moment in the whole.

How Determinate Identity Comes About

While in the foregoing the significance of understanding was stated from the point of view of the self-consciousness of substance, by what has been here stated we can see clearly its significance from the point of view of substance qua being.[14] Existence is quality, self-identical determinateness, or determinate simplicity, deter-

minate thought: this is existence from the point of view of understanding. On this account it is *voûs* [*nous*, or "mind"], as Anaxagoras[15] first thought reality to be. Those who succeeded him grasped the nature of existence in a more determinate way as ειδος [*eidos*, or "form"] or ιδέα ["idea," compare with Plato's Forms or Ideas],[16] that is, as determinate or specific universality, kind, or species. The term *species* or *kind* seems indeed too ordinary and inadequate for Ideas, for beauty, holiness, eternal, which are the vogue in these days. As a matter of fact, however, idea (ιδέα) means neither more nor less than kind, species. But we often find nowadays that a term that exactly designates a conception is despised and rejected, and another is preferred to it that hides and obscures the conception, and thus sounds more edifying, even though this is merely due to its being expressed in a foreign language.

Precisely for the reason that existence is designated a species or kind, it is a naked simple thought; *voûs*, simplicity, is substance. It is on account of its simplicity, its self-identity, that it appears steady, fixed, and permanent. But this self-identity is likewise negativity; hence, that fixed and stable existence carries the process of its own dissolution within itself.[17] The determinateness appears at first to be so solely

---

14 **substance qua being:** substance as being.

15 **Anaxagoras:** pre-Socratic philosopher (c. 500–428 BCE). Anaxagoras held that *nous*, or "mind," was a driving and unifying principle in metaphysics, taking on much the same role as Hegel attributes to mind or spirit (*Geist*).

16 **Forms or Ideas:** in earlier translations of Plato, "Idea" was used. Now "Form" is a more common translation. Here Hegel is connecting himself to the Greeks in much the same way as Heidegger will later.

17 **fixed and stable . . . within itself:** this is an example of Hegel's dialectical method at work.

through its relation to something else; and its process seems imposed and forced upon it externally. But its having its own otherness within itself, and the fact of its being a self-initiated process—these are implied in the very simplicity of thought itself. For this is self-moving thought, thought that distinguishes, is inherent inwardness, the pure notion. Thus, then, it is the very nature of understanding to be a process, and being a process, it is rationality.

In the nature of existence as thus described—to be its own notion and being in one—consists logical necessity in general. This alone is what is rational, the rhythm of the organic whole: it is as much knowledge of content as that content is notion and essential nature. In other words, this alone is the sphere and element of speculative thought. The concrete shape of the content is resolved by its own inherent process into a simple determinate quality. Thereby it is raised to logical form, and its being and essence coincide; its concrete existence is merely this process that takes place, and is *eo ipso* ("by that very fact") logical existence. It is therefore needless to apply a formal scheme to the concrete content in an external fashion; the content is in its very nature a transition into a formal shape, which, however, ceases to be formalism of an external kind, because the form is the indwelling process of the concrete content itself.

This nature of scientific method, which consists partly in being inseparable from the content and partly in determining the

rhythm of its movement by its own agency, finds its peculiar systematic expression in speculative philosophy. What is here stated describes in effect the essential principle but cannot stand for more at this stage than an assertion or assurance by way of anticipation. The truth it contains is not to be found in this exposition, which is in part historical in character. And just for that reason, too, it is not in the least refuted if anyone assures us on the contrary that this is not so, that the process instead is here so and so; if ideas we are all used to, being truths accepted or settled and familiar to everyone, are brought to mind and recounted; or, again, if something new is served up and guaranteed as coming from the inner sanctuaries of inspired intuition.

Such a view is bound to meet with opposition.[18] The first instinctive reaction on the part of knowing, when offered something unfamiliar, is usually to resist it. It seeks by that means to save freedom and native insight, to secure its own inherent authority—against alien authority—for that is the way anything apprehended for the first time appears. This attitude is adopted, too, in order to do away with the semblance of a kind of disgrace lying in the fact that something has had to be learnt. In like manner, again, when the unfamiliar or unknown is received with applause, the reaction is in the same way an exaltation of freedom and native authority. It consists in something analogous to ultra-revolutionary declamation and action.

––––––––––––

18 **bound to meet with opposition:** this is the concluding of the dialectic working on this problem.

■ READING AND DISCUSSION QUESTIONS

1. Go to the Internet and look up philosophical idealism. What sets it off as a distinct theory?
2. What does Hegel mean by Kant's empty formalism? How might Kant reply?
3. How do Hegel and Kant differ in their understanding of the way determinateness comes about?
4. How does negativity function in distinguishing and establishing existence?
5. What does Hegel mean when he says that true scientific knowledge claims to have "the inner necessity controlling the object"?
6. What is the self-identity of a substance?
7. How are being and thought related?
8. Describe the process of becoming.
9. How does Hegel see his metaphysical system in relation to that of the ancient Greeks?

■ CLASS EXERCISES

A. *Direct logical discourse:* Using the tools found in Chapter 2, outline the argument suggested by one of the reading and discussion questions. Based on your assessment of one key premise, write a one-page argument about why you agree or disagree with the argument's conclusion.

B. *Fictive-narrative philosophy:* Using the tools found in Chapter 3, begin with a claim that relates to the reading and discussion questions above. Then create a modern-day story about people or situations familiar to you that makes the logical claim you have identified. Three pages.

LORDSHIP AND BONDAGE

G. W. F. Hegel

Adapted from G. W. F. Hegel, *The Phenomenology of Mind,* trans. J. B. Baillie (London: G. Allen & Unwin, 1931), 228–240.* *Note on the translation:* English words found in brackets are inserted by the translator to make better sense of the English rendering.

"Lordship and Bondage" is one of the most famous subparts of the Phenomenology. *It is often called the "Master-Slave Dialectic." This passage suggests that there can exist in ethics and social and political philosophy a relation of a dominant figure and a subordinate. Whether we are talking about everyday interpersonal relationships or legal systems that subordinate others based on some conception of natural domination, the argument is roughly the same (though when the master possesses great power, the ability of the slave to change things is severely limited). Since this is one of the most perennial problems in ethics and social and political philosophy, this text has had much influence.*

Self- and Other Consciousness

Self-consciousness exists in itself and for itself, in that and by the fact that it exists for another self-consciousness; that is to say, it *is* only by being acknowledged or "recognized." The conception of this—its unity in its duplication of infinitude realizing itself in self-consciousness—has many sides to it and encloses within it elements of varied significance. Thus, its moments must on the one hand be strictly kept apart in detailed distinctiveness and, on the other, in this distinction must, at the same time, also be taken as not distinguished, or must always be accepted and understood in their opposite sense. This double meaning of what is distinguished lies in the nature of self-consciousness—of its being infinite, or directly the opposite of the determinateness in which it is fixed. The detailed exposition of the notion of this spiritual unity in its duplication will bring before us the process of *recognition.*[19]

Self-consciousness has before it another self-consciousness; it has come outside itself. This has a double significance. First, it has lost its own self since it finds itself as

---

* *This text is also translated under the title* The Phenomenology of Spirit *(according to how one wishes to translate the German word* Geist*).*

19 **recognition:** a key concept. It breaks the status quo. Without recognition the master-slave relation will continue.

an *other* being; secondly, it has thereby sublated [negated][20] that other, for it does not regard the other as essentially real but sees its own self in the other.

It must cancel this (its other). To do so is the sublation of that first double meaning and is therefore a second double meaning. First, it must set itself to sublate the other independent being, in order thereby to become certain of itself as true being, second, it thereupon proceeds to sublate its own self, for this other is itself.

This sublation in a double sense of its otherness in a double sense is at the same time a return in a double sense into its self. For, first, through sublation, it gets back itself because it becomes one with itself again through the canceling of *its* otherness; but second, it likewise gives otherness back again to the other self-consciousness, for it was aware of being in the other, it cancels this its own being in the other and thus lets the other again go free.

This process of self-consciousness in relation to another self-consciousness has in this manner been represented as the action of one alone. But this action on the part of the one has itself the double significance of being at once its own action and the action of that other as well. For the other is likewise independent, shut up within itself, and there is nothing in it that is not there through itself. The first does not have the object before it only in the passive form characteristic primarily of the object of desire but as an object existing independently for itself, over which therefore it has no power to do anything for its own benefit, if that object does not per se intrinsically do what the first does to it. The process then is absolutely the double process of both self-consciousnesses. Each sees the other do the same as itself; each itself does what it demands on the part of the other, and for that reason does what it does, only so far as the other does the same. Action from one side only would be useless because what is to happen can only be brought about by means of both.

Consequences of the Dual Sense of Self and Other

The action has then a *double entente* ("double meaning") not only in the sense that it is an act done to itself as well as to the other, but also in the sense that the act *simpliciter* ("by itself") is the act of the one as well as of the other regardless of their distinction.

In this movement we see the process repeated that came before us as the play of forces; in the present case, however, it is found in consciousness. What in the former had effect only for us [contemplating experience] holds here for the terms themselves. The middle term is self-consciousness, which breaks itself up into the extremes, and each extreme is this interchange of its own determinateness and complete transition into the opposite. While qua consciousness, it no doubt comes outside itself;

---

20 **sublated [negated]:** *Aufhebung* (often translated as "sublation") means literally to lift out, with the contradictory senses of both preservation and change. It is appropriate that dialectically inclined Hegel would use such a term, for it brings dynamism to his presentation. The reader must refer to the particular context for the meaning in that context.

still, in being outside itself, it is at the same time restrained within itself, it exists for itself, and its self-externalization is for consciousness. *Consciousness* finds that it immediately is and is not another consciousness, as also that this other is for itself only when it cancels itself as existing for itself and has self-existence only in the self-existence of the other. Each is the mediating term to the other, through which each mediates and unites itself with itself; and each is to itself and to the other an immediate self-existing reality, which, at the same time, exists thus for itself only through this mediation. They recognize themselves as mutually recognizing one another.

This pure conception of recognition, of duplication of self-consciousness within its unity, we must now consider in the way its process appears for self-consciousness. It will, in the first place, present the aspect of the disparity of the two, or the breakup of the middle term into the extremes, which, qua extremes, are opposed to one another, and of which one is merely recognized, while the other only recognizes.

Self-consciousness is primarily simple existence for self, self-identity by exclusion of every other from itself. It takes its essential nature and absolute object to be ego, and in this immediacy, in this bare fact of its self-existence, it is individual. That which for it is other stands as unessential object, as object with the impress and character of negation. But the other is also a self-consciousness; an individual makes its appearance in antithesis to an individual. Appearing thus in their immediacy, they are for each other in the manner of ordinary objects. They are independent individual forms, modes of consciousness

that have not risen above the bare level of life (for the existent object here has been determined as life). They are, moreover, forms of consciousness that have not yet accomplished for one another the process of absolute abstraction, of uprooting all immediate existence, and of being merely the bare, negative fact of self-identical consciousness; or, in other words, have not yet revealed themselves to each other as existing purely for themselves (that is, as self-consciousness). Each is indeed certain of its own self but not of the other, and hence its own certainty of itself is still without truth. For its truth would be merely that its own individual existence *for itself* would be shown to it to be an independent object, or, which is the same thing, that the object would be exhibited as this pure certainty of itself. By the notion of recognition, however, this is not possible, except in the form that as the other is for it, so *it is* for the other; each in its self through its *own action* and again through the *action of the other* achieves this pure abstraction of existence for self.

Dialectical Moment One: Dissolving the Abstraction

The presentation of itself, however, as pure abstraction of self-consciousness consists in showing itself as a pure negation of its objective form, or in showing that it is fettered to no determinate existence, that it is not bound at all by the particularity everywhere characteristic of existence as such, and is *not* tied up with life. The process of bringing all this out involves a twofold action—action on the part of the other and action on the part of itself. In so far as it is the other's action, each aims at the destruction and death of the other. But in this there is implicated also the second kind of action, self-activity; for the former implies that it risks its own life. The relation of both self-consciousnesses is in this way so constituted that they prove themselves and each other through a life-and-death struggle. They must enter into this struggle, for they must bring their certainty of themselves, the certainty of being for themselves, to the level of objective truth and make this a fact both in the case of the other and in their own case as well. And it is solely by risking life that freedom is obtained; only thus is it tried and proved that the essential nature of self-consciousness is not bare existence, is not the merely immediate form in which it at first makes its appearance, is not its mere absorption in the expanse of life. Rather it is thereby guaranteed that there is nothing present but what might be taken as a vanishing moment—that self-consciousness is merely pure self-existence, being-for-self. The individual, who has not staked his life, may, no doubt, be recognized as a *person*, but he has not attained the truth of this recognition as an independent self-consciousness. In the same way each must aim at the death of the other, as it risks its own life thereby; for that other is to it of no more worth than itself; the other's reality is presented to the former as an external other, as outside itself; it must cancel that externality. The other is a purely existent consciousness and entangled in manifold ways; it must view its otherness as pure existence for itself or as absolute negation.

This trial by death, however, cancels both the truth that was to result from it and therewith the certainty of self altogether. For just as life is the natural "position" of consciousness, independence without absolute negativity, so death is the natural "negation" of consciousness, negation without independence, which thus remains without the requisite significance of actual recognition. Through death, doubtless, there has arisen the certainty that both did stake their life and held it lightly both in their own case and in the case of the other; but that is not for those who underwent this struggle. They cancel their consciousness, which had its place in this alien element of natural existence; in other words, they cancel themselves and are sublated as terms or extremes seeking to have existence on their own account. But along with this there vanishes from the play of change the essential moment, namely, that of breaking up into extremes with opposite characteristics; and the middle term collapses into a lifeless unity that is broken up into lifeless extremes, merely existent and not opposed. And the two do not mutually give and receive one another back from each other through consciousness; they let one another go quite indifferently, like things. Their act is abstract negation, not the negation characteristic of consciousness, which cancels in such a way that it preserves and maintains what is sublated and thereby survives its being sublated.

Dialectical Moment Two: Creating Concrete Thinghood

In this experience self-consciousness becomes aware that *life* is as essential to it as pure self-consciousness. In immediate self-consciousness the simple ego is absolute object, which, however, is for us or in itself absolute mediation and has as its essential moment substantial and solid independence. The dissolution of that simple unity is the result of the first experience; through this there is posited a pure self-consciousness and a consciousness that is not purely for itself but for another, that is, as an existent consciousness, consciousness in the form and shape of thinghood. Both moments are essential since, in the first instance, they are unlike and opposed, and their reflexion into unity has not yet come to light, they stand as two opposed forms or modes of consciousness. The one is independent, and its essential nature is to be for itself; the other is dependent, and its essence is life or existence for another. The former is the master, or lord, the latter the bondsman.

The master is the consciousness that exists *for itself*, but no longer merely the general notion of existence for self. Rather, it is a consciousness existing on its own account that is mediated with itself through an other consciousness (that is, through an other whose very nature implies that it is bound up with an independent being or with thinghood in general). The master brings himself into relation to both these moments, to a thing as such, the object of desire, and to the consciousness whose essential character is thinghood. And since the master, is (a) qua notion of self-consciousness, an immediate relation of self-existence, but (b) is now moreover at the same time mediation, or a being-for-self that is for itself only through an other—he [the master] stands in relation (a) immediately to both (b) mediately to each through the other. The master relates himself to the bondsman mediately through

independent existence, for that is precisely what keeps the bondsman in thrall; it is his chain, from which he could not in the struggle get away, and for that reason he proved himself to be dependent, to have his independence in the shape of thinghood. The master, however, is the power controlling this state of existence, for he has shown in the struggle that he holds it to be merely something negative. Since he is the power dominating existence, while this existence again is the power controlling the other [the bondsman], the master holds, par consequence, this other in subordination. In the same way the master relates himself to the thing mediately through the bondsman. The [bondsman], being a self-consciousness in the broad sense, also takes up a negative attitude to things and cancels them; but the thing is, at the same time, independent for him, and, in consequence, he cannot, with all his negating, get so far as to annihilate it outright and be done with it; that is to say, he merely works on it. To the master, on the other hand, by means of this mediating process, belongs the immediate relation, in the sense of the pure negation of it; in other words, he gets the enjoyment. What mere desire did not attain, he now succeeds in attaining, namely, to have done with the thing and find satisfaction in enjoyment. Desire alone did not get the length of this because of the independence of the thing. The master, however, who has interposed the bondsman between it and himself, thereby relates himself merely to the dependence of the thing and enjoys it without qualification and without reserve. The aspect of its independence he leaves to the bondsman, who labors upon it.

The Master's Recognition

In these two moments, the master gets his recognition through an other consciousness, for in them the latter affirms itself as unessential, both by working upon the thing and, on the other hand, by the fact of being dependent on a determinate existence; in neither case can this other get the mastery over existence and succeed in absolutely negating it. We have thus here this moment of recognition, namely, that the other consciousness cancels itself as self-existent, and, ipso facto ("by that fact itself"), itself does what the first does to it. In the same way we have the other moment, that this action on the part of the second is the action proper of the first; for what is done by the bondsman is properly an action on the part of the master. The latter exists only for himself; that is his essential nature; he is the negative power without qualification, a power to which the thing is naught. And he is thus the absolutely essential act in this situation, while the bondsman is not so; he is an unessential activity. But for recognition proper there is needed the moment when what the master does to the other he should also do to himself, and what the bondsman does to himself, he should do to the other also. On that account a form of recognition has arisen that is one-sided and unequal.

In all this, the unessential consciousness is, for the master, the object that embodies the truth of his certainty of himself. But it is evident that this object does not correspond to its notion; for, just where the master has effectively achieved lordship, he really finds that something has come about quite different from an independent consciousness. It is not an independent, but rather a dependent, consciousness that he has achieved. He is thus not assured of self-existence as his truth; he finds that his truth is rather the unessential consciousness and the fortuitous unessential action of that consciousness.

The Twofold Consciousness

The truth of the independent consciousness is accordingly the consciousness of the bondsman. This doubtless appears in the first instance outside itself and not as the truth of self-consciousness. But just as lordship showed its essential nature to be the reverse of what it wants to be, so, too, bondage will, when completed, pass into the opposite of what it immediately is: being a consciousness repressed within itself, it will enter into itself and change round into real and true independence.

We have seen what bondage is only in relation to lordship. But it is a self-consciousness, and we have now to consider what it is, in this regard, in and for itself. In the first instance, the master is taken to be the essential reality for the state of bondage; hence, for it, the truth is the independent consciousness existing for itself, although this truth is not taken yet as inherent in bondage itself. Still, it does in fact contain within itself this truth of pure negativity and self-existence because it has experienced this reality within it. For this consciousness was not in peril and fear for this element or that, nor for this or that moment of time; it was afraid for its entire being; it felt the fear of death, the sovereign master. It has been in that experience melted to its inmost soul, has trembled throughout its every fiber, and all that was fixed and steadfast has quaked within it. This complete perturbation of its entire substance, this absolute dissolution of all its stability into fluent continuity, is, however, the simple, ultimate nature of self-consciousness, absolute negativity, pure self-referent existence, which consequently is involved in this type of consciousness. This moment of pure self-existence is moreover a fact for it; for in the master it finds this as its object. Further, this bondsman's consciousness is not only this total dissolution in a general way; in serving and toiling the bondsman actually carries this out. By serving he cancels in every particular aspect his dependence on and attachment to natural existence, and by his work removes this existence away.

The feeling of absolute power, however, realized both in general and in the particular form of service, is only dissolution implicitly; and albeit the fear of the lord is the beginning of wisdom, consciousness is not therein aware of being self-existent. Through work and labor, however, this consciousness of the bondsman comes to itself. In the moment that corresponds to desire in the case of the master's consciousness, the aspect of the nonessential relation to the thing seemed to fall to the lot of the servant, since the thing there retained its independence. Desire has reserved to itself the pure negating of the object and thereby unalloyed feeling of self. This satisfaction, however, just for that reason is itself only a state of evanescence, for it lacks objectivity or subsistence. Labor, on the other hand, is desire restrained and checked, evanescence

delayed and postponed; in other words, labor shapes and fashions the thing. The negative relation to the object passes into the *form* of the object, into something that is permanent and remains, because it is just for the laborer that the object has independence. This negative mediating agency, this activity giving shape and form, is at the same time the individual existence, the pure self-existence of that consciousness, which now in the work it does is externalized and passes into the condition of permanence. The consciousness that toils and serves accordingly attains by this means the direct apprehension of that independent being as its self.

The Third Dialectical Moment: The Resolution

But again, shaping or forming the object has not only the positive significance that the bondsman becomes thereby aware of himself as factually and objectively self-existent; this type of consciousness has also a negative import, in contrast with its first moment, the element of fear. For in shaping the thing, it only becomes aware of its own proper negativity, its existence on its own account, as an object, through the fact that it cancels the actual form confronting it. But this objective negative element is precisely the alien, external reality, before which it trembled. Now, however, it destroys this extraneous alien negative, affirms and sets itself up as a negative in the element of permanence, and thereby becomes for itself a self-existent being. In the master, the bondsman feels self-existence to be something external, an objective fact; in fear self-existence is present within himself; in fashioning the thing, self-existence comes to be felt explicitly as his own proper being, and he attains the consciousness that he himself exists in its own right and on its own account [*an und für sich*]. By the fact that the form is objectified, it does not become something other than the consciousness molding the thing through work; for just that form is his pure self-existence, which therein becomes truly realized. Thus, precisely in labor where there seemed to be merely some outsider's mind and ideas involved, the bondsman becomes aware, through this rediscovery of himself by himself of having and being a "mind of his own."

For this reflection of self into self the two moments, fear and service in general, as also that of formative activity, are necessary: and at the same time, both must exist in a universal manner. Without the discipline of service and obedience, fear remains formal and does not spread over the whole known reality of existence. Without the formative activity shaping the thing, fear remains inward and mute, and consciousness does not become ob-jective for itself. Should consciousness shape and form the thing without the initial state of absolute fear, then it has a merely vain and futile "mind of its own"; for its form or negativity is not negativity per se, and hence its formative activity cannot furnish the consciousness of itself as essentially real. If it has endured not absolute fear but merely some slight anxiety, the negative reality has remained external to it; its substance has not been through and through infected thereby. Since the entire content of its natural consciousness has not tottered and shaken, it is still inherently a determinate mode of being; having a "mind of its own" [*der eigene Sinn*] is simply stubbornness [*Eigensinn*], a type of freedom that does not get beyond the attitude of bondage. As little as the pure form can become its essential nature, so little is that form, considered as extending over particulars, a universal formative activity, an absolute notion; it is rather a piece of cleverness that has mastery within a certain range but not over the universal power nor over the entire objective reality.

■ READING AND DISCUSSION QUESTIONS

1. What is the domain of self-consciousness? How does it recognize another consciousness?
2. How does Hegel use sublation to incorporate senses of preservation and change? Review its role in the dialectic.
3. How is the pure abstraction of self-consciousness dissolved?
4. How does concrete thinghood come about?
5. What is the process behind the master's recognition?
6. What is twofold consciousness?
7. How is the dialectic resolved?

■ CLASS EXERCISES

A. *Direct logical discourse:* Using the tools found in Chapter 2, outline the argument from one of the dialectical moments. Based on your assessment of one key premise, write a one-page argument about why you agree or disagree with the argument's conclusion.

B. *Fictive-narrative philosophy:* Using the tools found in Chapter 3, begin with a claim that relates to the reading and discussion questions above. Then create a modern-day story about people or situations familiar to you that makes the logical claim you have identified. Three pages.

MORALITY AND THE ETHICAL COMMUNITY

G. W. F. Hegel

Translated and adapted by Michael Boylan from G. W. F. Hegel, *Grundlinien der Philosophie des Rechts*, ed. Georg Lasson (Leipzig: F. Meiner, 1911). *Note on the translation:* English words found in brackets are inserted by the translator to make better sense of the English rendering.

In this important work Hegel examines the relationship between the agent and his ethical community. The key terms at work are Sitten (Sittlichkeit),[21] *meaning "custom" (what is customarily done in a community) and originating from the existing ethical community, and* Moralität *(a universal code of ethics that applies to everyone). In this volume, the key texts on ethics and social and political philosophy that would argue with Hegel here are those by Thomas Aquinas, Buddha, Hannah Arendt, and Martin Luther King Jr.*

Morality (*Moralität*)

Actions require both content and an end to be achieved. Duties, as such, are abstractions without content. Because of this disparity, the question arises as to what is my duty? There are no good answers except to act rightly and to strive after personal and community welfare (a universalized sense).

Specific duties cannot be derived from the analysis of *duty*'s definition. This is because specific duties are not contained in the abstract definition though [the opposite] is the case since contained within the specific duties is the higher sphere of unconditioned duty. The moral consciousness contains within itself duty, which is the universal. When considered introspectively, solely by itself, there is only abstract universality: identity without content, abstractly positive, and indeterminate.

One the one hand, it is essential to give prominence to the pure unconditioned self-determination of the will as the source

---

21 **key terms . . . everyone:** though Kant's and Hegel's approaches to ethics are quite different (with Kant arguing for universal norms discovered via reason and its logical structure and Hegel beginning with the concrete ethical community), it is interesting to note that Kant's *Groundwork* uses *sitten* in the title: *Grundlegung zur Metaphysik der Sitten*. Kant could have used the Latin form *Moralität* (which would have reinforced his universal message) but did not do so. Nonetheless Hegel gets the point in his depiction of the two positions.

of duty and to give recognition to the role that knowledge plays in establishing a grounding based on infinite autonomy à la Kant's original work. On the other hand, to maintain the moral position [*Moralität*] without making a transition to the conception of ethics [*Sittlichkeit*] is to reduce the enterprise to empty formalism: the preaching of duty for duty's sake alone. From this standpoint no immanent doctrine of duties is possible. One could, perhaps, bring in content from the outside and then generate particular duties, but if one is to understand duty as being the absence of contradiction (coherence and abstract variety stabilized), then no [authentic] transition is possible concerning identifying particular duties. Further, if some particular moral problem is presented for consideration, there is no mechanism to dictate whether or not a duty is at stake. Because of this, one [may subsume the particular] under any [universal duty] and so any wrong or immoral direction might be justified.

Kant's [thought experiment] of visualizing the possibility of an action as a universal maxim is more concrete (due to the concrete nature of visualization). But [Kant's thought experiment] reduces to the abstract identity of "being without contradiction" (discussed above).

The absence of [concrete] property possesses just as little [actual] contradiction as one might find in the nonexistence of a family or nation, etc., or the death of the entire human race. However, if one presupposes that property and human life are to exist and to be respected (on other grounds), then indeed it is a contradiction to commit theft or murder.

But a contradiction must be a contradiction *of something*—in other words some content presupposed in a given principle. In that case, the proposed action at hand is related to that single principle by correspondence or contradiction. But if duty is willed solely for duty's sake and not for the sake of some content, it is only a formal identity that by nature excludes specification and [actual] content. . . .

Ethical Life (*Sittlichkeit*)

Ethical life comes from the idea of freedom. On the one hand, freedom is the good animated in life and endowed with self-consciousness in knowing and willing self-conscious action. On the other hand, self-consciousness has in the ethical community [*Sittlichkeit*] an absolute grounding and the end that actualizes its effort. Thus, ethical life [in the ethical community] [*Sittlichkeit*] is the concept of freedom that has been developed in the existing world [in existing communities]. This concept, so situated, is the nature of self-consciousness.

Because this unified concept of the will with its embodiment as the particular will is [exhibited] through knowing, the conscious distinction between these two moments of the Idea—[the good in self-consciousness and self-consciousness freely situated in a community]—exhibit themselves in such a way that these two moments become united in the totality of the Idea that has totality as its grounding and content.

The *objective ethical order* that presents itself in place of good (in the abstract) is substance made concrete by subjectivity through infinite form. Thus, it asserts within itself distinctions whose specific character is thus determined by the concept. The objective ethical order provides ethical order (*Sittlichkeit*) with a stable, independent content that gives it authority above subjective opinion and caprice. These distinctions give rise to absolutely valid laws and institutions.

When the self-consciousness actually attains the *substantial order*, it is known as an object of knowledge. This ethical substance and its laws and powers [beget] an object against the subject. This means from the subject's point of view that they *are* in the highest sense constitutive of self-subsistent being. This substantial order represents absolute authority and power infinitely more firmly established than the being of nature.

The bond of duty acts as a restriction only on indeterminate subjectivity (abstract freedom) and on the impulses of the natural or the moral will. This is because those impulses determine the will arbitrarily. The truth is that in duty the individual finds his liberation: (a) liberation from dependence upon natural impulse and the depression that would ensue from the prison of moral reflection about what ought to be and what might be, and (b) liberation from indeterminate subjectivity that never attains reality or objective determinacy of action but instead is subjectively cocooned and lacking actuality. In duty the individual acquires substantive freedom.

In an *ethical community* [*Sittlichkeit*], it is clear what an agent must do and what duties he must perform in order to be virtuous. He must follow the explicit, public, well-known rules that apply to his situation. Virtue is the general character demanded of him by law or custom. But from the standpoint of *morality* [*Moralität*], virtue often seems comparatively inferior. This is because morality suggests that there is something beyond [the ethical community] that makes higher demands upon the agent and his community. The source of this is the craving to be something special beyond the absolute and the universal. In this case the consciousness of peculiarity is only found in the exceptional.

■ READING AND DISCUSSION QUESTIONS

1. Go to the Internet and look up positions of moral relativism, moral absolutism, and moral contextualism. Explain each theory. What are the strengths and weaknesses of each?
2. How does Hegel's argument from the *Phenomenology of Mind [Spirit]* on "empty formalism" work here in the context of ethics and social and political philosophy?
3. What is the difference between the *Sittlichkeit* and the *Moralität* standpoints? Which do you support? Why? Give an example.
4. Take the Holocaust as an example. How might Kant and Hegel see things differently?
5. What is the advantage and the disadvantage of thinking of ethics and social and political philosophy from the standpoint of an individual contemplating what is

right and wrong on some independent standard versus the standpoint of an individual who seeks to accept the standards of his community as being decisive in the development of his personal worldview?

■ CLASS EXERCISES

A. *Direct logical discourse:* Using the tools found in Chapter 2, outline the argument behind one of the reading and discussion questions. Based on your assessment of one key premise, write a one-page argument about why you agree or disagree with the argument's conclusion.

B. *Fictive-narrative philosophy:* Using the tools found in Chapter 3, begin with a claim that relates to the reading and discussion questions above. Then create a modern-day story about people or situations familiar to you that makes the logical claim you have identified. Three pages.

ALIENATED LABOR

Karl Marx

Adapted from Karl Marx, "The Economic and Philosophical Manuscripts," in Karl Marx, *Early Writings*, trans. T. B. Bottomore (New York: McGraw-Hill, 1963), 120–134, 147–157. *Note on the translation:* English words found in brackets are inserted by the translator to make better sense of the English rendering.

This first of two early philosophical essays is part of a body of early writings that present Marx as a philosopher. Alienation through labor takes on four forms: (1) from the product that is taken from the worker as soon as it is produced, (2) from the labor itself that is not fulfilling but arduous and unpleasant, (3) from the species-life—humans produce without reference to what makes them human and so the individual is separated from his humanity—and (4) from other workers when the relation of exchange replaces the natural human satisfaction of reciprocity based on human need, resulting in the worker's becoming subjugated to a nonworker.

We have begun from the presuppositions of political economy. We have accepted its terminology and its laws. We presupposed private property; the separation of labor, capital, and land, as also of wages, profit and rent; the division of labor; competition; the concept of exchange value, etc. From political economy itself, in its own words, we have shown that the worker sinks to the level of a commodity, and to that of a most miserable commodity; that the misery of the worker increases with the power and volume of his production; that the necessary result of competition is the accumulation of capital in a few hands and thus a restoration of monopoly in a more terrible form; and finally that the distinction between capitalist and landlord and between agricultural laborer and industrial worker must disappear and the whole of society divide into the two classes of property owners and propertyless workers.

Political economy begins with the fact of private property; it does not explain it. It conceives the material process of private property, as this occurs in reality, in general and abstract formulas that then serve it as laws. It does not comprehend these laws; that is, it does not show how they arise out of the nature of private property. Political economy provides no explanation of the basis for the distinction of labor from capital, of capital from land. When, for example, the relation of wages to profits is defined, this is explained in terms of the interests of capitalists; in other words, what should be explained is assumed. Similarly, competition is referred to at every point and is explained in terms of external conditions. Political economy tells us nothing about the extent to which these external and apparently accidental conditions are simply the expression of a necessary development. We have seen how exchange itself seems an accidental fact. The only motive forces that political economy recognizes are avarice and the war between the avaricious, or competition.

Just because political economy fails to understand the interconnections within this movement, it was possible to oppose the doctrine of competition to that of monopoly, the doctrine of freedom of the crafts to that of the guilds, the doctrine of the division of landed property to that of the great estates; for competition, freedom of crafts, and the division of landed property were conceived only as accidental consequences brought about by will and force, rather than as necessary, inevitable, and natural consequences of monopoly, the guild system, and feudal property.

Thus, we have now to grasp the real connection between this whole system of alienation—private property; acquisitiveness; the separation of labor, capital, and land; exchange and competition; value and the devaluation of man; monopoly and competition—and the system of money.

Let us not begin our explanation, as does the economist, from a legendary primordial condition. Such a primordial condition does not explain anything; it merely removes the question into a grey and nebulous distance. It asserts as a fact or event what it should deduce, namely, the necessary relation between two things, for example, between the division of labor and exchange. In the same way theology explains the origin of evil by the fall of man; that is, it asserts as a historical fact what it should explain.

Alienation of the Laborer from the Product of Labor

We shall begin from a contemporary economic fact. The worker becomes poorer the more wealth he produces and the more his production increases in power and extent. The worker becomes an ever cheaper commodity the more goods he creates. The devaluation of the human world increases in direct relation with the increase in value of the world of things. Labor does not only create goods; it also produces itself and the worker as a commodity, and indeed in the same proportion as it produces goods.

This fact simply implies that the object produced by labor, its product, now stands opposed to it as an alien being, as a power independent of the producer. The product of labor is labor that has been embodied in an object and turned into a physical thing; this product is an objectification of labor. The performance of work is at the same time its objectification. The performance of work appears in the sphere of political economy as a vitiation of the worker, objectification as a loss and as servitude to the object, and appropriation as alienation.

So much does the performance of work appear as vitiation that the worker is vitiated to the point of starvation. So much does objectification appear as loss of the object that the worker is deprived of the most essential things not only of life but also of work. Labor itself becomes an object that he can acquire only by the greatest effort and with unpredictable interruptions. So much does the appropriation of the object appear as alienation that the more objects the worker produces the fewer he can possess and the more he falls under the domination of his product, of capital.

All these consequences follow from the fact that the worker is related to the product of his labor as to an alien object. For it is clear on this presupposition that the more the worker expends himself in work, the more powerful becomes the world of objects that he creates in face of himself, the poorer he becomes in his inner life, and the less he belongs to himself. It is just the same as in religion. The more of himself man attributes to God, the less he has left in himself. The worker puts his life into the object, and his life then belongs no longer to himself but to the object. The greater his activity, therefore, the less he possesses. What is embodied in the product of his labor is no longer his own. The greater this product is, therefore, the more he is diminished. The alienation of the worker in his product means not only that his labor becomes an object, assumes an external existence, but that it exists independently, outside himself, and alien to him and that it stands opposed to him as an autonomous power. The life that he has given to the object sets itself against him as an alien and hostile force.

Let us now examine more closely the phenomenon of objectification—the worker's production and the alienation and loss of the object it produces, which is involved in it. The worker can create nothing without nature, without the sensuous external world. The latter is the material in which his labor is realized, in which it is active, out of which and through which it produces things.

But just as nature affords the means of existence of labor, in the sense that labor cannot live without objects upon which it can be exercised, so also it provides the means of existence in a narrower sense, namely, the means of physical existence for the worker himself. Thus, the more the worker appropriates the external world of sensuous nature by his labor, the more he deprives himself of means of existence in two respects: first, that the sensuous external world becomes progressively less an object belonging to his labor or a means of existence of his labor, and secondly, that it becomes progressively less a means of existence in the direct sense, a means for the physical subsistence of the worker.

In both respects, therefore, the worker becomes a slave of the object: first, in that he receives an object of work, that is, receives work, and secondly, in that he receives means of subsistence. Thus, the object enables him to exist, first as a worker and secondly as a physical subject. The culmination of this enslavement is that he can only maintain himself as a physical subject so far as he is a worker, and it is only as a physical subject that he is a worker.

The alienation of the worker in his object is expressed as follows in the laws of political economy: the more the worker produces, the less he has to consume; the more value he creates, the more worthless he becomes; the more refined his product, the cruder and more misshapen the worker; the more civilized the product, the more barbarous the worker; the more powerful the work, the more feeble the worker; the more the work manifests intelligence, the more the worker declines in intelligence and becomes a slave of nature.

Political economy conceals the alienation in the nature of labor in so far as it does not examine the direct relationship between the worker (work) and production. Labor certainly produces marvels for the rich, but it produces privation for the worker. It produces palaces but hovels for the worker. It produces beauty but deformity for the worker. It replaces labor by machinery but casts some of the workers back into a barbarous kind of work and turns the others into machines. It produces intelligence but also stupidity and cretinism for the workers.

The direct relationship of labor to its products is the relationship of the worker to the objects of his production. The relationship of property owners to the objects of production and to production itself is merely a consequence of this first relationship and confirms it. We shall consider this second aspect later.

Thus, when we ask what the important relationship of labor is, we are concerned with the relationship of the worker to production.

Alienation of the Laborer from the Act of Production

So far we have considered the alienation of the worker only from one aspect: namely, his relationship with the products of his labor. However, alienation appears not merely in the result but also in the process of production, within productive activity itself. How could the worker stand in an alien relationship to the product of his activity if he did not alienate himself in the act of production itself? The product is indeed only the résumé [summary] of activity, of production. Consequently, if the product of labor is alienation, production itself must be active alienation—the alienation of activity and the activity of alienation. The alienation of the object of labor merely summarizes the alienation in the work activity itself.

What constitutes the alienation of labor? First, that the work is external to the worker, that it is not part of his nature; consequently, he does not fulfill himself in his work but denies himself, has a feeling of misery rather than well-being, does not develop freely his mental and physical energies but is physically exhausted and mentally debased. The worker, therefore, feels himself at home only during his leisure time, whereas at work he feels homeless. His work is not voluntary but imposed, forced labor. It is not the satisfaction of a need but only a means for satisfying other needs. Its alien character is clearly shown by the fact that as soon as there is no physical or other compulsion, it is avoided like the plague. External labor, labor in which man alienates himself, is a labor of self-sacrifice, of mortification. Finally, the external character of work for the worker is shown by the fact that it is not his own work but work for someone else, that in work he does not belong to himself but to another person.

We arrive at the result that man (the worker) feels himself to be freely active only in his animal functions—eating, drinking, and procreating—or at most also in his dwelling and in personal adornment, while in his human functions he is reduced to an animal. The animal becomes human, and the human becomes animal.

Eating, drinking, and procreating are of course also genuine human functions. But abstractly considered, apart from the environment of human activities and turned into final and sole ends, they are animal functions.

We have now considered the act of alienation of practical human activity, labor, from two aspects: (1) the relationship of the worker to the product of labor as an alien object that dominates him—this relationship is at the same time the relationship to the sensuous external world, to natural objects, as an alien and hostile world—and (2) the relationship of labor to the act of production within labor. This is the relationship of the worker to his own activity as something alien and not belonging to him, activity as suffering (passivity), strength as powerlessness, creation as emasculation, the personal physical and mental energy of the worker, his personal life (for what is life but activity?), as an activity that is directed against himself, independent of him and not belonging to him. This is self-alienation as against the above-mentioned alienation of the thing.

We have now to infer a third characteristic of alienated labor from the two we have considered.

Alienation from Species-Life

Man is a species-being not only in the sense that he makes the community (his own as well as those of other things) his object both practically and theoretically but also (and this is simply another expression of the same thing) in the sense that he treats himself as a present, living species, as a universal, and consequently free, being.

Species-life, for man as for animals, has its physical basis in the fact that man (like animals) lives from inorganic nature, and since man is more universal than an animal, so the range of inorganic nature from which he lives is more universal. Plants, animals, minerals, air, light, etc., constitute, from the theoretical aspect, a part of human consciousness as objects of natural science and art; they are man's spiritual inorganic nature, his intellectual means of life, which he must first prepare for enjoyment and perpetuation. So also, from the practical aspect, they form a part of human life and activity. In practice man lives only from these natural products, whether in the form of food, heating, clothing, housing, etc. The universality of man appears in practice in the universality that makes the whole of nature into his inorganic body: (1) as a direct means of life, and equally (2) as the material object and instrument of his life activity. Nature is the inorganic body of man; that is to say, nature excluding the human body itself. To say that man lives from nature means that nature is his body with which he must remain in a continuous interchange in order not to die. The statement that the physical and mental life of man and nature are interdependent means simply that nature is interdependent with itself, for man is a part of nature.

Since alienated labor (1) alienates nature from man, and (2) alienates man from himself, from his own active function, his life activity, so it alienates him from the species. It makes species-life into a means of individual life. In the first place, it alienates species-life and individual life, and secondly, it turns the latter, as an abstraction, into the purpose of the former, also in its abstract and alienated form.

For labor, life-activity (productive life), now appears to man only as means for the satisfaction of a need, the need to maintain his physical existence. Productive life is, however, species-life. It is life creating life. In the type of life-activity resides the whole character of a species, its species-character; and free, conscious activity is the species-character of human beings. Life itself appears only as a means of life.

The animal is one with its life-activity. It does not distinguish the activity from itself. It is its activity. But man makes his life-activity itself an object of his will and consciousness. He has a conscious life-activity. It is not a determination with which he is completely identified. Conscious life-activity distinguishes man from the life-activity of animals. Only for this reason is he a species-being. Or rather, he is only a self-conscious being—that is, his own life is an object for him—because he is a species-being. Only for this reason is his activity free activity. Alienated labor reverses the relationship in that man, because he is a self-conscious being, makes his life activity, his being, only a means for his existence.

It is just in his work upon the objective world that man really proves himself as a species-being. This production is his active species-life. By means of it, nature appears as his work and his reality. The object of labor is, therefore, the objectification of man's species-life; for he no longer reproduces himself merely intellectually, as in consciousness, but actively and in a real sense, and he sees his own reflection in a world that he has constructed. While, therefore, alienated labor takes away the object of production from man, it also takes away his species-life, his real objectivity as a species-being, and changes his advantage over animals into a disadvantage in so far as his inorganic body, nature, is taken from him.

Just as alienated labor transforms free and self-directed activity into a means, so it transforms the species-life of man into a means of physical existence.

Consciousness, which man has from his species, is transformed through alienation so that species-life becomes only a means for him. Thus, alienated labor turns the species-life of man, and also nature as his mental species-property, into an alien being and into a means for his individual existence. It alienates from man his own body, external nature, his mental life, and his human life. A direct consequence of the alienation of man from the product of his labor, from his life activity and from his species-life, is that man is alienated from other men. When man confronts himself he also confronts other men. What is true of man's relationship to his work, to the product of his work and to himself, is also true of his relationship to other men, to their labor and to the objects of their labor.

In general, the statement that man is alienated from his species-life means that each man is alienated from others and that each of the others is likewise alienated from human life.

Alienation from Other Workers and Subjugation to a Nonworker

Human alienation, and above all the relation of man to himself, is first realized and expressed in the relationship between each man and other men. Thus, in the relationship of alienated labor, every man regards other men according to the standards and relationships in which be finds himself placed as a worker.

We began with an economic fact, the alienation of the worker and his production. We have expressed this fact in conceptual terms as alienated labor, and in analyzing the concept we have merely analyzed an economic fact.

Let us now examine further how this concept of alienated labor must express and reveal itself in reality. If the product of labor is alien to me and confronts me as an alien power, to whom does it belong? If my own activity does not belong to me but is an alien, forced activity, to whom does it belong? To a being other than myself. And who is this being? The gods? It is apparent in the earliest stages of advanced production—for example, temple building, etc., in Egypt, India, Mexico—and in the service rendered to gods that the product belonged to the gods. But the gods alone were never the lords of labor. And no more was nature. What a contradiction it would be if the more man subjugates nature by his labor, and the more the marvels of the gods are rendered superfluous by the marvels of industry, the more he should abstain from his joy in producing and his enjoyment of the product for love of these powers.

The alien being to whom labor and the product of labor belong, to whose service labor is devoted, and to whose enjoyment the product of labor goes can only be man himself. If the product of labor does not belong to the worker but confronts him as an alien power, this can only be because it

belongs to a man other than the worker. If his activity is a torment to him, it must be a source of enjoyment and pleasure to another. Not the gods, nor nature, but only man himself can be this alien power over men.

Consider the earlier statement that the relation of man to himself is first realized, objectified, through his relation to other men. If he is related to the product of his labor, his objectified labor, as to an alien, hostile, powerful, and independent object, he is related in such a way that another alien, hostile, powerful, and independent man is the lord of this object. If he is related to his own activity as to unfree activity, then he is related to it as activity in the service, and under the domination, coercion, and yoke, of another man.

Every self-alienation of man, from himself and from nature, appears in the relation that he postulates between other men and himself and nature. Thus, religious self-alienation is necessarily exemplified in the relation between laity and priest, or, since it is here a question of the spiritual world, between the laity and a mediator. In the real world of practice, this self-alienation can only be expressed in the real, practical relation of man to his fellow men. The medium through which alienation occurs is itself a practical one. Through alienated labor, therefore, man not only produces his relation to the object and to the process of production as to alien and hostile men but also produces the relation of other men to his production and his product, as well as the relation between himself and other men. Just as he creates his own production as a vitiation, a punishment, and his own product as a loss, as a product that does not belong to him, so he creates the domination of the nonproducer over production and its product. As he alienates his own activity, so he bestows upon the stranger an activity that is not his own.

We have so far considered this relation only from the side of the worker, and later we shall consider it also from the side of the nonworker.

Thus, through alienated labor the worker creates the relation of another man, who does not work and is outside the work process, to this labor. The relation of the worker to work also produces the relation of the capitalist (or whatever one likes to call the lord of labor) to work. Private property is, therefore, the product, the necessary result, of alienated labor, of the external relation of the worker to nature and to himself. Private property is thus derived from the analysis of the concept of alienated labor—that is, alienated man, alienated labor, alienated life, and estranged man.

Private Property

We have, of course, derived the concept of alienated labor (alienated life) from political economy, from an analysis of the movement of private property. But the analysis of this concept shows that although private property appears to be the basis and cause of alienated labor, it is rather a consequence of the latter, just as the gods are fundamentally not the cause but the product of confusions of human reason. At a later stage, however, there is a reciprocal influence.

Only in the final stage of the development of private property is its secret revealed, namely, that it is on one hand the product of alienated labor, and on the other hand the means by which labor is alienated, the realization of this alienation.

This elucidation throws light upon several unresolved controversies:

1. Political economy begins with labor as the real soul of production and then goes on to attribute nothing to labor and everything to private property. Proudhon,[22] faced by this contradiction, has decided in favor of labor against private property. We perceive, however, that this apparent contradiction is the contradiction of alienated labor with itself and that political economy has merely formulated the laws of alienated labor.

   We also observe, therefore, that wages and private property are identical, for wages, like the product or object of labor itself remunerated, are only a necessary consequence of the alienation of labor. In the wage system labor appears not as an end in itself but as the servant of wages. We shall develop this point later and here only bring out some of the consequences.

   An enforced increase in wages (disregarding the other difficulties, especially that such an anomaly could only be maintained by force) would be nothing more than a better remuneration of slaves and

---

22 **Proudhon:** Pierre-Joseph Proudhon (1809–1865), French politician, philosopher, and socialist.

would not restore, either to the worker or to the work, their human significance and worth.

Even the equality of incomes that Proudhon demands would only change the relation of the present-day worker to his work into a relation of all men to work. Society would then be conceived as an abstract capitalist.

2. From the relation of alienated labor to private property, it also follows that the emancipation of society from private property, from servitude, takes the political form of the emancipation of the workers, not in the sense that only the latter's emancipation is involved but because this emancipation includes the emancipation of humanity as a whole. For all human servitude is involved in the relation of the worker to production, and all the types of servitude are only modifications or consequences of this relation.

As we have discovered the concept of private property by an analysis of the concept of alienated labor, so with the aid of these two factors we can evolve all the categories of political economy, and in every category, for example trade, competition, capital, and money, we shall discover only a particular and developed expression of these fundamental elements.

■ READING AND DISCUSSION QUESTIONS

1. In your own words, find an example in contemporary society that might illustrate each of Marx's four stages of alienation.
2. How does objectification lead to worker alienation and loss?
3. Compare Marx's fourth form of alienation and compare his account of subjugation with Hegel's master-slave dialectic. How are they similar? How are they different?
4. Go to the Internet and look up Pierre-Joseph Proudhon and Fabian socialism. What did Proudhon and Fabian socialists advocate? How were they similar and different from Marx?

■ CLASS EXERCISES

A. *Direct logical discourse:* Using the tools found in Chapter 2, outline the argument on one of the four stages of alienation. Based on your assessment of one key premise, write a one-page argument about why you agree or disagree with the argument's conclusion.

B. *Fictive-narrative philosophy:* Using the tools found in Chapter 3, begin with a claim that relates to the reading and discussion questions above. Then create a modern-day story about people or situations familiar to you that makes the logical claim you have identified. Three pages.

PRIVATE PROPERTY AND LABOR

Karl Marx

Adapted from Karl Marx, "The Economic and Philosophical Manuscripts," in Karl Marx, *Early Writings*, trans. T. B. Bottomore (New York: McGraw-Hill, 1963), 147–157. *Note on the translation:* English words found in brackets are inserted by the translator to make better sense of the English rendering.

In studying this second work on private property and labor, it is important for readers to challenge their preconceptions about capitalism and the relative values of labor and capital (money). This is really a question of distributive justice. Since most readers of this book (I would guess) live in countries that like to think of themselves as capitalistic, they will find that Marx calls into question the relative values of fundamental concepts and how they operate within a society.

The subjective essence of private property, private property as activity for itself, as subject, as person, is labor. It is evident, therefore, that only the political economy that recognized labor as its principle (Adam Smith[23]) and no longer regarded private property as merely a condition external to man can be considered as both a product of the real dynamism and development of private property, a product of modern industry, and a force that has accelerated and extolled the dynamism and development of industry and has made it a power in the domain of consciousness.

Thus, from the viewpoint of this enlightened political economy, which has discovered the subjective essence of wealth within the framework of private property, the partisans of the monetary system and the mercantilist system, who consider private property as a purely objective being for man, are fetishists and Catholics. Engels[24] is right, therefore, in calling Adam Smith the Luther[25] of political economy. Just as Luther recognized religion and faith as the essence of the real world, and for that reason took up a position against Catholic paganism; just as he annulled external reli-

---

23 **Adam Smith:** Scottish philosopher and political economist (1723–1790); author of *The Wealth of Nations* (1776).

24 **Engels:** Friedrich Engels (1820–1895), German philosopher and social activist; coauthor with Karl Marx of *The Communist Manifesto* (1848).

25 **Luther:** Martin Luther (1483–1546), German theologian and initiator of the Protestant Reformation.

giosity while making religiosity the inner essence of man; just as he negated the distinction between priest and layman because he transferred the priest into the heart of the layman; so wealth external to man and independent of him (and thus only to be acquired and conserved from outside) is annulled. That is to say, its external and mindless objectivity is annulled by the fact that private property is incorporated in man himself, and man himself is recognized as its essence. But as a result, man himself is brought into the sphere of private property, just as, with Luther, he is brought into the sphere of religion.

Under the guise of recognizing man, political economy, whose principle is labor, carries to its logical conclusion the denial of man. Man himself is no longer in a condition of external tension with the external substance of private property; he has himself become the tension-ridden being of private property. What was previously a phenomenon of being external to oneself, a real external manifestation of man, has now become the act of objectification, of alienation. This political economy seems at first, therefore, to recognize man with his independence, his personal activity, etc. It incorporates private property in the very essence of man, and it is no longer, therefore, conditioned by the local or national characteristics of private property regarded as existing outside itself. It manifests a cosmopolitan, universal activity that is destructive of every limit and every bond and substitutes itself as the only policy, the only universality, the only limit, and the only bond.

But in its further development, it is obliged to discard this hypocrisy and to show itself in all its cynicism. It does this, without any regard for the apparent contradictions to which its doctrine leads, by showing in a more one-sided fashion, and thus with greater logic and clarity, that labor is the sole essence of wealth and by demonstrating that this doctrine, in contrast with the original conception, has consequences that are inimical to man. Not only does the cynicism of political economy increase from Smith, through Say, to Ricardo, Mill,[26] et al. inasmuch as for the latter the consequence of industry appeared more and more developed and contradictory; from a positive point of view they become more alienated, and more consciously alienated, from man, in comparison with their predecessors. This is only because their science develops with greater logic and truth. Since they make private property in its active form the subject, and since at the same time they make man as a nonbeing into a being, the contradiction in reality corresponds entirely with the contradictory essence that they have accepted as a principle. The divided reality of industry is far from refuting, but instead confirms, its self-divided principle. Its principle is in fact the principle of this division.

The physiocratic[27] doctrine of Quesnay[28] forms the transition from the mercantilist

---

26 **Say . . . Mill:** Jean-Baptiste Say (1767–1832), French economist; David Ricardo (1772–1823), English political economist; John Stuart Mill (1806–1873), English philosopher and political economist.

27 **physiocratic:** believing that the source of wealth lies in land and agriculture.

28 **Quesnay:** François Quesnay (1694–1774), French economist and physiocrat.

system to Adam Smith. Physiocracy is in a direct sense the economic decomposition of feudal property, but for this reason it is equally directly the economic transformation, the reestablishment, of this same feudal property, with the difference that its language is no longer feudal but economic. All wealth is reduced to land and cultivation (agriculture). Land is not yet capital but is still a particular mode of existence of capital, whose value is claimed to reside in, and derive from, its natural particularity; but land is nonetheless a natural and universal element, whereas the mercantilist system regarded only precious metals as wealth. The object of wealth, its matter, has therefore been given the greatest universality within natural limits—inasmuch as it is also, as nature, directly objective wealth. And it is only by labor, by agriculture, that land exists for man. Consequently, the subjective essence of wealth is already transferred to labor. But at the same time agriculture is the only productive labor. Labor is, therefore, not yet taken in its universality and its abstract form; it is still bound to a particular element of nature as its matter and is only recognized in a particular mode of existence determined by nature. Labor is still only a determinate, particular alienation of man, and its product is also conceived as a determinate part of wealth due more to nature than to labor itself. Land is still regarded here as something that exists naturally and independently of man and not yet as capital, that is, as a factor of labor. On the contrary, labor appears to be a factor of nature. But since the fetishism of the old external wealth, existing only as an object, has been reduced to a very simple natural element, and since its essence has

been partially, and in a certain way, recognized in its subjective existence, the necessary advance has been made in recognizing the universal nature of wealth and in raising labor in its absolute form, that is, in abstraction, to the principle. It is demonstrated against the physiocrats that from the economic point of view (that is, from the only valid point of view), agriculture does not differ from any other industry and that it is not, therefore, a specific kind of labor, bound to a particular element, or a particular manifestation of labor, but labor in general that is the essence of wealth.

Physiocracy denies specific, external, purely objective wealth, in declaring that labor is its essence. For the physiocrats, however, labor is in the first place only the subjective essence of landed property. They merely turn landed property into alienated man. They annul its feudal character by declaring that industry (agriculture) is its essence, but they reject the industrial world and accept the feudal system by declaring that agriculture is the only industry.

It is evident that when the subjective essence—industry in opposition to landed property, industry forming itself as industry—is grasped, this essence includes within itself the opposition. For just as industry incorporates the superseded landed property, its subjective essence incorporates the subjective essence of the latter.

Landed property is the first form of private property, and industry first appears historically in simple opposition to it, as a particular form of private property (or rather, as the liberated slave of landed property); this sequence is repeated in the scientific study of the subjective essence of private property, and labor appears at first only as agricultural labor but later establishes itself as labor in general.

All wealth has become industrial wealth, the wealth of labor, and industry is realized labor—just as the factory system is the realized essence of industry (that is, of labor) and as industrial capital is the realized objective form of private property. Thus, we see that it is only at this stage that private property can consolidate its rule over man and become, in its most general form, a world historical power.

■ READING AND DISCUSSION QUESTIONS

1. What does Marx mean by the political economy?
2. Go to the Internet and look up François Quesnay's physiocratic doctrine. Why does Marx see this as a link between the mercantile system and Adam Smith's laissez-faire capitalism?
3. When someone invests money to buy and build a manufacturing plant, does his capital risk rightly put him first in line for profits when those manufactured goods are sold? What of the value of the workers who fabricate the product? Do they have a primary claim? Should it be equal?
4. Go to the Internet and find a particular Native American traditional understanding about property that eschews private ownership. Why did this particular people believe the way they did (do)? Compare and contrast this stance to the one Marx is taking. How would the world be different if we all thought and acted this way today?
5. Can any of Marx's insights be adopted in some form in today's world without starting a revolution and changing everything? Give an example.

■ CLASS EXERCISES

A. *Direct logical discourse:* Using the tools found in Chapter 2, outline the argument suggested by one of the reading and discussion questions. Based on your assessment of one key premise, write a one-page argument about why you agree or disagree with the argument's conclusion.

B. *Fictive-narrative philosophy:* Using the tools found in Chapter 3, begin with a claim that relates to the reading and discussion questions above. Then create a modern-day story about people or situations familiar to you that makes the logical claim you have identified. Three pages.

CHAPTER ELEVEN

Heidegger and Arendt

Martin Heidegger (1889–1976) was a celebrated (though controversial) German philosopher. Though he wrote on a number of topics, his best known work is Being and Time *(1927), in which he attempts to use phenomenology to give a temporal understanding of human existence. He ended up having an affair with one of his early students, Hannah Arendt, a Jewish woman. Heidegger became a Nazi shortly after his becoming rector in April 1933 of Freiburg University, which he helped make into a model Nazi university. One year later he resigned the post and ceased his public political activities. In 1945 (after the war) Heidegger was prohibited from teaching and a year later was forced to resign his chair of philosophy because of alleged Nazi sympathies. The ban was lifted in 1949.*

Hannah Arendt (1906–1975) was a political philosopher. She went to Marburg in 1924 and studied philosophy with Martin Heidegger. In 1925 the relationship became romantic but broke off the following year when she moved to Heidelberg to study with Karl Jaspers. Her two major works in academic political philosophy are The Origins of Totalitarianism *(1951) and* The Human Condition *(1958). These works address a variety of particular problems using not only theoretical analysis but also empirical data. Her most widely read book was* Eichmann in Jerusalem *(1963), in which she attends the trial of Adolf Eichmann in Jerusalem. It was the last of the major trials for the Nazi atrocities.*

EICHMANN AND HEIDEGGER IN JERUSALEM*

Michael Boylan

This story begins with a rite of passage at American universities: the senior thesis exercise. In order to fulfill the requirements of the major, students have to write a substantial essay or engage in an academic project and then orally respond to criticism from members of the department. In this story the narratives of three characters emerge: Heidegger, Arendt, and Eichmann. Many narrative frames are presented to understand the action. Be sure to acknowledge which narrative frame is which when viewing the action.

The room was packed. There was a sense of anticipation. Several in the audience glanced over to the person sitting in the glass booth. The expression on his face was intense. He was keenly aware of his judges watching, but he didn't want to let them see his anxiety. This was about an event that had shaken human history. Everyone was deadly serious in anticipation.

Then the philosophy thesis director, Christian Tode, stood up and addressed the Bard College students. "Good afternoon, everyone. It was good of you all to have tramped through the newly fallen snow to the Weis Cinema in order to view Patrick's senior project in philosophy (which will also be his senior project in film). As you are all aware, he has made a dramatic rendition of Hannah Arendt's book *Eichmann in Jerusalem*. However, it is not just a reenactment. It is set in the context of the life and influences upon Dr. Arendt.

"Mr. O'Neil will demonstrate these as he selects certain hypertexts at key points in the presentation. The hypertext home is in a birdcage that will be atop the screen as he presents his film. Periodically, during the presentation, Patrick will click on the birdcage and certain special scenes will appear to help explain or give counterpoint to the courtroom drama. Afterwards, he will be available for a few general questions from the audience before his committee and I will commandeer him to Aspinwall[1] to grill him with some pointed questions about the presentation and the paper we required him to

---

* *This short story makes use of material from Hannah Arendt,* Eichmann in Jerusalem, *rev. ed. (New York: Penguin Books, 1965), and Ursula Ludz, ed.* Letters 1925–1975: Hannah Arendt and Martin Heidegger, *trans. Andrew Shields (New York: Harcourt, 1998).*

1 **Aspinwall:** the building that is home to Bard's philosophy department.

prepare." Then the forty-five-year-old philosophy professor, rail thin from chain smoking, sat down and ran his hand through his short black hair and the recalcitrant cowlick at the crown.

The film room in the Bertelsmann Campus Center blackened and the movie began as Patrick, inside the control booth, started the DVD on his computer, which was connected to a ceiling-mounted projector.

The scene opened with a female holding an old-style microphone. Sarah, a Bard drama major (who has appeared briefly in professional film and stage productions), tilted her head. "This is Hannah Arendt reporting to you from Jerusalem. The date is April 11, 1961. The place is the courtroom in Jerusalem [which looks a lot like a classroom at Bard College]. I will be covering this trial for *XYZ News* and for *The New Yorker.*"[2] Then Hannah was interrupted by the court usher, who yelled at the top of his voice, "Beth Hamishpath!" (the House of Justice). These words created silence for the entrance of the judges.

Then the three judges entered. They were bare headed and wore black robes. They marched into the courtroom from outside the camera's view to take their elevated places above the fray. The judges were Justice Moshe Landau, Dr. Benjamin Halevi, and Dr. Yitzhak Raveh. Israel's attorney general, Gideon Hausner, headed the prosecution. Adolf Eichmann sat alone, bald headed with heavy, dark-framed glasses, in a protective cage of bulletproof glass. His defense lawyer was Dr. Robert Servatius, a stout man with short-cropped hair and silver-rimmed glasses. Everyone listened as Judge Landau read the fifteen charges.[3]

> Charge 1: Eichmann was ultimately responsible for the murder of millions of Jews.
> Charge 2: He placed these Jews, before they were murdered, in living conditions designed to kill them.
> Charge 3: He caused them grave physical and mental harm.
> Charge 4: He took actions that resulted in the sterilization of Jews and otherwise prevented childbirth.
> Charge 5: He caused the enslavement, starvation, and deportation of millions of Jews.
> Charge 6: He caused general persecution of Jews on national, racial, religious, and political grounds.

---

2 **The New Yorker:** of course, Hannah Arendt was only a reporter for *The New Yorker*. This added role is fictional for the purposes of this story.

3 **fifteen charges:** I would like to emphasize that this is a work of fiction and that actual testimony is retained in spirit but not in literalness. For exact transcripts of the trial, see *The Trial of Adolf Eichmann: Record of Proceedings in the District Court of Jerusalem*, 9 vols. (Jerusalem: Trust for the Publication of the Proceedings of the Eichmann Trial, 1992–1995).

Charge 7: He spoiled Jewish property by inhuman measures involving compulsion, robbery, terrorism, and violence.

Charge 8: All of the above were punishable war crimes.

Charge 9: He deported a half-million Poles.

Charge 10: He deported 14,000 Slovenes.

Charge 11: He deported tens of thousands of gypsies.

Charge 12: He deported and murdered one hundred Czech children from the village of Lidice.

Charges 13 to 15: He was a member of the SD, Gestapo, and SS,[4] which were determined to be criminal organizations according to the Nüremberg trials.

The first twelve counts of the indictment each carried the death penalty as the maximum punishment.

When Judge Landau had finished, he took off his glasses and set his oblong face so that his sagging jowls seemed to disappear. Then he turned to the defendant and asked, "And how do you plead to these counts that have been brought against you?"

Instantly, defense attorney Servatius sprang up and, instead of answering, declared, "Your Honor, we move for a dismissal based upon the fact that the three of you cannot possibly claim to be unbiased in this case. No Jewish judge could be."

The three judges huddled together and discussed the issue in animated fashion. Then Judge Landau, wearing his thin-rimmed black glasses, declared in level tones, "I believe it may be true that yours is a difficult case to try. No judge (Jewish or otherwise) could be completely without feeling when confronted with the horrors of genocide. However, we will take your motion under advisement. This court is now in recess."

And that was all for the first day.

Patrick moved the wireless mouse to click the birdcage atop the screen. It was a place that afforded a privileged view.

"Herr Professor!" said the undergraduate student as her teacher put his hand behind her head and kissed her.

"Fraulein, would you like to see 'Being's flash of light'?"

"And would this be Herr Hegel's Geist[5] *or the phenomenology of Herr Husserl[6]?"*

"Neither," he said as he kissed her deeply again. "First, I have to show you and then I may be able to uncover it."

"Herr Professor!"

---

4 **SD . . . SS:** SD (Sicherheitsdienst), the intelligence service of the Nazi party; Gestapo, the secret police of Nazi Germany; SS (Schutzstaffel), an elite Nazi militia.

5 **Herr Hegel's *Geist*:** *Herr* means "mister" in German. *Geist* is the concept of mind or spirit in *Phenomenology of Spirit* (1807) by German philosopher G. W. F. Hegel (1770–1831).

6 **Herr Husserl:** Edmund Husserl (1859–1938), Austrian philosopher and founder of phenomenology, the study of conscious experience. Martin Heidegger (1889–1976) was Husserl's student.

"*Call me Martin,*" *he said as he began unbuttoning her blouse.*

Later, when they were both smoking cigarettes, he said, "I am working on some very important projects that will put my name on the map."

Hannah took a long drag on her cigarette and rested her eighteen-year-old head on the shoulder of the man twice her age. Martin was growing a moustache, which was quite the rage (besides it softened his hawklike nose). His black hair was thick and combed up and straight back from his high forehead. His dark eyes had a look of great intensity.

*"It is my conjecture that the essence of man belongs to the disclosing that our own being (*Dasein*) is connected to Being itself—not unlike the relation of the individuals to the Forms of Plato. I think I will call this phenomenological ontology."*

"I am just a neophyte in all of this, Herr Professor—"

"Not at all. I'm still trying to put this all together. I've seen my way past Husserl to another method of describing authentic everyday existence."

"And is all that about the light of being?"

"Let's call it Being's flash of light!"

Hannah laughed, put her cigarette down, and kissed her lover again. He broke off the kiss and asked, "So what do you think about this emphasis upon Being itself as opposed to individual beings? And the major problem in the disclosure of Being itself?"

"I will have to think about this. It seems a lot like Hegel's Geist *involved in Plato's third man.[7] Are your maneuvers between* Dasein, Sein, *and* Da-sein[8] *really anything different?"*

"Think about it, Hannah. At the moment I'm seeing this from another direction."

"Well, I'll wait a week and see what you say then."

A week later Judge Landau addressed the court. "The court has thought about your plea, Dr. Servatius, and we have decided that in any trial a judge may have opinions and judgments on the legal and moral principles that might be involved. However, in those cases as well as in this case, the jurists must distance themselves from their personal opinions and act as objective fact finders within the context of the law."

---

7 **Plato's third man:** an argument in Plato's dialogue, *Parmenides*, meant to show difficulties in Plato's theory of Forms. The argument begins with two entities: the Form of man and some particular man. How can the two connect? It would seem that what is needed is a connecting Form between the two. But then what connects the connecting Form to the two extremes (the Form of Man and the particular man)? Of course, two more Forms at either side of the connecting Form. But then what connects these two new, second-order connecting Forms to the first-order connecting Form? Of course, four third-order connecting Forms. This goes on to infinity (which is a nonsense concept to the ancient Greeks). This is a form of argument to absurdity and is meant to show Plato's theory of Forms to be false.

8 ***Dasein, Sein, and Da-sein:*** *Sein* refers to "being." *Da* ("there") situates being to become *da-Sein*, which later transmutes to *Dasein*, the being that we, ourselves, are. This is a complicated term for Heidegger. In ordinary German the word means "life." But with Heidegger the "*da*" situates it to mean the disclosure of being that is uniquely human: we are the only being that through our existence seeks to understand the significance of our place among other beings and in relation to the foundational idea of Being itself.

238 ‡ Chapter 11: Heidegger and Arendt

Servatius frowned and sat down.

Judge Landau then read the charges again. "How do you plead?"

"In the sense of the indictment—not guilty."

Judge Landau then scratched a note on a pad to himself: his plea hasn't changed.

It was time for Hausner's opening statement. The bald man with the egg-shaped head, dark-framed glasses, and ears that protruded like wings on the side set his expressive mouth carefully. He walked in front of the judges but really talked to everyone in the room. "I address myself to history, as well as to the particulars of this case. I am not a Holocaust survivor. I did not sit in the death camps waiting for my turn to enter the showers of death. How is it that I am able to make this case against a man who bore great responsibility for one of the most murderous acts in history? Almost by necessity, I will diminish the horror and the evil done because I was not a firsthand witness." Hausner paused. Was he overcome with emotion? He let out a slow sigh. His prominent lower jaw seemed to jut forward. "Even though I have a mountain of evidence, I thought that I had to become—even secondhand—a personal witness. I went to the Fighters' Kibbutz and spoke personally with Yitzhak Zuckerman and his wife about the Warsaw Ghetto Uprising.[9] I had to feel it personally."

"You have to feel it personally." Martin leaned back and lit a cigarette. They were sitting at their bench on campus. It was one of their public places of rendezvous.

"What do you mean?" replied Hannah as she took a cigarette too.

"Well, you are already in the world. You are my student and my lover. These are facts. But your personal reaction is to make the world your own. Yet, this existentiality leads to forfeiture if we become so wrapped up in our own being that we forget Being itself."

"Forgive me, Martin, but what is to stop your notion of Being from taking on a metaphorical meaning as the state itself."

"What are you talking about?"

"I'm sure you know that some people bring forth Hegel's Geist *to justify anything the state does because it is the State. And what of those politicians who cite Nietzsche's will to power[10] to amount to the same thing. Aren't you afraid of this?"*

Heidegger tossed down his cigarette and ground it underfoot. This was unlike him. He was generally a frugal fellow. He ran his hands through his thick, dark brown hair, which stood several inches above his head. The action almost doubled the height of his hair. Hannah thought he looked almost ghoulish. She dropped her cigarette, too, but was not aware of its absence.

---

9 **Fighters' Kibbutz . . . Warsaw Ghetto Uprising:** Yitzhak Zuckerman (1915–1981) was one of the leaders of the Warsaw Ghetto Uprising (1943), the largest case of Jewish armed resistance to the German occupation of Poland and the subsequent transportation of Jews to the extermination camps. After the war, Zuckerman and his wife, Zivia Lubetkin, helped found the Ghetto Fighters' Kibbutz, a community in Israel.

10 **Nietzsche's will to power:** German philosopher Friedrich Wilhelm Nietzsche (1844–1900) posited that a "will to power" was a fundamental motive in human behavior, even more primary than the "will to live."

"Look, Hannah. You're my student. How many times have you heard me talk about Geist *in my lectures?"*

"Hardly ever."

"Then what in heaven's name are you talking about?"

"I AM."[11]

"Bist-du? Come on. This is a charade."

"The trial is a charade," returned Servatius. "Prosecutor Hausner, you speak of your need to recreate ersatz personal involvement in the internal activities of the German Republic during the last war. You do this by speaking to those who have a vested interest in the outcome of this trial. You speak of citing grave 'atrocities' (that have not been fully documented). These may or may not have anything to do with my client. He was (after all) under the command and direction of Reinhard Heydrich, the Obergruppen Führer[12] for the SS. Herr Heydrich was (according to most) second in command to the Füh—I mean Herr Hitler, himself. By all accounts it was Heydrich who conceived of the 'Final Solution.' The credit or blame is his and his alone."

"No, you have to take responsibility for how you will be interpreted. People may twist your words against you for bad purposes." Hannah was passionate. She gestured with both hands in concert.

"Hannah, this is PHILOSOPHY! We aren't engaged in the world of action. We are above all that."

"And when you get onto your high horse and declare that in addition to your normal trial duties, you see your task as preserving for the world's memory the horrors of the Holocaust—especially for this younger generation that thankfully was not born during those troubling times—I put it to you that you are assuming what you are trying to prove. This is an error in elementary logic. We are about the facts of the case and not some high-browed philosophical speculation. A man's life is at stake!" Servatius pointed his index finger directly at Hausner.

"All I'm saying, Martin, is that you can't hide behind the ivory tower of academia. What we say and do can make a difference."

"Of course it makes a difference—"

"But that means that we must be careful of how the assertion of a groundwork of Being might be misinterpreted by those who want to take advantage of our fragile democracy. Martin, there are lives at stake!"

"This is not my concern."

"This is not the court's concern," put in Dr. Moshe Landau. "We are investigators of the Truth, but no person on earth could honestly say he was 'disinterested.' We are formally fair according to the law. It is to our credit that we have as our goal NOT to make this a show trial—the likes of which were famous in Nazi Germany. No. We are

---

11 **I AM:** compare to Exodus 3:14 and the Hebrew account of the ground of all being, Yahweh.

12 **Obergruppen Führer:** senior group officer.

above that. We, the victims, will give *your* client what he denied *us*: a trial under the rule of law."

The next time they met, Hannah told Martin that she was going to study with Karl Jaspers.[13] *Martin didn't take it very well. "What can you get from him? I've taught him everything he knows—except for his psychiatric nonsense, of course. Would you rather get the Truth straight from me or secondhand from him?"*

"Look, Martin, we've had our ups and downs, but if I'm going to prosper as a student of philosophy, I've got to do it outside your dominating influence. I must find a venue where I can explore for myself what I see as the imperatives of philosophy. I want to submit myself totally to this rule of law. I cannot do that so long as I am a student of yours. Were I to attempt it, I'm afraid that the conflict of interests would entangle me in a web of self-deception."

"Your honor, the claims of the defendant are either bold lies or instances of clear self-deception." Hausner was working his incredibly expressive facial muscles to superb effect. "He claims that he was a follower of Kant's categorical imperative.[14] His idealized general society was the Third Reich—it was Being itself to him. Whatever it dictated, he performed as an absolute duty. This is how he understood Kant." Hausner shook his head and walked back to the prosecution's table to drink from his water glass. Then he screwed up those expressive lips and looked right at the man in the bulletproof cage. "How could he possibly understand the philosopher Kant in this way? The leading contemporary scholars of Kant—like Norman Kemp Smith,[15] who before the war published some amazing translations of the German philosopher—all agree that Kant's second form of the categorical imperative dictates we do not use another as a means only but must always recognize his dignity as a human being. How can you do that and kill that very person, all at the same time? Only by being a liar. There are two sort of liars: those who lie to others to get some advantage and those who lie to themselves."

"Don't you understand, Martin, that if I were to stay—feeling the way I do—I'd be deceiving myself."

"Your Honors," put Servatius. "What does this have to do with the case at hand? Eichmann was a benevolent bureaucrat who did what he thought was his duty to the state. He saw the state, as many patriots do, as almost a secular religion: it was Being itself. He was not at the top—though he was at a high level. Obedience was essential. How many of you, when put into a similar situation, wouldn't do just as Herr Eichmann did?"

---

13 **Karl Jaspers:** German philosopher and psychiatrist (1883–1969).

14 **Kant's categorical imperative:** for German philosopher Immanuel Kant (1724–1804), a *categorical imperative* is a moral act according to a universal law: an act that would be right for any person in similar circumstances.

15 **Norman Kemp Smith:** Scottish philosopher (1872–1958) and influential translator of Kant's *Critique of Pure Reason.*

In 1961 shortly after the Adolf Eichmann trial, a Yale psychologist, Stanley Milgram, wanted to test Eichmann's assertion that other people, set in a situation in which there is a conflict between obeying orders and acting ethically, will perform just as Eichmann did. Milgram devised an experiment that involved giving phony electric shocks to a test subject called "the learner" (really an actor). Milgram found that most of his real test subjects (called "the teachers") followed the model that Eichmann described as they administered increasingly severe electric shocks to the test subject—even when the subject complained of pain and a heart condition. For the most part, the teachers were willing to follow whatever they were directed to do by the stern (phony) research director, even when this seemed to entail torturing the learner. Others have also verified these findings, and parallel experiments have yielded similar results.[16]

What are we to think of this? Does this alter our judgment of Eichmann? Is he excused because most would act as he did, or does this suggest that the standard of just behavior requires the following of a different sort of "duty": the duty to act ethically?

"So, how does Augustine[17] actually describe evil actions if Evil, itself, does not exist?" Hannah took a drink of coffee as she sat across from Karl Jaspers, her dissertation director. He was a pleasantly plump man of medium height who brushed his thin hair straight back. His straight nose was not sharp but complemented the soft roundness of his mouth and chin. He was a man with whom it was easy to talk.

"The genius of Augustine was that he was able to see that there is really no such thing as 'Evil itself' as an ontological force. Evil is created by the failings of mediocre men."

"But what about the great diabolical figures in history?"

"They represent ordinary people who are promoted far past their ability." Jaspers signaled for the waiter to refill his tea.

"But what about the very top? The truly terrible figures?"

"Well, they are different. You are right. They are the stupidest of all. They are characterized psychologically in their worldview as 'stubborn,' 'intellectually noninquisitive,' and 'pathologically narcissistic.' This presents itself in their latching onto an action plan or policy either because they see no other way or because someone else presented it to them. Once they see this direction (rather arbitrarily adopted), they don't question it and persevere. From their point of view, they are virtuous because they are accepting a standard and carrying it

---

16 **Others have . . . similar results:** details of this and similar experiments can be found in Stanley Milgram, *Obedience to Authority: An Experimental View* (New York: Harper Collins, 2004); Thomas Blass, *The Man Who Shocked the World* (New York: Basic Books, 2004); Solomon Asch, "Effects of Group Pressure upon the Modification and Distortion of Judgment," in *Groups, Leadership, and Men,* ed. H. Buetzkov (Pittsburgh, PA: Carnegie Press, 1951); and Philip Zimbardo and Ken Musen, *Quiet Rage: The Stanford Experiment* (New York: Insight Media, 2004).

17 **Augustine:** St. Augustine of Hippo (354–430 CE), Berber philosopher and theologian in what is now Algeria; author of *On the Free Choice of the Will,* which was a crucial part of Arendt's dissertation.

out. But because they are so stupid, they do not see that the very standard or policy itself demands rational scrutiny before one acts on it.

"For Augustine, the only way out of this dilemma is via love, which occasions rational and emotional connection to the people at hand."

Hannah was about to light a cigarette but dropped it onto the table. She didn't look up but watched her cigarette rolling about on the table. When it stopped, she reached across the table and grabbed her director's hand. "I now concur that evil is only the mistake of the ordinary and the stupid. How do we keep these creeps out of public office?"

Karl smiled at his student. "As you know, I started out in psychiatry. This is a discipline of care and connection. Although I have now come over to philosophy, I cannot reject this essential inclination. It is the only authentic way out of our existential dilemma."

Hannah pursed her lips and nodded her head.

"This is Hannah Arendt reporting for *XYZ News* from the war-crimes trial of Adolf Eichmann. The defense and prosecution have now rested. The summary of the prosecution's case is twofold. In the *first place* were the procedural arguments, such as, on the one hand, only Hitler was responsible for the murder of the Jews. But then, on the other hand, Hitler had sovereign immunity and couldn't have been prosecuted had he lived. Thus, there would have been no justice. The state of affairs of there being 'no justice' is impermissible, so Hitler's subordinates had to be held accountable.

"Then there was also a question of venue. The defense said that the trial should have been held in Germany by Germans. But Germany never sought extradition. QED.[18]

"In the *second place* are the testimonies of death camp survivors describing the horrors of those conditions. A witness quoted Eichmann, himself, bragging, 'I will jump into my grave laughing, because the fact that I have the death of five million Jews [or "enemies of the Reich,"[19] as he always claimed to have said] on my conscience gives me extraordinary satisfaction.'[20] This and other quotes showed Eichmann's passion for killing Jews. This passion was documented in Nüremberg through thousands of documents—many of them personally signed by Eichmann.

"The defense strategy centered on the issue of responsibility. They contended that Eichmann was lawfully fulfilling the statutes that were in place within his country. He was only following orders handed down to him by others superior to himself. If he was guilty of anything, it was merely of aiding and abetting.

"Besides this central theme, the defense also tried to defuse the rhetorical force of all firsthand accounts of the undeniable mayhem and murder that took place by shifting to theoretical questions of jurisdiction, venue, and the impartiality of the judges themselves.

---

18 **QED:** quod erat demonstrandum ("which was to be proved"); an abbreviation at the end of a formal proof, indicating that the last proposition deduced is the one that was to be demonstrated, thus completing the proof.

19 **Reich:** the Third Reich ("Empire"), the Nazi's name for their regime (1933–1945).

20 Arendt, *Eichmann in Jerusalem*, 46.

"It's impossible to guess for sure what the outcome will be, but if there is any outcome other than a guilty sentence and the death penalty, I believe there will be civil unrest.

"In the end, history will be the ultimate judge of whether Adolf Eichmann is merely a simple dumb man who was promoted far above his competence or was a raving disciple of evil much on the model of Satan, himself. Which is the real Adolf Eichmann?"

Eichmann was found guilty. On Friday, December 15, 1961, at nine o'clock in the morning, the death sentence was pronounced. The appeal judgment was read on May 29, 1962. On the same day Eichmann beseeched the president of Israel, Itzhak Ben-Zvi, for mercy. After considering Eichmann's and others' pleas for clemency, the president rejected them all on Thursday, May 31, 1962. That very day, shortly before midnight, Eichmann was hanged, his body cremated, and his ashes scattered over the Mediterranean Sea in international waters. The purpose of this disposal of the body was so that he might have no permanent marker of his life and no enduring resting place in Israel.

Eichmann's last words were, "Long live Germany. Long live Austria. Long live Argentina. I owe a lot to these countries, and I shall not forget them. I had to obey the rules of war and my flag." Thus, ends the story of Eichmann.

Martin Heidegger faced charges in the denazification hearings after the war.* These charges focused first on his acceptance of the Nazi-influenced promotion to the post of rector at Freiburg University and his inaugural address, "The Self-Assertion of the German University"; second, on his Nazi sympathies; third, on his allegedly turning in four philosophy students (one of whom was gassed at Auschwitz). In his own defense, Heidegger cited that the Nazi doctrine of "biologism" (biological determinism) was one he attacked in his published writings—though he attacked "biologism" and not "the Nazi doctrine of biologism." Heidegger was accused by Hans Jonas and Karl Löwith,[21] who testified that Heidegger supported Nazi thought. Hannah Arendt defended her former professor and resumed their lifelong correspondence. Karl Jaspers denounced Heidegger.

As a result of these hearings, in 1945 Heidegger was forced to step down from his chair and resign from teaching. Four years later the restriction against his teaching was lifted. Shortly thereafter, Heidegger became a professor emeritus until his death in 1976.

Heidegger's Nazi membership card number was 312589.

Patrick exited out of his program, turned off the projector, and turned up the lights. Then he made his way out of the booth and up the main aisle to the front of the room. He paused slightly before saying anything. The six-foot-two-inch philosophy and film

---

* *Some material from this section of the story comes from Victor Farias,* Heidegger and Nazism *tr. Paul Burrell (1987; rpt. Philadelphia, PA: Temple University Press, 1991). For some discussion of this controversial book, see Richard Wolin, ed.* The Heidegger Controversy: A Critical Reader *(Cambridge, MA: MIT Press, 1992).*

21 **Hans Jonas and Karl Löwith:** German philosophers and former students of Heidegger.

double major was thin and good-looking. His face was accented with several days of unshaven beard. The hair on the top of his head spiked up, making his face seem even thinner. "I want to thank you all for coming. Several of you helped me in making the film—a special thanks to Dr. Tode for his constructive comments and to Professor Lux for her help with the filming. Then there was Miss Sophia in the library and the Arendt Collection. Next, a thanks to Sarah, Josh, Josie, and the entire existentialism seminar, who all lent a hand. Without your help, this wouldn't have been possible."

Then, Professor Tode stood up. "We only have time for a couple of questions before the formal oral defense. Who would like to ask Patrick a question?"

The professor looked around the room. No one was moving. The silence was breeding tension. Then a hand shot up in the back row. It was a male sporting tiny bottle-bottom glasses and close-cropped hair, "Hey, I wanted to know how long it took you to do this? I mean you must have put in a lot of time in this. It was very realistic."

Patrick smiled. "Yes. And I had to do a paper too! If I had just settled for a paper, it would have been a lot easier. But some messages you just can't put into the sort of arguments Professor Tode requires. That's why I just *had* to make this film."

Then three more hands shot up.

"What made you think of the hyperlink feature?" asked a freshman girl with a bright red streak in her punk hairdo.

"I don't know how to answer that. It just seemed that everything was so complicated that I wanted to show several different vantage points."

"Why didn't you just put them into the film itself instead of having to stop and start so many times?"

"Well, that's a good point. I guess this way you are all made aware that I am there in the booth telling the story. It's a personal involvement—à la Walter Benjamin.[22] Did you like the effect?"

"Yeah," she replied. "It just kind of makes my head swim."

"Are you sure that's from the film?" said a boy from across the room.

The punk-haired freshman responded with a hand gesture.

"Why didn't you go farther in the sex scene? I mean just unbuttoning two buttons?" blurted a senior boy with long frizzy blonde hair and a gold nose ring.

Patrick laughed along with the rest of the audience, as Professor Tode looked impatient. "Hey, this is Bard, you know. Only tame-frame on the official screen."

This caused a general murmuring of discontent.

Patrick lifted both hands to frame the side of his head in anxiety. "Hey, guys, you wouldn't want Professor Tode to kill me, would you?"

The murmur transferred to a tittering of laughter. Professor Tode looked like he was ready to explode. His very round blue eyes bulged out of their sockets, "One last question. Yes, Shelby."

---

22 **Walter Benjamin:** German-Jewish philosopher and literary critic (1892–1940).

Shelby was a well-known English major on campus who often performed his off-beat poetry. He was rather short and plump. "Hey, Patrick. Good job. I really liked it. I'm glad you made the film and that I came to see it. To tell you the truth, I had never even heard of Adolf Eichmann before your film. He seems like one crazy wacko, if you ask me."

There was a general murmur of assent. Patrick started to mount a reply when Professor Tode grabbed him by the arm and headed him out of the room.

It wasn't over yet.

■ READING AND DISCUSSION QUESTIONS

1. Go to the Internet and look up Adolf Eichmann. Who was he, and what was his role in the Holocaust?
2. Go to the Internet and look up Hannah Arendt's connection to Bard College. Does this information affect the way you read the story?
3. Who are the senior thesis judges in this story? What other judges enter the picture? Are all types of judges different, or is there some level of similarity in the act of judging?
4. Arendt refers to the rule of law in talking to Heidegger. Which rule of law does she mean? How would Socrates in the "Crito" or Thomas Aquinas's natural law or Hegel's *Sittlichkeit* react to this? Compare their reactions with defense attorney Servatius's comments.
5. How do the various narratives comment on each other? Give three examples.
6. How did Arendt's work on Augustine inform her idea that evil is banal?
7. The character of Martin Heidegger says philosophy is above the fray of day-to-day events. Hannah Arendt takes a different stance. Evaluate the two positions. Which one do you agree with?

■ FICTIVE-NARRATIVE PHILOSOPHY FEEDBACK

What claims are made in this story? Write them out in a bulleted list and include whether they are made through dialogue, dramatic action, or the presentation of the scene (including descriptive detail). One page. Then choose either a short direct-discourse response (according to the rules in Chapter 2) or a short fictive-narrative presentation (according to the rules in Chapter 3).

THE EXPOSITION OF THE QUESTION OF THE MEANING OF BEING

Martin Heidegger

Translated and adapted by Michael Boylan from Martin Heidegger, *Sein und Zeit* (Halle: M. Niemeyer, 1929). *Note on the translation:* English words found in brackets are inserted by the translator to make better sense of the English rendering. German words found in brackets are given for clarity in certain key situations.

In Being and Time, *Heidegger changes the direction of phenomenology away from Edmund Husserl. In the work Heidegger explores various ways that we exist and encounter being. This is done not only in the abstract (the direct connection with things in themselves that Husserl believes is possible) but via our lived experience—especially as we become conscious of our anxiety about living in the world (angst). This starting point of being in the world is captured by the term* Dasein *(a combination of being, or* sein, *and* da, *which gives the being signification of "here" and "there": thus "being here and there"). Ontology is the philosophical study of being. Thus, it is correct to think of this exercise as an exploration of how our own being is connected to Being itself. In this depiction, Heidegger is engaged in a novel sort of phenomenological ontology.*

Today, in our world that smugly considers itself progressive, the question of affirming metaphysics has been forgotten. We feel that [by omission] we are spared the great battle of giants concerning being. But this is no arbitrary question. It was central to Plato and Aristotle. But afterwards this question ceased to be treated as a thematic question of philosophical investigation. In the history of philosophy these two philosophers have been distorted and put in disguise up until the writing of Hegel's *Logic*.[23] Even then what was presented through great effort were merely fragments that have since been trivialized.

Not only that, but in the face of the groundwork of the Greek's point of departure, a dogmatic attitude has stated

(a) the question of the meaning of Being is superfluous, and
(b) the neglect [of this question] is wrong.

---

23 **Hegel's *Logic*:** *Science of Logic* (3 volumes; 1811, 1812, 1816) by German philosopher Georg Wilhelm Friedrich Hegel (1770–1831).

It is said that Being is the most universal yet the emptiest of concepts. Because of this, it resists each attempt at definition. Nor does this most universal and indefinable concept need any definition. Everyone uses the concept of Being and understands what is meant by it. Thus, pursuing [such questions] made the ancient philosophers anxious because of its inherent obscurity. [It] has now taken on clarity so that whoever pursues questions [of Being] is guilty of methodological error.

Three Primary Suppositions About Being

These prejudices against questioning Being that have been planted and that continually sprout anew (which I referred to above) cannot here be discussed in detail. They foster the belief that questions about Being are unnecessary—they were planted in classical ontology[24] itself. That ontology can only be properly interpreted from the standpoint of Being that has already been conceptually clarified. One must begin from the original soil that gave rise to these ontological concepts, which gave rise to the appropriate demonstration of categories and completeness. We shall carry the discussion of these presuppositions only to the point necessary for clearly restating [or recapturing] the question about the meaning of being. There are three [primary presuppositions]:

1. Being is the most universal concept. "An understanding of Being is contained within our every apprehension of beings."[25] However, the *universality* of Being is not that of a *type*. Being does not modify or constrain the domain of beings in as much as they are conceived according to [the Aristotelian categories of] genus and species. Thus, Being is not a genus. Instead, the universality of Being transcends the universality of genus. Thus, in the language of the medievals, Being is a *transcendens*. Aristotle understood the unity of the transcendent universal[26] as the unity of *analogy* (in contrast to the multiplicity of universals generated from those concepts with material content). With this discovery, Aristotle moved the question of Being to a new level. Now it is true that Aristotle did not clarify these categorical connections. This task was left to medieval ontologists. They proposed many possibilities—most prominent being the Thomistic and Scotist schools.[27] But fundamental clarity

---

24 **ontology:** the study of the nature of being and existence.

25 Thomas Aquinas, *Summa Theologiae* II–I q.94, a.2.

26 **transcendent universal:** Heidegger here is referring to Aristotle's *The Categories*, which presents a group of categories (similar to those presented by Kant in this volume). Unlike Kant's, Aristotle's categories have one aspect that ascends in generality: Socrates → man → animal → living thing → thing → substance.

27 **Thomistic and Scotist schools:** followers of theologians St. Thomas Aquinas (c. 1225–1274) and John Duns Scotus (c. 1266–1308), respectively.

was not achieved. Hegel finally defines Being as the indeterminate immediate. Hegel then makes this definition the groundwork of all his additional categorization and explication in his *Logic*. [In this way], Hegel remains within the tradition of classical ontology. However, Hegel does relinquish the problem (raised by Aristotle) of the unity of Being in contrast to the manifold of categories that possess material content. Therefore, if it is said that Being is the most universal of concepts, this cannot mean that it is so clear as to obviate discussion. Rather, the concept of Being is the most obscure concept of all.

2. The concept of Being cannot be defined. This conclusion comes from its transcendent universality. This would be true if definition is only achieved via [Aristotelian] genus + species difference. Then Being cannot be understood as a being, and Being cannot be depicted as predicating beings to it (since it does not add a natural property). [Further], Being cannot be derived from higher concepts; nor can it be represented by lower ones. So, does this indicate that the concept of Being is not a problem? No, we can only conclude that Being is not like a being. We cannot apply to Being the concept of *definition* within traditional [Aristotelian] logic (that itself is rooted in classical ontology). But

though Being cannot be defined in a conventional way, this does not mean that its *meaning* does not force itself upon us.

3. Being is the self-evident concept. Being is implied in all knowing and in every predicating relation to beings. It is in each subject-object relation and its expression is understood without any additional exposition. All people understand such propositions as "The sky is blue" or "I am happy," etc. But this common understandability demonstrates its nonunderstandability because a conundrum lies in wait, a priori: every relation between beings is in the context of some partial understanding of Being (shrouded in darkness). This dynamic proves the fundamental imperative of recapitulating the question, What is Being?

Within the realm of self-understandability—especially when we come to the concept of Being—is the dubious procedure to invoke *self-evidence*, even if it is the "implicit judgments of common reason" (Kant[28]) to become *explicit* as a goal of our business in philosophical analysis.

Formulating the Question of Being

By considering these prejudices, we have made plain that the answer to the question of Being is incomplete and that the posing of the question itself is direction-

---

28 **Kant:** German philosopher Immanuel Kant (1724–1804).

less. Therefore, to summarize: the question of Being means first to develop an adequate way to formulate the question.

The question on the meaning of Being needs specification. If it is *a* (or even *the*) fundamental question, then such questioning needs to be clear and thoughtfully undertaken. Therefore, we ought to discuss briefly what belongs to any question in general so that from this standpoint the question of Being can be made clear and distinctive.

Each inquiry is a quest [*Suchen*]. Every quest takes its direction initially from what is sought. Inquiry is a conscious search for beings in their *thatness* and *whatness* regarding its Being. The conscious search can become an investigation as the inquiry reveals its direction. Any inquiry, as an inquiry, is about something that has [the content of] what it asks. All inquiry is in some way an inquisition of something. So in addition to that which is asked, an inquiry also has *what is interrogated.* In questions that are specifically theoretical (investigative questions), what is asked about is determined and conceptualized. Further, in what is asked about there lies that which can only be found in the asking. This is intended, and it is here that the inquiry reaches its goal. As an attitude adopted by a being, the inquirer in his inquiry has his own character of Being. Inquiry can arise informally in common queries or via explicitly formulated inquiries. What is proper to the latter is the fact that inquiry only becomes lucid to the latter when all the above named characteristics of the inquiry have become clear.

The question about the meaning of Being is what [the inquiry] must formu-late. We must thus discuss it keeping in mind these structural issues.

Inquiry, as a kind of quest, needs initial guidance about its end. The meaning of Being must therefore already be available in some sense. We suggested earlier that we are always engaged [in the context of] an understanding of Being. From this understanding develops the explicit question of the meaning of Being and the attraction to its concept. We do not know the meaning of Being, but even when we ask, "What is Being?" we possess an understanding of the "is." This is the case despite not being able to provide a concept of the "is." We do not even know the horizon that will allow us to further specify meaning. This common and vague understanding of Being is a fact. . . .

The "Being of Beings"

Inasmuch as Being is what is asked about, and inasmuch as Being means the "Being of beings," then it turns out that beings themselves are the source of interrogation in the inquiry about Being. The beings are, in a manner, interrogated regarding their Being. But if the beings are to truly display the characteristics of their Being, they must have become accessible in advance as they are in themselves. When we come to what is to be interrogated, the question of Being demands that the proper access to beings be gained and secured prior to the interrogation. We may call various things "existent" [*seind*] in different ways. Everything we talk about or are related to in daily life is through being. What and how we ourselves exist [in the world] is also via being. Being is found in the "this" and the "what" realities: the objective presence of things, subsistence, validity, and existence [*Dasein*], and in the [existential] given [*es gibt*].[29] In which being is the meaning of Being to be found? How does the disclosure of Being come about? Is the starting point arbitrary, or is there in a particular being a [hierarchical] set of preconditions that [properly] elaborate Being? If so, then whence is this being, and in what manner does it have priority?

If the inquiry into Being is to be clearly formulated and developed to its optimal clarity, then the elaboration of this inquiry requires explication of the modes of regarding Being according to what has already been said. This includes understanding and grasping conceptually Being's meaning. Also, we must ponder the potential right choice of an exemplary being and develop a mode to access this being. The constitutive attitudes of inquiry are understanding, grasping, choosing, and obtaining access to. These are modes of Being for *the* beings about which we inquire. Therefore, to work out the inquiry into being means to make a being: one who questions [and through this intellectual activity] is conscious of his Being. Asking this question as a mode of *being* in being structures what is asked about it, that is, Being. This being (which we all are individually) includes in its inquiry the many possibilities of Being (which we will now term as *Dasein*). The explicit formulation of the inquiry of the meaning of Being requires a prior explication of being (*Dasein*) with respect to Being. . . .

Formulating the Inquiry

According to the guideline of the question's per se formal structure, the characteristics of the inquiry into Being have made it clear that this question is a singular one. This is because its elaboration and solution require a series of fundamental inquiries. The distinctiveness of this inquiry into Being will only become clear when the question is sufficiently delineated regarding function, intention, and motives.

Until now the need to recapitulate the inquiry was motivated both by the dignity of its origin and by there being a lack of a definite answer or even an adequate formulation of the question. One can demand to know what purpose this inquiry serves. Is it solely (or in whole) an inquiry that is amorphous speculation about the most general of the general? Or [on the other hand] is it the most basic, and at the same time the most concrete, of inquiries?

Being is always the Being of a being. The sum of beings can become (relative to its domains) the field where definite areas of knowledge are entertained and examined. These areas of knowledge (for example, history, nature, space, life, *Dasein*, language, etc.) can themselves become themes in scientific [systematic] inquiry. Scientific [*wissenschaftliche*] research engages roughly and naively in cartography as it first establishes these areas of knowledge according to commonsense beginning. The elaboration of the area in its fundamental structures is an approach of

---

29 **the [existential] given:** how we find ourselves in the world: what is our given and how do we find ourselves situated? The answer at the level of the individual is very particular. Each of us is different, and our situations in the world are unique.

the prescientific [philosophical] experience and interpretation of the domain of Being about which the area of subject matter is confined. The resulting basic concepts comprise the guidelines for the first concrete disclosure. Though this research may lean toward a positive [scientific] approach, the importance of this research is not so much in establishing concepts that are collected and sorted into handbooks but rather in the imperative to ask questions about the essential constitution [*Grundverfassungen*] of each of these areas. This inquiry is chiefly a reaction against the [requirement] merely to increase knowledge in each area.

The real movement of the sciences [that is, exact philosophy] takes place in the more or less radical revision of these basic concepts transparent to itself. This revision is more or less successful with regard to itself. An exact level of development is determined by the extent to which it is able to ascertain [the meaning of] a crisis of basic concepts. In these immanent crises, the relation begins to become unstable between the positive investigative inquiry and those things that are under interrogation questions (to the matter at hand). Today tendencies to place philosophical investigation on a new foundation have mushroomed in a variety of disciplines. . . .

The Grounding of Scientific Inquiry

Fundamental concepts are determinations in [the development] of knowledge. These fundamental concepts are the groundwork for all thematic objects of a science. Through them one attains an understanding that precedes and guides all positive investigation. Accordingly, these concepts first receive their evidential grounding in a corresponding preliminary research into knowledge itself. But since each of these areas arises from the domain of beings themselves, this preliminary research (from which the basic concepts are drawn) amounts to nothing other than interpreting these beings with reference to the essential constitution of Being. This sort of inquiry must precede the positive sciences. It is able to do so. The work of Plato and Aristotle confirms this. Setting out the groundwork of the sciences in this way is different, in principle, from a logic limping along behind with haphazard investigations in search of a method. Formulating a [definitive] groundwork is productive logic in the sense that it leaps ahead, so to speak, into a definite realm of Being. It discloses for the first time its constitutive Being and makes the acquired structures available to the positive sciences as clear protocols for further inquiry. Therefore (to give an example), what is philosophically primary is neither a theory of concept formation told in historiology[30] nor a theory of historiological knowledge. It is not even a theory of history as an object of historiology. Rather, the interpretation of actual historical beings, historically situated, is what is primary. Similarly, the positive result of Kant's *Critique of Pure Reason* is what it contributes toward the working out of what belongs to any nature. This is not a theory of knowledge but [an application of] a

---

30 **historiology:** the study of (the discipline of) history.

transcendental logic as an a priori logic in the realm of Being called nature.

and conceived of this clarification as its primary task. . . .

Ontological Inquiry

This inquiry [called] ontology, taken in its broadest sense without reference to specific ontological directions, still needs [for itself] some guideline. Ontological inquiry is more original than the ontic[31] inquiry of the positive sciences. But it is still naive and opaque if its investigations into the Being of beings leaves the meaning of Being [as such] unexamined. It is this ontological task of constructing a genealogy of the different possible modes of Being (that is not deductively construed) [that needs to be undertaken]. This first requires a meaning of what is really meant by the expression "Being."

The inquiry into Being thus aims not only at ascertaining an a priori condition of the possibility of scientific investigation of beings of such and such sort (and in so doing already proceeds with an understanding of Being) but also it aims at the threshold of possible ontologies that proceed *from* and are found *in* the ontic sciences (and provide their foundations). All ontology, regardless of the elegance of categories it has at its disposal, will be fundamentally blind. This blindness perverts the deepest intent if it has not previously clarified the meaning of Being properly

Dasein

Dasein is a being that does not simply occur among other beings but is ontically distinguished by the fact that in its Being this being is keen [to perceive the nature] of its very Being. Therefore, it is constitutive of *Dasein*'s Being to have in its Being a relation toward that Being that is a relationship of Being. This means that *Dasein* understands itself in its Being in some way and with some exactness. It is proper to this being that it be disclosed to itself with and through its Being. *The understanding of Being is a determination of* Dasein's *Being. Dasein* is ontically distinctive because it is ontological.

To be ontological does not mean that an ontology has been developed. The term *ontology* will be reserved for the explicit theoretical question of the meaning of beings. The intended ontological character of *Dasein* may be termed "pre-ontological." This does not mean it is simply ontical; rather, it refers to a being's manner of understanding of Being.

We shall call the very Being to which *Dasein* can relate in one way or another (and it always does) "existence" [*Existenz*].[32] Because the essential definition of *Dasein* cannot be realized by ascribing to it

---

31 **Ontological . . . ontic:** the term *ontologisch* ("ontological") is contrasted with *ontisch* ("ontical"), with the former denoting inquiry into Being, while the latter concerns the plain simple facts of physical beings.

32 **Existenz:** here it is important to note that the normal words for "existence" and "existential" (meaning a reflected life) are to be contrasted with a merely lived life that ignores its own meaning (via Heidegger's coined word *existenziell*[*e*]).

a "what"[33] that specifies its material content, and because its essence lies in the fact that in each case it has its Being to be, that Being always must be known through itself. The term *Dasein* is a pure expression of Being and therefore has been chosen to designate this being.

Dasein always understands itself in terms of its existence: its possibility to be or not to be itself. *Dasein* has either chosen these possibilities or has accidentally come upon them or has grown up in them. Existence is decided only by each *Dasein* itself in the manner of seizing upon or neglecting such possibilities. We come to terms with the question of existence always and only through existence itself. We shall call this sort of self-understanding "existential [*existenziell*] understanding." The question of existence is an ontic affair of *Dasein*. To obtain this theoretical clarity of the ontological structure of existence is not necessary. The inquiry about structure seeks an analysis of what constitutes existence. The coherence of these structures can be termed "existentiality." The analysis of existentiality does not have character of vital lived [*existenzielle*] understanding but rather an understanding of reflective experience. The proper job of an existential analysis of *Dasein* is prescribed through its possibility and necessity in the ontic character of *Dasein*.

Since existence defines *Dasein*, the ontological analysis of this being always requires a previous existential glimpse. However, we understand existentiality as the constitution of being's Being that exists. But the idea of Being already lies in the idea of such a constitution of Being. Thus, there is the possibility of carrying out the analysis of *Dasein* according to the prior elaboration of the question of Being in general.

Sciences and those [sorts of] disciplines are ways of being in which *Dasein* also relates to beings that it may not *itself* be. But being in a world belongs essentially to *Dasein*. . . .

Ontologies that have beings unlike *Dasein* as their theme are driven and derived in the ontic structure of *Dasein* itself. This structure includes (through itself) the determination of a preontological understanding of Being. Therefore, fundamental ontology, from which alone all other ontologies can originate, must be sought in the existential analysis of *Dasein*.

---

33 **"what":** ascribing a "what" refers to giving a definition via genus + species difference (Aristotelian definition). Heidegger finds this approach wanting for ontology. It is not rich enough for Heidegger's taste. His critique is similar to Hegel's critique of Kant.

■ READING AND DISCUSSION QUESTIONS

1. What does Heidegger mean by *Dasein*?
2. Contrast Heidegger's use of "ontic" and "ontological."
3. How does existence reveal *Dasein*?
4. What are the three primary presuppositions about Being? What do earlier thinkers get right, and what do they get wrong?

5. How do "being" and "Being" relate?
6. How does positive science proceed? What is this useful for? What are its limitations?
7. Why are ontologies that are driven merely by ontic depictions of *Dasein* called "preontological"? Give an example.
8. Why, if Being is the most universal of concepts, is it the most obscure concept of all?

■ CLASS EXERCISES

A. *Direct logical discourse:* Using the tools found in Chapter 2, outline the argument from one of the subsections above. Based on your assessment of one key premise, write a one-page argument about why you agree or disagree with the argument's conclusion.

B. *Fictive-narrative philosophy:* Using the tools found in Chapter 3, begin with a claim that relates to the reading and discussion questions above. Then create a modern-day story about people or situations familiar to you that makes the logical claim you have identified. Three pages.

AN EXPERT ON THE JEWISH QUESTION

Hannah Arendt

From Hannah Arendt, *Eichmann in Jerusalem: A Report on the Banality of Evil* (New York: Viking Press, 1963), 36–55.

In this very influential book, Arendt adapts her academic political philosophy to a more popular audience as she covers the trial of Adolf Eichmann in Jerusalem. One of the book's most startling theses is that instead of being an "evil genius" who wreaked death and destruction on millions, Adolf Eichmann was a rather ordinary man who merely wanted to get ahead in the Nazi state. He was a joiner who hid behind official clichés and euphemisms. This notion of evil as ignorance and banality follows Arendt's doctoral dissertation on Augustine's On the Free Choice of the Will *under Karl Jaspers. If Arendt is correct in her assessment, then the possibility of another Holocaust is real and requires our constant vigilance to prevent.*

In 1934, when Eichmann[34] applied successfully for a job, the SD was a relatively new apparatus in the SS,[35] founded two years earlier by Heinrich Himmler to serve as the Intelligence service of the Party and now headed by Reinhardt Heydrich,[36] a former Navy Intelligence officer, who was to become, as Gerald Reitlinger put it, "the real engineer of the Final Solution" (*The Final Solution,* 1961). Its initial task had been to spy on Party members, and thus to give the SS an ascendancy over the regular Party apparatus. Meanwhile it had taken on some additional duties, becoming the information and research center for the Secret State Police, or Gestapo. These were the first steps toward the merger of the SS and the police, which, however, was not carried out until September, 1939, although Himmler held the

---

34 **Eichmann:** Adolf Eichmann (1906–1962), Nazi official executed for his role in managing extermination camps during World War II.

35 **SD . . . SS:** SD (for Sicherheitsdienst, meaning "security service"), Nazi intelligence organization; SS (for Schutzstaffel, meaning "protective echelon"), elite Nazi militia.

36 **Heinrich Himmler . . . Reinhardt Heydrich:** Himmler (1900–1945), head of the SS; Heydrich (1904–1942), chief of the SD.

double post of Reichsführer SS and Chief of the German Police from 1936 on. Eichmann, of course, could not have known of these future developments, but he seems to have known nothing either of the nature of the SD when he entered it; this is quite possible, because the operations of the SD had always been top secret. As far as he was concerned, it was all a misunderstanding and at first "a great disappointment. For I thought this was what I had read about in the *Münchener Illustrierten Zeitung*[37]; when the high Party officials drove along, there were commando guards with them, men standing on the running boards of the cars. . . . In short, I had mistaken the Security Service of the Reichsführer SS for the Reich Security Service . . . and nobody set me right and no one told me anything. For I had had not the slightest notion of what now was revealed to me." The question of whether he was telling the truth had a certain bearing on the trial, where it had to be decided whether he had volunteered for his position or had been drafted into it. His misunderstanding, if such it was, is not inexplicable; the SS, or *Schutzstaffeln*, had originally been established as special units for the protection of the Party leaders.

His disappointment, however, consisted chiefly in that he had to start all over again, that he was back at the bottom, and his only consolation was that there were others who had made the same

mistake. He was put into the Information department, where his first job was to file all information concerning Freemasonry (which in the early Nazi ideological muddle was somehow lumped with Judaism, Catholicism, and Communism) and to help in the establishment of a Freemasonry museum. He now had ample opportunity to learn what this strange word meant that Kaltenbrunner[38] had thrown at him in their discussion of Schlaraffia.[39] (Incidentally, an eagerness to establish museums commemorating their enemies was very characteristic of the Nazis. During the war, several services competed bitterly for the honor of establishing anti-Jewish museums and libraries. We owe to this strange craze the salvage of many great cultural treasures of European Jewry.) The trouble was that things were again very, very boring, and he was greatly relieved when, after four or five months of Freemasonry, he was put into the brand-new department concerned with Jews. This was the real beginning of the career which was to end in the Jerusalem court.

It was the year 1935 when Germany, contrary to the stipulations of the Treaty of Versailles,[40] introduced general conscription and publicly announced plans for rearmament, including the building of an air force and a navy. It was also the year when Germany, having left the League of Nations in 1933, prepared neither quietly nor secretly for the occupation of the de-

---

37 ***Münchener Illustrierten Zeitung:*** *Munich Illustrated Times* (newspaper).

38 **Kaltenbrunner:** Ernst Kaltenbrunner (1903–1946), high-ranking SS leader.

39 **Schlaraffia:** German-speaking men's social organization with local clubs spread worldwide.

40 **Treaty of Versailles:** the 1919 treaty ending World War I between Germany and the Allied powers.

militarized zone of the Rhineland. It was the time of Hitler's peace speeches—"Germany needs peace and desires peace," "We recognize Poland as the home of a great and nationally conscious people," "Germany neither intends nor wishes to interfere in the internal affairs of Austria, to annex Austria, or to conclude an *Anschluss*[41]"—and, above all, it was the year when the Nazi regime won general and, unhappily, genuine recognition in Germany and abroad, when Hitler was admired everywhere as a great national statesman. In Germany itself, it was a time of transition. Because of the enormous rearmament program, unemployment had been liquidated, the initial resistance of the working class was broken, and the hostility of the regime, which had at first been directed primarily against "anti-Fascists"—Communists, Socialists, left-wing intellectuals, and Jews in prominent positions—had not yet shifted entirely to persecution of the Jews qua Jews.[42]

To be sure, one of the first steps taken by the Nazi government back in 1933 had been the exclusion of Jews from the Civil Service (which in Germany included all teaching positions, from grammar school to university, and most branches of the entertainment industry, including radio, the theater, the opera, and concerts) and, in general, their removal from public offices. But private business remained almost untouched until 1938, and even the legal and medical professions were only gradually abolished, although Jewish students were excluded from most universities and were nowhere permitted to graduate. Emigration of Jews in these years proceeded in a not unduly accelerated and generally orderly fashion, and the currency restrictions that made it difficult, but not impossible, for Jews to take their money, or at least the greater part of it, out of the country were the same for non-Jews; they dated back to the days of the Weimar Republic.[43] There were a certain number of *Einzelaktionen*—individual actions putting pressure on Jews to sell their property at often ridiculously low prices—but these usually occurred in small towns and, indeed, could be traced to the spontaneous, "individual" initiative of some enterprising Storm Troopers, the so-called SA[44] men, who, except for their officer corps, were mostly recruited from the lower classes. The police, it is true, never stopped these "excesses," but the Nazi authorities were not too happy about them, because they affected the value of real estate all over the country. The emigrants, unless they were political refugees, were young people who realized that there was no future for them in Germany. And since they soon found out that there was hardly any future for them in other European countries either, some Jewish emigrants actually returned during this period. When Eichmann was asked how he had reconciled his personal feelings about Jews

---

41 *Anschluss*: annexation (of Austria).

42 **Jews qua Jews:** Jews as Jews.

43 **Weimar Republic:** the parliamentary government (1919–1933) that governed Germany between the end of World War I and the Nazi Third Reich.

44 **SA:** Sturmabteilung ("assault detachment" or "stormtroopers"), Nazi paramilitary organization.

with the outspoken and violent anti-Semitism of the Party he had joined, he replied with the proverb: "Nothing's as hot when you eat it as when it's being cooked"—a proverb that was then on the lips of many Jews as well. They lived in a fool's paradise, in which, for a few years, even Streicher[45] spoke of a "legal solution" of the Jewish problem. It took the organized pogroms[46] of November, 1938, the so-called *Kristallnacht* or Night of Broken Glass, when seventy-five hundred Jewish shop windows were broken, all synagogues went up in flames, and twenty thousand Jewish men were taken off to concentration camps, to expel them from it.

The frequently forgotten point of the matter is that the famous Nuremberg Laws,[47] issued in the fall of 1935, had failed to do the trick. The testimony of three witnesses from Germany, high-ranking former officials of the Zionist organization who left Germany shortly before the outbreak of the war, gave only the barest glimpse into the true state of affairs during the first five years of the Nazi regime. The Nuremberg Laws had deprived the Jews of their political but not of their civil rights; they were no longer citizens (*Reichsbürger*), but they remained members of the German state (*Staatsange-hörige*). Even if they emigrated, they were not automatically stateless. Sexual intercourse between Jews and Germans, and the contraction of mixed marriages, were forbidden. Also, no German woman under the age of forty-five could be employed in a Jewish household. Of these stipulations, only the last was of practical significance; the others merely legalized a *de facto* situation.

Hence, the Nuremberg Laws were felt to have stabilized the new situation of Jews in the German Reich. They had been second-class citizens, to put it mildly, since January 30, 1933; their almost complete separation from the rest of the population had been achieved in a matter of weeks or months—through terror but also through the more than ordinary connivance of those around them. "There was a wall between Gentiles and Jews," Dr. Benno Cohn of Berlin testified. "I cannot remember speaking to a Christian during all my journeys over Germany." Now, the Jews felt, they had received laws of their own and would no longer be outlawed. If they kept to themselves, as they had been forced to do anyhow, they would be able to live unmolested. In the words of the *Reichs-vertretung* of the Jews in Germany (the national association of all communities and organizations, which had been founded in September, 1933, on the initiative of the Berlin community, and was in no way Nazi-appointed), the intention of the Nuremberg Laws was "to establish a level on which a bearable relationship between the German and the Jewish people [became] possible," to which a member of the Berlin community, a radical Zionist, added: "Life is possible under every law. However, in

---

45 **Streicher:** Julius Streicher (1885–1946), Nazi propagandist.

46 **pogroms:** riots directed at Jews.

47 **Nuremberg Laws:** anti-Semitic laws passed by the Nazis.

complete ignorance of what is permitted and what is not one cannot live. A useful and respected citizen one can also be as a member of a minority in the midst of a great people" (Hans Lamm, *Über die Entwicklung des deutschen Judentums*, 1951). And since Hitler, in the Röhm purge[48] in 1934, had broken the power of the SA, the Storm Troopers in brown shirts who had been almost exclusively responsible for the early pogroms and atrocities, and since the Jews were blissfully unaware of the growing power of the black-shirted SS, who ordinarily abstained from what Eichmann contemptuously called the "*Stürmer*[49] methods," they generally believed that a *modus vivendi*[50] would be possible; they even offered to cooperate in "the solution of the Jewish question." In short, when Eichmann entered upon his apprenticeship in Jewish affairs, on which, four years later, he was to be the recognized "expert," and when he made his first contacts with Jewish functionaries, both Zionists and Assimilationists[51] talked in terms of a great "Jewish revival," a "great constructive movement of

German Jewry," and they still quarreled among themselves in ideological terms about the desirability of Jewish emigration, as though this depended upon their own decisions.

Eichmann's account during the police examination of how he was introduced into the new department—distorted, of course, but not wholly devoid of truth—oddly recalls this fool's paradise. The first thing that happened was that his new boss, a certain von Mildenstein,[52] who shortly thereafter got himself transferred to Albert Speer's[53] *Organisation Todt*, where he was in charge of highway construction (he was what Eichmann pretended to be, an engineer by profession), required him to read Theodor Herzl's *Der Judenstaat*,[54] the famous Zionist classic, which converted Eichmann promptly and forever to Zionism. This seems to have been the first serious book he ever read and it made a lasting impression on him. From then on, as he repeated over and over, he thought of hardly anything but a "political solution" (as opposed to the later "physical solution," the

48 **Röhm purge:** political executions carried out by the Nazis, targeting especially SA members and their leader, Ernst Röhm; also called the "Night of the Long Knives."

49 **Stürmer:** *Der Stürmer* (*The Attacker*), a weekly Nazi newspaper published by Julius Streicher.

50 *modus vivendi:* "way of living"; an accommodation between disputants in which they agree to disagree.

51 **Assimilationists:** Jews seeking to shed much of their cultural and religious distinctiveness in order to fit inconspicuously into the national culture of the countries in which they lived.

52 **von Mildenstein:** Baron Itz von Mildenstein, Nazi and SS official, who hoped to expel German Jews to Palestine.

53 **Albert Speer:** (1905–1981); during the Third Reich, head of the Ministry of Armaments and War Production, into which the Organization Todt, a civil and military engineering group, was absorbed.

54 **Theodor Herzl's *Der Judenstaat*:** *The Jewish State* (1896), in which Herzl (1860–1904), the father of modern Zionism, advocated a state for Jews in Palestine.

first meaning expulsion and the second extermination) and how to "get some firm ground under the feet of Jews." (It may be worth mentioning that, as late as 1939, he seems to have protested against desecrators of Herzl's grave in Vienna, and there are reports of his presence in civilian clothes at the commemoration of the thirty-fifth anniversary of Herzl's death.) Strangely enough, he did not talk about these things in Jerusalem, where he continuously boasted of his good relations with Jewish officials.

In order to help in this enterprise, he began spreading the gospel among his SS comrades, giving lectures and writing pamphlets. He then acquired a smattering of Hebrew, which enabled him to read haltingly a Yiddish newspaper—not a very difficult accomplishment, since Yiddish, basically an old German dialect written in Hebrew letters, can be understood by any German-speaking person who has mastered a few dozen Hebrew words. He even read one more book, Adolf Böhm's *History of Zionism* (during the trial he kept confusing it with Herzl's *Judenstaat*), and this was perhaps a considerable achievement for a man who, by his own account, had always been utterly reluctant to read anything except newspapers, and who, to the distress of his father, had never availed himself of the books in the family library. Following up Böhm, he studied the organizational setup of the Zionist movement, with all its parties, youth groups, and different programs. This did not yet make him an "authority," but it was enough to earn

him an assignment as official spy on the Zionist offices and on their meetings; it is worth noting that his schooling in Jewish affairs was almost entirely concerned with Zionism.

His first personal contacts with Jewish functionaries, all of them well-known Zionists of long standing, were thoroughly satisfactory. The reason he became so fascinated by the "Jewish question," he explained, was his own "idealism"; these Jews, unlike the Assimilationists, whom he always despised, and unlike Orthodox Jews, who bored him, were "idealists," like him. An "idealist," according to Eichmann's notions, was not merely a man who believed in an "idea" or someone who did not steal or accept bribes, though these qualifications were indispensable. An "idealist" was a man who *lived* for his idea—hence he could not be a businessman—and who was prepared to sacrifice for his idea everything and, especially, everybody. When he said in the police examination that he would have sent his own father to his death if that had been required, he did not mean merely to stress the extent to which he was under orders, and ready to obey them; he also meant to show what an "idealist" he had always been. The perfect "idealist," like everybody else, had of course his personal feelings and emotions, but he would never permit them to interfere with his actions if they came into conflict with his "idea."

The greatest "idealist" Eichmann ever encountered among the Jews was Dr. Rudolf Kastner,[55] with whom he negotiated during the Jewish deportations from Hun-

---

55 **Rudolf Kastner:** (1906–1957); negotiated with Eichmann to exchange some 1,700 Hungarian Jews for money and valuables.

gary and with whom he came to an agreement that he, Eichmann, would permit the "illegal" departure of a few thousand Jews to Palestine (the trains were in fact guarded by German police) in exchange for "quiet and order" in the camps from which hundreds of thousands were shipped to Auschwitz. The few thousand saved by the agreement, prominent Jews and members of the Zionist youth organizations, were, in Eichmann's words, "the best biological material." Dr. Kastner, as Eichmann understood it, had sacrificed his fellow-Jews to his "idea," and this was as it should be. Judge Benjamin Halevi, one of the three judges at Eichmann's trial, had been in charge of the Kastner trial in Israel, at which Kastner had to defend himself for his cooperation with Eichmann and other high-ranking Nazis. In Halevi's opinion, Kastner had "sold his soul to the devil." Now that the devil himself was in the dock he turned out to be an "idealist," and though it may be hard to believe, it is quite possible that the one who sold his soul had also been an "idealist."

Long before all this happened, Eichmann was given his first opportunity to apply in practice what he had learned during his apprenticeship. After the *Anschluss* (the incorporation of Austria into the Reich), in March, 1938, he was sent to Vienna to organize a kind of emigration that had been utterly unknown in Germany, where up to the fall of 1938 the fiction was maintained that Jews, if they so desired, were permitted, but were not forced, to leave the country. Among the reasons German Jews believed in the fiction was

the program of the NSDAP,[56] formulated in 1920, which shared with the Weimar Constitution the curious fate of never being officially abolished; its Twenty-Five Points had even been declared "unalterable" by Hitler. Seen in the light of later events, its anti-Semite provisions were harmless indeed: Jews could not be full-fledged citizens, they could not hold Civil Service positions, they were to be excluded from the press, and all those who had acquired German citizenship after August 2, 1914—the date of the outbreak of the First World War—were to be denaturalized, which meant they were subject to expulsion. (Characteristically, the denaturalization was carried out immediately, but the wholesale expulsion of some fifteen thousand Jews, who from one day to the next were shoved across the Polish border at Zbaszyn, where they were promptly put into camps, took place only five years later, when no one expected it any longer.) The Party program was never taken seriously by Nazi officials; they prided themselves on belonging to a movement, as distinguished from a party, and a movement could not be bound by a program. Even before the Nazis' rise to power, these Twenty-Five Points had been no more than a concession to the party system and to such prospective voters as were old-fashioned enough to ask what was the program of the party they were going to join. Eichmann, as we have seen, was free of such deplorable habits, and when he told the Jerusalem court that he had not known Hitler's program he very likely spoke the truth: "The Party program did not matter,

---

56 **NSDAP:** Nationalsozialistische Deutsche Arbeiterpartei (National Socialist German Workers' Party); that is, the Nazi Party.

you knew what you were joining." The Jews, on the other hand, were old-fashioned enough to know the Twenty-Five Points by heart and to believe in them; whatever contradicted the legal implementation of the Party program they tended to ascribe to temporary, "revolutionary excesses" of undisciplined members or groups.

But what happened in Vienna in March, 1938, was altogether different. Eichmann's task had been defined as "forced emigration," and the words meant exactly what they said: all Jews, regardless of their desires and regardless of their citizenship, were to be forced to emigrate—an act which in ordinary language is called expulsion. Whenever Eichmann thought back to the twelve years that were his life, he singled out his year in Vienna as head of the Center for Emigration of Austrian Jews as its happiest and most successful period. Shortly before, he had been promoted to officer's rank, becoming an *Untersturmführer*, or lieutenant, and he had been commended for his "comprehensive knowledge of the methods of organization and ideology of the opponent, Jewry." The assignment in Vienna was his first important job, his whole career, which had progressed rather slowly, was in the balance. He must have been frantic to make good, and his success was spectacular: in eight months, forty-five thousand Jews left Austria, whereas no more than nineteen thousand left Germany in the same period; in less than eighteen months, Austria was "cleansed" of close to a hundred and fifty thousand people, roughly sixty per cent of its Jewish population, all of whom left the country "legally"; even after the outbreak of the war, some sixty thousand Jews could escape. How did he do it? The basic idea that made all this possible was of course not his but, almost certainly, a specific directive by Heydrich, who had sent him to Vienna in the first place. (Eichmann was vague on the question of authorship, which he claimed, however, by implication; the Israeli authorities, on the other hand, bound to the fantastic "thesis of the all-inclusive responsibility of Adolf Eichmann" and the even more fantastic "supposition that one [that is, Eichmann's] mind was behind it all," helped him considerably in his efforts to deck himself in borrowed plumes, for which he had in any case a great inclination.) The idea, as explained by Heydrich in a conference with Goring[57] on the morning of the *Kristallnacht*, was simple and ingenious enough: "Through the Jewish community, we extracted a certain amount of money from the rich Jews who wanted to emigrate. By paying this amount, and an additional sum in foreign currency, they made it possible for poor Jews to leave. The problem was not to make the rich Jews leave, but to get rid of the Jewish mob." And this "problem" was not solved by Eichmann. Not until the trial was over was it learned from the Netherlands State Institute for War Documentation that Erich Rajakowitsch, a "brilliant lawyer" whom Eichmann, according to his own testimony, "employed for the handling of legal ques-

57 **Goring:** Hermann Göring or Goering (1893–1946), high-ranking member of the Nazi Party and commander of the German air force.

tions in the central offices for Jewish emigration in Vienna, Prague, and Berlin," had originated the idea of the "emigration funds." Somewhat later, in April, 1941, Rajakowitsch was sent to Holland by Heydrich in order to "establish there a central office which was to serve as a model for the 'solution of the Jewish question' in all occupied countries in Europe."

Still, enough problems remained that could be solved only in the course of the operation, and there is no doubt that here Eichmann, for the first time in his life, discovered in himself some special qualities. There were two things he could do well, better than others: he could organize and he could negotiate. Immediately upon his arrival, he opened negotiations with the representatives of the Jewish community, whom he had first to liberate from prisons and concentration camps, since the "revolutionary zeal" in Austria, greatly exceeding the early "excesses" in Germany, had resulted in the imprisonment of practically all prominent Jews. After this experience, the Jewish functionaries did not need Eichmann to convince them of the desirability of emigration. Rather, they informed him of the enormous difficulties which lay ahead. Apart from the financial problem, already "solved," the chief difficulty lay in the number of papers every emigrant had to assemble before he could leave the country. Each of the papers was valid only for a limited time, so that the validity of the first had usually expired long before the last could be obtained. Once Eichmann understood how the whole thing worked, or, rather, did not work, he "took counsel with himself" and "gave birth to the idea which I thought would do justice to both parties." He imagined "an assembly line, at whose beginnings the first document is put, and then the other papers, and at its end the passport would have to come out as the end product." This could be realized if all the officers concerned— the Ministry of Finance, the income tax people, the police, the Jewish community, etc.—were housed under the same roof and forced to do their work on the spot, in the presence of the applicant, who would no longer have to run from office to office and who, presumably, would also be spared having some humiliating chicaneries practiced on him, and certain expenses for bribes. When everything was ready and the assembly line was doing its work smoothly and quickly, Eichmann "invited" the Jewish functionaries from Berlin to inspect it. They were appalled: "This is like an automatic factory, like a flour mill connected with some bakery. At one end you put in a Jew who still has some property, a factory, or a shop, or a bank account, and he goes through the building from counter to counter, from office to office, and comes out at the other end without any money, without any rights, with only a passport on which it says: 'You must leave the country within a fortnight. Otherwise you will go to a concentration camp.'"

This, of course, was essentially the truth about the procedure, but it was not the whole truth. For these Jews could not be left "without any money," for the simple reason that without it no country at this date would have taken them. They needed, and were given, their *Vorzeigegeld*, the amount they had to show in order to obtain their visas and to pass the immigration controls of the recipient country. For this amount, they needed foreign currency, which the Reich had no intention of wasting on its Jews. These needs could not be met by Jewish accounts in foreign countries, which, in any event, were difficult to get at because they had been illegal for many years; Eichmann therefore sent Jewish functionaries abroad to solicit funds from the great Jewish organizations, and these funds were then sold by the Jewish community to the prospective emigrants at a considerable profit—one dollar, for instance, was sold for 10 or 20 marks when its market value was 4.20 marks. It was chiefly in this way that the community acquired not only the money necessary for poor Jews and people without accounts abroad, but also the funds it needed for its own hugely expanded activities. Eichmann did not make possible this deal without encountering considerable opposition from the German financial authorities, the Ministry [of Finance] and the Treasury, which, after all, could not remain unaware of the fact that these transactions amounted to a devaluation of the mark.

Bragging was the vice that was Eichmann's undoing. It was sheer rodomontade when he told his men during the last days of the war: "I will jump into my grave laughing, because the fact that I have the death of five million Jews [or "enemies of the Reich," as he always claimed to have said] on my conscience gives me extraordinary satisfaction." He did not jump, and if he had anything on his conscience, it was not murder but, as it turned out, that he

had once slapped the face of Dr. Josef Löwenherz, head of the Vienna Jewish community, who later became one of his favorite Jews. (He had apologized in front of his staff at the time, but this incident kept bothering him.) To claim the death of five million Jews, the approximate total of losses suffered from the combined efforts of all Nazi offices and authorities, was preposterous, as he knew very well, but he had kept repeating the damning sentence *ad nauseam* to everyone who would listen, even twelve years later in Argentina, because it gave him "an extraordinary sense of elation to think that [he] was exiting from the stage in this way." (Former Legationsrat[58] Horst Grell, a witness for the defense, who had known Eichmann in Hungary, testified that in his opinion Eichmann was boasting. That must have been obvious to everyone who heard him utter his absurd claim.) It was sheer boasting when he pretended he had "invented" the ghetto system or had "given birth to the idea" of shipping all European Jews to Madagascar. The Theresienstadt ghetto,[59] of which Eichmann claimed "paternity," was established years after the ghetto system had been introduced into the Eastern occupied territories, and setting up a special ghetto for certain privileged categories was, like the ghetto system, the "idea" of Heydrich. The Madagascar plan seems to have been "born" in the bureaus of the German Foreign Office, and Eichmann's own contribution to it turned out to owe a good deal to his beloved Dr. Löwenherz,

58 **Legationsrat:** counselor at an embassy.

59 **Theresienstadt ghetto:** a concentration camp in Czechoslovakia, presented by the Germans to outsiders as a model Jewish community; also called Terezin.

whom he had drafted to put down "some basic thoughts" on how about four million Jews might be transported from Europe after the war—presumably to Palestine, since the Madagascar project was top secret. (When confronted at the trial with the Löwenherz report, Eichmann did not deny its authorship; it was one of the few moments when he appeared genuinely embarrassed.) What eventually led to his capture was his compulsion to talk big—he was "fed up with being an anonymous wanderer between the worlds"—and this compulsion must have grown considerably stronger as time passed, not only because he had nothing to do that he could consider worth doing, but also because the postwar era had bestowed so much unexpected "fame" upon him.

But bragging is a common vice, and a more specific, and also more decisive, flaw in Eichmann's character was his almost total inability ever to look at anything from the other fellow's point of view. Nowhere was this flaw more conspicuous than in his account of the Vienna episode. He and his men and the Jews were all "pulling together," and whenever there were any difficulties the Jewish functionaries would come running to him "to unburden their hearts," to tell him "all their grief and sorrow," and to ask for his help. The Jews "desired" to emigrate, and he, Eichmann, was there to help them, because it so happened that at the same time the Nazi authorities

had expressed a desire to see their Reich *judenrein*. The two desires coincided, and he, Eichmann, could "do justice to both parties." At the trial, he never gave an inch when it came to this part of the story, although he agreed that today, when "times have changed so much," the Jews might not be too happy to recall this "pulling together" and he did not want "to hurt their feelings."

The German text of the taped police examination, conducted from May 29, 1960, to January 17, 1961, each page corrected and approved by Eichmann, constitutes a veritable gold mine for a psychologist—provided he is wise enough to understand that the horrible can be not only ludicrous but outright funny. Some of the comedy cannot be conveyed in English, because it lies in Eichmann's heroic fight with the German language, which invariably defeats him. It is funny when he speaks, *passim*,[60] of "winged words" (*geflügelte Worte*, a German colloquialism for famous quotes from the classics) when he means stock phrases (*Redensarten*, or slogans, *Schlagworte*). It was funny when, during the cross-examination on the Sassen documents,[61] conducted in German, by the presiding judge, he used the phrase *"kontra geben"* (to give tit for tat), to indicate that he had resisted Sassen's efforts to liven up his stories; Judge Landau, obviously ignorant of the mysteries of card games, did not understand, and Eichmann could not think of any other way to

60 *passim:* "here and there" or "in many places." "Chapter 4 et passim" means the topic is discussed in chapter 4 and in throughout the rest of the work in passing.

61 **Sassen documents:** papers and tapes of Wilhelm Sassen (1918–2001), Dutch collaborator with the Nazis who interviewed Eichmann in Argentina before his capture; extracts of the interviews were published in *Life* magazine.

put it. Dimly aware of a defect that must have plagued him even in school—it amounted to a mild case of aphasia—he apologized, saying, "Officialese [*Amtssprache*] is my only language." But the point here is that officialese became his language because he was genuinely incapable of uttering a single sentence that was not a cliché. Was it these clichés that the psychiatrists thought so "normal" and "desirable"? Are these the "positive ideas" a clergyman hopes for in those to whose souls he ministers? Eichmann's best opportunity to show this positive side of his character in Jerusalem came when the young police officer in charge of his mental and psychological well-being handed him *Lolita*[62] for relaxation. After two days Eichmann returned it, visibly indignant: "Quite an unwholesome book," he told his guard. To be sure, the judges were right when they finally told the accused that all he had said was "empty talk"—except that they thought the emptiness was feigned, and that the accused wished to cover up other thoughts which, though hideous, were not empty. This supposition seems refuted by the striking consistency with which Eichmann, despite his rather bad memory, repeated word for word the same stock phrases and self-invented clichés (when he did succeed in constructing a sentence of his own, he repeated it until it became a cliché) each time he referred to an incident or event of importance to him. Whether writing his memoirs in Argentina or in Jerusalem, whether speaking to the

police examiner or to the court, what he said was always the same, expressed in the same words. The longer one listened to him, the more obvious it became that his inability to speak was closely connected with an inability to *think*, namely, to think from the standpoint of somebody else. No communication was possible with him, not because he lied but because he was surrounded by the most reliable of all safeguards against the words and the presence of others, and hence against reality as such.

Thus, confronted for eight months with the reality of being examined by a Jewish policeman, Eichmann did not have the slightest hesitation in explaining to him at considerable length, and repeatedly, why he had been unable to attain a higher grade in the SS, that this was not his fault. He had done everything, even asked to be sent to active military duty— "Off to the front, I said to myself, then the *Standartenführer* [colonelcy] will come quicker." In court, on the contrary, he pretended he had asked to be transferred because he wanted to escape his murderous duties. He did not insist much on this, though, and, strangely, he was not confronted with his utterances to Captain Less,[63] whom he also told that he had hoped to be nominated for the *Einsatzgruppen*, the mobile killing units in the East, because when they were formed, in March, 1941, his office was "dead"— there was no emigration any longer and deportations had not yet been started. There was, finally, his greatest ambition—

---

62 **Lolita:** a novel (1955) by Vladimir Nabokov (1899–1977) in which the middle-aged protagonist becomes sexually obsessed with a twelve-year-old girl.

63 **Captain Less:** Avner Less (1916–1987), German-born Israeli who interrogated Eichmann after his capture.

to be promoted to the job of police chief in some German town; again, nothing doing. What makes these pages of the examination so funny is that all this was told in the tone of someone who was sure of finding "normal, human" sympathy for a hard-luck story. "Whatever I prepared and planned, everything went wrong, my personal affairs as well as my years-long efforts to obtain land and soil for the Jews. I don't know, everything was as if under an evil spell; whatever I desired and wanted and planned to do, fate prevented it somehow. I was frustrated in everything, no matter what." When Captain Less asked his opinion on some damning and possibly lying evidence given by a former colonel of the SS, he exclaimed, suddenly stuttering with rage: "I am very much surprised that this man could ever have been an SS *Standartenführer.* That surprises me very much indeed. It is altogether, altogether unthinkable. I don't know what to say." He never said these things in a spirit of defiance, as though he wanted, even now, to defend the standards by which he had lived in the past. The very words "SS," or "career," or "Himmler" (whom he always called by his long official title: Reichsführer SS and Chief of the German Police, although he by no means admired him) triggered in him a mechanism that had become completely unalterable. The presence of Captain Less, a Jew from Germany and unlikely in any case to think that members of the SS advanced in their careers through the exercise of high moral qualities, did not for a moment throw this mechanism out of gear.

Now and then, the comedy breaks into the horror itself, and results in stories, presumably true enough, whose macabre humor easily surpasses that of any Surrealist invention. Such was the story told by Eichmann during the police examination about the unlucky Kommerzialrat Storfer[64] of Vienna, one of the representatives of the Jewish community. Eichmann had received a telegram from Rudolf Höss, Commandant of Auschwitz, telling him that Storfer had arrived and had urgently requested to see Eichmann. "I said to myself: OK, this man has always behaved well, that is worth my while. . . . I'll go there myself and see what is the matter with him. And I go to Ebner [chief of the Gestapo in Vienna], and Ebner says—I remember it only vaguely—'If only he had not been so clumsy; he went into hiding and tried to escape,' something of the sort. And the police arrested him and sent him to the concentration camp, and, according to the orders of the Reichsführer [Himmler], no one could get out once he was in. Nothing could be done, neither Dr. Ebner nor I nor anybody else could do anything about it. I went to Auschwitz and asked Höss to see Storfer. 'Yes, yes [Höss said], he is in one of the labor gangs.' With Storfer afterward, well, it was normal and human, we had a normal, human encounter. He told me all his grief and sorrow: I said: 'Well, my dear old friend, we certainly got it! What rotten luck!' And I also said: 'Look, I really cannot help you, because according to orders from the Reichsführer nobody can get out. I can't get you out. Dr. Ebner can't get you out. I hear you made a mistake, that you

<hr>

64 **Kommerzialrat Storfer:** Berthold Storfer, Jewish businessman who worked with Eichmann to organize the exodus of Jews from Austria to Palestine; *Kommerzialrat* is an honorary Austrian title.

went into hiding or wanted to bolt, which, after all, *you* did not need to do.' [Eichmann meant that Storfer, as a Jewish functionary, had immunity from deportation.] I forget what his reply to this was. And then I asked him how he was. And he said, yes, he wondered if he couldn't be let off work, it was heavy work. And then I said to Höss: 'Work—Storfer won't have to work!' But Höss said: 'Everyone works here.' So I said: 'OK,' I said, 'I'll make out a chit to the effect that Storfer has to keep the gravel paths in order with a broom,' there were little gravel paths there, 'and that he has the right to sit down with his broom on one of the benches.' [To Storfer] I said: 'Will that be all right, Mr. Storfer? Will that suit you?' Whereupon he was very pleased, and we shook hands, and then he was given the broom and sat down on his bench. It was a great inner joy to me that I could at least see the man with whom I had worked for so many long years, and that we could speak with each other." Six weeks after this normal human encounter, Storfer was dead—not gassed, apparently, but shot.

Is this a textbook case of bad faith, of lying self-deception combined with outrageous stupidity? Or is it simply the case of the eternally unrepentant criminal (Dostoevski[65] once mentions in his diaries that in Siberia, among scores of murderers, rapists, and burglars, he never met a single man who would admit that he had done wrong) who cannot afford to face reality because his crime has become part and parcel of it? Yet Eichmann's case is different from that of the ordinary criminal, who can shield himself effectively against the reality of a noncriminal world only within the narrow limits of his gang. Eichmann needed only to recall the past in order to feel assured that he was not lying and that he was not deceiving himself, for he and the world he lived in had once been in perfect harmony. And that German society of eighty million people had been shielded against reality and factuality by exactly the same means, the same self-deception, lies, and stupidity that had now become ingrained in Eichmann's mentality. These lies changed from year to year, and they frequently contradicted each other; moreover, they were not necessarily the same for the various branches of the Party hierarchy or the people at large. But the practice of self-deception had become so common, almost a moral prerequisite for survival, that even now, eighteen years after the collapse of the Nazi regime, when most of the specific content of its lies has been forgotten, it is sometimes difficult not to believe that mendacity has become an integral part of the German national character. During the war, the lie most effective with the whole of the German people was the slogan of "the battle of destiny for the German people," coined either by Hitler or by Goebbels, which made self-deception easier on three counts: it suggested, first, that the war was no war; second, that it was started by destiny and not by Germany; and, third, that it was a matter of life and death for the Germans, who must annihilate their enemies or be annihilated.

---

65 **Dostoevski:** Fyodor Doestoevsky, or Dostoyevsky (1821–1881), Russian writer, author of *A Writer's Diary* as well as the novels *Crime and Punishment* and *The Brothers Karamazov*.

Eichmann's astounding willingness, in Argentina as well as in Jerusalem, to admit his crimes was due less to his own criminal capacity for self-deception than to the aura of systematic mendacity that had constituted the general, and generally accepted, atmosphere of the Third Reich. "Of course" he had played a role in the extermination of the Jews; of course if he "had not transported them, they would not have been delivered to the butcher." "What," he asked, "is there to 'admit'?" Now, he proceeded, he "would like to find peace with [his] former enemies"—a sentiment he shared not only with Himmler, who had expressed it during the last year of the war, or with the Labor Front leader Robert Ley (who, before he committed suicide in Nuremberg, had proposed the establishment of a "conciliation committee" consisting of the Nazis responsible for the massacres and the Jewish survivors), but also, unbelievably, with many ordinary Germans, who were heard to express themselves in exactly the same terms at the end of the war. This outrageous cliché was no longer issued to them from above, it was a self-fabricated stock phrase, as devoid of reality as those clichés by which the people had lived for twelve years; and you could almost see what an "extraordinary sense of elation" it gave to the speaker the moment it popped out of his mouth.

Eichmann's mind was filled to the brim with such sentences. His memory proved to be quite unreliable about what had actually happened; in a rare moment of exasperation, Judge Landau asked the accused: "What *can* you remember?" (if you don't remember the discussions at the so-called Wannsee Conference, which dealt with the various methods of killing) and the answer,

of course, was that Eichmann remembered the turning points in his own career rather well, but that they did not necessarily coincide with the turning points in the story of Jewish extermination or, as a matter of fact, with the turning points in history. (He always had trouble remembering the exact date of the outbreak of the war or of the invasion of Russia.) But the point of the matter is that he had not forgotten a single one of the sentences of his that at one time or another had served to give him a "sense of elation." Hence, whenever, during the cross-examination, the judges tried to appeal to his conscience, they were met with "elation," and they were outraged as well as disconcerted when they learned that the accused had at his disposal a different elating cliché for each period of his life and each of his activities. In his mind, there was no contradiction between "I will jump into my grave laughing," appropriate for the end of the war, and "I shall gladly hang myself in public as a warning example for all anti-Semites on this earth," which now, under vastly different circumstances, fulfilled exactly the same function of giving him a lift.

These habits of Eichmann's created considerable difficulty during the trial—less for Eichmann himself than for those who had come to prosecute him, to defend him, to judge him, and to report on him. For all this, it was essential that one take him seriously, and this was very hard to do, unless one sought the easiest way out of the dilemma between the unspeakable horror of the deeds and the undeniable ludicrousness of the man who perpetrated them, and declared him a clever, calculating liar—which he obviously was not. His own convictions in this matter were far from modest: "One of the few gifts fate bestowed upon me is a capacity for truth insofar as it depends upon myself." This gift he had claimed even before the prosecutor wanted to settle on him crimes he had not committed. In the disorganized, rambling notes he made in Argentina in preparation for the interview with Sassen, when he was still, as he even pointed out at the time, "in full possession of my physical and psychological freedom," he had issued a fantastic warning to "future historians to be objective enough not to stray from the path of this truth recorded here"—fantastic because every line of these scribblings shows his utter ignorance of everything that was not directly, technically and bureaucratically, connected with his job, and also shows an extraordinarily faulty memory.

Despite all the efforts of the prosecution, everybody could see that this man was not a "monster," but it was difficult indeed not to suspect that he was a clown. And since this suspicion would have been fatal to the whole enterprise, and was also rather hard to sustain in view of the sufferings he and his like had caused to millions of people, his worst clowneries were hardly noticed and almost never reported. What could you do with a man who first declared, with great emphasis, that the one thing he had learned in an ill-spent life was that one should never take an oath ("Today no man, no judge could ever persuade me to make a sworn statement, to declare something under oath as a witness. I refuse it. I refuse it for moral reasons. Since my experience tells me that if one is loyal to his oath, one day he has to take the consequences, I have made up my mind once and for all that no judge in the world or any other authority will ever be capable of making me swear an oath, to give sworn testimony. I won't do it voluntarily and no one will be able to force me"), and then, after being told explicitly that if he wished to testify in his own defense he might "do so under oath or without an oath," declared without further ado that he would prefer to testify under oath? Or who, repeatedly and with a great show of feeling, assured the court, as he had assured the police examiner, that the worst thing he could do would be to try to escape his true responsibilities, to fight for his neck, to plead for mercy—and then, upon instruction of his counsel, submitted a handwritten document, containing his plea for mercy?

As far as Eichmann was concerned, these were questions of changing moods, and as long as he was capable of finding, either in his memory or on the spur of the moment, an elating stock phrase to go with them, he was quite content, without ever becoming aware of anything like "inconsistencies." As we shall see, this horrible gift for consoling himself with clichés did not leave him in the hour of his death.

■ READING AND DISCUSSION QUESTIONS

1. Go to the Internet and read about events in Germany between 1933 and 1939. Cite three events that were key assaults against the Jews. Theorize as to why ordinary Germans allowed this to happen.

2. What does the proverb "Nothing's as hot when you eat it as when it is being cooked" mean? How might the same proverb be understood differently by Nazis and German Jews?

3. What were the Nüremberg Laws of 1935? What was their significance?

4. Why did Eichmann claim that he supported the "political solution" (forced emigration) over the "physical solution" (death camps)? What did his support of Theodor Herzl mean? Was Eichmann's inability to effect forced emigration due to his lack of ability or lack of interest?

5. Arendt says that bragging was Eichmann's undoing. Examine this passage and close-read it for various levels of meaning. What sorts of people boast and exaggerate? Does their doing so involve self-deception?

6. Arendt says Eichmann could not see events from another's point of view (empathy). How did this flaw exhibit itself in the Vienna episode?

7. Was Eichmann adept at using German? Were his "winged words" intelligent insights or banal euphemisms? What does this tell you about Eichmann? What sorts of people become immersed in officialese so that they are entrapped in it?

8. If anyone repeats a phrase over and over again, does it diminish his ability to understand its actual content? Explore how this works in politics and advertising.

9. Eichmann claimed that he tried to achieve advancement in the SS so that he could leave his murderous duties, but Arendt suggests that promotion was denied because of Eichmann's limited intelligence. How would this fill in the way we understand Eichmann?

10. Was Eichmann a man of bad faith who lied to himself and others and was outrageously stupid or was he a monstrous unrepentant criminal? What would the argument for each position look like?

11. How does the expression "the battle of destiny for the German people" make mass self-deception easier? Can you compare it to any other political slogans that created public support for morally evil policies?

■ CLASS EXERCISES

A. *Direct logical discourse:* Using the tools found in Chapter 2, outline the argument suggested by one of the reading questions. Based on your assessment of one key premise, write a one-page argument about why you agree or disagree with the argument's conclusion.

B. *Fictive-narrative philosophy:* Using the tools found in Chapter 3, begin with a claim that relates to the reading and discussion questions above. Then create a modern-day story about people or situations familiar to you that makes the logical claim you have identified. Three pages.

one is not responsible for one's fate,
however one can face and confront their fate.

Analytic / narrative philosophy = nature of
philosophy [Logical + narrative]
    Combine Lit + Phil.

CHAPTER TWELVE

Murdoch

Iris Murdoch (1919–1999) was an Irish-born British philosopher and novelist. Her early philosophy tried to come to terms with Jean-Paul Sartre's metaphysics and ethics. These two concentrations stayed with her throughout her philosophical career. She also had a keen interest in Plato and his views on art and ethics. As a novelist, she took on a variety of viewpoints of British society (such as in The Black Prince, The Sacred and Profane Love Machine, *and* The Sea, The Sea). *She also connected literary traditions in* The Green Knight *and Socrates's famous argument from the "Crito" in* An Accidental Man.

AN ACCIDENTAL WOMAN*

Michael Boylan

In this story we confront Iris Murdoch at a critical moment in her life. She is just about to publish in the same year an important work in philosophy and a novel. It was always her tenet that the problem that she wished to address would dictate whether the expression would be best accomplished via fictive-narrative philosophy or direct-discourse philosophy. This made her something of a rebel and outsider.

Iris got onto her bicycle for a ride. She thought that she was heading for the swimming hole of her youth in the Thames above Oxford, but she knew that wasn't true. What *was* she doing? It was nearly the middle of June. The sun was out, but there were some clouds to hide her. Trinity term[1] would be ending soon. The humidity was still light. It was almost the longest day of the year. It was almost the longest day of her life.

They say that turning fifty puts the fear of God in you. But what does it have to do with longing for Good? Perhaps it means moving God to the Good? Oh well!

Iris was riding an old black Raleigh with high handlebars and a basket in the front. It was what they used to call a "man's bicycle." There was only one speed and two sorts of brakes (pedal and hand): each worked perfectly well. As she rode the narrow road, there wasn't much traffic. It was 1970, and there were still few motorcars on the road. She rode her bike to a familiar wheat field. They no longer used the old farming methods of her youth. Then they used to mow the hay in a strip system that hadn't significantly changed for eight hundred years! There was a magical rhythm to that. It was that magic that used to draw her swimming—or rather floating about under the grasses that overhung the bank's edges. She could become almost invisible and at one with nature. She was like a water rat: silently moving about. In those days the sedge warblers would sing their ancient incantations as cuckoos and kingfishers crossed across the rushes.

She thought back to Frank Thompson. Was that a different lifetime? When he was killed in the Balkans in 1944, things altered. The War changed everyone alive at the time. It even affected the children and grandchildren: nothing like it before or since. Even the Great War (WWI) was only an entrée.

---

* I would like to acknowledge Peter J. Conradi, Iris Murdoch: A Life *(New York: Norton, 2001), and John Bayley,* Elegy for Iris *(New York: St. Martins, 1999), in my creation of the character of Iris Murdoch.*

1 **Trinity term:** the last of the three regular terms at Oxford University, England, running from late April to the middle of June.

For the most part, there is a natural order of things. Iris loved to submit to the order and then to emerge and rub against it just a bit. But the War changed many things. Demons entered her life and tormented her in the guise of pleasure. She was adrift. Her social service didn't help at all. It only irritated the wound.

When she returned to England, she welcomed the chance to be a pivotal part of St. Anne's.[2] She amazed her students within the context of the patriarchal community at Oxford. Women weren't supposed to be philosophers. Right? Their brains were configured differently, inclining them to domestic tasks like cooking, cleaning, and taking care of hubby. Service and self-sacrifice were what women were made for.

Well, Iris had just had her fill of service in the postwar refugee camps hearing terrible stories of Nazi atrocities. It was within this context that she met Jean-Paul Sartre.[3] This was a man who sat in the middle of the whole thing. He knew the terrible trade-offs—such as caring for an ailing mother versus fighting against a tyranny the world had never known. A social collective response was in order. She became a Communist. But she didn't know just what a Communist was apart from what Sartre preached.

She was saved by her devotion to an idea. As soon as she fully recognized its existence, she had to describe it so that she might know it more intimately. It was then that she decided that there were parts of this that had to come out in her traditional philosophy. Iris resolved to write a book on Sartre.

However, that was not enough. At the same time she would try to capture recognition of an authentic worldview. This could only come about through a novel. Was it possible to do both at the same time?

Iris started pedaling hard on the very slight hill. It was something she always did on this stretch of road. This time it was different. The *thymos*[4] requisite to be her old self just wasn't there. She was someone else. Things had again changed.

Iris decided to get off her bike and lay it on the ground while she walked about in the modern fields of rows and annual crop rotation. She situated herself between two nameless rows. She was anonymous in the mechanically efficient system of modern farming. The ground was dry beneath her thin wool skirt. Against her calves she felt the aerated dirt against her skin gently cushion her leg. Thank god that they still didn't use irrigation in this area of England.

Her mind started to drift to a tea she'd had with Elizabeth Anscombe[5] the week before at the Randolph Hotel. The dining room was very spacious and filled with light

---

2 **St. Anne's:** St. Anne's College at Oxford. Founded as a women-only college in 1952, it became coeducational in 1979.

3 **Jean-Paul Sartre:** French existentialist philosopher and political activist (1905–1980).

4 ***thymos***: spiritedness; one element of Plato's tripartite divisions of the soul, along with reason and desire.

5 **Elizabeth Anscombe:** Irish-born British philosopher (1919–2001), who studied with Austrian British philosopher Ludwig Wittgenstein (1889–1951), was an Oxford fellow at Sommerville College, and later became a Cambridge professor (an exalted position at that school).

from the floor-to-ceiling windows. Near to the door was a baby grand piano that was played during dinner to slow down the guests as they ate and added to their bill of fare.

They were to meet at four. Iris was twenty minutes late. She scanned the room and then was told by the headwaiter that her friend was in the back corner.

Iris walked briskly to the table, getting there before the headwaiter. The two women hugged, and Iris sat down with a wave toward the piano. "They say that's the C. S. Lewis piano from his Joy Gresham[6] moment."

Elizabeth smiled.

"I rather like to think of the time you took down the old sot in your debate on naturalism at the Socratic Club."[7]

Elizabeth replied, "Iris, please have some tea." The table was already set. There were two Royal Dalton off-white teapots with a row of red flowers around the top. Each had a green dot in the center of five starlike petals. One pot was brewing tea. The other was full of hot water. A little stainless steel stand held various jams, a pot of clotted cream, soft butter, scones, muffins, and assorted breads.

Iris sat down and immediately prepared her food with rapid dexterity. When she had finished, she looked at her friend. "Well, Gertrude Elizabeth, you're certainly doing well for yourself: a chair at Cambridge. Quite impressive." Iris handed her companion a pot of clotted cream.

Anscombe took the gift and slathered her scone with the clotted cream over the layer of strawberry jam. Anscombe was a stout woman with a very intense gaze. "Well, I've always loved the place since studying with Wittgenstein. He was a dear. Rather a queer bird, but a darling nonetheless."

"Well, I know nothing about odd characters, don't you know."

Elizabeth laughed and took a rather large bite out of her carefully prepared scone. Iris reached out and poured herself a full cup of tea. She didn't strain or add anything to it, but took a long drink. The two engaged in a bit of small talk about Elizabeth's move when Iris said, "You know when I returned from the Royal Academy[8] a couple of years ago, they wanted me to get back into the philosophy swing of things again. I just couldn't do it. I was too tired. But I think it caused some problems."

Elizabeth started to gag rather violently. Iris moved to get up when her friend stopped. Anscombe then very deliberately picked up her strainer and poured her teacup half full. Then she reached for the hot water pot and filled it one quarter more. Finally she reached for the cream and settled the deal. She didn't take sugar.

"There, that's better," said Elizabeth taking a short sip. "So sorry."

Iris waved a hand.

---

6 **Joy Gresham:** later married C. S. Lewis. This moment in the Randolph is cited as key in their courting.

7 **Socratic Club:** Oxford Socratic Club, founded in 1941 for the discussion of intellectual issues related to religion.

8 **Royal Academy:** Royal Academy of Arts in London.

"It's just that I was at a conference last month on action theory. Donald Davidson[9] was there, and it was very cutthroat."

"Oh, I know. Academics, who lead the most sheltered of lives, are the most acerbic to their own kind—though I should say that it was *lucky* that Bernard Williams[10] wasn't there." Iris began to smile but then put her heavy linen napkin to her lips. She hadn't eaten much; nor were there any crumbs about her mouth.

"Well, I was sitting at one of those long tables they have at Corpus Christi, and a few spaces over were Alfred and Isaiah[11] talking to some new fixed-term assistant lecturers. They were holding court. The young boys were agog."

"I wasn't paying too much attention except when I heard your name."

"Oh, really?"

"Yes, they seemed a bit peeved that you did that bit at the Royal Academy and that your books have been getting so much attention."

"My books?" asked Iris taking a short drink of tea and then pouring herself another cup.

"Well, actually, your novels."

"I thought so."

"They didn't really see the point of spending so much time writing stories when you have a real gift in philosophy," Elizabeth poured herself another cup of tea as meticulously as the first.

Iris brought her napkin again to her lips. "Rather a difficult point, actually: philosophy and literature. As I've talked and written incessantly, Plato was the first bloke to get it all wrong. He thought of art as basically instrumental even when his own art wasn't merely that."

Elizabeth nodded as she prepared a sweet bread with some soft butter.

"You know, that's why I wanted to lecture at the Royal Academy. I had to get some things straight in my head in the company of sympathetic people who didn't challenge the practice of art from the outset."

"Is it as bad as all that?"

Iris didn't respond but merely gave a half nod of her head.

The two didn't say anything right away. It was Elizabeth who broke the silence. "Well, I assume that it was all initiated because they all care deeply about you as a colleague working in philosophy."

"Well, I haven't exactly given up philosophy, don't you know. This year I've a philosophy book coming out entitled *The Sovereignty of the Good* and a novel, *A Fairly Honorable Defeat*. How could I be more evenhanded than that?"

---

9 **Donald Davidson:** American philosopher (1917–2003).

10 **Bernard Williams:** Sir Bernard Williams (1929–2003), English moral philosopher.

11 **Alfred and Isaiah:** Sir A. J. Ayer (1910–1989) and Sir Isaiah Berlin (1909–1997), British philosophers. This conversation is fictional but is based on material in Conradi, *Iris Murdoch*.

"Oh, I don't know. These academics are very jealous of what they do. It's sort of a marriage. When you step out on them, they come back at you with the religious zeal of a scorned lover."

"Well, I know a bit about that," replied Iris. This time it was Elizabeth's turn to smile. Iris picked up a muffin, broke it in half, and began nibbling on one half without any butter.

There was another silence, this time broken by Iris. "Was Philippa[12] there?"

Elizabeth didn't answer at first. Iris fixed a stare on her tea companion that had its effect. Elizabeth finally said, "Yes, she was there. Yes, she nodded her head to the kings of court. By all signs she seemed to be in agreement—but she didn't say *anything*."

"Naturally. She wouldn't."

"Now don't take this so hard, Iris."

"Look, there are polar opposites working here. What they are saying about *me* is not really about me but about ways of expressing philosophical claims. Their methodology is to try to simplify. Find a claim. Strip it bare to its logical skeleton. Then count the ribs and you're done. But what if it isn't that simple.

"This distinct possibility is what the French philosophers talk about. They are much more open to examining the presentation of the problem with its empirical particularity. This is what you can do in narrative. Narrative is about nuance. It isn't about bare, simplistic expression: that's bad art. Is simplistic, elemental expression bad thinking? I believe the result is actually more complex. There is no clean, simple result, and philosophy does more than leave everything as it is." Iris set aside her tea and half-eaten muffin.

Elizabeth was quick to respond. "Well, you know, I'm very sympathetic to your program of writing in both direct and indirect discourse. It follows from your love of Plato. Personally, I rather think that is how religious texts work. Most of that work has been done on the Continent, too. But the majority of analytic philosophers don't really think with those parts of their brains. It's their fault and not yours."

Iris smiled. This time she didn't bring the napkin to her mouth. "Well, what you say doesn't surprise me. There are these essential poles that pull us in different directions. With me it's between writing philosophical novels and writing direct philosophy. The former for me is sympathetic to more complex and nuanced worldviews. It is more authentic to the quest for truth.

"When I employ the latter, I concern myself with the direct exploration of aesthetics, metaphysics, ethics—by themselves and in society."

"So you see yourself torn, but in your heart you have really made a choice."

Iris reached again for the half muffin and started to nibble on it. "Yes, that's right. You know me too well, Elizabeth. One of these days I'll dedicate a book to you— probably a philosophy book to honor you for your fine work on Wittgenstein, on in-

---

12 **Philippa:** Philippa Foot (born 1920), British philosopher.

tentionality, and your well-regarded morality article that really got us thinking about Aristotle again. Well done."

Elizabeth reached out and grabbed the hands of her friend. Iris smiled and noticed that all the sweet condiments were at Elizabeth's end of the table.

As Iris sat in the fields in an unnamed row of wheat, she heard a wee scuttling sound. She moved her gaze slowly until she saw a light-brown field mouse. It stopped in its journey to look at this huge figure occupying the space of its intended path. The mouse was stone still when suddenly, without a noise, a cat leg stretched out and the paw fell upon the mouse's tail. Instantly, the mouse began to struggle. But the physical fact that the tail was firmly attached to the body made such attempts at escape useless. The cat brought its body closer until the mouse stopped fighting. Then the cat lifted the restraining paw and stared at the mouse. The two were motionless until the mouse moved around in what looked like a little dance—all the time keeping within inches of the powerful predator. After a few jazzy numbers the cat grew bored, did the deed, and exited (without any acknowledgement of Iris's presence). *Cheeky cat,* she thought.

The event had an effect on Iris. How unfortunate for the mouse to have stopped when it confronted her. It was very bad "mouse luck." But such an epithet wasn't good enough. Was it really luck at all? This was a fashionable topic in philosophy circles just now. Much is made between luck and accident and whether moral blame can ever be attached to it. The whole discussion harkens back to Aristotle's presentation of the topic as involving two sorts of luck. On the one hand, there was some event that occurs despite any planning on the agent's part. It would be like being hit on the head by a branch in a high wind. No one planned it this way. It just happened by accident.

The other sort of luck occurred when two sorts of purposive actions collided. Aristotle talks about person A going to the market to buy some food. Person B does the same thing at that same time. Now it just so happens that A owes B two quid, five and three. B confronts A and asks for payment. Here it is an accident that B finds A and is lucky to get his money back.

The first sort of case involves fate: the lucky (or unlucky) draw of the cards. One is not responsible for one's fate (unless one is a Hindu). But still, even here there is the reality that one can face her fate and confront it in some way. Sartre was on the right track here. Iris wished she could have her book back to develop this idea further.

The second sort of case involves accidental success or failure. Human freedom is fully engaged, along with blame and culpability. But the outcomes themselves are not necessarily just. At times the good guy gets crushed while the slacker is rewarded without desert. It is just this sort of situation that confronts one daily on the front pages of the tabloids. It is the fodder for many novels—good and bad.

So what sort of luck or accident applied to the mouse? Surely the first sort since mice must have a low cognitive threshold. They cannot freely act. Suddenly, Iris's thoughts were no longer about mice but of rodents of a different kind. The concept presented itself in pieces dealing with the politics of the day and a story she had recently read in

The Times. The components were these: the Vietnam War, the American lottery draft, dual citizenship, Edward Heath,[13] and Socrates. Might these characters be accidental too? Aristotle, get on your horse that Alexander gave you to honor your Macedonian heritage! No more Platonic notions of absolute freedom that were accepted by the likes of Sartre and Churchill[14] (at the extremes).

Iris was excited. She had been waiting for her next novel to come to her. It could never be forced, or it wasn't any good. The idea had to present itself and call you to attention. Once you made its acquaintance, you started writing it out as either narrative or philosophy as demanded by the idea.

Where was that bicycle? She felt lost. Then she saw it lying there quietly.

Iris mounted her aged black machine and peddled back home inspired to contrive some accident—one way or the other—or possibly both!

---

13 **Edward Heath:** Sir Edward ("Ted") Heath (1916–2005), prime minister of England (1970–1974).

14 **Winston:** Sir Winston Churchill (1874–1965), prime minister of England (1940–1945, 1951–1955).

■ READING AND DISCUSSION QUESTIONS

1. What is the significance of Murdoch's choosing to ride a "man's bicycle"?
2. What might attract a philosopher or novelist (Murdoch was both) to nature? Compare Aquinas's use of nature (in his writing) with Murdoch's (from this story)?
3. Go to the Internet and look up John-Paul Sartre and his theory of freedom. Sartre created the logical dilemma about caring for an ailing mother versus joining the French Resistance to fight against the Nazi occupation of France. Why is this a dilemma? How does it test his idea of freedom? How do Murdoch's actions in the story reflect this?
4. How might Murdoch convey an authentic worldview through a novel?
5. Go to the Internet and look up Elizabeth Anscombe. Like Murdoch she was an outsider in the Oxford philosophical establishment. Why was this?
6. As Murdoch and Anscombe have their tea, their philosophical careers are going in different directions. How do these dynamics allow you to close-read their tea ceremony?
7. Why were people gossiping at Corpus Christi about Murdoch? How does she react? What does it mean?
8. Go to the Internet and look up the terms *analytic philosophy* and *continental philosophy*. How do they differ? Which one might be more inclined to explore narrative philosophy? Why?
9. Did Murdoch ever dedicate a book to Elizabeth Anscombe? If so, what is the title? If not, then why not? (*Hint:* limit your exploration to Murdoch's publications in philosophy.)

10. What is the significance of the cat and mouse? In the context of the story, which is Murdoch and who plays the other role?
11. What is the significance of luck in the context of Murdoch's musings?

■ FICTIVE-NARRATIVE PHILOSOPHY FEEDBACK

What claims are made in this story? Write them out in a bulleted list and include whether they are made through dialogue, dramatic action, or the presentation of the scene (including descriptive detail). One page. Then choose either a short direct-discourse response (according to the rules in Chapter 2) or a short fictive-narrative presentation (according to the rules in Chapter 3).

LUDWIG'S CONUNDRUM

Iris Murdoch

From Iris Murdoch, *An Accidental Man* (New York: Viking, 1971), 70–84.

This excerpt from Murdoch's novel An Accidental Man *takes place during the Vietnam War era. In this time period, all males had to register for the draft at age eighteen and were subject to being called for military duty in the war. In this story Ludwig Leferrier is in a rather complicated position. He has dual citizenship (US and UK), so he does not have to serve if he does not want to. He could renounce his US citizenship and content himself with a nice job at Oxford and marriage to a woman whom he loves and who is also wealthy. Through this series of letters, some of the complications become evident as Ludwig shows himself to be a man who wants to make the right choice.*

My dear Ludwig,

Your last letter has filled your mother and myself with consternation. When you spoke of this matter earlier we did not, I am afraid, realize how serious you were. This step which, led by understandable feelings, you propose to take seems to us not only injudicious but wrong. We are fortunate enough to live in a democratic state and should surely obey or at least confront its laws however temporarily repugnant, as Socrates did with the laws of Athens. The accident of your birth in England seems a quite insufficient reason for this grave step, which must be seen by the English authorities themselves as a mere device or subterfuge. The United States government has a long arm. Are you certain that you cannot be extradited as a deserter? Your letter was vague on this point. We are very alarmed indeed about your position and feel uncomfortable about your motivation. You know how with gratitude your mother and I regard our deliverance in this land of freedom. Naturally we share your horror of this terrible war, though we cannot agree with you that it is wrong to wage it. Some wars are less evil than what they combat, in the present case totalitarian government, which we have experienced and you have not. Naturally too we do not want to see you in uniform. You are our only child. Perhaps you do not realize how ardently we have prayed that this cup might pass from us,[15]

---

15 **we have prayed . . . pass from us:** an allusion to the prayer of Jesus the night before his capture and crucifixion: "O my Father, if this cup may not pass away from me, except I drink it, thy will be done" (Matthew 26:42).

and that you would not in fact be drafted, as this seemed at some time likely. Of this I say no more. Duty has nothing to do with what we however passionately desire. We feel in this eventuality that you cannot adopt what seems so odd and makeshift a solution without in the long run thinking ill of yourself, even apart from the danger of your being extradited. We understand about your work and about the pleasantness and ease of life in England, but you are not an English person. You have the precious privilege of an American passport which must not be lightly given away, and there are claims which America has upon you because of us, because of your education, because of the true ideals for which, however imperfectly, this country stands. You are young and young people are greedy. But you have many years ahead, God willing, and England and a time of work there can be enjoyed later. If you do not now somehow make yourself straight with the American power, you will be unable to return here for many years or perhaps ever without severe penalties, such as imprisonment, and you know what terrible places are these prisons, where you could even be killed by the other prisoners. You must know that if you do not meet this matter properly now, in some way, and meet it right here at home, you are choosing exile from what you are fortunate enough to call your homeland. You would be certain to wish to return later, we feel sure, and to come whatever the cost, this we fear. Your suggestion that we should, at

our age, remove our home yet again seems to us merely thoughtless. We do not want to return to Europe where we have no happy memory. We have so far managed to keep your decision from the neighbors, who about your return constantly inquire, but we have discussed the matter with Mr. Livingstone. Having regard to the date of drafting, he advises that you profess to have been travelling in continental Europe and not to have received the papers. This untruth, though as such repugnant, seems the best method to put yourself right with the law. When you have come back here we can consider best what to do with regard to your attempting to get perhaps exemption. The tribunals are more sympathetic now and there are a lot of different possible courses, but these must be arranged for over here. Above all you must come back soon, or any further delay is now very dangerous and we so terribly fear your being extradited, which would be the ruin of your life. Will you please send a cable to say that you are coming. You are causing us very great anxiety and pain. Your mother sends her love and hopes you will soon be with us once more.

Your affectionate father,
J. P. H. LEFERRIER

Dearest Karen,[16]

Will you be my bridesmaid? This is my way of letting you know that I am engaged, affianced, a *promessa sposa!* No, not to—But to that American boy I told you of, Ludwig Leferrier, the young ancient

---

16 **Karen:** Karen Arbuthnot, bridesmaid to Gracie. Karen loves Sebastian Odmore. She calls herself his "slave."

historian! So I am to be a don's wife after all! (Do you remember "tinker, tailor" in the dorm and Ann crying because she always got "thief"?)[17] I didn't expect it, when I first met him I thought him awfully censorious, and then suddenly I started seeing him as Sir Lancelot. I feel rather frightened and old but fearfully happy. He's handsome in a grave sort of way but sort of furry too, he's awfully clever and serious, not a bit like—Do you remember saying let's never get married unless we feel fantastically lucky to get him? I feel like that about Ludwig. May you, darling, be equally blessed. I have always regarded you as my sister since that first morning at boarding school when you told me I didn't *really* have to turn my mattress every day! I gather you are still down at the Mill House. Let me know when you'll be in town and we'll talk clothes and love! Lots and lots of the latter from your childhood pal,

G.[18]

Sebastian,[19]

What did I tell you? Please see the enclosed cutting from *The Times*.[20] You know what your tactical mistake was of course? Interested as I was, I even gave you, on *that* evening, a hint of advice. I was *then* almost resigned. I know I have been a complete idiot where you are concerned. I gratuitously confessed my love (which men despise) and I let you have me when I was sure you loved another (which is genuinely contemptible) and you can do what you like with me and you know it. However, since this morning there is a new world in which it still remains, oddly enough, for you and me to make each other's acquaintance. We did rather start at the end, didn't we? I think now something rather formal would be in order. The parents are still much involved in their childish pursuits, Pa with his pigs and Mama with organizing her terrible boutique, but I can give them the slip on Monday. Let us then lunch at an expensive restaurant of your choosing, yes? I shall probably be staying with Ann Colindale, not at the parental mansion. She is in love, by the way, but not, wise girl, with you. Don't tell Gracie I'll be in town.

Your slave,
KAREN

Are you really very sad about Gracie?? My darling.

Dearest Sis,

I have told the parents that I cannot, because of an examination (a fiction this), attend the funeral games, I hope you enjoy them. Poor old Grandma.[21] Everyone will be rejoicing, won't they, especially

---

17 **"tinker, tailor" . . . "thief":** items in a counting rhyme that, in one version, has the lines "Tinker, tailor, / soldier, sailor, / rich man, poor man, / beggar man, thief."

18 **G:** Gracie Tisbourne. High school–educated but very wealthy, she is the fiancée of Ludwig.

19 **Sebastian:** Sebastian Odmore; loved Gracie, but the relationship did not develop from his point of view; studying to be a charted accountant at Oxford.

20 **The Times:** national newspaper in the United Kingdom; sometimes referred to as the *London Times*.

21 **Grandma:** Alison Ledgard, mother to Clara (Ledgard) Tisbourne and Charlotte Ledgard.

Aunt Char.[22] What news of the carve-up[23]? Aunt Char will be able to act out her fantasy of cocking a snook[24] at the family. Us I am afraid she has never liked since the days when she babysat us while the Ps were out on the tiles. Now maybe she'll light out for Monte Carlo. I would if I were her.

About the egregious Leferrier. (What does "egregious" mean exactly? I must look it up.) He is decent and clever and too good for you and I respect his decision not to return to that ghastly place. Perhaps now at last you'll stop flirting. I have had to speak to you about this before. Flirtatiousness cuts you off from people. Some women (for example, our mother) are eternally cut off from the world by a flirtatious temperament, only they never realize it. Yes, he's decent and I'm glad. Or am I? Am I not a little jealous? Will not our old alliance suffer? Ralph Odmore[25] says that Sebastian (ought I to tell you this?) is dashed.

Ralph still doesn't know how I feel about him. We have dignified conversations about European history. God. I confess I'm relieved you aren't wedding Sebastian. Foresuffering all, like the Grecian sage,[26] I know that whatever the fate of my passion for Ralph all will in a year or two be dust and ashes. So young and so untender, love's victim though I be. I pant for Ralph, yet panting know that all is vanity. A family connection would prove an embarrassment.

Talking of embarrassment I have had another of *those* letters from Mum, partly tosh about Grandma (faugh!) and also about the Gibson Grey biz about which she is agog, and into which pie she proposes to plunge up to the elbow with the highest of motives. (People like our ma should be forbidden to write letters.) God, how I think one should leave other people's things alone and not crawl all over them. I see our dear Ps as two giant snails with waggling inquisitive eyes leaving long slimy trails behind. Do not let us be like them. Fear it, sweet Gracie, fear it, my dear sister. Aunt Char *is* at least a decent sardonic letter-alone. I now have an appointment with Ralph in the cricket pavilion of which nothing will come. Look after yourself, my child. What you and Ludwig have so far *done* about it I forbear to ask, though I should certainly like to know.

Ever your loving sibling,
PATROCLUS TIRESIAS TISBOURNE[27]

---

22 **Aunt Char:** Charlotte Ledgard, elder sister to Clara (Ledgard) Tisbourne. Charlotte is middle-aged and gave her life to care for her mother but was cut out of the will.

23 **carve-up:** division of the estate.

24 **cocking a snook:** thumbing her nose.

25 **Ralph Odmore:** brother to Sebastian Odmore and lover of Patrick Tisbourne (Gracie's brother).

26 **Grecian sage:** the blind prophet Tiresias in T. S. Eliot's *The Wasteland* (1922), who "sees" only the future: "And I Tiresias have foresuffered all" (Section III, line 243).

27 **Patrick Tiresias Tisbourne:** brother of Gracie. Patrick is a college student and loves Ralph Odmore, brother to Sebastian.

My dear Dorina,[28]

Thank you very much for your little note about poor Mama. Expected though it was, we are all very grieved and will miss her sorely. I will not dwell on this further. She was a wonderful person, and as you may imagine our hearts are full. And Gracie's engagement, in a happier way, has made us feel the fateful passage of time.

May I take this little chance to say something? We were very sorry indeed to hear about Austin's[29] misfortune about his job, of which I gather you have now learnt. George, who sends his best regards by the way, is scouting around for a suitable post and has told Austin this, which has relieved Austin's mind very much indeed, so don't you worry either. Job-hunting can be so depressing. Meanwhile, may I suggest that you yourself should come and stay with us for a while? There are times when it may be better to be away from one's own family, on neutral ground as it were, and in a new scene! Even lucky I feel this now and then! Regard it as a holiday, as a treat. Also I am sure it could help you to talk a bit to an outside well-wisher. You understand. And we could invite Austin or not as you pleased. You know how very sincerely we hope for both your happinesses. To see you here would, I need hardly say, gladden our hearts after our recent troubles. Do say I may fix with Mavis for you to come.

Ever, with love,

CLARA[30]

P.S. We have just heard that Matthew[31] has come home! What a surprise! Austin tells us he came straight to Austin from the airport in the most touching way. Austin seems delighted about his return and one cannot but think this a happy augury!

Dearest Gracie,

All my congratulations! I have just seen it in *The Times*. May you be happy and glorious! Nor will I withhold the tribute of saying that the news caused me pain, I will not specify how much! I will always feel something special about you, even when we are both ninety. Why it didn't come off with us I think we both very well understand, though it would be hard to say and now will be never said. I like your intended a great deal. I understand you will in all likelihood be decorating the Oxford scene? When a decent interval has elapsed I will invite you both to lunch. That will occasion another pang. Dare I hope in your bosom too a little? I say no more. All greatest happiness to you, dear Gracie, and love from,

Yours, a good loser,

SEBASTIAN

---

28 **Dorina:** Dorina (Argyll) Grey, second wife of Austin Gibson Grey, currently living with her sister. Dorina is experiencing a bout of mental illness.

29 **Austin:** Austin Gibson Grey, a man of much misfortune. Austin's first wife, Betty, killed herself, and his second wife, Dorina, has left to live with her sister, Mavis, while she goes through a bout of mental disorder.

30 **Clara:** Clara Tisbourne, middle-aged mother of Gracie and Patrick. George, her husband, is getting on in his civil service job.

31 **Matthew:** Matthew Gibson Grey, brother to Austin Gibson Grey. Matthew went to Asia, made a fortune, and earned a knighthood. His brother, Austin, accuses him of having had an affair with his wife, Betty (when he really had the affair with Betty's sister, Mavis Argyll).

Dear Louis,[32]

I have heard of your engagement and write to congratulate you so much upon it. Gracie is a lovely girl, and we are all so glad that you will stay in England. I expect you will now be very busy as engaged people are. But I hope you will still find time to come and see me. I have expected you on several days but you did not come, though I understood from Austin that you would come. Your visits are precious because I know you are on Austin's side and with many other people I am not sure what side they are on. This connects with what we spoke of when you were last here. I am sorry to be so sunk in my own concerns. I know I am not important except to myself and I suppose to Austin and Mavis but I am at a loss. I am sorry this letter which was meant to be very short is getting incoherent. I just meant to say that I value you because of Austin and because you are a good person and have been a good friend to me. Please continue to visit me now and then if you can find time. I am rather depressed. With my very best wishes to you and Gracie,

Ever,

Dorina

Dear Leferrier,

I believe I may be the first to bring you the glad news, since the Master's letter won't get into the post till tomorrow, that you have (of course) been elected to the fellowship in ancient history. We immensely look forward to you and are in a fever lest you may have changed your mind about us! I personally tremendously enjoyed our arguments. The school of Lit. Hum.[33] is, as you know, trinitarian in form, its pillars being in this case yours truly, as the Greek and Latin language hand, MacMurraghue, whom you didn't meet, as the philosopher, and now yourself as the ancient history merchant. MacMurraghue is incomprehensible and distinguished. Our joint pupils will be lucky men. Our common room, though not quite a small Athenian state, is a gay enough place. May I say how glad I and MacMurraghue (and also the Master, who I fear designs you to be Dean!) are that you are a single man. There are too few merry bachelor dogs left among us young Turks. I did enjoy getting drunk with you on that second evening and I shall take pleasure in returning to the charge about your heresy concerning the *De Rerum Natura*[34] and the Delphic Oracle![35] And I hope you have forgiven me for describing your interest in Aristophanes as limited to his value as a source of information about the price of sausages! In anticipation, in short, of larks, this being I fear not the sort of solemn letter you may have expected to receive from a prospective colleague and an Oxford dignitary,

I nevertheless sign myself,

Yours sincerely,

Andrew Hilton

Fellow and tutor

---

32 **Louis:** nickname for Ludwig.

33 **Lit. Hum.:** *literae humaniores,* the core classics curriculum at Oxford; also called "the Greats."

34 ***De rerum natura*:** "On the Nature of Things," a poem on Epicurean philosophy by Lucretius, a Roman philosopher of the first century BCE.

35 **Delphic Oracle:** priestess of Apollo at Delphi (Greece), who delivered prophecies from the god while in a trance.

My dear Austin,

I am sorry that I visited you so precipitately and so late on the evening of my arrival. My heart was full of you and I had to come to you directly, it could not have waited till the morning. Please forgive my rather abrupt appearance and departure. I have called twice since but got no reply, though I think Miss Ricardo[36] was in on the second occasion. Your telephone appears to be out of order. May I suggest that we have lunch soon, somewhere quiet, perhaps my club? I think I should tell you this much of my plans. I am looking for a house and propose to settle here for good, I do not intend to hunt for old acquaintances and I shall not be calling at Valmorana. I have diplomatic cronies in London if I crave for company, which I do not expect to do. But I very much want to see you. I found (this condenses a long story which I will tell you at more leisure) that it was impossible to settle elsewhere with any peace of mind while our old difficulties remained as an unresolved cloud upon the horizon. I do not presume to imagine that I can help you. But you can certainly help me. And if I speak in this context of fraternal affection these are not, as far as I am concerned, empty words.

As ever,
Your devoted brother,
MATTHEW

Dear Ludwig,

I'm sorry we've kept missing each other. I hope you got the note which I left on the door of the flat. I shall be back there on Friday. I've been in the East End job-hunting. I want to find something straightforward to do for other people. I can't express to you how sick I got of philosophy, much more so than when we last talked. I said then it was rubbish. I think now it is muck. More of this when we meet. I haven't said, and I say now, how good it is that you are marrying Gracie Tisbourne. Good for her, since she is getting a first-class chap, and good for you since you are getting what you want. I wish you happiness, and the things which are more important than happiness. You know what they are. About my father: I cannot think very highly of Miss Ricardo as a companion for him, but I am glad that he is where you are. My intuitions about him and you at Cambridge, Mass., were just ones. Do stay by him. At present I can do nothing for him, except keep clear of him and also of Dorina and Uncle Matthew. In families people are often automatically gifted with an ability to cause awful pain by moves which are innocent in themselves. I don't know how much you have studied, and if so understood, our curious scene. Anyway, *stick to Dorina* whatever happens as well as to Father. She is probably best at Valmorana for the moment and so long as you go there Father will feel easier about her. Excuse all this family rot. When we meet let us talk about quite other things.

Yours,
GARTH[37]

---

36 **Miss Ricardo:** the landlady.

37 **Garth:** Garth Grey, son of Austin Grey. He studied at Harvard, where he med Ludwig (who did his undergraduate studies there before going for his DPhil at Oxford).

My little bird,

How is it with you? I think about you constantly, I will send Ludwig over with some flowers. When you have the flowers, will you please send one back to me the way you used to? Your husband is still a sentimental old silly where you are concerned. I miss you horribly day and night. You know I told you in that note about having chucked up my job. Well, I think I will stay on a little longer in the Ricardo lodging house so as to get some money by letting the flat while I look for a better job. Mitzi is a blousy old whore but kindly and lets me have the room cheap. I believe she is having some sort of romance with her photographer. As I expect you have heard Matthew has turned up again. He came round late one evening, rather hang-dog. I'm afraid I was somewhat brisk with him and indicated in the politest possible way that he should keep clear of my affairs. I rely on you to support me in this. (Please, Dorina. Important.) I haven't seen him since but he has written me a hypocritical letter wherein he says incidentally that he would rather hobnob with "diplomatic cronies" than be seen dead with "old acquaintances." (That might interest Mavis.) I fear he has become quite incurably grand and will not be met with in our little world any more. About us, it may be better at the moment to continue things as they are. I feel you are *resting* at Valmorana and you are safe there. If the Tisbournes suggest you're going to their place, for God's sake don't go, they are prying peepers and first-class trouble-makers. George very kindly announced he would find me a job! I told him to go to hell. Rest well, dear child, and become better in your heart and your soul. Quietness will make you feel whole again and will dispel those anxieties which made us both so naughty. Then you will come back to your tiresome old husband who loves you— who loves his dearest little bird so much. Let me know, as always, how your days go, what you do. I so much want to know that, to be able to picture you.

Ever, ever, ever,

AUSTIN

Dearest Patrick,

Grandma's funeral was a riot. I wish you'd been there. The graveyard bit was gloomy of course and I found myself shedding tears. Poor old thing, she never had much fun. Aunt Charlotte cried and Mama patted her face (her own face not Aunt Char's) with a *black* hankie. Papa wept a bit, would you believe it, I was quite shaken. He is very *sensible*. (The French word.) He never got on with Grandma of course, but he took it all in a literary sense. He was talking about mortality and so on in the car, the brevity of life and all that. That was in the car *going*. In the car coming back he was enormously cheerful, as indeed we all were. Aunt Char looked twenty years younger. Mama was chattering about the Spode dinner service and the Georgian silver. Then everyone came back to our house and there was a sort of *party*. Sir *Charles* had come. (I cannot get used to his elevation.) (We were spared Hester, Sebastian, and your beloved.) And a lot of rather chic people I didn't know, and some of the linen people from Ulster, only they sheered off when they saw the *drink*! You see, everyone stood around for a while trying to be solemn, and then we heard a burst of gay laughter from the kitchen where Papa and Sir Charles had opened a bottle of champagne. Then we all converged on the kitchen and there were drinks all round, and people were sitting on the kitchen table and draped round the hall and stairs with glasses in their hands and corks were popping, it was quite a wake. Ludwig was there of course and he obviously rather disapproved, but he had a drink to please me and then cheered up. Yes, of course he is too good for me, and I thank heaven fasting.[38] He will be a good *husband*—dread word—you see how old I have become that I can even utter it. He is clever and wise and sweet, and if he is solemn his other half will provide the laughs. I am glad, chicken, that you are jealous! But fear not for our alliance, that is eternal, and a brother is forever. Oh dear, Ludwig wants me to write to his parents and I don't know how. I suspect they are *difficult* (religious!), so unlike our dear parents whom you were so idly knocking. *Ours* have, so far as I know, never prevented either of us from doing anything that we wanted ever, which is not bad for aged Ps. As for your *curiosity* about what Lud and I are *doing,* you must *reck your own rede*[39] and be contained! Best of luck with Ralph Odmore, whom I always think of (sorry, lover boy) as a grubby urchin. But of course he's huge now. I suspect he's cleverer than Sebastian. Only I can't help hoping your being hooked on your own sex is just a phase, and you aren't going to be like Oliver. I think the other sex is always more fun. Write soon. Much love, little one. Your matronly sister,

    G.

Yes, about the aged Ps not getting imbrued in the Gibson Grey mess. As I think Ma told you telephone-wise, Matthew is back. There's another man I want in my net! I'm told he's got fat, though.

Dearest Clara,

    I was glad and sad to hear of Gracie's engagement. Our age-old plan for our young had something too-good-to-be-true about it, hadn't it? I think, probably from some time ago, they had both deeply decided otherwise, and I daresay they are being sensible and it serves middle-aged dreamers right! As Charles is always telling me, one shouldn't dream too much about other people's destinies, even if they are one's children. I hope Gracie will be very very happy and I look forward to meeting the boy.

    I am told Matthew Gibson Grey is in England. Is this true? Do you know his address? Charles is very keen to get hold of him about some government thing, to serve on a commission or something. I thought he was going to join a religious order in the East? I suppose that was just a legend. Matthew is the sort of person who generates legends. Poor Austin can't be too pleased. Even if the old story about Betty isn't true, Austin can hardly want Big Brother as a spectator of his current catastrophes. But perhaps Matthew is only passing by? Will we see you at the Mill House this weekend? Mollie says she has invited Penny Sayce again but *not* Oliver and Henrietta! (Apparently Geoffrey cannot stand

---

38 **thank heaven fasting:** allusion to "Down on your knees, and thank Heaven, fasting, for a good man's love" (*As You Like It* 3.5.60–61).

39 ***reck your own rede*:** follow your own advice; after "recks not his own rede" (*Hamlet* 1.3.51).

Oliver.) We count on you for the weekend following, of course. Charles sends love. He *did* enjoy himself at the funeral!

Au revoir and love,

HESTER[40]

I gather Garth Gibson Grey is home too and has become a dropout. I'm so terrified Ralph will be one. Thank heavens he and Patrick are pals now. Patrick will be such a steadying influence.

My dear Charlotte,

I should have written to you much sooner to say how sorry I was to hear of your mother's death. These are not empty words, and it is not just that in every death we mourn our own. I saw little of her lately, but I recall with gratitude her vigour and directness in the days when she used to help me financially with my girls. Her charity was always judicious. I only wish I could have recruited her as a fellow worker. She came of a good breed, and it is only sad that so much energy and character had to be confined to the narrow field of family life. What a general she would have made!

On another topic. I am so worried about Dorina. Clara has invited her. She won't go. (You know why.) I think indeed she cannot go to Clara's, but she does desperately need to see somebody other than me. In a way I am the last person who can help her at present. She is fond of you and respects you. Will you not come and see us, especially now that you are more free? Ring up soon about this. Only don't tell D. I asked you to come!

I hope it's in place to add that I am so glad that you will now be in easier financial circumstances! One does like to see the big money going, for once, to those who deserve it and are one's friends! Forgive this faintly cynical note, which issues, as you know, from affection! Come soon. With love,

MAVIS

P.S. Is it true that Matthew has come home? Could you let me know if you hear anything about him?

My dear Father,

I grieve deeply at the pain which I am causing to you and to my mother, and I beg you to forgive me and to try to understand. This is not anything hasty and surely you know me well enough to realize that "the pleasantness and ease" of England is not something which could tempt me away from my duty if I thought that it lay elsewhere. I cannot be an active partner in an iniquitous proceeding. That this war is an unjust war and a crime I have many times argued to you and I will not rehearse the arguments. We see this differently. All right. But granted that I believe what I do believe, I cannot be morally justified in donning the American uniform. I should regard myself with abhorrence, as a murderer, if I were to let conventional attitudes or public opinion or even my love for you lead me to be a slaughterer of the innocent. If ever I saw my duty plain before my face it is here, and I cannot do otherwise than refuse this summons into a place of wickedness.

---

40 **Hester:** Hester Odmore, mother of Ralph Odmore.

As for obtaining exemption, I do not see that, since I am not a pacifist, I could do so on any ground allowable by the tribunals. This is a matter on which I have reflected for years and about which I feel clear. Meanwhile do not fear that I shall be extradited. The British government is very unwilling to extradite any American "objectors," and my having been born here makes extradition unthinkable in my case. I feel there is moreover nothing improper in my now presuming upon the "accident" of my "English" birth, for it seems, in all the circumstances of my having come to study in London, together with the crisis which has overtaken me here, to be no accident after all but a disposal of destiny for which I should be humbly grateful.

It is indeed arguable that I ought to come home and be martyred, tear up my draft card, refuse to join up, as many others have so admirably done, and then let them do their worst. That would be to act the Socratic part. Socrates did not allow the laws of Athens to force him into wrongdoing. He kept on speaking the truth and was prepared to take the consequences. I have thought long and carefully about this and have decided that this particular martyrdom is not enjoined upon me. I do not dread, indeed I would welcome, a term in prison, but if I were to drink of this cup I should lose my passport, my access to Europe, and possibly any further chance of pursuing my studies. I would find myself forced to become a full-time protester. And this, I am certain, is not my task in life. You, who have so often bid me ponder the parable of the talents,[41] should understand this. Plato said that justice was doing one's own job. I must pursue my chosen studies and develop my mind and make it fruitful or else perish in my soul. I could not live the life of protest. I am not in any sense a group man. I should become rancorous and ultimately vapid. I am a contemplative and could never be a man of action. I know myself, and the *duties* which being myself imposes. Please please understand that this is not an idle or frivolous decision, but engages all the deepest things that I am. I make it as before God.

I have a piece of news which I hope will give you pleasure and seem to you like a hopeful sign of some later time when we shall have survived these woes. I have become engaged to be married to an English girl. Her name is Grace Tisbourne. I enclose, as you will have seen, a photograph of her. (It isn't a very good one. She is much more beautiful than that.) Her family are very good, her father is a high civil servant, her brother is at a private school (what they call a public school over here) and she is a wonderful and sweet girl. She would like very much to write to you and will probably do so in a little while. Do rejoice with me if you can in this. And see that now I *must* envisage a time when we shall all be united in peace and happiness

---

41 **parable of the talents:** in Matthew 25:14–30, Jesus's parable of the master who left sums of money (talents) with his servants while away on a trip and demanded an accounting of the servants' use of the money on his return. The servants who invested the money productively were rewarded; the one who merely hid the money till the master's return was thrown out. A talent is a large sum of money, but the word also lends itself to the meaning of "skill" or "ability." That is, one's abilities should be used productively.

in Europe. Please see it this way. I love you and I honour you and if I could obey you I would. But I must first obey my conscience, as you yourselves have always taught me to do. Please understand that my decision is firmly taken. And please write soon and forgivingly to

Your loving son,
LUDWIG

My darling husband,

Thank you for your sweet letter. No Louis and no flowers however. Never mind. I miss you terribly too. In a little while we'll meet, but not yet. You are very understanding, who else would understand so well? There is a sort of nothing here, a nothing in me—I'm sure everyone else thinks that something definite is up, whereas—Oh I am a troublesome girl to you and you must forgive me! I just have to be alone for just a bit longer, just breathing, existing. You like to know what I do. I do little things. Today I worked in the garden. I clipped the privet hedge[42] and mowed the lawn. And I painted a cupboard and stuck some pictures from magazines onto the door of it. It is very pretty. You shall see it. I will do one for us. I am rather worried about your letting the flat, though I suppose it is necessary, is it? It seems silly to say it, but it sort of cuts off our retreat for the moment. I mean it is home after all. I know I left it but it is there. You will think I am being very stupid, but I feel suddenly homeless. Please let this time be short, and don't let anyone get into the flat that you can't easily get out again, will

you. Had you not better take legal advice about it? And do be careful who it is, the tenant I mean, there's so much of *our* things in the flat, there's letters and things and all your old stuff in that trunk and private things. Don't destroy anything please, but lock it all up somehow won't you. I do hope you will soon get a better job, I'm sure you were right to throw up the other one, and go back to the flat again. I liked to think of you there in *our* place. I hope you are comfortable where you are. I think Mitzi Ricardo[43] is a nice person. Give her my best wishes. And give my love to Garth. Don't worry about Matthew. He won't come here. So we are in our seclusion and all is well. And of course I won't go to the Tisbournes. I am not too troubled with the strange things, and I am reading a lot. I will send you a book at the weekend. I would like us to be reading the same book. Forgive me and don't stop loving me, as indeed ever and ever I love you.

Your nothing-wife,
DORINA

My dear Dorina,

Thank you for your letter and your kind wishes. I am sorry not to have seen you, but I am afraid I am terribly busy at present. I have to be a lot in Oxford where I am to take up that college appointment that I told you of. So I am afraid I shall have to resign my task as messenger! I hope all will be well with you, and I trust we shall meet again later on. With best affectionate wishes,

LOUIS

---

42 **privet hedge:** a hedge formed from privet, a shrub.

43 **Mitzi Ricardo:** a former athlete now gone to seed due to a freak injury. She runs a rooming house where Ludwig and Austin stay. Mitzi has her romantic eye on Austin.

■ READING AND DISCUSSION QUESTIONS

1. What sort of reasons does Ludwig's father use to support his claim that Ludwig should return to the United States? How strong are these reasons?
2. What does Gracie Tisbourne reveal about herself and her worldview in her letter to Karen? Is it the same as her letter to Ludwig?
3. What do you make of Andrew Hilton's letter to Ludwig? How does Andrew assess Ludwig as a person?
4. When Matthew writes his brother Austin, how does he present himself? If Matthew shines in the eyes of the world through his peerage and wealth but is more controversial in his private life, then what claim is Murdoch making concerning how the world values things?
5. Garth writes a letter to his former friend from Harvard days about his father (Austin) and uncle (Matthew). What does Garth's letter tell you about how Ludwig is regarded by others?
6. When Ludwig writes back to his father, what argument does he make? Do you agree with it?

■ CLASS EXERCISES

A. *Direct logical discourse:* Using the tools found in Chapter 2, outline the argument from either of the two letters between Ludwig and his father. Based on your assessment of one key premise, write a one-page argument about why you agree or disagree with the argument's conclusion.

B. *Fictive-narrative philosophy:* Using the tools found in Chapter 3, begin with a claim that relates to the reading and discussion questions above. Then create a modern-day story about people or situations familiar to you that makes the logical claim you have identified. Three pages.

CHAPTER THIRTEEN

King

The Reverend Dr. Martin Luther King Jr. was the most prominent figure in the American civil rights movement of the 1950s and 1960s. The 1964 Civil Rights Act and the 1965 Voting Rights Act are national examples of his exceptional influence. His "I Have a Dream" speech modeled a vision of racial equality that has defined not only the United States but other racially and ethnically diverse countries as well. King came from a family with a long tenure at the Ebenezer Baptist Church in Atlanta. He attended segregated public schools in Georgia and graduated high school at age fifteen. After receiving a bachelor of arts from Morehouse, he received a bachelor of divinity from Crozer Theological Seminary and subsequently received his doctorate from Boston University in 1955. King chose a strategy of social and political protest that owed much to the tactics of Gandhi. He was very successful in achieving results at the grassroots and national levels. At the age of thirty-five, King was the youngest person to have received the Nobel Peace Prize. He donated the money for the prize to further the cause of civil rights in America. On the evening of April 4, 1968, while standing on the balcony of his hotel room in Memphis, Tennessee, where he was to lead a protest march in sympathy with striking garbage workers of that city, King was assassinated.

DR. KING'S REFRIGERATOR

Charles Johnson

In the story we meet a twenty-five-year-old Martin Luther King Jr. as he returns home after a long day's work. Many thoughts are jumbled about in his mind, from his work in the Church, to his ongoing dissertation, to his involvement with civil rights organizations, to being attentive to his young, attractive wife. Martin moves to the refrigerator with the intent of making a snack to help him sleep. Little does he realize that what he finds will awaken him profoundly.

अन्नाद् भवन्ति भूतानि

Beings exist from food.
BHAGAVAD GITA, BOOK 3, CHAPTER 14

In September, the year of Our Lord 1954, a gifted, young minister from Atlanta named Martin Luther King Jr. accepted his first pastorate at the Dexter Avenue Baptist Church in Montgomery, Alabama. He was twenty-five years old, and in the language of the Academy he took his first job when he was ABD at Boston University's School of Theology—*All But Dissertation*—which is a common and necessary practice for scholars who have completed their coursework and have families to feed. If you are offered a job when still in graduate school, you snatch it and, if all goes well, you finish the thesis that first year of your employment when you are in the thick of things, trying mightily to prove—in Martin's case—to the staid, high-toned laity at Dexter that you really are worth the $4,800 salary they were paying you. He had, by the way, the highest-paying job of any minister in the city of Montgomery, and the expectations for his daily performance—as a pastor, husband, community leader, and the son of Daddy King— were equally high.

But what few people tell the eager ABD is how completing the doctorate from a distance means wall-to-wall work. There were always meetings with the local NAACP,[1] ministers' organizations, and church committees; or, failing that, the budget and treasury to balance; or, failing that, the sick to visit in their homes, the ordination of dea-

---

1 **NAACP:** National Association for the Advancement of Colored People, one of the oldest civil rights organizations in the United States.

cons to preside over, and a new sermon to write *every* week. During that first year away from Boston, he delivered forty-six sermons to his congregation, and twenty sermons and lectures at other colleges and churches in the South. And, dutifully, he got up every morning at 5:30 to spend three hours composing the thesis in his parsonage, a white frame house with a railed-in front porch and two oak trees in the yard, after which he devoted another three hours to it late at night, in addition to spending sixteen hours each week on his Sunday sermons.

On the Wednesday night of December first, exactly one year before Rosa Parks[2] refused to give up her bus seat, and after a long day of meetings, writing memos and letters, he sat entrenched behind a roll-top desk in his cluttered den at five minutes past midnight, smoking cigarettes and drinking black coffee, wearing an old fisherman's knit sweater, his desk barricaded in by books and piles of paperwork. Naturally, his in-progress dissertation, "A Comparison of the Conceptions of God in the Thinking of Paul Tillich and Henry Nelson Wieman," was itching at the edge of his mind, but what he really needed this night was a theme for his sermon on Sunday. Usually, by Tuesday Martin at least had a sketch, by Wednesday he had his research and citations—which ranged freely over five thousand years of Eastern and Western philosophy—compiled on note cards, and by Friday he was writing his text on a pad of lined, yellow paper. Put bluntly, he was two days behind schedule.

A few rooms away, his wife was sleeping under a blue corduroy bedspread. For an instant he thought of giving up work for the night and climbing into sheets warmed by her body, curling up beside this heartbreakingly beautiful and very understanding woman, a graduate of the New England Conservatory of Music, who had sacrificed her career back east in order to follow him into the Deep South. He remembered their wedding night on June 18th a year ago in Perry County, Alabama, and how the insanity of segregation meant he and his new bride could not stay in a hotel operated by whites. Instead, they spent their wedding night at a black funeral home and had no honeymoon at all. Yes, he probably *should* join her in their bedroom. He wondered if she resented how his academic and theological duties took him away from her and their home (many an ABD's marriage ended before the dissertation was done)—work like that infernal, unwritten sermon, which hung over his head like the sword of Damocles.[3]

Weary, feeling guilty, he pushed back from his desk, stretched out his stiff spine, and decided to get a midnight snack.

---

2 **Rosa Parks:** African American civil rights activist (1913–2005) whose refusal in 1955 to yield her bus seat to a white passenger sparked the Montgomery (Alabama) Bus Boycott and became an iconic moment in the American civil rights movement.

3 **sword of Damocles:** a constant, if indeterminate, threat; by extension, a looming burden. In legend, Damocles changed places with his king for a day in order to experience a life of ease but relinquished his new position hastily when he noticed a sword hanging by a single thread over the throne on which he sat.

Now, he *knew* he shouldn't do that, of course. He often told friends that food was his greatest weakness. His ideal weight in college was 150 pounds, and he was aware that, at 5 feet, 7 inches tall, he should not eat between meals. His bantam weight ballooned easily. Moreover, he'd read somewhere that the average American will in his (or her) lifetime eat 60,000 pounds of food. To Martin's ethical way of thinking, consuming that much tonnage was downright obscene, given the fact that there was so much famine and poverty throughout the rest of the world. He made himself a promise—a small prayer—to eat just a little, only enough tonight to replenish his tissues.

He made his way cautiously through the dark, seven-room house, his footsteps echoing on the hardwood floors like he was in a swimming pool, scuffing from the smoke-filled den to the living room, where he circled round the baby grand piano his wife practiced on for church recitals, then past her choices in decorations—two African masks on one wall and West Indian gourds on the mantle above the fireplace—to the kitchen. There, he clicked on the overhead light, and drew open the door to their refrigerator.

Scratching his stomach, he gazed—and gazed—at four, well-stocked shelves of food. He saw a Florida grapefruit and a California orange. On one of the middle shelves he saw corn and squash, both native to North America, and introduced by Indians to Europe in the fifteenth century through Columbus. To the right of that, his eyes tracked bright yellow slices of pineapple from Hawaii, truffles from England and a half-eaten Mexican *tortilla*. Martin took a step back, cocking his head to one side, less hungry now than curious about what his wife had found at public market, and stacked inside their refrigerator without telling him.

He began to empty the refrigerator and heavily packed food cabinets, placing everything on the table and kitchen counter and, when those were filled, on the flower-printed linoleum floor, taking things out slowly at first, his eyes squinted, scrutinizing each item like an old woman on a fixed budget at the bargain table in a grocery store. Then he worked quickly, bewitched, chuckling to himself as he tore apart his wife's tidy, well-scrubbed, Christian kitchen. He removed all the beryline olives from a thick, glass jar and held each one up to the light, as if perhaps he'd never really *seen* an olive before, or seen one so clearly. Of one thing he was sure: no two olives were the same. Within fifteen minutes, Martin stood surrounded by a galaxy of food.

From one corner of the kitchen floor to the other, there were popular American items such as pumpkin pie and hotdogs, but also heavy, sour-sweet dishes like German sauerkraut and *schnitzel* right beside Tibetan rice, one of the staples of the Far East, all sorts of spices, and the macaroni, spaghetti, and ravioli favored by Italians. There were bricks of cheese and wine from French vineyards, coffee from Brazil, and from China and India black and green teas that probably had been carried from fields to far-away markets on the heads of women, or the backs of donkeys, horses and mules. All of human culture, history and civilization lay unscrolled at his feet, and he had only to step into his kitchen to discover it. No one people or tribe, living in one place on this planet, could produce the endless riches for the palate that he'd just pulled from his refrigerator. He looked around the disheveled room, and he saw in each succulent fruit, each slice of bread, and each grain of rice a fragile, inescapable network of mutuality in which all earthly creatures were co-dependent, integrated, and tied in a single garment of destiny. He recalled Exodus 25:30,[4] and realized all this before him was showbread. From the floor Martin picked up a Golden Delicious apple, took a bite from it, and instantly he apprehended the haze of heat from summers past, the roots of the tree from which the fruit was taken, the cycles of sun and rain and seasons, the earth and even those who tended the orchard. Then he slowly put the apple down, feeling not so much hunger now as a profound indebtedness and thanksgiving—to everyone and everything in Creation. For was not *he*, too, the product of infinite causes and the full, miraculous orchestration of Being stretching back to the beginning of time?

At that moment his wife came into the disaster area that was their kitchen, half-asleep, wearing blue slippers and an old housecoat over her nightgown. When she saw what her philosopher husband had done, she said, *Oh!* And promptly disappeared from the room. A moment later, she was back, having composed herself and put her glasses on, but her voice was barely above a whisper:

"Are you all right?"

"Of course, I am! I've *never* felt better!" he said. "The whole universe is inside our refrigerator!"

She blinked.

"Really? You don't mean that, do you? Honey, have you been drinking? I've told you time and again that orange juice and vodka you like so much isn't good for you, and if anyone at church smells it on your breath . . . "

"If you *must* know, I was hard at work on my thesis an hour ago. I didn't drink a drop of *any*thing—except coffee."

"Well, that explains," she said.

"No, you don't understand! I was trying to write my speech for Sunday, but—but—I couldn't think of anything, and I got hungry . . . "

She stared at food heaped on the floor. "*This* hungry?"

"Well, *no*." His mouth wobbled, and now he was no longer thinking about the metaphysics of food but instead how the mess he'd made must look through her eyes. And, more importantly, how *he* must look through her eyes. "I think I've got my sermon, or at least something I might use later. It's so obvious to me now!" He could tell by the tilt of her head and twitching of her nose that she didn't think any of this was obvious at all. "When we get up in the morning, we go into the bathroom where we reach for a sponge provided for us by a Pacific Islander. We reach for soap created by a Frenchman. The towel is provided by a Turk. Before we leave for our jobs, we are beholden to more than half the world."

---

4 **Exodus 25:30:** "And thou shalt set upon the table showbread before me always." Showbread is bread set aside on a special table as an offering to God.

"Yes, dear." She sighed. "I can *see* that, but what about my kitchen? You *know* I'm hosting the Ladies Prayer Circle today at eight o'clock. That's seven hours from now. Please tell me you're going to clean up everything before you go to bed."

"But I have a sermon to write! What I'm saying—*trying* to say—is that whatever affects *one* directly, affects *all* indirectly!"

"Oh, yes, I'm sure all this is going to have a remarkable affect on the Ladies Prayer Circle . . . "

"Sweetheart . . . ," he held up a grapefruit and a head of lettuce, "I had a *revelation* tonight. Do you know how rare that is? Those things don't come easy. Just ask Meister Eckhart or Martin Luther[5]—you know Luther experienced enlightenment on the toilet, don't you? Ministers only get maybe one or two revelations in a lifetime. But *you* made it possible for me to have a vision when I opened the refrigerator." All at once, he had a discomforting thought. "How much *did* you spend for groceries last week?"

"I bought extra things for the Ladies Prayer Circle," she said. "Don't ask how much and I won't ask why you've turned the kitchen inside-out." Gracefully, like an angel, or the perfect wife in the Book of Proverbs,[6] she stepped toward him over cans and containers, plates of leftovers and bowls of chili. She placed her hand on his cheek, like a mother might do with her gifted and exasperating child, a prodigy who had just torched his bedroom in a scientific experiment. Then she wrapped her arms around him, slipped her hands under his sweater, and gave him a good, long kiss—by the time they were finished her glasses were fogged. Stepping back, she touched the tip of his nose with her finger, and turned to leave. "Don't stay up too late," she said. "Put everything back before it spoils. And come to bed—I'll be waiting."

Martin watched her leave and said, "Yes, dear," still holding a very spiritually understood grapefruit in one hand and an ontologically clarified head of lettuce in the other. He started putting back everything on the shelves, deciding as he did so that while his sermon could wait until morning, his new wife definitely should not.

---

5 **Meister Eckhart or Martin Luther:** Eckhart von Hochheim (c. 1260–c. 1328) and Martin Luther (1483–1546), German theologians.

6 **the perfect wife . . . Proverbs:** the poem in Proverbs 31:10–31 describing how an exemplary woman behaves. It begins, "Who can find a virtuous woman? For her price is far above rubies."

■ READING AND DISCUSSION QUESTIONS

1. At the beginning of the story we meet a twenty-five-year-old ABD ("all but dissertation") who has a new job. What do King's educational situation and marital status tell us about his day-to-day life? Does the fact that he was the highest-paid clergyman in Montgomery, Alabama, make a difference in the pressures he puts on himself?

2. Go to the Internet and look up NAACP and the Southern Christian Leadership Conference. What were these organizations about? What did they do? How did King participate in these two organizations?

3. After King began his doctoral studies, he still worked as a preacher. He delivered almost one new sermon per week. In the story how many hours did King spend each week on his job that allowed him to follow his career goals? How do the duties of a rigorous job affect the worldview of an aspiring man of the cloth?

4. Where did Coretta Scott King and Martin spend their wedding night? What foreshadowing does this suggest on a life (Martin's) cut short?

5. Look up on the Internet the figures Paul Tillich, Henry Nelson Wieman (the themes of King's dissertation), and Mahatma Gandhi. What do these thinkers have in common? How do they reveal insights to the young Martin Luther King?

6. What is King's weakness? What does King see when he opens the refrigerator? What do the adjectives convey? How is the refrigerator a microcosm of the United States? What does it mean when King "tore apart his wife's tidy, well-scrubbed Christian kitchen"?

7. Go to the Internet and look up Exodus 25:30. What does the passage say? What is the meaning here?

8. When Coretta Scott King sees what Martin has done to the kitchen, she at first only says, "Oh." Then she returns and asks Martin whether he is all right. What does this question refer to? How is Coretta's empathy for her husband (whom she gave up her career to support) challenged at this moment?

9. Go to the Internet and look up Meister Eckhart and Martin Luther (the protagonist's namesake). Why are they mentioned in the closing passages of the story?

10. Go to the Internet and read *Hamlet*, act 5, scene 1. Hamlet takes a skull and says, "Alas, poor Yorick! I knew him, Horatio." King takes up a grapefruit in his hand in a similar fashion. What would mapping these two scenes upon each other add to Johnson's story?

■ FICTIVE-NARRATIVE PHILOSOPHY FEEDBACK

What claims are made in this story? Write them out in a bulleted list and include whether they are made through dialogue, dramatic action, or the presentation of the scene (including descriptive detail). One page. Then choose either a short direct-discourse response (according to the rules in Chapter 2) or a short fictive-narrative presentation (according to the rules in Chapter 3). You may want to add to Johnson's story and pick up at a point after the story leaves off.

LETTER FROM A BIRMINGHAM JAIL

Martin Luther King Jr.

The 16th Street Baptist Church in Birmingham, Alabama, was used as a meeting place for civil rights leaders like Martin Luther King Jr., Ralph David Abernathy, and Fred Shuttlesworth. Tensions were high in 1963 as the Southern Christian Leadership Conference and the Congress of Racial Equality became involved in a campaign to register African American citizens to vote in Birmingham. This resulted in the bombing of the church by white segregationists and the death of four young women: Denise McNair (eleven years old), Addie Mae Collins (fourteen years old), Carole Robertson (fourteen years old), and Cynthia Wesley (fourteen years old). Eugene "Bull" Connor was a focal point of this controversy as he used German shepherds and high-powered water hoses to attack peaceful black men and women marching and singing Christian hymns in nonviolent protest against the apartheid racism of the city of Birmingham, Alabama. Martin Luther King was also arrested for his role in the protests (his thirteenth time). While in jail he wrote this letter, which was widely disseminated.

In "Letter from a Birmingham Jail" King creates a direct-discourse logical argument with the following conclusion: "King, his followers, and all people should break the unjust Birmingham law now (even though they may go to jail) for the sake of real law and justice." Critical to his inference are the dual tenets holding that (a) injustice anywhere is a threat to justice everywhere, and (b) unjust laws ought not to be obeyed. Along the way King tries to address various objections to his argument from both the white and black communities.

April 16, 1963

My Dear Fellow Clergymen:

While confined here in the Birmingham city jail, I came across your recent statement calling my present activities "unwise and untimely." Seldom do I pause to answer criticism of my work and ideas. If I sought to answer all the criticisms that cross my desk, my secretaries would have little time for anything other than such correspondence in the course of the day, and I would have no time for constructive

302

work. But since I feel that you are men of genuine good will and that your criticisms are sincerely set forth, I want to try to answer your statement in what I hope will be patient and reasonable terms.

I think I should indicate why I am here in Birmingham, since you have been influenced by the view which argues against "outsiders coming in." I have the honor of serving as president of the Southern Christian Leadership Conference, an organization operating in every southern state, with headquarters in Atlanta, Georgia. We have some eighty-five affiliated organizations across the South, and one of them is the Alabama Christian Movement for Human Rights. Frequently we share staff, educational and financial resources with our affiliates. Several months ago the affiliate here in Birmingham asked us to be on call to engage in a nonviolent direct-action program if such were deemed necessary. We readily consented, and when the hour came we lived up to our promise. So I, along with several members of my staff, am here because I was invited here. I am here because I have organizational ties here.

But more basically, I am in Birmingham because injustice is here. Just as the prophets of the eighth century BC left their villages and carried their "thus saith the Lord" far beyond the boundaries of their home towns, and just as the Apostle Paul left his village of Tarsus and carried the gospel of Jesus Christ to the far corners of the Greco-Roman world, so am I compelled to carry the gospel of freedom beyond my own home town. Like Paul, I must constantly respond to the Macedonian call for aid.[7]

Moreover, I am cognizant of the interrelatedness of all communities and states. I cannot sit idly by in Atlanta and not be concerned about what happens in Birmingham. Injustice anywhere is a threat to justice everywhere. We are caught in an inescapable network of mutuality, tied in a single garment of destiny. Whatever affects one directly, affects all indirectly. Never again can we afford to live with the narrow, provincial "outside agitator" idea. Anyone who lives inside the United States can never be considered an outsider anywhere within its bounds.

You deplore the demonstrations taking place in Birmingham. But your statement, I am sorry to say, fails to express a similar concern for the conditions that brought about the demonstrations. I am sure that none of you would want to rest content with the superficial kind of social analysis that deals merely with effects and does not grapple with underlying causes. It is unfortunate that demonstrations are taking place in Birmingham, but it is even more unfortunate that the city's white power structure left the Negro community with no alternative.

In any nonviolent campaign there are four basic steps: collection of the facts to determine whether injustices exist; negotiation; self-purification; and direct action. We have gone through all these steps in Birmingham. There can be no gainsaying the fact that racial injustice engulfs this community. Birmingham is probably the

---

7 **the Macedonian call for aid:** "And a vision appeared to Paul in the night; There stood a man of Macedonia, and prayed him, saying, 'Come over into Macedonia, and help us'" (Acts 16:9).

most thoroughly segregated city in the United States. Its ugly record of brutality is widely known. Negroes have experienced grossly unjust treatment in the courts. There have been more unsolved bombings of Negro homes and churches in Birmingham than in any other city in the nation. These are the hard, brutal facts of the case. On the basis of these conditions, Negro leaders sought to negotiate with the city fathers. But the latter consistently refused to engage in good-faith negotiation.

Then, last September, came the opportunity to talk with leaders of Birmingham's economic community. In the course of the negotiations, certain promises were made by the merchants—for example, to remove the stores' humiliating racial signs. On the basis of these promises, the Reverend Fred Shuttlesworth and the leaders of the Alabama Christian Movement for Human Rights agreed to a moratorium on all demonstrations. As the weeks and months went by, we realized that we were the victims of a broken promise. A few signs, briefly removed, returned; the others remained.

As in so many past experiences, our hopes had been blasted, and the shadow of deep disappointment settled upon us. We had no alternative except to prepare for direct action, whereby we would present our very bodies as a means of laying our case before the conscience of the local and the national community. Mindful of the difficulties involved, we decided to undertake a process of self-purification. We began a series of workshops on nonviolence, and we repeatedly asked ourselves: "Are you able to accept blows without retaliating?" "Are you able to endure the ordeal of jail?" We decided to schedule our direct-action program for the Easter season, realizing that except for Christmas, this is the main shopping period of the year. Knowing that a strong economic-withdrawal program would be the by-product of direct action, we felt that this would be the best time to bring pressure to bear on the merchants for the needed change.

Then it occurred to us that Birmingham's mayoral election was coming up in March, and we speedily decided to postpone action until after election day. When we discovered that the Commissioner of Public Safety, Eugene "Bull" Connor,[8] had piled up enough votes to be in the run-off, we decided again to postpone action until the day after the run-off so that the demonstrations could not be used to cloud the issues. Like many others, we waited to see Mr. Connor defeated, and to this end we endured postponement after postponement. Having aided in this community need, we felt that our direct-action program could be delayed no longer.

You may well ask: "Why direct action? Why sit-ins, marches and so forth? Isn't negotiation a better path?" You are quite right in calling for negotiation. Indeed, this is the very purpose of direct action. Nonviolent direct action seeks to create such a crisis and foster such a tension that a community which has constantly refused

---

8 **Eugene "Bull" Connor:** (1897–1973); public safety commissioner of Birmingham, Alabama, whose aggressive tactics against integration backfired by capturing national attention and catalyzing social change.

to negotiate is forced to confront the issue. It seeks so to dramatize the issue that it can no longer be ignored. My citing the creation of tension as part of the work of the nonviolent-resister may sound rather shocking. But I must confess that I am not afraid of the word *tension.* I have earnestly opposed violent tension, but there is a type of constructive, nonviolent tension which is necessary for growth. Just as Socrates felt that it was necessary to create a tension in the mind so that individuals could rise from the bondage of myths and half-truths to the unfettered realm of creative analysis and objective appraisal, so must we see the need for nonviolent gadflies to create the kind of tension in society that will help men rise from the dark depth's of prejudice and racism to the majestic heights of understanding and brotherhood.

The purpose of our direct-action program is to create a situation so crisis-packed that it will inevitably open the door to negotiation. I therefore concur with you in your call for negotiation. Too long has our beloved Southland been bogged down in a tragic effort to live in monologue rather than dialogue.

One of the basic points in your statement is that the action that I and my associates have taken in Birmingham is untimely. Some have asked: "Why didn't you give the new city administration time to act?" The only answer that I can give to this query is that the new Birmingham administration must be prodded about as much as the outgoing one, before it will

act. We are sadly mistaken if we feel that the election of Albert Boutwell as mayor will bring the millennium to Birmingham. While Mr. Boutwell is a much more gentle person than Mr. Connor, they are both segregationists, dedicated to maintenance of the status quo. I have hope that Mr. Boutwell will be reasonable enough to see the futility of massive resistance to desegregation. But he will not see this without pressure from devotees of civil rights. My friends, I must say to you that we have not made a single gain in civil rights without determined legal and nonviolent pressure. Lamentably, it is an historical fact that privileged groups seldom give up their privileges voluntarily. Individuals may see the moral light and voluntarily give up their unjust posture; but, as Reinhold Niebuhr[9] has reminded us, groups tend to be more immoral than individuals.

We know through painful experience that freedom is never voluntarily given by the oppressor; it must be demanded by the oppressed. Frankly, I have yet to engage in a direct-action campaign that was "well timed" in the view of those who have not suffered unduly from the disease of segregation. For years now I have heard the word "Wait!" It rings in the ear of every Negro with piercing familiarity. This "Wait" has almost always meant "Never." We must come to see, with one of our distinguished jurists, that "justice too long delayed is justice denied."[10]

We have waited for more than 340 years for our constitutional and God-given

---

9 **Reinhold Niebuhr:** American theologian (1892–1971).

10 **"justice delayed . . . justice denied":** King may have had Oliver Wendell Holmes in mind as the "distinguished jurist" who uttered this maxim, though the saying has an older history than that.

rights. The nations of Asia and Africa are moving with jetlike speed toward gaining political independence, but we still creep at horse-and-buggy pace toward gaining a cup of coffee at a lunch counter. Perhaps it is easy for those who have never felt the stinging darts of segregation to say, "Wait." But when you have seen vicious mobs lynch your mothers and fathers at will and drown your sisters and brothers at whim; when you have seen hate-filled policemen curse, kick, and even kill your black brothers and sisters; when you see the vast majority of your twenty million Negro brothers smothering in an airtight cage of poverty in the midst of an affluent society; when you suddenly find your tongue twisted and your speech stammering as you seek to explain to your six-year-old daughter why she can't go to the public amusement park that has just been advertised on television, and see tears welling up in her eyes when she is told that Funtown is closed to colored children, and see ominous clouds of inferiority beginning to form in her little mental sky, and see her beginning to distort her personality by developing an unconscious bitterness toward white people; when you have to concoct an answer for a five-year-old son who is asking: "Daddy, why do white people treat colored people so mean?"; when you take a cross-country drive and find it necessary to sleep night after night in the uncomfortable corners of your automobile because no motel will accept you; when you are humiliated day in and day out by nagging signs reading "white" and "colored"; when your first name becomes "nigger," your middle name becomes "boy" (however old you are), and your last name becomes "John," and your wife and mother are never given the respected title "Mrs.";

when you are harried by day and haunted by night by the fact that you are a Negro, living constantly at tiptoe stance, never quite knowing what to expect next, and are plagued with inner fears and outer resentments; when you are forever fighting a degenerating sense of "nobodiness"—then you will understand why we find it difficult to wait. There comes a time when the cup of endurance runs over, and men are no longer willing to be plunged into the abyss of despair. I hope, sirs, you can understand our legitimate and unavoidable impatience.

You express a great deal of anxiety over our willingness to break laws. This is certainly a legitimate concern. Since we so diligently urge people to obey the Supreme Court's decision of 1954 outlawing segregation in the public schools, at first glance it may seem rather paradoxical for us consciously to break laws. One may well ask: "How can you advocate breaking some laws and obeying others?" The answer lies in the fact that there are two types of laws; just and unjust. I would be the first to advocate obeying just laws. One has not only a legal but a moral responsibility to obey just laws. Conversely, one has a moral responsibility to disobey unjust laws. I would agree with St. Augustine that "an unjust law is no law at all."

Now, what is the difference between the two? How does one determine whether a law is just or unjust? A just law is a man-made code that squares with the moral law or the law of God. An unjust law is a code that is out of harmony with the moral law. To put it in the terms of St. Thomas Aquinas: An unjust law is a human law that is not rooted in eternal and natural law. Any law that uplifts human personality is just. Any law that degrades human personality is unjust. All segregation statutes are unjust because segregation distorts the soul and damages the personality. It gives the segregator a false sense of superiority and the segregated a false sense of inferiority. Segregation, to use the terminology of the Jewish philosopher Martin Buber, substitutes an "I-it" relationship for an "I-thou" relationship and ends up relegating persons to the status of things. Hence segregation is not only politically, economically, and sociologically unsound, it is morally wrong and sinful. Paul Tillich[11] has said that sin is separation. Is not segregation an existential expression of man's tragic separation, his awful estrangement, his terrible sinfulness? Thus it is that I can urge men to obey the 1954 decision of the Supreme Court, for it is morally right; and I can urge them to disobey segregation ordinances, for they are morally wrong.

Let us consider a more concrete example of just and unjust laws. An unjust law is a code that a numerical or power majority group compels a minority group to obey but does not make binding on itself. This is *difference* made legal. By the same token, a just law is a code that a majority compels a minority to follow and that it is willing to follow itself. This is *sameness* made legal.

Let me give another explanation. A law is unjust if it is inflicted on a minority that, as a result of being denied the right to vote, had no part in enacting or devising the law. Who can say that the legislature of Alabama which set up that state's segregation laws was democratically elected? Throughout Alabama all sorts of devious methods are used to prevent Negroes from becoming registered voters, and there are some counties in which, even though Negroes constitute a majority of the population, not a single Negro is registered. Can any law enacted under such circumstances be considered democratically structured?

Sometimes a law is just on its face and unjust in its application. For instance, I have been arrested on a charge of parading without a permit. Now, there is nothing wrong in having an ordinance which requires a permit for a parade. But such an ordinance becomes unjust when it is used to maintain segregation and to deny citizens the First-Amendment privilege of peaceful assembly and protest.

I hope you are able to see the distinction I am trying to point out. In no sense do I advocate evading or defying the law, as would the rabid segregationist. That would lead to anarchy. One who breaks an unjust law must do so openly, lovingly, and with a willingness to accept the penalty. I submit that an individual who breaks a law that conscience tells him is unjust, and who willingly accepts the penalty of imprisonment in order to arouse the conscience of the community over its injustice, is in reality expressing the highest respect for law.

Of course, there is nothing new about this kind of civil disobedience. It was evidenced sublimely in the refusal of Shadrach, Meshach, and Abednego to obey the laws of Nebuchadnezzar,[12] on the ground

---

11 **Paul Tillich:** German American theologian (1886–1965).

12 **Shadrach . . . Nebuchadnezzar:** King Nebuchadnezzar of Babylon had the young Hebrew men Shadrach, Meshach, and Abednego thrown into a fiery furnace for refusing to worship an idol. The young men, protected by an angel, emerged from the furnace unscathed (Daniel 3:1–30).

that a higher moral law was at stake. It was practiced superbly by the early Christians, who were willing to face hungry lions and the excruciating pain of chopping blocks rather than submit to certain unjust laws of the Roman Empire. To a degree, academic freedom is a reality today because Socrates practiced civil disobedience. In our own nation, the Boston Tea Party represented a massive act of civil disobedience.

We should never forget that everything Adolf Hitler did in Germany was "legal" and everything the Hungarian freedom fighters did in Hungary was "illegal." It was "illegal" to aid and comfort a Jew in Hitler's Germany. Even so, I am sure that, had I lived in Germany at the time, I would have aided and comforted my Jewish brothers. If today I lived in a Communist country where certain principles dear to the Christian faith are suppressed, I would openly advocate disobeying that country's anti-religious laws.

I must make two honest confessions to you, my Christian and Jewish brothers. First, I must confess that over the past few years I have been gravely disappointed with the white moderate. I have almost reached the regrettable conclusion that the Negro's great stumbling block in his stride toward freedom is not the White Citizens' Councilor or the Ku Klux Klanner,[13] but the white moderate, who is more devoted to "order" than to justice; who prefers a negative peace which is the absence of tension to a positive peace which is the presence of justice; who constantly says: "I agree with you in the goal you seek, but I cannot agree with your methods of direct action"; who paternalistically believes he can set the timetable for another man's freedom; who lives by a mythical concept of time and who constantly advises the Negro to wait for a "more convenient season." Shallow understanding from people of good will is more frustrating than absolute misunderstanding from people of ill will. Lukewarm acceptance is much more bewildering than outright rejection.

I had hoped that the white moderate would understand that law and order exist for the purpose of establishing justice and that when they fail in this purpose they become the dangerously structured dams that block the flow of social progress. I had hoped that the white moderate would understand that the present tension in the South is a necessary phase of the transition from an obnoxious negative peace, in which the Negro passively accepted his unjust plight, to a substantive and positive peace, in which all men will respect the dignity and worth of human personality. Actually, we who engage in nonviolent direct action are not the creators of tension. We merely bring to the surface the hidden tension that is already alive. We bring it out in the open, where it can be seen and dealt with. Like a boil that can never be cured so long as it is covered up but must be opened with all its ugliness to the natural medicines of air and light, injustice must be exposed, with all the tension its exposure creates, to the light of human

---

13 **White Citizens' Councilor or the Ku Klux Klanner:** members of two prominent white supremacist groups.

conscience and the air of national opinion before it can be cured.

❧ In your statement you assert that our actions, even though peaceful, must be condemned because they precipitate violence. But is this a logical assertion? Isn't this like condemning a robbed man because his possession of money precipitated the evil act of robbery? Isn't this like condemning Socrates because his unswerving commitment to truth and his philosophical inquiries precipitated the act by the misguided populace in which they made him drink hemlock? Isn't this like condemning Jesus because his unique God-consciousness and never-ceasing devotion to God's will precipitated the evil act of crucifixion? We must come to see that, as the federal courts have consistently affirmed, it is wrong to urge an individual to cease his efforts to gain his basic constitutional rights because the quest may precipitate violence. Society must protect the robbed and punish the robber.

I had also hoped that the white moderate would reject the myth concerning time in relation to the struggle for freedom. I have just received a letter from a white brother in Texas. He writes: "All Christians know that the colored people will receive equal rights eventually, but it is possible that you are in too great a religious hurry. It has taken Christianity almost two thousand years to accomplish what it has. The teachings of Christ take time to come to earth." Such an attitude stems from a tragic misconception of time, from the strangely irrational notion that there is something in the very flow of time that will inevitably cure all ills. Actually, time itself is neutral; it can be used either destructively or constructively. More and more I feel that the people of ill will have used time much more effectively than have the people of good will. We will have to repent in this generation not merely for the hateful words and actions of the bad people but for the appalling silence of the good people. Human progress never rolls in on wheels of inevitability; it comes through the tireless efforts of men willing to be co-workers with God, and without this hard work, time itself becomes an ally of the forces of social stagnation. We must use time creatively, in the knowledge that the time is always ripe to do right. Now is the time to make real the promise of democracy and transform our pending national elegy into a creative psalm of brotherhood. Now is the time to lift our national policy from the quicksand of racial injustice to the solid rock of human dignity.

You speak of our activity in Birmingham as extreme. At first I was rather disappointed that fellow clergymen would see my nonviolent efforts as those of an extremist. I began thinking about the fact that I stand in the middle of two opposing forces in the Negro community. One is a force of complacency, made up in part of Negroes who, as a result of long years of oppression, are so drained of self-respect and a sense of "somebodiness" that they have adjusted to segregation; and in part of a few middle-class Negroes who, because of a degree of academic and economic security and because in some ways they profit by segregation, have become insensitive to the problems of the masses. The other force is one of bitterness and hatred, and it comes perilously close to advocating violence. It is expressed in the various black nationalist groups that are springing up across the nation, the largest and best-known being Elijah Muhammad's Muslim movement.[14] Nourished by the Negro's frustration over the continued existence of racial discrimination, this movement is made up of people who have lost faith in America, who have absolutely repudiated Christianity, and who have concluded that the white man is an incorrigible "devil."

I have tried to stand between these two forces, saying that we need emulate neither the "do-nothingism" of the complacent nor the hatred and despair of the black nationalist. For there is the more excellent way of love and nonviolent protest. I am grateful to God that, through the influence of the Negro church, the way of nonviolence became an integral part of our struggle.

If this philosophy had not emerged, by now many streets of the South would, I am convinced, be flowing with blood. And I am further convinced that if our white brothers dismiss as "rabble-rousers" and "outside agitators" those of us who employ nonviolent direct action, and if they refuse to support our nonviolent efforts, millions of Negroes will, out of frustration and despair, seek solace and security in black-nationalist ideologies—a development that would inevitably lead to a frightening racial nightmare.

Oppressed people cannot remain oppressed forever. The yearning for freedom eventually manifests itself, and that is what has happened to the American Negro. Something within has reminded him of his birthright of freedom, and something without has reminded him that it can be gained. Consciously or unconsciously, he has been caught up by the *Zeitgeist*,[15] and with his black brothers of Africa and his brown and yellow brothers of Asia, South America, and the Caribbean, the United States Negro is moving with a sense of great urgency toward the promised land of racial justice. If one recognizes this vital urge that has engulfed the Negro community, one should readily understand why public demonstrations are taking place. The Negro has many pent-up resentments and latent frustrations, and he must release them. So let him march; let him make prayer pilgrimages to the city hall; let him go on freedom rides[16]—and try to understand why he must do so. If his repressed emotions are not released in nonviolent ways, they will seek expression through violence; this is not a threat but a fact of history. So I have not said to my people: "Get rid of your discontent." Rather, I have tried to say that this normal and healthy discontent can be channeled into the creative outlet of nonviolent direct action. And now this approach is being termed extremist.

---

14 **Elijah Muhammad's Muslim movement:** Elijah Muhammad (1897–1975) led the Nation of Islam, sometimes referred to (with other groups) as Black Muslims.

15 *Zeitgeist*: spirit of the time.

16 **freedom rides:** excursions by bus into the South by black and white civil rights activists ("Freedom Riders") in order to challenge local laws that enforced segregation.

But though I was initially disappointed at being categorized as an extremist, as I continued to think about the matter I gradually gained a measure of satisfaction from the label. Was not Jesus an extremist for love: "Love your enemies, bless them that curse you, do good to them that hate you, and pray for them which despitefully use you, and persecute you." Was not Amos an extremist for justice: "Let justice roll down like waters and righteousness like an everflowing stream." Was not Paul an extremist for the Christian gospel: "I bear in my body the marks of the Lord Jesus." Was not Martin Luther an extremist: "Here I stand; I cannot do otherwise, so help me God." And John Bunyan: "I will stay in jail to the end of my days before I make a butchery of my conscience." And Abraham Lincoln: "This nation cannot survive half slave and half free." And Thomas Jefferson: "We hold these truths to be self-evident, that all men are created equal. . . . " So the question is not whether we will be extremists, but what kind of extremists we will be. Will we be extremists for hate or for love? Will we be extremists for the preservation of injustice or for the extension of justice? In that dramatic scene on Calvary's hill three men were crucified. We must never forget that all three were crucified for the same crime—the crime of extremism. Two were extremists for immorality, and thus fell below their environment. The other, Jesus Christ, was an extremist for love, truth, and goodness, and thereby rose above his environment. Perhaps the South, the nation, and the world are in dire need of creative extremists.

I had hoped that the white moderate would see this need. Perhaps I was too optimistic; perhaps I expected too much. I suppose I should have realized that few members of the oppressor race can understand the deep groans and passionate yearnings of the oppressed race, and still fewer have the vision to see that injustice must be rooted out by strong, persistent, and determined action. I am thankful, however, that some of our white brothers in the South have grasped the meaning of this social revolution and committed themselves to it. They are still all too few in quantity, but they are big in quality. Some—such as Ralph McGill, Lillian Smith, Harry Golden, James McBride Dabbs, Ann Braden, and Sarah Patton Boyle—have written about our struggle in eloquent and prophetic terms. Others have marched with us down nameless streets of the South. They have languished in filthy, roach-infested jails, suffering the abuse and brutality of policemen who view them as "dirty nigger-lovers." Unlike so many of their moderate brothers and sisters, they have recognized the urgency of the moment and sensed the need for powerful "action" antidotes to combat the disease of segregation.

Let me take note of my other major disappointment. I have been so greatly disappointed with the white church and its leadership. Of course, there are some notable exceptions. I am not unmindful of the fact that each of you has taken some significant stands on this issue. I commend you, Reverend Stallings, for your Christian stand on this past Sunday, in welcoming Negroes to your worship service on a nonsegregated basis. I commend the Catholic leaders of this state for integrating Spring Hill College several years ago.

But despite these notable exceptions, I must honestly reiterate that I have been disappointed with the church. I do not say this as one of those negative critics who can always find something wrong with the church. I say this as a minister of the gospel, who loves the church; who was nurtured in its bosom; who has been sustained by its spiritual blessings and who will remain true to it as long as the cord of life shall lengthen.

When I was suddenly catapulted into the leadership of the bus protest in Montgomery, Alabama, a few years ago, I felt we would be supported by the white church. I felt that the white ministers, priests, and rabbis of the South would be among our strongest allies. Instead, some have been outright opponents, refusing to understand the freedom movement and misrepresenting its leaders; all too many others have been more cautious than courageous and have remained silent behind the anesthetizing security of stained-glass windows.

In spite of my shattered dreams, I came to Birmingham with the hope that the white religious leadership of this community would see the justice of our cause and, with deep moral concern, would serve as the channel through which our just grievances could reach the power structure. I had hoped that each of you would understand. But again I have been disappointed.

I have heard numerous southern religious leaders admonish their worshippers to comply with a desegregation decision because it is the law, but I have longed to hear white ministers declare: "Follow this decree because integration is morally right and because the Negro is your brother." In the midst of blatant injustices inflicted upon the Negro, I have watched white churchmen stand on the sidelines and mouth pious irrelevancies and sanctimonious trivialities. In the midst of a mighty struggle to rid our nation of racial and economic injustice, I have heard many ministers say: "Those are social issues, with which the gospel has no real concern." And I have watched many churches commit themselves to a completely otherworldly religion which makes a strange, unbiblical distinction between body and soul, between the sacred and the secular.

I have traveled the length and breadth of Alabama, Mississippi, and all the other southern states. On sweltering summer days and crisp autumn mornings I have looked at the South's beautiful churches with their lofty spires pointing heavenward. I have beheld the impressive outlines of her massive religious education buildings. Over and over I have found myself asking: "What kind of people worship here? Who is their God? Where were their voices when the lips of Governor Barnett[17] dripped with words of interposition and nullification? Where were they when Governor Wallace[18] gave a clarion call for defiance and hatred? Where were their voices

---

17 **Governor Barnett:** Ross Barnett (1898–1987), governor of Mississippi and a staunch segregationist.

18 **Governor Wallace:** George Wallace (1919–1998), four-time governor of Alabama. In his first inaugural speech (January 1963), just three months before King wrote his "Letter," Wallace declared, "Segregation now, segregation tomorrow, segregation forever."

of support when bruised and weary Negro men and women decided to rise from the dark dungeons of complacency to the bright hills of creative protest?"

Yes, these questions are still in my mind. In deep disappointment I have wept over the laxity of the church. But be assured that my tears have been tears of love. There can be no deep disappointment where there is not deep love. Yes, I love the church. How could I do otherwise? I am in the rather unique position of being the son, the grandson, and the great-grandson of preachers. Yes, I see the church as the body of Christ. But, oh! How we have blemished and scarred that body through social neglect and through fear of being nonconformists.

There was a time when the church was very powerful—in the time when the early Christians rejoiced at being deemed worthy to suffer for what they believed. In those days the church was not merely a thermometer that recorded the ideas and principles of popular opinion; it was a thermostat that transformed the mores of society. Whenever the early Christians entered a town, the people in power became disturbed and immediately sought to convict the Christians for being "disturbers of the peace" and "outside agitators." But the Christians pressed on, in the conviction that they were "a colony of heaven,"[19] called to obey God rather than man. Small in number, they were big in commitment. They were too God-intoxicated to be "astronomically intimidated." By

their effort and example they brought an end to such ancient evils as infanticide and gladiatorial contests.

Things are different now. So often the contemporary church is a weak, ineffectual voice with an uncertain sound. So often it is an archdefender of the status quo. Far from being disturbed by the presence of the church, the power structure of the average community is consoled by the church's silent—and often even vocal—sanction of things as they are.

But the judgment of God is upon the church as never before. If today's church does not recapture the sacrificial spirit of the early church, it will lose its authenticity, forfeit the loyalty of millions, and be dismissed as an irrelevant social club with no meaning for the twentieth century. Every day I meet young people whose disappointment with the church has turned into outright disgust.

Perhaps I have once again been too optimistic. Is organized religion too inextricably bound to the status quo to save our nation and the world? Perhaps I must turn my faith to the inner spiritual church, the church within the church, as the true *ekklesia*[20] and the hope of the world. But again I am thankful to God that some noble souls from the ranks of organized religion have broken loose from the paralyzing chains of conformity and joined us as active partners in the struggle for freedom. They have left their secure congregations and walked the streets of Albany, Georgia, with us. They

19 **"a colony of heaven":** "But we are a colony of heaven, and from heaven we expect our deliverer to come" (Philippians 3:20).

20 *ekklesia:* church; the root of the English word "ecclesiastical."

have gone down the highways of the South on tortuous rides for freedom. Yes, they have gone to jail with us. Some have been dismissed from their churches, have lost the support of their bishops and fellow ministers. But they have acted in the faith that right defeated is stronger than evil triumphant. Their witness has been the spiritual salt that has preserved the true meaning of the gospel in these troubled times. They have carved a tunnel of hope through the dark mountain of disappointment.

I hope the church as a whole will meet the challenge of this decisive hour. But even if the church does not come to the aid of justice, I have no despair about the future. I have no fear about the outcome of our struggle in Birmingham, even if our motives are at present misunderstood. We will reach the goal of freedom in Birmingham and all over the nation, because the goal of America is freedom. Abused and scorned though we may be, our destiny is tied up with America's destiny. Before the pilgrims landed at Plymouth, we were here. Before the pen of Jefferson etched the majestic words of the Declaration of Independence across the pages of history, we were here. For more than two centuries our forebears labored in this country without wages; they made cotton king; they built the homes of their masters while suffering gross injustice and shameful humiliation—and yet out of a bottomless vitality they continued to thrive and develop. If the inexpressible cruelties of slavery could not stop us, the opposition we now face will surely fail. We will win our freedom because the sacred heritage of our nation and the eter-

nal will of God are embodied in our echoing demands.

Before closing I feel impelled to mention one other point in your statement that has troubled me profoundly. You warmly commended the Birmingham police force for keeping "order" and "preventing violence." I doubt you would have so warmly commended the police force if you had seen its dogs sinking their teeth into unarmed, nonviolent Negroes. I doubt that you would so quickly commend the policemen if you were to observe their ugly and inhumane treatment of Negroes here in the city jail; if you were to watch them push and curse old Negro women and young Negro girls; if you were to see them slap and kick old Negro men and young boys; if you were to observe them, as they did on two occasions, refuse to give us food because we wanted to sing our grace together. I cannot join you in your praise of the Birmingham police department.

It is true that the police have exercised a degree of discipline in handling the demonstrators. In this sense they have conducted themselves rather "nonviolently" in public. But for what purpose? To preserve the evil system of segregation. Over the past few years I have consistently preached that nonviolence demands that the means we use must be as pure as the ends we seek. I have tried to make clear that it is wrong to use immoral means to attain moral ends. But now I must affirm that it is just as wrong, or perhaps even more so, to use moral means to preserve immoral ends. Perhaps Mr. Connor and his policemen have been rather nonviolent in public, as was Chief Pritchett in Albany, Georgia, but they have used the moral means of nonviolence to maintain the immoral end of racial injustice. As T. S. Eliot has said: "The last temptation is the greatest treason: To do the right deed for the wrong reason."

I wish you had commended the Negro sit-inners and demonstrators of Birmingham for their sublime courage, their willingness to suffer, and their amazing discipline in the midst of great provocation. One day the South will recognize its real heroes. They will be the James Merediths,[21] with the noble sense of purpose that enables them to face jeering and hostile mobs, and with the agonizing loneliness that characterizes the life of the pioneer. They will be old, oppressed, battered Negro women, symbolized in a seventy-two-year-old woman in Montgomery, Alabama, who rose up with a sense of dignity and with her people decided not to ride segregated buses, and who responded with ungrammatical profundity to one who inquired about her weariness: "My feets is tired, but my soul is at rest." They will be the young high school and college students, the young ministers of the gospel, and a host of their elders, courageously and nonviolently sitting in at lunch counters and willingly going to jail for conscience' sake. One day the South will know that when these disinherited children of God sat down at lunch counters, they were in reality standing up for what is best in the American dream and for the most sacred values in our Judaeo-Christian heritage, thereby bringing our nation back to those great wells of democracy which were dug deep by the founding fathers in their formulation of the Constitution and the Declaration of Independence.

Never before have I written so long a letter. I'm afraid it is much too long to take your precious time. I can assure you that it would have been much shorter if I had been writing from a comfortable desk, but what else can one do when he is alone in a narrow jail cell, other than write long letters, think long thoughts, and pray long prayers?

If I have said anything in this letter that overstates the truth and indicates an unreasonable impatience, I beg you to forgive me. If I have said anything that understates the truth and indicates my having a patience that allows me to settle for anything less than brotherhood, I beg God to forgive me.

---

21 **James Meredith:** American civil rights activist (born 1933). He was the first African American to enroll at the University of Mississippi, one of the key events of the civil rights movement.

■ READING AND DISCUSSION QUESTIONS

1. To whom does King address his letter? Why is it important to keep this audience in mind? Are some of his arguments particularly directed to this audience as opposed to a general audience?
2. Part of King's argument involves the premises that just laws ought to be obeyed and unjust laws ought *not* to be obeyed. Contrast King's argument with that of

Socrates in the "Crito" and Iris Murdoch's depiction of Ludwig's parent in *An Accidental Man.*

3. Another key premise of King's argument is, "The laws that perpetuated the brutality and abuse of segregation in Birmingham, Alabama, are not in accord with moral law or God's law." How is this distinction similar to the argument that Thomas Aquinas makes in Chapter 7?

4. Why does Martin Luther King Jr., a citizen of Atlanta, Georgia, feel compelled to involve himself in Birmingham, Alabama? What does King mean by interrelatedness? What follows from accepting such a premise?

5. What are the four basic steps in moving toward nonviolent direct action? Explain, in order, how each step works.

6. Go to the Internet and research Eugene "Bull" Connor. What was his role in these historical events? How did he justify his actions to the public?

7. What were the impediments posed by the white community that King cites? What is King's response?

8. What were the impediments posed by the black community that King cites? What is King's response?

9. Examine the premise that "freedom is never voluntarily given by the oppressor; it must be demanded by the oppressed." How is this similar to G. W. F. Hegel's position in the master/slave dialectic? How is this premise relevant to the audience of King's letter?

■ CLASS EXERCISES

A. *Direct logical discourse:* Using the tools found in Chapter 2, outline the argument from "Letter from a Birmingham Jail" that has as its conclusion that "King, his followers, and all people should break the unjust Birmingham law now (even though they may go to jail) for the sake of real law and justice." Based on your assessment of one key premise, write a one-page argument about why you agree or disagree with the argument's conclusion.

B. *Fictive-narrative philosophy:* Using the tools found in Chapter 3, begin with a claim that relates to the reading and discussion questions above. Then either create a modern-day story about people or situations familiar to you that makes the logical claim you have identified or create a story involving King in his jail cell making his argument in front of other inmates there. Three pages.

❧ FINAL PROJECT

A. *Direct logical discourse:* Expand on one of your direct-discourse evaluations in the second half of the course, reexamining three premises in the reconstructed argument in order to write either a pro or a con response to the argument's conclusion. Be sure to show that you understand what the opposite side might say against your argument and counter-refute the hypothetical objector. Eight pages.

B. *Fictive-narrative philosophy:* Expand upon one of your narratives (a different one from the argument examined in "A"). In this expanded version, strive for greater development of characters, scene, and/or dramatic action. To help keep you on track, use your previous responses to the pertinent "Fictive-Narrative Philosophy Feedback" section. Six pages.

APPENDIX

▚ Some Philosophy Games

Directions: The traditional division of philosophy is into four areas: logic, ethics, epistemology, and metaphysics. Each of these, in turn, has many subcategories and has had various expressions over the years according to the many writers who have enhanced our understanding of problems addressed from these standpoints.[1] Below are nine games that will require entering into one of the four areas of philosophy to formulate an answer. These games are intended to stimulate further study in philosophy in order that readers might acquire better facility in coming to terms with the particular problems. Good luck! (At the end of this appendix, there is a short feedback section.)

Logic: Deductive Coherence

Mr. white = center

Problem #1: Using Deductive Coherence as Your Methodology, Solve This Thought Problem[2]

Mr. Green, Mr. Black, Mr. White, Mr. Red, and Mr. Yellow all play basketball for the Arlington Warriors. The positions on the basketball team are center, point guard, off guard, and two forwards. Who plays where?

   Mr. Green and Mr. Black took the forwards and their wives to dinner one night. The off guard loves Italian food. Mr. White's wedding ring is silver. The center is a homosexual who lives by himself. Mr. White always eats alone and never goes out with other members of the team. Mr. Black beat the point guard in poker one night.

---

1 The function of philosophy is to criticize and examine first principles. When this is applied to any discipline, then a new department is formed, such as "philosophy of art" or "philosophy of economics." With a little effort one could force these into the traditional categories, but why bother? Just add these under a different mode of classification.

2 This particular problem is original to this author. However, the type of problem is very common among various logic textbooks.

1. What position does Mr. Green play?
2. What position does Mr. Black play?
3. What position does Mr. White play?
4. What position does Mr. Red play?
5. What position does Mr. Yellow play?

Problem #2: What Do You Make of the Following Proposition?[3]

α: "Epimenides, a Cretan (one who lives in Crete), says, 'All Cretans are liars.'"

What sorts of problems do you see occurring? What do they mean? Does this paradox affect the way you think about deductive coherence?

Ethics

The Trolley Problem[4]

1. You are the engineer of a trolley.
2. The trolley has gotten almost out of control.
3. Your only choice is to switch at Lincoln Junction between A track and B track.
4. You are approaching Lincoln Junction and on the RIGHT track is a school bus filled with fifty innocent young children whose bus is caught in the trolley tracks.
5. The LEFT track is occupied by a homeless person whose poor-fitting shoe has gotten caught in the trolley tracks.
6. As the engineer, you have the choice of moving your lethal train to the right or to the left. This is your only choice. What should you do?

---

3 This is a problem from classical philosophy that has come to be known as the Liars Paradox. Various forms of this paradox have affected thinkers like Bertrand Russell in his theory of types (explained in W. V. O. Quine, *Methods of Logic* [New York: Holt, 1950]) and Kurt Gödel in his famous theorem on the inherent limitations of the axiomatic method, "Über formal unentscheidbare Sätz der Principia Mathematica und verwanter Systeme," in *Monatschefte für Mathematik und Physik* 38 (1931): 173–198, translated by J. van Heijenoort, *From Frege to Gödel, Sourcebook on Mathematical Logic* (Cambridge, MA: Harvard University Press, 1967).

4 The trolley problem has been a perennial question that queries ethical problem solving when aggregate outcomes are at stake. For further exploration of this topic, see Francis Kamm, *Intricate Ethics: Rights, Responsibilities, and Permissible Harm* (New York: Oxford University Press, 2007); Joseph Shaw, "Intentions and Trolleys," *Philosophical Quarterly* 56, no. 222 (2006): 63–83; Gilbert Harmon, "Three Trends in Moral and Political Philosophy," *Journal of Value Inquiry* 37, no. 3 (2003): 415–425; and Michael Boylan, *Basic Ethics*, 2nd ed. (Upper Saddle River, NJ: Prentice Hall, 2008), ch. 12.

The Rationing Problem[5]

You have been appointed chairperson of the governor's task force on health-care allocations for the next four years. The state is divided into four large health-care regions, but at this moment you are thinking about region #2, which encompasses a major city. One of the findings that has interested you is that allocation requests from impoverished inner-city areas differ from those from affluent suburban areas. Requests from the inner cities are for basic medical supplies and low-tech medical delivery. This group needs more physicians, subsidized pharmaceuticals (such as medicine for hypertension), and extensive prenatal and pediatric care, along with basic health-care information so that patients in this area can make informed health-care decisions that will affect their lives.

The suburbs request sophisticated diagnostic and surgical facilities to meet high-tech needs in sports medicine, cosmetic surgery, and less-invasive operating procedures.

The committee's decisions must go through the normal political process. At the moment, many on the committee believe that the affluent areas should get the major share of this money. They reason that the affluent people in the suburbs (1) support the society with their taxes and therefore should be cared for first, (2) vote in much higher numbers and so are more important in political decisions, and (3) have lobbying groups that will support their interests. Because they "put their money where their mouths are," they should be rewarded with funding.

In contrast, the poor in the inner city (1) pay fewer taxes, (2) vote in small numbers and therefore have little influence in political decisions, and (3) are not the movers and the shakers of society. They are disproportionately female, black, Hispanic, and Native American, and many of them are children. These groups do not have a powerful constituency.

How should you balance the needs of these two groups in the report you are writing? Include in your answer recognition of moral and practical considerations.

Epistemology

Clifford's Slave Ship[6]

There was once a shipowner who sent a ship to sea full of people to be exiled from Britain. It was an old ship and rather cheaply built to begin with. It was suggested to

---

5 Versions of this case study have appeared in my edited volume, *Medical Ethics* (Upper Saddle River, NJ: Prentice Hall, 2000), and *Basic Ethics*. See also Norman Daniels and James Sabin, *Setting Limits Fairly: Can We Learn to Share Medical Resources* (New York: Oxford University Press, 2002), and Michael Boylan, *A Just Society* (Lanham, MD: Rowman & Littlefield, 2004), ch. 3.

6 This is adapted from William Kingdom Clifford, "The Ethics of Belief," in *Lectures and Essays* (London: Macmillan & Co., 1901), 2:163–205. For a contemporary reaction to Clifford, see William James, "The Sentiment of Rationality," in *The Will to Believe and Other Essays* (New York: Longmans, Green & Co., 1897), 63–110. For a discussion of this question in a contemporary context, see Michael Boylan, *The Good, The True, and The Beautiful* (London: Continuum, 2008), ch. 4.

him that the ship might not be seaworthy. But the ship had been on many voyages and had always come back, so the shipowner decided to trust in the sincerity of his conviction that all was well with the ship full of exiles. He waved at the ship when it set sail. Later, when the ship went down in the middle of the ocean with all onboard lost, the shipowner received his insurance money, and no one was the wiser.

What should we think about the shipowner? At the very least the man was negligent in the care of his ship. This negligence was criminal because it resulted in the death of all the exiles (people being shipped from Britain). Most would say that the shipowner should be sent to jail for his failure to have the ship inspected and kept in proper repair. But what if the shipowner said that he had a *sincere conviction* that the ship was seaworthy? Does this make any difference? What sorts of obligations do we have to make sure that the propositions we call "facts" really are true? Is this a case of epistemology bumping up against ethics?

Berkeley's Vase [7]

Bishop George Berkeley was looking at the vase in his study. The vase was rather singular. It stood about eighteen inches high. It was straight on the sides starting from a square base that was two inches by four inches. It expanded to an apex of one foot by four inches. The material was Belleek clay. The thin vase was glazed in off-white and sported a theme from the Red Branch. Berkeley could describe all the physical features of the vase, but he could not say for sure that there was any underlying substratum— real material—that was the vase. What difference would it make if we all accepted that our unaided, naive empirical experience of the world was just that: sense impressions and nothing more? What would it mean to our understanding of the existence of objects-to-us? If all depends upon our subjective sense impressions, then what happens to the vase when we leave the room? Does it disappear?

Metaphysics

The Nature of Being #1 [8]

Consider the following two propositions: α "God exists"; β "Harry Potter exists."

Now, some would say that because they fully understand the meaning of α and β and because the internal sensibility of both subjects is clear and distinct to

---

7 This is a rather free adaptation by Boylan from George Berkeley, *A Treatise Concerning the Principles of Human Knowledge* (London: J. Tonson, 1734). For a contemporary reaction, see Immanuel Kant, "The Refutation of Idealism," in *The Critique of Pure Reason*, trans. Norman Kemp Smith (New York: St. Martins, 1929), 244–256, B274–B294. Contemporary opinions can be sampled in Kenneth Winkler, *The Cambridge Companion to Berkeley* (Cambridge: Cambridge University Press, 2007).

8 This is a compilation by Boylan of various old adages in philosophy. For further work on this, see Descartes, *Meditations*, III, V; Kant, "The Ontological Argument," in *The Critique of Pure Reason*,

them, this is sufficient to confidently declare that either God or Harry Potter exists or both do.

Is there any difference between the declarations found in α and β? If so, where does the difference come from?

The Nature of Being #2 [9]

Most readers of this book go to university. Let us pick a random university as fitting for our example: Oxford University. Now, say a visitor to Oxford were to visit Christ Church, the Bodleian Library, and the Ashmolean Museum and observe students walking about and an occasional don, and so forth, and then asked, "Where is the university? I want to see the real Oxford University."

What is the nature of this query? What possibilities are there and what counts as supporting one against the other?

The Nature of Being #3 [10]

Once there were three Buddhist monks building a fire to cook their dinner. While they were building the fire, one of them, Xi, heard the other two arguing about subjectivity and objectivity. Xi joined them and said, "Observe before you." He began pointing with his emaciated, aged index finger. "Before you is a big stone. Do you consider it to be inside or outside your mind?"

Yoshi, the youngest monk, replied, "From the Buddhist viewpoint, everything is an objectification of mind, so I would say that the stone is inside my mind."

"Then I must say that your head must feel very heavy," observed Xi, "if you are carrying around a stone like that in your mind."

What does this parable say about the metaphysical problem of being?

500–506, B620–B630; and Bertrand Russell, "On Denoting," *Mind* 14 (1905): 479–493, reprinted in Bertrand Russell, *Essays in Analysis* (London: Allen and Unwin, 1973), 103–119. For some views of fictive characters, see Paisley Livingston, *Art and Intention: A Philosophical Study* (Oxford: Clarendon Press, 2005), and Amie L. Thomasson, "Fictional Characters and Literary Practices," *British Journal of Aesthetics* 43, no. 2 (2003): 138–157.

9 This comes from Gilbert Ryle, *The Concept of Mind* (London: Hutchinson & Co., 1949), esp. 11–24. See also the short discussion by Simon Blackburn, *Think* (Oxford: Oxford University Press, 1999), 50–52.

10 This is a reformulation of a traditional Zen koan. The thrust of any koan is to throw into question the way we conceptualize various problems. For further study of this mode of expression, see Scott R. Stroud, "How to Do Things with Art," *Southern Journal of Philosophy* 44, no. 2 (2006): 341–364, and Steven Heine, *Opening a Mountain: Koans of the Zen Masters* (Oxford: Oxford University Press, 2004).

Feedback Section

This section is intended to give either answers or a few more follow-up questions to assist the reader who is pondering these issues. For further readings on these games, consult the footnote associated with that game.

Logic

Problem #1: Mr. Green is the point guard; Mr. Black is the center; Mr. White is the off guard; Mr. Red is the forward; Mr. Yellow is the forward.

Problem #2: This sort of problem is called a self-referential sentence. It creates a never-ending feedback loop. The critical question is whether this feedback loop is just a silly artifact of an artificial problem or a deep problem about formal structures of truth claims. One point for consideration: Does the problem change when I add different labels?

α "Epimenides, a Cretan (one who lives in Crete), says, β 'All Cretans are liars.'"

What is the relationship between the activities in α and the content of β considered separately?

Ethics

The trolley problem: The key question to ask is whether one has any *moral/ethical* justification for going to the right or to the left? To answer this question you must ask further whether human life is additive? Is it morally worse to be the agent of more deaths than fewer deaths? Why? Should we think about the difference between children in the bus versus a homeless person on the other track? Is the normal path of the train important?

The rationing problem: This is a case study and will probably stretch most college students toward their particular major for input on how to answer this conundrum.

Epistemology

Clifford's slave ship: The key questions are: 1. whether there is an ethical duty to hold true beliefs, 2. whether one should first consult externalist-based sources of knowledge first and only afterwards examine internalist-based beliefs based upon reliablist structures.

Berkeley's vase: George Berkeley was a Christian theist. This means he believed in a God who knew all and was all-powerful. The question posed may be different when we consider the perspective of any given human observer versus the perspective of a God who sees all. The vase disappears to the observer, but it is ever present because of God. But what happens if you are an atheist?

Metaphysics

The nature of being #1: One must distinguish the various influences upon why we believe some proposition or not. Some of these are grammatical. Aristotle said that the subject of a sentence had a strong inclination toward existential import. Others demur. They want to cleanse the grammatical force and concentrate upon the concepts themselves. But is this really any help—especially with characters who are introduced to us in books?

The nature of being #2: Those who believed in dualism, like Plato and Descartes, thought that the primary entity was nonphysical. Thus, for these philosophers, understanding the esprit de corps is not a vain endeavor. This game pushes one into answering the ontological question, How many sorts of things are there? If there is one sort of thing, then is it material (as per the slant of the game) or spiritual (as in Berkeley's vase). Descartes and Plato opted for two sorts of things: material and spiritual, with the latter as more important than the former.

The nature of being #3: Some might say that this example violates the terms of acceptable narrative (see the introductory essay in Chapter 1). This might be because of the obvious silliness of the consequence of a person carrying a real rock inside his head. But in this situation the very issue involved (the nature of acquaintance with being) is at stake. Some might say that the koan begs the question. Others might say that the bizarre consequence acts to prove its point. What do you say?

CREDITS

Chapter 4 (Plato)

Charles Johnson, "The Cynic." Copyright © by Charles Johnson. Reprinted by permission of the author. All rights reserved.

Plato, "The Myth of the Charioteer." Adapted from Plato, "Phaedrus," in *The Dialogues of Plato*. Vol. 1 translated by B. Jowett. New York: Random House, 1892.

Plato, "Crito." Adapted from Plato, "Crito," in *The Complete Dialogue of Plato*. Vol. 1 translated by B. Jowett. New York: Random House, 1897.

Chapter 5 (Aristotle)

Michael Boylan, "Aristotle the Outsider." Copyright © 2010 by Michael Boylan. Reprinted by permission of the author. All rights reserved.

Aristotle, "On the Soul." Adapted from Aristotle, *De Anima*. Translated by J. A. Smith. Oxford: Oxford University Press, 1910.

Chapter 6 (Buddha)

Charles Johnson, "The Prince of the Ascetics" (also previously published as "Night Watch"). Copyright © by Charles Johnson. Reprinted by permission of the author. All rights reserved.

Buddha, "From the *Dhammapada*." Adapted from *Dhammapada*. Translated by F. Max Müller. Oxford: Oxford University Press, 1881.

Chapter 7 (Aquinas)

Michael Boylan, "The Murder of Thomas Aquinas." Copyright © 2010 by Michael Boylan. Reprinted by permission of the author. All rights reserved.

Thomas Aquinas, "On the Natural law." Adapted from Thomas Aquinas, *Summa Theologica*, I–II, q93, a2; q93, a3; q94, a4. Rome: Typographia Forzani, 1894. Translated by Michael Boylan. Reprinted by permission of the translator. English translation copyright © 2010 by Michael Boylan. All rights reserved.

Chapter 8 (Descartes)

Charles Johnson, "The Queen and the Philosopher." Copyright © 2005 by Charles Johnson. Reprinted with the permission of Scribner, a Division of Simon & Schuster, Inc., from *Dr. King's Refrigerator and Other Bedtime Stories* by Charles Johnson. All rights reserved.

René Descartes, "Finding a Foundation for Knowledge." Adapted from René Descartes, "Meditations on First Philosophy." In *The Philosophical Writings of Descartes*. Vol. 1. Translated by Elizabeth S. Haldane and G. R. T. Ross. Cambridge: Cambridge University Press, 1911, reprinted 1931.

Chapter 9 (Kant)

Michael Boylan, "Kant Awakened." Reprinted by permission of the author. Copyright © 2010 by Michael Boylan. All rights reserved.

Gottfried Leibniz, "On Geometrical Method and the Method of Metaphysics." Adapted from Gottfried Leibniz, *Discourse on Metaphysics*. Translated by George Montgomery (1902). Revised by Albert R. Chandler. LaSalle, IL: Open Court, 1924.

Christian Wolff, "Three Types of Human Knowledge: History, Philosophy, and Mathematics." Adapted from Christian Wolff, *Preliminary Discourse on Philosophy in General*. Translated by Richard J. Blackwell, 3–14. Indianapolis, IN: Bobbs-Merrill, 1963.

David Hume, "Of the Academical or Skeptical Philosophy." Adapted from David Hume, *An Enquiry Concerning Human Understanding*. London, 1748.

Immanuel Kant, "The Possibility of Metaphysics." Adapted from Immanuel Kant, *Prolegomena [to any Future Metaphysics]*. Translated by Paul Carus. Chicago: Open Court, 1902.

Chapter 10 (Marx)

Michael Boylan, "A Game of Chess in Paris." Copyright © 2010 by Michael Boylan. Reprinted by permission of the author. All rights reserved.

G. W. F. Hegel, "Preface." Adapted from G. W. F. Hegel, *The Phenomenology of Mind*. Translated by J. B. Baillie, 107–111. London: G. Allen & Unwin, 1931.

G. W. F. Hegel, "Lordship and Bondage." Adapted from G. W. F. Hegel, *The Phenomenology of Mind*. Translated by J. B. Baillie, 228–240. London: G. Allen & Unwin, 1931.

G. W. F. Hegel, "Morality and the Ethical Community." Adapted from G. W. H. Hegel, *Grundlinien der Philosophie des Rechts*. Edited by Georg Lasson. Leipzig: F. Meiner, 1911. Translated by Michael Boylan. Reprinted by permission of the translator. English translation copyright © 2010 by Michael Boylan. All rights reserved.

Karl Marx, "Alienated Labor." Adapted from "The Economic and Philosophical Manuscripts," in Karl Marx, *Early Writings*. Translated by T. B. Bottomore, 120–134, 147–157. New York: McGraw-Hill, 1963. Reproduced with permission of the McGraw-Hill Companies.

Karl Marx, "Private Property and Labor." Adapted from "The Economic and Philosophical Manuscripts," in Karl Marx, *Early Writings*. Translated by T. B. Bottomore, 147–157. New York: McGraw-Hill, 1963. Reproduced with permission of the McGraw-Hill Companies.

Chapter 11 (Heidegger and Arendt)

Michael Boylan, "Eichmann and Heidegger in Jerusalem." Copyright © 2010 by Michael Boylan. Reprinted by permission of the author. All rights reserved.

Martin Heidegger, "The Exposition of the Question of the Meaning of Being." Translated and adapted by Michael Boylan from Martin Heidegger, *Sein und Zeit*. Halle, Germany: M. Niemeyer, 1929. English translation copyright © 2010 by Michael Boylan. Reprinted by permission of the translator. All rights reserved.

Hannah Arendt, "An Expert on the Jewish Question." From *Eichmann in Jerusalem* by Hannah Arendt. Copyright © 1963, 1964 by Hannah Arendt, copyright renewed © 1991, 1992 by Lotte Kohler. Used by permission of Viking Penguin, a division of Penguin Group (USA) Inc.

Chapter 12 (Murdoch)

Michael Boylan, "An Accidental Woman." Copyright © 2010 by Michael Boylan. Reprinted by permission of the author. All rights reserved.

Iris Murdoch, "Ludwig's Conundrum." From *An Accidental Man* by Iris Murdoch, published by Chatto & Windus. Copyright © 1971 by Iris Murdoch. Reprinted by permission of the Random House Group Ltd. and by kind permission of the Estate of Iris Murdoch.

Chapter 13 (King)

Charles Johnson, "Dr. King's Refrigerator." Copyright © 2005 by Charles Johnson. Reprinted with the permission of Scribner, a Division of Simon & Schuster, Inc., from *Dr. King's Refrigerator and Other Bedtime Stories* by Charles Johnson. All rights reserved.

Martin Luther King, Jr., "Letter from a Birmingham Jail." Copyright © 1963 by Dr. Martin Luther King Jr.; copyright renewed © 1991 by Coretta Scott King. Reprinted by arrangement with the Heirs to the Estate of Martin Luther King Jr., c/o Writers House as agent for the proprietor New York, NY.

ABOUT THE AUTHORS

Michael Boylan is professor of philosophy at Marymount University. His recent book, *The Good, The True, and The Beautiful* (2008), is a popular application of his worldview theory to many of the traditional problems in philosophy. His other books include *The Extinction of Desire* (2007), a bold experiment in narrative philosophy, and *A Just Society* (2004), his manifesto on ethics and social and political philosophy. He is the general editor of a series on public philosophy and the ethics editor for the *Internet Encyclopedia of Philosophy*. He is currently writing one volume of the forthcoming *Morality and Global Justice* while also editing a companion reader, which together extend his worldview theory to international problems.

Charles Johnson is a novelist, essayist, literary critic, short story writer, cartoonist, and professor emeritus at the University of Washington, Seattle. A MacArthur fellow, he holds a PhD in philosophy and received the 1990 National Book Award for his novel *Middle Passage*. He is the author of three other novels (*Faith and the Good Thing, Oxherding Tale*, and *Dreamer*) and three story collections, the most recent of which is *Dr. King's Refrigerator and Other Bedtime Stories*. His essays and articles are widely anthologized. A survey conducted by the University of Southern California named him one of the ten best short story writers in America.

INDEX